Street-Level Architecture

This book provides the tools to maintain and rebuild the interaction between architecture and public space. Despite the best intentions of designers and planners, interactive frontages have dwindled over the past century in Europe and North America. This book demonstrates why even our best intentions for interactive frontages are currently unable to turn a swelling tide of economic and technological evolution, land consolidation, introversion, stratification, and contagious decline. It uses these lessons to offer concrete locational, programming, design, and management strategies to maximize street-level interaction and trust among street-level architecture, its inhabitants, and the city.

This book demonstrates that designers, developers, planners, and managers ultimately have to create the right preconditions for inhabitants and passersby to bring frontages to life. These preconditions connect architecture to its urban, social, economical, and technological context. Only the right frontage in the right context, with the right design, the right inhabitation, and the right attitude to the city will become part of the ecosystem of trust and interaction that supports public life. This book empowers the many participants in this ecosystem to build, inhabit, and enjoy truly urbane architecture.

Conrad Kickert, PhD, is an assistant professor at the University at Buffalo's School of Architecture and Planning. Conrad has a background in urbanism and architecture from the TU Delft (the Netherlands) and holds a PhD in architecture from the University of Michigan. He has worked as an urban researcher and designer for various design offices, property developers, and nonprofit organizations in the Netherlands, the United Kingdom, and the United States. His research focuses on the evolving relationship between urban form, urban life, and the urban economy. Dr. Kickert has authored peer-reviewed articles, edited books on bottom-up urbanism and urban retail, and recently authored the award-winning book *Dream City – Creation, Destruction and Reinvention in Downtown Detroit*. His research and studio work has been supported by numerous corporations, foundations, and the National Endowment for the Arts.

Hans Karssenberg is a partner at STIPO, a team for urban development, with offices in Amsterdam, Rotterdam, and Athens and projects throughout Europe. Hans has extensive experience developing, programming, and managing interactive frontages. In partnership with nearly 100 practitioners, scholars, and regulators, STIPO has compiled successful strategies for frontage reactivation in the open-source online and print book series *The City at Eye Level*. The practical applicability and extensive reach of *The City at Eye Level* has not just generated readership across the globe but also fueled professional projects on frontages across Europe. STIPO is at the heart of the growing European placemaking network, and has partnered with UN Habitat, Project for Public Spaces, and various universities and foundations.

Street-Level Architecture

The Past, Present and Future of Interactive Frontages

Conrad Kickert
with
Hans Karssenberg

NEW YORK AND LONDON

Cover image: Conrad Kickert

First published 2023
by Routledge
605 Third Avenue, New York, NY 10158

and by Routledge
4 Park Square, Milton Park, Abingdon, Oxon, OX14 4RN

Routledge is an imprint of the Taylor & Francis Group, an informa business

© 2023 Conrad Kickert with Hans Karssenberg

The right of Conrad Kickert with Hans Karssenberg to be identified as authors of this work has been asserted in accordance with sections 77 and 78 of the Copyright, Designs and Patents Act 1988.

All rights reserved. No part of this book may be reprinted or reproduced or utilised in any form or by any electronic, mechanical, or other means, now known or hereafter invented, including photocopying and recording, or in any information storage or retrieval system, without permission in writing from the publishers.

Trademark notice: Product or corporate names may be trademarks or registered trademarks, and are used only for identification and explanation without intent to infringe.

Library of Congress Cataloging-in-Publication Data
Names: Kickert, Conrad, author. | Karssenberg, Hans, author.
Title: Street-level architecture : the past, present and future of
  interactive frontages / Conrad Kickert with Hans Karssenberg.
Description: Abingdon, Oxon : Routledge, 2022. | Includes
  bibliographical references and index. |
Identifiers: LCCN 2021061768 (print) | LCCN 2021061769 (ebook) |
  ISBN 9780367486112 (hardback) | ISBN 9780367486105
  (paperback) | ISBN 9781003041887 (ebook)
Subjects: LCSH: Public spaces. | Architecture—Human factors. |
  Architecture and society. | Street life.
Classification: LCC NA9053.S6 K53 2022 (print) | LCC NA9053.S6
  (ebook) | DDC 720.1/03—dc23/eng/20220414
LC record available at https://lccn.loc.gov/2021061768
LC ebook record available at https://lccn.loc.gov/2021061769

ISBN: 978-0-367-48611-2 (hbk)
ISBN: 978-0-367-48610-5 (pbk)
ISBN: 978-1-003-04188-7 (ebk)

DOI: 10.4324/9781003041887

Typeset in Adobe Caslon
by Apex CoVantage, LLC

Contents

Preface: Turning a Corner   vi
Hans Karssenberg
Acknowledgements   viii

1	Introduction	1
2	Detroit – Eye-Level Death and Resurrection	21
3	Birmingham – The Concrete Collar Unleashed	41
4	The Hague – The Layered City at Eye Level	63
5	Vancouver – The Frontage Formula	81
6	The Frontage Ecosystem	103
7	Commercial Life – Eye-Level Transactions in the City	129
8	Life Beyond Transactions – New Destinations in the City	155
9	Living at Eye Level – Prospect and Refuge	175
10	Conclusion – Living it Up	193

Index   209

Preface

Turning a Corner

We all have that feeling of discovering a new city while walking around. We look around us, and all of a sudden feel that we should turn right onto that great street. That gut feeling is telling us we want to explore this street, be there, and spend time.

In the past decade, with our research program called The City at Eye Level, we have been trying to catch this gut feeling. Because if we understand the criteria and the mechanisms behind our gut telling us to turn, we can repeat it in the new parts of the city we develop and the existing parts of the city that we redevelop.

Unfortunately, it is not at all self-evident that we create attractive streets with our new developments. There are many mechanisms working against eye-level excitement and vitality: standardization, lack of frameworks, lack of attention, short-term profit orientation, to mention just a few of them.

Nor was it self-evident in the past decades. Car-oriented urbanism, modernism, an increasing scale of development, and policies giving priority to large-scale urban functions have created urban areas that we certainly wouldn't turn a corner for. Modernism has brought us a more efficient urban development model of light, air, and green space, but also deliberately only treated the city from a rational point of view. But us human beings, walking through the city, really have two parts of our brains. Not only do we want the street to be efficient, but we also want to be inspired and feel at home.

The streets we want to turn a corner for have great street-level architecture with both great buildings and great programs, both great form and great functions, both hardware and software that interacts with us, giving us a sense of trust, care, and safety. This book explores the interaction between this hardware and software. While our built hardware is certainly changing, perhaps even more is changing in the software of life that fills these buildings. For example, with the rise of the internet, small-scale retail is under pressure. Changing cultures are similarly challenging the traditional urban office. However, an abundance of other functions are waiting to get into our street-level spaces – if we let them, and find out the mechanisms behind them.

The streets we want to turn a corner for are hardly ever only planned from the top-down, but they are co-created with professionals and end users. Both the planned and the lived city contribute. In his recent works, sociologist Richard Sennett has been writing about the incomplete city: a city that is not too finished, that allows space for users to shape it to their needs. An incomplete city invites the users to co-create, brings diversity for the pedestrian walking at five kilometers per hour, watching the details, and brings mental ownership, community involvement, human scale, and a sense of place.[1]

The streets we want to turn a corner for develop through time. Urban development is an intriguing profession, in which we deal with different life cycles. We create structures for 40 to 100 years, while the economy turns upside down every five years, and the city population changes over every ten years. If our public spaces and the lining street-level spaces are resilient enough, urban life can adapt to urban space through the decades. Resilient public space and architecture allows the city to breathe, to be flexible and adaptable through time, without the urban environment becoming a jumble of mismatches between space and inhabitation. Strong streets hold this resilience together. And once a street has been created, it is likely to be there for hundreds of years.

The streets we want turn a corner for have great hardware and software, but also great 'orgware'. Creating a great street or place takes time, an iterative process of testing, discovering and reinforcing what works, a process that can only be done by generations of users and professionals each making their small contributions. Great streets and places ripen over time, if curated well by communities, active street coalitions, and consistent policies. This book mostly focuses on the hardware and software of interactive cities at eye level. There is certainly enough to discover here first – but who knows, a next book could dive into the organizational mechanisms of creating and maintaining interaction between buildings and public space.

Street-level architecture is crucial for creating a sustainably functioning city, for investors and users to co-invest in, to make more streets we want to turn a corner for. In order to achieve this, we also need to turn a corner in our profession: to include street-level architecture in our policies, developments, and investment systems. This book calls on cities to include criteria for the street level into their urban development frameworks, and to include new functions in their economic policies and zoning. It calls on designers to combine their bird's eye view with the eye-level view on the street into their architecture and urban designs. It calls on real estate developers, investors, and owners to include the street-level perspective in their projects, the way they commission their design teams, and include long-term value creation caused by the active street level into their business models. This book provides the elements for turning these corners.

Hans Karssenberg
Founding partner of STIPO urban development and
initiator of The City at Eye Level

Note

1 Richard Sennett, *Building and Dwelling: Ethics for the City* (New York: Farrar, Straus and Giroux, 2018).

Acknowledgements

The authors would like to thank the many people that have provided invaluable assistance to gather, synthesize, and provide input on the data at the heart of this book. The mapping for our four case study cities required thousands of hours of meticulous data collection and mapping, for which we specifically thank Paul van Veen, Jon Moore, Molly Grote, Binita Mahato, Maureen Curran, Wen Zhang, Yajie Hu, and Shannon Gillie for their assistance. We thank the staff at a wide range of libraries, most notably the University of Michigan Library, The Hague's Municipal Archives, the Netherlands Architecture Institute, Kraaijvanger Architects, the Detroit Public Library and its Burton Historical Collection, the Birmingham Public Library, the Vancouver Archives, and the Vancouver Public Library for helping us find what we need. We thank Conrad Kickert's dissertation committee – Dr. Linda Groat, Dr. Robert Fishman, Dr. June Manning Thomas, and Henco Bekkering – for helping to lay the groundwork of the frontage research in this book. We thank the many scholars at the University of Michigan and TU Delft that have helped Kickert's dissertation research along the way. We thank a multitude of researchers and practitioners that have shared their thoughts about the subject matter in this book, including Aart Jan van Duren, Arno Ruigrok, Danilo Palazzo, Emily Talen, Heather Arnold, Heraldo Borges, Joost Nicasie, Leonie Kuepers, Martijn van Dam, Nico Larco, Pim van den Berg, Sander van der Ham, Tina Govan, Victor Joosten, and Vikas Mehta. We thank the many people and organizations that we feature in this book as exemplars for revitalizing frontages, often giving us their time, their ideas, and, not unimportantly, their image permissions. We thank the editors at Routledge for giving us the opportunity and the knowledge to pursue this project, most notably our editors Christine Bondira and Krystal Racaniello. We would like to thank Tigran Haas, Peter Elmlund and the Ax:son Johnson Foundation for supporting this research project. Last but certainly not least, we would like to thank Kelly Anne Gregg for her support and wisdom.

1 INTRODUCTION

Figure 1.0 The Passage in The Hague

DOI: 10.4324/9781003041887-1

More than ever before, the future of our cities depends on their quality of life. Much of this quality comes from exciting destinations, walkable, fine-grained neighborhoods, and vibrant sidewalks. Oddly enough, we have come to know so much about how to design and plan for walkability and high-quality public space over the past decades, but hardly anything about the street-level architecture that feeds it. Quite a shame, as well-designed and well-inhabited ground floors give our walks purpose and a sense of safety, care, and excitement.

A city comes to life by interactions among citizens, which take place along squares and sidewalks but also inside and through the buildings of a city. Subconsciously, we can read the pulse of a city by reading its buildings as we pass by them. If buildings open up to the city, whether through inviting storefronts, social stoops, or welcoming lobbies, we sense trust and care. If buildings hide from the city behind walls, ramps, and parked cars, we sense distrust and a lack of care. On so many levels, we yearn for porous, *interactive frontages*. They give us destinations to walk to, feeding sidewalks with visitors.[1] On the way, they make our walks more interesting by providing sensorial stimulation. By evolution, our ears and eyes tend to focus on what is right in front of us, making the first few feet or meters of a building much more experientially significant than the floors above it. At eye level, interactive frontages allow us to communicate, to socialize, to consume, to grow, to share. They allow us to embrace the city, while giving us space to withdraw and transition into our private realms.

Planners, designers, and regulators have come to love interactive frontages. For decades, lead urbanists and designers like Team 10 in the 1950s; Jane Jacobs in the 1960s; Christopher Alexander, Jan Gehl, and the Structuralists from the 1970s onward; Donald Appleyard and William Whyte in the 1980s; and New Urbanists from the 1990s onward have extolled the virtues of interactive frontages. Each from their own perspective and with their own empirical backing, argued and proved that interactive frontages bring life to public space, create destinations, please the eye, encourage socialization, and reinforce safety.[2] Their collective call to action has yielded swaths of design guidelines, blueprints, and toolkits to encourage or even mandate transparent street-level architecture. From Adelaide to Zurich, no self-respecting new urban project now meets the street without an abundance of expectant plate glass.[3] Then again, many dreams of transparency still wait to find the life that gives it meaning (Figure 1.1). Just around the corner, older buildings sit vacant at eye level, and a block away, we may only see parking lots and colossal structures with blank walls. If we like interactive frontages so much, why can't we seem to build them and, more problematically, fill them with urban life?

It is not a lack of best intentions that kills off our ground floors. After studying miles of blank walls in New York in the 1980s, urbanist William Whyte exasperatedly concluded he did not know who would fix them: "[N]o one is for [blank walls]. There are no civic debates whether to have them or not."[4] We seem to know and agree why we are fighting for interactive frontages – we just do not know exactly what we are fighting *for*, nor who or what we are fighting *against*.

Ask any professional who is to blame for inactive frontages, and the first culprit is likely another professional. Many of us especially blame architects for failing to connect their work with the street. Indeed, after decades of proclaiming 'bigness', certain stars still have a knack for putting their work on literal and figurative pedestals, to be admired from a distance rather than enjoyed from up close. However, most architects are simply forced to respond to a variety of larger societal, economic, and cultural forces that obstruct interactive frontages. Developers are eager to consolidate fine-grained urbanism into large sites that preferably internalize and filter profitable urban functions like shops, restaurants, and offices, and leave parking, logistics, but also crime for the city to solve. This privatization also feeds and responds to urban inequality, which propagates an 'architecture of fear' by some accounts.[5] With growing social inequality, we see diminishing trust between citizens reflected in the design and the inhabitation of street-level spaces. Cars have a curious role in this cycle of distrust, as they filter movement and force buildings to accommodate or succumb to their needs. Moving and parked cars not only take up the majority of our public spaces, but also take up the majority of new construction in cities like Detroit.[6] Nevertheless, it would be too simplistic to ascribe the deactivation of our cities to disconnected architecture, developer greed, distrust, and drivers. There is much more at play.

We need to overcome three key common misconceptions to truly come to an urbane architecture that supports and reflects interactive urban life. First, we focus too much on the form of frontages, perhaps because it is the easiest lever to pull as designers and planners. Yes, buildings usually transition to the city at street level with windows and doors, which we can and often do regulate. But beyond form, frontages should harbor the right function at street level, fostering an inhabitation that communicates and reinforces trust. Only the right street-level inhabitant with the right mindset will bring a transparent, permeable space to life. Which brings us to our second common pitfall: we tend to conflate interactive frontages with storefronts. Frontages can and should do far more than just host transactions; they should build and reinforce interaction and trust among citizens, architecture, and the city. It would be a shame if we consider anything but a storefront inactive, as so much of our interaction happens in front of homes, workshops, and other street-level spaces. Last, we focus on interactive frontages by designing and regulating

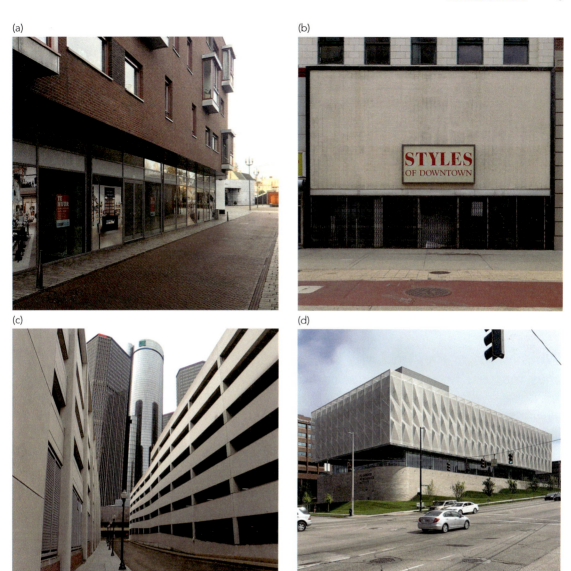

Figure 1.1a–d Despite our best intentions, new frontages stay vacant, existing frontages don't find new life, and many existing and new buildings turn themselves away from the street. Why? Source: Image (a) by Conrad Kickert in Goes, 2020; image (b) by Conrad Kickert in Buffalo, 2021; image (c) by Matteo Marrocco in Detroit, 2021; image (d) by Conrad Kickert in Cincinnati, 2020.

single buildings. However, trust and interaction can only blossom at a critical mass, a scale certainly beyond the singular building. It takes a city and its society to trust one another, and it takes at least a block of interactive frontages the fine-grained ecosystem of trust and mutual support that will bring them to life. Most importantly, it takes a team of designers, planners, but also developers, managers, and especially inhabitants to build a critical mass of frontages with the right form, the right function, and the right communication. Only then will we achieve frontages that enable supervision and transaction, but especially interaction and trust to the street (Figure 1.2).

This book delves beyond the platitudes of the merits of interactive frontages or the culprits of their demise, equipping us with knowledge on what forces and trends truly influence our street-level architecture. A detailed analysis of a century of frontage change in four countries on both sides of the Atlantic demonstrates how frontages make up a delicate ecosystem of external forces and internal patterns that have affected not only their form but also their inhabitation and their connotations of trust and care. By understanding how our frontages represent form, life, and meaning, this book concludes with a series of strategies to regain the vibrant public architecture our cities deserve.

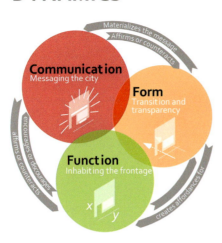 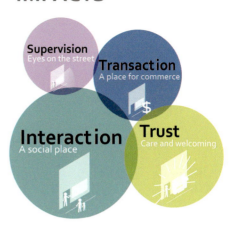

Figure 1.2 Interactive frontages are about far more than form or transactions – they form an ecosystem in which the dynamics of form, function, and communication enable supervision, transactions, interaction, and trust.
Source: Diagram by Conrad Kickert, 2021.[7]

What are frontages and why do they matter?

Street-level frontages are key to our urban experience, but they are rather elusive in our urban dictionary. We cannot even agree on what to call the connection between our buildings and public spaces, whether they are on the ground floor in the United Kingdom or on the first floor in the United States. The Dutch call them the *plinths* of buildings, a reference to the interior connection between wall and floor. The French ground-floor translation, *rez-de-chaussée*, directly refers the building ground floor to the *chaussée*, the street and its pavement. Our confusion goes beyond definition, as our knowledge of frontages has also fallen between the cracks of the many disciplines that design, govern, and inhabit them. Architects discuss ground floors but usually neglect the public spaces that line them. Similarly, developers and businesses study how to optimize their use of ground floors, mostly stopping at the doorstep. Conversely, planners, landscape architects, and traffic engineers discuss how to improve the quality of public spaces but underestimate the role that buildings play in this amelioration. Worst of all, each profession has a wealth of knowledge on their part of frontages, but their insights are rarely interconnected (Figure 1.3).

The main body of knowledge on frontages comes from the revival of professional and academic interest in making urban environments more human centered over the past decades. Past the axioms of urbanist thought leaders like Jane Jacobs, William Whyte, and Jan Gehl, an increasing amount of research demonstrates and models that urban vibrancy and success is linked to interactive frontages. Researchers regard frontages as a key element of walkable, compact cities, which are healthier, more sustainable, and more socially inclusive than sprawling, car-oriented urbanism, and have therefore thrived as places to live, work, and visit.[8] The world's most successful cities focus on improving their walkability to improve their quality of life and attract new residents, workers, and investors. To help this cause, traffic engineers, landscape architects, environmental psychologists, and urban planners have crafted a wide range of studies, policies, and tools for walkable environments, from nearby destinations to safe, useful, and exciting streets.[9] As a result, walkability is now a lively field in academia, with strong debates on underlying agendas, methodology, and implementation.[10] Curiously, the influence of frontages on walkability is underexposed in most walkability discussions. Even in the most advanced models, ground-floor architecture is seen as a small portion of a comprehensive index, either defining destinations or conflated with visual quality.[11] Most other models of walkability keep their eyes on the pavement, focusing on traffic safety and road design, forgoing architecture altogether.[12] The study of frontages warrants a look up to the buildings that line these walkable environments.

At the physical level, frontages are simply the street-level spaces where we transition from public space into the private space of a building. This transition can be by physically entering a building, but also by being able to see, hear, smell, and even touch what lies inside. The more a frontage can engage our senses, the more exciting it is as a destination, but also as a space to pass by or through. Our field of view is mostly horizontal, and we can only smell or hear from shorter distances. Hence, our close encounters with buildings happen mostly on the ground floor. Humans value environments with a certain level of sensory stimulation to make their environments

Figure 1.3a–c Demonstration of the disciplinary gap that focuses on active frontages: urban designers focus on public space and public life (a); architects focus on buildings (b); frontages need to encompass the connection between both (c).
Source: Image by Conrad Kickert, 2014.

positively challenging and appealing.[13] Over the past centuries, most urban environments across the globe have offered a surprisingly consistent fine-grained ground-floor architecture to satisfy this need for sensory stimulation, demonstrating a long-standing congruence between architecture and human desires.[14] The physical form of frontages need not only offer us entry; it can also shelter us from adverse weather, and provide us with an edge from which we can observe the city – a prospect and a refuge.[15]

Besides offering us physical stimulation, frontages enable us to interact not only with buildings but also with one another. Interactive frontages hold many of the spaces that we use to socialize and share ideas and culture with others. Street-level spaces hold what sociologist Ray Oldenburg coined the "third places", the crucial coffee shops, bars, libraries, and barber shops that allow us to meet people away from home or work.[16] But even beyond public amenities, the vast majority of our neighborhood social bonds are built right in front of our homes.[17] Frontages hold walkable destinations that promote health, decrease our need to drive, prevent loneliness, and build social capital.[18] Furthermore, street-level spaces offer large cohorts of underrepresented people job and entrepreneurial opportunities, and they are the spaces where we exchange ideas and innovate.[19] Interactive frontages are therefore cornerstones to healthy, sustainable, sociable, vibrant, and inclusive cities – with the right use, the right location, and the right attitude toward the city.

Inhabitation, meaning, and trust

The right use, location, and attitude of interactive frontages depends on far more than the right design. It strongly depends on who inhabits frontages, and how they view and interact with the city. The reason that we so easily conflate interactive frontages with street-level business is that retailers, bars, and restaurants enliven streets in their aim to draw in passersby and convert them into paying customers or patrons. They frame our eye-level view with fantasy worlds of consumption, communicating the best sale, the latest fashion, and the best experiences to an urban audience – a fine-tuned architecture of seduction.[20] These street-level businesses make the inviting storefronts and patios we all love. Nevertheless, as our stores become bigger, dominated by global brands, and oriented to automobile shoppers, window displays shift from engagement to mere branding, dwindling into dullness or even hostility (Figure 1.4).

The majority of our urban frontages are not occupied by businesses but by residents. Residents have a more ambiguous relationship to passersby and the city, as they balance a ground-floor desire for expression and sociability with their demand for privacy. Residential frontages need to offer a prospect into the city, but also a refuge for residents. Interactive street-level dwellings are the cornerstones of vibrant sidewalk life, but dwellings need to be designed and inhabited to allow this interaction to happen. Amsterdam architect Milos Bobić discovered that street-level residents directly respond to their perceptions of public space, materializing and reinforcing a sense of trust or distrust. In Denmark, architect and urbanist Jan Gehl demonstrated the vital importance of 'soft edges' to promote social interaction, finding that strategically placed front stoops, garden benches, and vegetation can strongly promote neighborhood cohesion by conveying trust and enabling daily conversations between neighbors.[21] Residents will go to great lengths to fit their physical environments to suit their social

Figure 1.4a–b Some storefronts invite passersby on a journey of discovery through displaying merchandise (a); others dull down this journey to a mere brand (b).
Source: Both images by Conrad Kickert; image (a) in Paris, 2012; image (b) in The Hague, 2012.

needs for privacy, safety, sociability, and expression (Figure 1.5).[22]

Our urban walks will also inevitably pass by office frontages – which is unlikely to be an exciting experience. A combination of land value growth, organizational evolution, technological innovations in telecommunication, construction, lighting, and elevators has consolidated our most central urban blocks into large office buildings. Earlier generations of offices faced the street with lavish lobby entrances, accessible arcades, or an array of ground-floor retailers, which served not only upstairs office workers but also the bottom lines of building owners. However, contemporary office architecture has become far more introverted due to an increasing focus on corporate image and security over urbanity.[23] The fine-grained transactions that used to take place in street-level workshops and retailers are now overseen by consolidated offices, which by the account of British architect Richard MacCormac represents "the discipline of work, its hermetic form safeguarding its productivity from the disorder of the world outside".[24] Beleaguered as they may be from shifting workplace culture, how can we better integrate offices in our cities at eye level?

Inevitably, we will also walk by parking garages and parking lots, which are almost certain not to excite us. The motor age has not been kind to our cities, blighting and superseding their eye-level experience with wide streets,

Figure 1.5 Residential frontages balance privacy, safety, sociability, and expression. The right transition between homes and the street is fertile ground for interactions between homes and the city.
Source: Image in Washington D.C. by ctj71081 via Flickr, CC-BY-SA-2.0.

parking lots, and garages. Parking had already become a staple in most American downtowns by the early 20th century, but the car has certainly left its mark in European downtowns over the past half century as well.[25] Parking

Figure 1.6a–b Whether in a lot (a) or in a garage (b), car parking disrupts walkability and the interaction between buildings and public space. Nevertheless, our thirst for cars is unlikely to go away soon.
Source: Both images by Conrad Kickert; image (a) in Birmingham, 2017, image (b) in The Hague, 2014.

is a paradox, as it feeds our cities with visitors, while simultaneously serving as voids in the urban fabric.[26] Even in an age of rapid transportation evolution, cars are unlikely to vanish from our cities (Figure 1.6). Similarly, our thirst for rapid delivery and local products is bolstering the rise of small manufacturing and warehousing to our urban cores. Can we turn these street-level uses from voids to interactive neighbors in our cities?

What kind of frontage inhabitant (and hence, what kind of frontage shape) we pass by relates strongly to where we find ourselves in a city. Street-level functions such as retail, bars, restaurants, offices, residents, and vacancy cluster, disperse, stratify, or diversify along lines of accessibility, agglomeration, and land values. The most central streets of our cities hold the uses that need this centrality the most, like national retailers or office headquarters. The same thirst for accessibility has replaced many historical buildings at the heart of our cities with office lobbies, and have seen American downtown functions relocate to the new centrality of freeway corridors.[27] Ground-floor tenants do not only disperse through the city, they also tend to cluster. Especially retailers benefit from being close to other retailers, but so do residents prefer to have more neighbors that they can rely on and socialize with.[28] The dynamics of our street-level functions are rapidly shifting, as dwindling street-level retail consumption makes way for new spaces of production, like co-working spaces and small manufacturing. We need to understand these trends and remain aware of how to connect new street-level inhabitants to the city.

The right connections between street-level inhabitants and the city is crucial for our urban experience. The way a city presents itself at street level is a sign of how its citizens perceive and trust public life. Trust shapes architecture, and architecture shapes trust. If citizens distrust one other, and by proxy, distrust public space, street-level architecture will follow suit and put up barricades. If a city trusts the vitality and diversity of its streets, its architecture will encourage a seamless interaction between private and public spaces. This is why sociologist Richard Sennett argues that true urbane architecture is about more than form or function, but about 'porosity', which hinges on urban trust.[29] Underlying connotations of society govern not only the designed form but the everyday inhabitation of street-level architecture, which in turn shape the meaning and connotation of public life. Frontages are hence shaped by designers, inhabitants, and passersby alike. They simultaneously read the city and feed the city.

Frontages are not just designed spaces or containers for inhabitants. They actively communicate and reinforce meaning, influencing the way we experience, evaluate, and shape our cities.[30] As frontages demarcate the boundary between public and private space, they communicate trust in how they reject, embrace, or even coopt the street. Inspired by the Structuralist movement, architect and urbanist Kris Scheerlinck demonstrates how street-level architecture marks its territory according to its trust in society, with strict demarcation promoting social control and safety, and more gradual transitions to denote various levels of privacy and socialization.[31] Others have similarly measured and connected public-private transitions as signs of urban connectivity and trust.[32] Frontages reflect a level of trust between private and public spaces, but in turn also influence this trust as people pass them by.

Figure 1.7a–b Frontages reflect and perpetuate trust between private and public space, no matter what inhabitants they have. A barricaded retailer in Birmingham signals and perpetuates a sense of distrust and unsafety (a), while residents in Raleigh connect with passersby (b). Image (a) by Conrad Kickert 2017, image (b) by Tina Govan, 2020.

Blank walls and barricades not only demonstrate a fear of crime, but they perpetuate crime in a self-fulfilling cycle, as connections between neighbors, natural surveillance, and social investment into the street falters.[33] Frontages also communicate care and culture, as they can convey what an inhabitant believes in. They can provide streets with a sense of place, appealing to our desire for enduring experiences, collective memories, and unique identities.[34]

The main currency in our quest for interactive frontages is not transparency or transactions – it is trust. Plate glass windows offer views, not necessarily access. Merchants make sales, not necessarily connections (Figure 1.7). Our architecture should not only allow citizens to connect and interact with buildings, it should allow citizens to connect and interact with one another.

What prevents our architecture from fostering these connections and interactions, and how can we turn the tide?

The past, present, and future of frontages – a reading guide

This book will provide you with insights and strategies to mend the relationship between buildings and public space, building and maintaining a street-level architecture that feeds city life. This is not a book about style. It provides design lessons, but street-level interactivity depends on far more than the right form; it depends on a symbiosis between the right design, the right inhabitation, and the right trust in the city. This requires connecting architecture with the city, its society, its culture, and its economy. Many challenges and opportunities for frontages go far beyond the typical scope of architecture, as they involve urban dynamics that require understanding and collaboration with policy makers, developers, business owners, inhabitants, passersby, and many others. Many of the lessons in this book come from these movers and shapers of frontages. Only by broadening our horizons will we be able to create the right preconditions for urban life at eye level.

This book continues in two stages. It first delves into the question of what we are fighting against: the forces and patterns that deactivate street-level architecture. It does so by studying how frontages have deactivated, and often reactivated, in four cities on both sides of the Atlantic (Chapters 2 through 5). The second part of the book then addresses these forces and patterns with strategies for frontage reactivation, learning from best practices. This book therefore bridges the past, the present, and the future of interactive frontages in a Western context. By synthesizing our mistakes and successes, we can take a sharper aim at building and maintaining interactive frontages.

Chapters 2 to 6 will demonstrate that our street-level architecture has drastically deactivated over the past century. These chapters will delve into the reasons why they have deactivated; and will study the patterns of how they deactivated. After all, in our battle for interactive frontages, we need to know the forces and patterns we need to upend to substantiate better designs, developments, and policies for frontage reactivation. To unveil these forces and patterns, these chapters track the transformation of frontages in four cities on both ends of the Atlantic: Birmingham (United Kingdom), Detroit (United States), The Hague (the Netherlands), and Vancouver (Canada). These cities have been chosen as representative of their cultural, political, and economic context (Figure 1.8). The transformation in these four cities reflects the street-level transformation of far more cities in their countries, and in the Anglo-Saxon world in general. They have transformed *sufficiently* to enable a meaningful study of the forces and patterns behind their transformations (for example disqualifying historic cities like Amsterdam, Bruges, or Oxford), but have also transformed *consistently* over the past century, without any major external shocks such as war or natural disasters (for example disqualifying war-damaged cities like Rotterdam and Coventry). At first sight, these cities seem to have

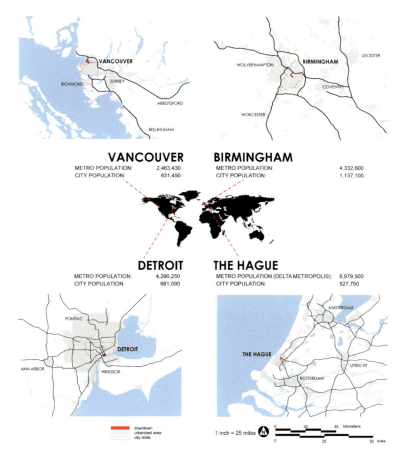

Figure 1.8 The four case study cities in their global and regional context.

undergone vastly different fates, and reflect a wide array of urban conditions.

However, these four cities actually reflect a balance of political, social, economic, and physical differences and similarities. The case study cities represent different levels of public involvement in urban affairs; different roles of cities in society; different economic transformations; and different resulting physical conditions. Furthermore, these four cities have been deliberately chosen on both sides of the Atlantic, representing positive and negative European and North American trajectories. Despite their differences, these case studies also represent similarities in their Anglo-Saxon cultural context, which assumes (or has assumed) cultural value to ground-floor commerce and street-level social interaction, a significant (if fleeting) level of public involvement in the shaping of public and private space, a strong role of automobility in streetscapes, and profound economic and physical changes over the past century. This balance between differences and similarities allows us to find generalizable patterns between cases, while still allowing us to learn unique lessons from each case. Future research is needed to delve into non-Western frontage dynamics.[35]

This book analyzes the urban cores of these four cities, as these have undergone the most consistent and profound transformations, and reflects the greatest diversity in ground-floor land uses. Whereas residential districts often only gradually change with their socioeconomic characteristics, urban cores and commercial districts continue to transform in a constant negotiation for space, commerce, and meaning.[36] As a result, urban cores present us with a fascinatingly layered spatial and functional landscape, rapidly evolving in response to social, economic, technological, and cultural forces. Urban cores often contain the city's oldest buildings next to their newest, their most mundane next to their most elaborate.[37] At eye level, urban cores present us with an array of ground floors, from hyperactive storefronts to sheltered front porches, aloof office lobbies, blank walls, and vacant lots. Urban cores hence are the ideal environment in which to study the gamut of ground-floor conditions. To ensure that all of these conditions are present, the case studies venture beyond central commercial blocks to include the fringe zone of the core, and the first blocks of areas surrounding this fringe (Figure 1.9). The fringe zone of an urban core corresponds to the highly dynamic area right outside its most central streets – the zone where commerce makes way for parking, vibrancy makes way for quiet, and growth often makes way for stagnation or even decline. Beyond

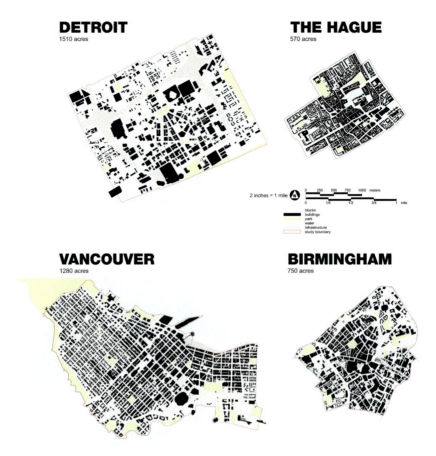

Figure 1.9 The four studied urban cores to scale.

the fringe, we find residential dynamics akin to urban districts further afield. The different frontage dynamics between the urban core, its fringe, and the surrounding neighborhoods unveil how differently buildings relate to public spaces depending on their location within the city.

Maps will track the frontage transformation in each city over the span of a century in roughly 25-year intervals. This century-long time frame allows us to recognize some of the more persistent, longue-durée forces that have shaped our frontages, like economic change and the rise of new technology like the automobile. The maps give life to an otherwise abstract narrative of frontage change and demonstrate how surprisingly consistent frontages have changed in all the studied cities over the past century. They provide us with empirical insights on the long-term dynamics of frontage deactivation that we need to address to achieve substantive improvements. The maps are based on a combination of historic mapping and business directories, economic databases, and other archival records, showing the inhabitation of street-level spaces.

As we have discussed, the type of person or organization that inhabits a frontage strongly affects how a frontage interacts with the street. Furthermore, frontage inhabitation is the only reliable indicator of this interactivity over the span of a century. The congruence between a frontage inhabitant and its interaction with the street (rather than the commonly assumed congruence between a frontage *form* and its interaction with the street) is best illustrated when inhabitation and form collide. Inhabitants will almost always reshape a frontage to suit their desired relationship with the street. When residents and office workers settle into vacant storefronts, they almost invariably shutter them with blinds and curtains to protect their privacy and focus. Conversely, when shops open up in former residential buildings, they seek to approach the street to lure in pedestrian customers by building additions right up to the sidewalk or retrofitting smaller windows with large storefronts. In both cases, architecture (at least in its formal incarnation) has taken a back seat to the everyday needs of the building tenant, which most closely relates to the function the space serves. At street level, form indeed follows function (Figure 1.10).[38]

As a result, the type of frontage inhabitant – retail, bar, restaurant, residential, office, wholesaler, manufacturer, and so on – is translated into three tiers of frontage interactivity, from highest to lowest. The connection of frontage interactivity to their use relates to their "transactional value", a term coined by British architect MacCormac to denote the extent to which certain ground-floor uses interact with public space.[39] Interactive

INTRODUCTION   11

(a)

(b)

(c)

Figure 1.10a–c Many former retail stores in The Hague now serve as offices (a) or dwellings (b) by decreasing the visual permeability of former store windows. Conversely, this record store has taken over the front yard of a former home in Buffalo, New York (c).
Source: All images by Conrad Kickert.

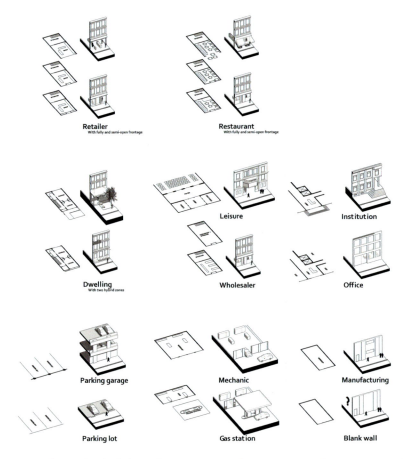

Figure 1.11 Each type of street-level inhabitant has its own spatial requirements and its own interaction with the street, from highly active retailers and restaurants at the top to inactive parking, mechanics, and blank walls at the bottom. The most common types are outlined here.
Source: Diagram by Conrad Kickert, 2021.

frontage functions such as shops or restaurants will result in highly permeable frontages that evoke a sense of a low threshold between public and private space, welcoming passersby. Conversely, highly inactive ground-floor functions such as parking garages or factories face public space with blank or impenetrable frontages, which evoke a sense of inactivity and impermeability. A functional typology of frontage interactivity has been created after pilot studies, examples of which are illustrated in Figure 1.11, and their categorization is illustrated in Figure 1.12. Together with the number of entrances per block, this indicates the level of interaction between buildings and public space. For a few areas, a more detailed analysis of the form of frontages demonstrates the changing relationship between buildings and public space at a finer grain; see Chapter 6.[40]

The first part of the book will study the dynamics of ground-floor frontages by combining maps and historical narratives of these four cities to form conclusions on the *forces* that deactivate frontages. Furthermore, these changes themselves also have internal *patterns* that warrant a closer statistical look. Do frontages decline more in certain areas than in others? Is frontage decline contagious? Does decline tend to self-accelerate? What is the role of large urban plans on frontage decline? Many of these questions are answered by further study of the frontages, both comparing them within their cities over time and between cities. Chapter 6 in this book will explain these forces and patterns, why they matter, and how they are surprisingly similar between cities that may seem different at first sight.

The second part of the book answers to the forces and patterns of frontage deactivation found in our four case study cities with strategies for frontage reactivation. These strategies learn from the successes in these four case study cities, expanding them with best practices from across the Atlantic and beyond. Oftentimes, these best practices hail from stakeholders other than architects, including regulators, managers, developers, and, most frequently, inhabitants in their everyday efforts and endless creativity to engage with the city. The strategies approach frontages from the perspective of their inhabitation types, as each

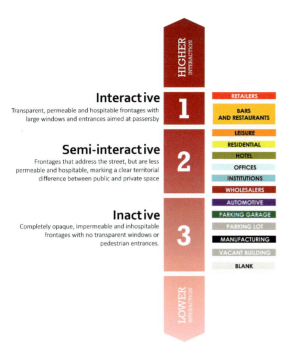

Figure 1.12 The extent to which certain inhabitants will interact with the city can be categorized into three tiers: interactive, semi-interactive, and inactive.
Source: Diagram by Conrad Kickert, 2021.

have their own dynamics of change, their own approach to the city, and their own strategies to steer this change and approach toward urbanity. Commercial frontage reactivation (Chapter 7) requires deeper insight into the internal functioning of commercial economics, feeding proposals that leverage the benefits of not only agglomeration and accessibility but also street management and storefront layout and design. The following chapter demonstrates that street-level spaces can serve as urban destinations far beyond hosting transactions. Whether in repurposed vacant storefronts or new spaces, street-level architecture can and should also enable us to socialize, grow, heal, produce new ideas and products, and learn. Chapter 8 will provide us with inspiration, and study the viability, design, and management strategies to ensure this inspiration can connect with the city. The unique dynamics of residential frontages are discussed in Chapter 9, focusing on the spatial and social conditions for residents to engage with the city in a balance of expression, socialization, and privacy. Each strategy focuses on architectural and urban design for built structure (defined as 'hardware'); the inhabitation of this structure (defined as 'software'); and the organizational, management, and inhabitant strategies to build and maintain active frontages (defined as 'orgware').[41] Beyond just a reference guide of good ideas, these chapters distill and frequently cross-pollinate their main lessons to connect new and existing inhabitants and the city.

Through ten chapters of research and strategies, this book will lay out the dynamics of street-level architecture in unprecedented detail to substantiate more targeted architectural, urban design, policy, and management strategies toward an architecture of public life. To truly change our cities at eye level, this book will bridge research and practice; connect architecture, urbanism, development, and management; and synthesize form, function, and meaning. Welcome on the journey to the past, present, and future of interactive frontages.

Notes

1 J. Gehl, "Soft Edges in Residential Streets," *Housing, Theory and Society* 3, no. 2 (1986); J. Gehl, "Close Encounters with Buildings," *Urban Design International* 11 (2006); T. G. Lopez, *Influence of the Public-Private Border Configuration on Pedestrian Behaviour. The Case of the City of Madrid* (Madrid: La Escuela Tecnica Superior de Arquitectura de Madrid, 2003).

2 Jane Jacobs, *The Death and Life of Great American Cities* (New York: Random House, 1961); Christopher Alexander, Sara Ishikawa, and Murray Silverstein, *A Pattern Language: Towns, Buildings, Construction* (New York: Oxford University Press, 1977); Jan Gehl, F Brack, and S. Thornton, "The Interface Between Public and Private Territories in Residential Areas," In *Department of Architecture and Building* (Melbourne: University of Melbourne, 1977); J. Gehl, *Life between Buildings: Using Public Space* (New York: Van Nostrand Reinhold, 1987); D. Appleyard, M. S. Gerson, and M. Lintell, *Livable Streets* (Berkeley, CA: University of California Press, 1982); Andres Duany, Elizabeth Plater-Zyberk, and Jeff Speck, *Suburban Nation: The Rise of Sprawl and the Decline of the American Dream* (New York: North Point Press, 2000); Jeff Speck, *Walkable City: How Downtown Can Save America, One Step at a Time* (New York: Farrar, Straus and Giroux, 2012); W. H. Whyte, *The Social Life of Small Urban Spaces* (Washington, DC: Conservation Foundation, 1980); W. H. Whyte, *City: Rediscovering the Center*, 1st ed. (New York: Doubleday, 1988); Alison Margaret Team Smithson, *Team 10 Primer* (London: Whitefriars Press, 1964).

3 Lopez, *Influence of the Public-Private Border Configuration on Pedestrian Behaviour. The Case of the City of Madrid*; Gehl, "Close Encounters with Buildings"; Vikas Mehta and Jennifer K. Bosson, "Third Places and the Social Life of Streets," *Environment and Behavior* 42, no. 6 (2010). For examples on frontage regulations, see A. Lehnerer, *Grand Urban Rules* (Rotterdam: 010 Publishers, 2009).

4 Whyte, *City: Rediscovering the Center*, 228.

5 Trevor Boddy, "Underground and Overhead: Building the Analogous City," in *Variations on a Theme Park: The New American City and the End of Public Space*, ed. Michael Sorkin (New York: Hill and Wang, 1992); Nan Ellin, *Postmodern Urbanism* (Cambridge, MA: Blackwell, 1996); Alison Isenberg, *Downtown America: A History of the Place and the People Who Made It* (Chicago: University of Chicago Press, 2004).

6 Conrad Kickert, *Dream City: Creation, Destruction, and Reinvention in Downtown Detroit* (Chicago: University of Chicago, 2019).

7 The tri-partite perspective on place between form, function and connotation or meaning has been developed by environmental psychologist David Canter to unveil how people memorize, use, and evaluate environments. See David V. Canter, *The Psychology of Place* (London: Architectural Press, 1977); David V. Canter, "Putting Situations in Their Place," in *Social Behaviour in Context*, ed. A. Furnham (Boston: Allyn & Bacon, 1983).

8 On the walkable city: Speck, *Walkable City: How Downtown Can Save America, One Step at a Time*. On the economic success of walkability: Christopher B. Leinberger, *The Option of Urbanism: Investing in a New American Dream* (Washington, DC: Island Press, 2008); C. B. Leinberger and M. Alfonzo, *Walk This Way: The Economic Promise of Walkable Places in Metropolitan Washington, D.C.*, ed. Metropolitan Policy Program (Washington, DC: Brookings Institution, 2012); R. Methorst, "Assessing Pedestrians' Needs," in *Walk21* (Conference Proceedings; The Hague, Netherlands, 2009).

9 Among others: M. A. Alfonzo, "To Walk or Not to Walk? The Hierarchy of Walking Needs," *Environment and Behavior* 37, no. 6 (2005); R. Ewing and S. Handy, "Measuring the Unmeasurable: Urban Design Qualities Related to Walkability," *Journal of Urban Design* 14, no. 1 (2009); C. C. Kickert, *The Urban Shopping Arcade* (Delft: TU Delft, 2007); Methorst, "Assessing Pedestrians' Needs."

10 Ann Forsyth and Michael Southworth, "Cities Afoot – Pedestrians, Walkability and Urban Design," *Journal of Urban Design* 13, no. 1 (2008): 1–3; Ann Forsyth, "What Is a Walkable Place? The Walkability Debate in Urban Design," *Urban Design International* 20, no. 4 (2015).

11 K. J. Clifton, A. D. Livi Smith, and D. Rodriguez, "The Development and Testing of an Audit for the Pedestrian Environment," *Landscape and Urban Planning* 80, no. 1 (2007); K. Day et al., "The Irvine – Minnesota Inventory to Measure Built Environments: Development," *American Journal of Preventive Medicine* 30, no. 2 (2006); Ewing and Handy, "Measuring the Unmeasurable: Urban Design Qualities Related to Walkability."; J. Heeling, H. Meyer, and J. Westrik, *Het Ontwerp Van De Stadsplattegrond*, vol. 1 (Nijmegen: Sun, 2002); A. B. Jacobs, *Great Streets* (Cambridge, MA: MIT Press, 1993).

12 D. Sauter, M. Wedderburn, and C. Buchanan, "Measuring Walking: Towards Internationally Standardised Monitoring Methods of Walking and Public Space" (8th International Conference on Survey Methods in Transport Annecy, France, 2008). For more information on walkability models, see Conrad Kickert, "Active Centers – Interactive Edges" (PhD Thesis, University of Michigan, 2014); Forsyth, "What Is a Walkable Place? The Walkability Debate in Urban Design."

13 Gehl, "Close Encounters with Buildings."; S. Kaplan, "Aesthetics, Affect and Cognition: Environmental Preference from an Evolutionary Perspective," *Environment and Behavior* 19, no. 1 (1987). For a background on the demand for stimuli on human performance, see R. M. Yerkes and J. D. Dodson, "The Relation of Strength of Stimulus to Rapidity of Habit-Formation," *Journal of Comparative Neurology and Psychology* 18 (1908). Visual complexity is one of four elements that humans prefer in their environments, the other being coherence, legibility, and mystery: J. L. Nasar, "The Evaluative Image of the City," *Journal of the American Planning Association* 56, no. 1 (1990); Kaplan, "Aesthetics, Affect and Cognition: Environmental Preference from an Evolutionary Perspective."; R. Kaplan, S. Kaplan, and T. Brown, "Environmental Preference," *Journal of the American Planning Association* 56, no. 5 (1989).

14 Amos Rapoport, *History and Precedent in Environmental Design* (New York: Plenum Press, 1990).

15 Gehl, "Close Encounters with Buildings."

16 Ray Oldenburg, *The Great Good Place: Cafes, Coffee Shops, Bookstores, Bars, Hair Salons, and Other Hangouts at the Heart of a Community* (Philadelphia, PA: Da Capo Press, 1999).

17 Oddvar Skjaeveland and Tommy Garling, "Effects of Interactional Space on Neighbouring," *Journal of Environmental Psychology* 17, no. 3 (1997).

18 Forsyth, "What Is a Walkable Place? The Walkability Debate in Urban Design."; Andrew Rundle et al., "Neighborhood Food Environment and Walkability Predict Obesity in New York City," *Environmental Health Perspectives* 117, no. 3 (2008); Samuel Stroope et al., "College Graduates, Local Retailers, and Community Belonging in the United States," *Sociological Spectrum* 34, no. 2 (2014); Stephan J. Goetz and Anil Rupasingha, "Wal-Mart and Social Capital," *American Journal of Agricultural Economics* 88, no. 5 (2006).

19 On job and entrepreneurial opportunities, see Robert W. Fairlie and Alicia M Robb, *Race and Entrepreneurial Success: Black-, Asian-, and White-Owned Businesses in the United States* (Cambridge, MA: MIT Press, 2010); Sharon Zukin, Philip Kasinitz, and Xiangming Chen, *Global Cities, Local Streets: Everyday Diversity from New York to Shanghai* (New York; London: Routledge, 2016). On innovation and idea exchange, see Bruce Katz and Julie Wagner, "The Rise of Innovation Districts: A New Geography of Innovation in America," in *Metropolitan Policy Program* (Washington, DC: Brookings Institution, 2014); Julie Wagner, Bruce Katz, and Thomas Osha, *The Evolution of Innovation Districts* (Washington, DC and Lugano: Global Institute on Innovation Districts, 2019); Nate Storring, *Placemaking and the Evolution of Innovation Districts* (Project for Public Spaces, 2019).

20 Leonard S. Marcus, *The American Store Window* (New York: Whitney Library of Design, 1978). A. Alfred Taubman, *Threshold Resistance: The Extraordinary Career of a Luxury Retailing Pioneer* (New York: Collins, 2007). J. Holck, *The Shops and the Living Cities. An Investigation of the Relational Complexity in Urban Shopping Environments* (University of Copenhagen, 2010); L. W. Turley and R. E. Milliman, "Atmospheric Effects on Shopping Behavior: A Review of the Experimental Evidence," *Journal of Business Research* 49, no. 2 (2000).

21 Milos Bobic, *Between the Edges: Street-Building Transition as Urbanity Interface* (Bussum Netherlands: Thoth Publishers, 2004), 57; Anne Matan and Peter Newman, *People Cities: The Life and Legacy of Jan Gehl* (Washington, DC: Island Press, 2016); Gehl, "Soft Edges in Residential Streets."

22 Eric van Ulden, Daniel Heussen, and Sander van der Ham, *De Stoep: Ontmoetingen Tussen Huis En Straat* (Rotterdam: 010 Publishers, 2015).

23 Street-level shops generated five to six times the rent of upper floor office space in the early 20th century. This rental calculation is provided in Cecil Calvert Evers, *The Commercial Problem in Buildings; A Discussion of the Economic and Structural Essentials of Profitable Building, and the Basis for Valuation of Improved Real Estate* (New York: Record and Guide Co., 1914), 185. For more information, see Carol Willis, *Form Follows Finance: Skyscrapers and Skylines in New York and Chicago* (New York: Princeton Architectural Press, 1995), 58–59.

24 R. MacCormac, "Fitting in Offices," *The Architectural Review* 181, no. 1083 (1987): 64.

25 John A. Jakle and Keith A. Sculle, *Lots of Parking: Land Use in a Car Culture* (Charlottesville: University of Virginia Press, 2004); Shannon Sanders McDonald, *The Parking Garage: Design and Evolution of a Modern Urban Form* (Washington, DC: Urban Land Institute, 2007).

26 McDonald, *The Parking Garage: Design and Evolution of a Modern Urban Form*, 176.

27 This stratification of land uses according to centrality was modeled as a "bid-rent" curve: E. B. Burgess, "Concentric Zone Model of Urban Structure and Land Use," *Landmark Publication* 125 (1925); Johann Heinrich Von Thünen, *Der Isolierte Staat in Beziehung Auf Landwirtschaft Und Nationalökonomie*, vol. 1 (Berlin: Wiegant, Hempel & Parey, 1875). It has since been followed by more advanced models, e.g. Hillier and J. Hanson, *The Social Logic of Space* (Cambridge [Cambridgeshire] and New York: Cambridge University Press, 1984); Hillier, *Space Is the Machine: A Configurational Theory of Architecture* (Cambridge and New York, NY: Cambridge University Press, 1996).

28 For retail clustering theory, see Stephen Brown, "Retail Location Theory: Evolution and Evaluation," *International Review of Retail, Distribution and Consumer Research* 3, no. 2 (1993). For the residential need for neighbors, see e.g. Gehl, "Soft Edges in Residential Streets"; Ulden, Heussen, and Ham, *De Stoep: Ontmoetingen Tussen Huis En Straat.*

29 Richard Sennett, *Building and Dwelling: Ethics for the City* (2018).

30 Matthew Carmona, *Public Places, Urban Spaces: The Dimensions of Urban Design* (Oxford; Boston: Architectural Press, 2003); Ulric Neisser, *Cognition and Reality: Principles and Implications of Cognitive Psychology* (San Francisco: W. H. Freeman, 1976). T. Cresswell, *Place: A Short Introduction*, vol. 3 (Chichester, West Sussex; Malden, MA: Wiley-Blackwell, 2004), 10. E. C. Relph, *Place and Placelessness*, Research in Planning and Design (London: Pion, 1976); Canter, *The Psychology of Place.*

31 K. Scheerlinck, *Depth Configurations. Proximity, Permeability and Territorial Boundaries in Urban Projects* (Barcelona: URL Barcelona, 2012). On structuralist analyses of the public-private boundary: N. J. Habraken and Jonathan Teicher, *The Structure of the Ordinary: Form and Control in the Built Environment* (Cambridge, MA: MIT Press, 1998); Heeling, Meyer, and Westrik, *Het Ontwerp Van De Stadsplattegrond*, 1; Ali Madanipour, *Public and Private Spaces of the City* (London and New York: Routledge, 2003).

32 Structuralist John Habraken measures the relation between homes and the city through their 'territorial' or 'topological depth': Habraken and Teicher, *The Structure of the Ordinary: Form and Control in the Built Environment*, 139. Architectural researchers Bill Hillier and Julienne Hanson demarcate the number and type of building entrances to public space as the

"constitutedness" of a street, an important indicator of sociability and vibrancy: Hillier and Hanson, *The Social Logic of Space*, 82–142, Chapter 3. See also G. Palaiologou and L. Vaughan, *Urban Rhythms: Historic Housing Evolution and Socio-Spatial Boundaries* (Santiago de Chile: 8th International Space Syntax Symposium, 2012).

33 Hillier and Hanson, *The Social Logic of Space*; Hillier, *Space Is the Machine: A Configurational Theory of Architecture*; S. Shu and J. Huang, "Spatial Configuration and Vulnerability of Residential Burglary: A Case Study of a City in Taiwan" (Paper presented at the Proceedings of 4th International Space Syntax Symposium. London, 2003); A. Van Nes and M. J. J. López, *Micro Scale Spatial Relationships in Urban Studies: The Relationship between Private and Public Space and Its Impact on Street Life* (Istanbul: 6th International Space Syntax Symposium, 2007).

34 On collective memory, see David Lowenthal, "Past Time, Present Place: Landscape and Memory," *Geographical Review* (1975): 1–36; M. Christine Boyer, *The City of Collective Memory: Its Historical Imagery and Architectural Entertainments* (Cambridge, MA: MIT Press, 1994); M. Hebbert, "The Street as Locus of Collective Memory," *Environment and Planning D* 23, no. 4 (2005); H. Meyer, L. Van den Burg, and H. C. Bekkering, eds., *Het Geheugen Van De Stad / the Memory of the City* (Amsterdam: SUN, 2006). On non-places and their conception, see Lefebvre in Dolores Hayden, *The Power of Place: Urban Landscapes as Public History* (Cambridge, MA: MIT Press, 1995), 21; Hans Ibelings, *Supermodernism: Architecture in the Age of Globalization* (Rotterdam: NAi, 1998); Marc Augé, *Non-Places: Introduction to an Anthropology of Supermodernity* (London; New York: Verso, 1995).

35 The balance between similarities and differences is the cornerstone of case study research methodology, described by social scientist Robert K. Yin. He states that case study research "needs to state the conditions under which a particular phenomenon is likely to be found (a literal replication [between case studies]) as well as the conditions when it is not likely to be found (a theoretical replication)" R. K. Yin, "Case Study Research," *Design and Methods* 5 (1994): 48.

36 Urban morphologist Brenda Scheer likens residential fabric with 'static fabric', inherently resistant to change. Conversely, commercial districts embrace change and evolution. Kiril Stanilov and Brenda Case Scheer, *Suburban Form: An International Perspective* (New York: Routledge, 2004). On the dynamics of urban cores, see Robert M. Fogelson, *Downtown: Its Rise and Fall, 1880–1950* (New Haven: Yale University Press, 2001); Isenberg, *Downtown America: A History of the Place and the People Who Made It*; Cor Wagenaar, *Town Planning in the Netherlands since 1800: Responses to Enlightenment Ideas and Geopolitical Realities* (Rotterdam: 010 Publishers, 2011).

37 This dichotomy has been aptly described in Rem Koolhaas, "Whatever Happened to Urbanism?" *Design Quarterly*, no. 164 (1995).

38 On the correlation between morphological types and functional requirements into "function-types", see Philip Steadman, *Building Types and Built Forms* (Kibworth: Matador, 2014). Although Steadman argues for a relative consistency of this correlation through history, others disagree: Daniel Koch, "Changing Building Typologies: The Typological Question and the Formal Basis of Architecture," *The Journal of Space Syntax* 5, no. 2 (2014).

39 R. MacCormac, "Urban Reform: Maccormac's Manifesto," *Architects Journal* 15 (1983); Richard MacCormac, "The Dignity of Office," *The Architectural Review* 190, no. 1143 (1992).

40 The research methodology behind the diachronic study of frontages in all four cities is explained in more detail in Kickert, "Active Centers – Interactive Edges"; Conrad C. Kickert, "Active Centers – Interactive Edges: The Rise and Fall of Ground Floor Frontages," *Urban Design International* 21, no. 1 (2016).

41 Meredith Glaser et al., *The City at Eye Level: Lessons for Street Plinths* (Delft: Eburon Uitgeverij BV, 2012).

Bibliography

Alexander, Christopher, Sara Ishikawa, and Murray Silverstein. *A Pattern Language: Towns, Buildings, Construction.* New York: Oxford University Press, 1977.

Alfonzo, M. A. "To Walk or Not to Walk? The Hierarchy of Walking Needs." *Environment and Behavior* 37, no. 6 (2005): 808–36.

Appleyard, D., M. S. Gerson, and M. Lintell. *Livable Streets.* Berkeley, CA: University of California Press, 1982.

Augé, Marc. *Non-Places: Introduction to an Anthropology of Supermodernity.* [in English] London and New York: Verso, 1995.

Bobic, Milos. *Between the Edges: Street-Building Transition as Urbanity Interface.* [in English] Bussum: Thoth Publishers, 2004.

Boddy, Trevor. "Underground and Overhead: Building the Analogous City." In *Variations on a Theme Park: The New American City and the End of Public Space*, edited by Michael Sorkin, 123–53. New York: Hill and Wang, 1992.

Boyer, M. Christine. *The City of Collective Memory: Its Historical Imagery and Architectural Entertainments.* [in English] Cambridge, MA: MIT Press, 1994.

Brown, Stephen. "Retail Location Theory: Evolution and Evaluation." *International Review of Retail,*

Distribution and Consumer Research 3, no. 2 (1993): 185–229.

Burgess, E. B. "Concentric Zone Model of Urban Structure and Land Use." *Landmark Publication* 125 (1925).

Canter, David V. *The Psychology of Place*. London: Architectural Press, 1977.

———. "Putting Situations in Their Place." In *Social Behaviour in Context*, edited by A. Furnham. Boston: Allyn & Bacon, 1983.

Carmona, Matthew. *Public Places, Urban Spaces: The Dimensions of Urban Design*. [in English] Oxford and Boston: Architectural Press, 2003.

Clifton, K. J., A. D. Livi Smith, and D. Rodriguez. "The Development and Testing of an Audit for the Pedestrian Environment." *Landscape and Urban Planning* 80, no. 1 (2007): 95–110.

Cresswell, T. *Place: A Short Introduction*. Vol. 3. Hoboken, NJ: Wiley-Blackwell, 2004.

Day, K., M. Boarnet, M. Alfonzo, and A. Forsyth. "The Irvine – Minnesota Inventory to Measure Built Environments: Development." *American Journal of Preventive Medicine* 30, no. 2 (2006): 144–52.

Duany, Andres, Elizabeth Plater-Zyberk, and Jeff Speck. *Suburban Nation: The Rise of Sprawl and the Decline of the American Dream*. [in English] New York: North Point Press, 2000.

Ellin, Nan. *Postmodern Urbanism*. [in English] Cambridge, MA: Blackwell, 1996.

Evers, Cecil Calvert. *The Commercial Problem in Buildings: A Discussion of the Economic and Structural Essentials of Profitable Building, and the Basis for Valuation of Improved Real Estate*. [in English] New York: Record and Guide Co., 1914.

Ewing, R., and S. Handy. "Measuring the Unmeasurable: Urban Design Qualities Related to Walkability." *Journal of Urban Design* 14, no. 1 (2009): 65–84.

Fairlie, Robert W., and Alicia M. Robb. *Race and Entrepreneurial Success: Black-, Asian-, and White-Owned Businesses in the United States*. Cambridge, MA: MIT Press, 2010.

Fogelson, Robert M. *Downtown: Its Rise and Fall, 1880–1950*. [in English] New Haven: Yale University Press, 2001.

Forsyth, Ann. "What Is a Walkable Place? The Walkability Debate in Urban Design." *Urban Design International* 20, no. 4 (2015): 274–92.

Forsyth, Ann, and Michael Southworth. "Cities Afoot – Pedestrians, Walkability and Urban Design." *Journal of Urban Design* 13, no. 1 (2008): 1–3.

Gehl, J. "Close Encounters with Buildings." *Urban Design International* 11 (2006): 29–47.

———. *Life Between Buildings: Using Public Space*. New York: Van Nostrand Reinhold, 1987.

———. "Soft Edges in Residential Streets." *Housing, Theory and Society* 3, no. 2 (1986): 89–102.

Gehl, J., F. Brack, and S. Thornton. *The Interface Between Public and Private Territories in Residential Areas*. Melbourne: Department of Architecture and Building, University of Melbourne, 1977.

Glaser, Meredith, Mattijs van 't Hoff, Hans Karssenberg, Jeroen Laven, and Jan van Teeffelen. *The City at Eye Level: Lessons for Street Plinths*. Delft: Eburon Uitgeverij BV, 2012.

Goetz, Stephan J., and Anil Rupasingha. "Wal-Mart and Social Capital." *American Journal of Agricultural Economics* 88, no. 5 (2006): 1304–10.

Habraken, N. J., and Jonathan Teicher. *The Structure of the Ordinary: Form and Control in the Built Environment*. [in English] Cambridge, MA: MIT Press, 1998.

Hayden, Dolores. *The Power of Place: Urban Landscapes as Public History*. [in English] Cambridge, MA: MIT Press, 1995.

Hebbert, M. "The Street as Locus of Collective Memory." *Environment and Planning D* 23, no. 4 (2005): 581.

Heeling, J., H. Meyer, and J. Westrik. *Het Ontwerp Van De Stadsplattegrond*. Vol. 1. Nijmegen: Sun, 2002.

Hillier. *Space Is the Machine: A Configurational Theory of Architecture*. Cambridge and New York: Cambridge University Press, 1996.

Hillier, and J. Hanson. *The Social Logic of Space*. Cambridge [Cambridgeshire] and New York: Cambridge University Press, 1984.

Holck, J. *The Shops and the Living Cities. An Investigation of the Relational Complexity in Urban Shopping Environments*. Copenhagen: Dissertation at the University of Copenhagen, 2010.

Ibelings, Hans. *Supermodernism: Architecture in the Age of Globalization*. [in English] Rotterdam: NAi, 1998.

Isenberg, Alison. *Downtown America: A History of the Place and the People Who Made It*. [in English] Chicago: University of Chicago Press, 2004.

Jacobs, A. B. *Great Streets*. Cambridge, MA: MIT Press, 1993.

Jacobs, Jane. *The Death and Life of Great American Cities*. New York: Random House, 1961.

Jakle, John A., and Keith A. Sculle. *Lots of Parking: Land Use in a Car Culture*. Charlottesville: University of Virginia Press, 2004.

Kaplan, R., S. Kaplan, and T. Brown. "Environmental Preference." *Environment and Behavior* 21, no. 5 (1989): 509.

Kaplan, S. "Aesthetics, Affect and Cognition: Environmental Preference from an Evolutionary Perspective." *Environment and Behavior* 19, no. 1 (1987): 3–32.

Katz, Bruce, and Julie Wagner. "The Rise of Innovation Districts: A New Geography of Innovation in America." In *Metropolitan Policy Program*. Washington, DC: Brookings Institution, 2014.

Kickert, C. C. *The Urban Shopping Arcade*. Delft: TU Delft, 2007.

Kickert, C. C. "Active Centers – Interactive Edges." PhD Thesis, University of Michigan, 2014.

———. "Active Centers – Interactive Edges: The Rise and Fall of Ground Floor Frontages." *Urban Design International* 21, no. 1 (2016): 55–77.

———. *Dream City: Creation, Destruction, and Reinvention in Downtown Detroit*. [In English] Chicago: University of Chicago, 2019.

Koch, Daniel. "Changing Building Typologies: The Typological Question and the Formal Basis of Architecture." *The Journal of Space Syntax* 5, no. 2 (2014): 168–89.

Koolhaas, Rem. "Whatever Happened to Urbanism?" *Design Quarterly*, no. 164 (1995): 28–31.

Leinberger, C. B. *The Option of Urbanism: Investing in a New American Dream*. [in English] Washington, DC: Island Press, 2008.

Leinberger, C. B., and M. Alfonzo. *Walk This Way: The Economic Promise of Walkable Places in Metropolitan Washington, D.C.* Edited by Metropolitan Policy Program. Washington, DC: Brookings Institution, 2012.

Lopez, T. G. *Influence of the Public-Private Border Configuration on Pedestrian Behaviour. The Case of the City of Madrid*. Madrid: La Escuela Tecnica Superior de Arquitectura de Madrid, 2003.

Lowenthal, David. "Past Time, Present Place: Landscape and Memory." *Geographical Review* (1975): 1–36.

MacCormac, R. "Fitting in Offices." *The Architectural Review* 181, no. 1083 (1987): 62–67.

———. "Urban Reform: MacCormac's Manifesto." *Architects Journal* 15 (1983): 59–77.

———. "The Dignity of Office." *The Architectural Review* 190, no. 1143 (1992): 76–82.

Madanipour, Ali. *Public and Private Spaces of the City*. [in English] London and New York: Routledge, 2003.

Marcus, Leonard S. *The American Store Window*. [in English] New York: Whitney Library of Design, 1978.

Matan, Anne, and Peter Newman. *People Cities: The Life and Legacy of Jan Gehl*. Washington, DC: Island Press, 2016.

McDonald, Shannon Sanders. *The Parking Garage: Design and Evolution of a Modern Urban Form*. [in English] Washington, DC: Urban Land Institute, 2007.

Mehta, Vikas, and Jennifer K. Bosson. "Third Places and the Social Life of Streets." *Environment and Behavior* 42, no. 6 (2010): 779–805.

Methorst, R. "Assessing Pedestrians' Needs." In *Walk21*. Conference Proceedings, The Hague, Netherlands, 2009.

Meyer, H., L. Van den Burg, and H. C. Bekkering, eds. *Het Geheugen Van De Stad/the Memory of the City*. Amsterdam: SUN, 2006.

Nasar, J. L. "The Evaluative Image of the City." *Journal of the American Planning Association* 56, no. 1 (1990): 41–53.

Neisser, Ulric. *Cognition and Reality: Principles and Implications of Cognitive Psychology*. San Francisco: W. H. Freeman, 1976.

Oldenburg, Ray. *The Great Good Place: Cafes, Coffee Shops, Bookstores, Bars, Hair Salons, and Other Hangouts at the Heart of a Community*. Philadelphia: PA Da Capo Press, 1999.

Palaiologou, G., and L. Vaughan. "Urban Rhythms: Historic Housing Evolution and Socio-Spatial Boundaries." Santiago de Chile: Eighth International Space Syntax Symposium, 2012.

Pivo, G., and J. D. Fisher. "The Walkability Premium in Commercial Real Estate Investments." *Real Estate Economics* 39, no. 2 (2011): 185–219.

Rapoport, Amos. *History and Precedent in Environmental Design*. New York: Plenum Press, 1990.

Relph, E. C. *Place and Placelessness*. Research in Planning and Design. London: Pion, 1976.

Rundle, Andrew, Kathryn M. Neckerman, Lance Freeman, Gina S. Lovasi, Marnie Purciel, James Quinn, Catherine Richards, Neelanjan Sircar, and Christopher Weiss. "Neighborhood Food Environment and Walkability Predict Obesity in New York City." *Environmental Health Perspectives* 117, no. 3 (2008): 442–47.

Sauter, D., M. Wedderburn, and C. Buchanan. "Measuring Walking: Towards Internationally Standardised Monitoring Methods of Walking and Public Space." 8th International Conference on Survey Methods in Transport Annecy, France, May 25–31, 2008.

Scheerlinck, K. "Depth Configurations. Proximity, Permeability and Territorial Boundaries in Urban Projects." PhD Thesis, URL Barcelona, 2012.

Sennett, Richard. *Building and Dwelling: Ethics for the City*. New York: Farrar, Straus and Giroux, 2018.

Shu, S., and J. Huang. "Spatial Configuration and Vulnerability of Residential Burglary: A Case Study of a City in Taiwan." Paper presented at the Proceedings of 4th International Space Syntax Symposium, London, 2003.

Skjaeveland, Oddvar, and Tommy Garling. "Effects of Interactional Space on Neighbouring." *Journal of Environmental Psychology* 17, no. 3 (1997): 181–98.

Smithson, Alison Margaret Team. *Team 10 Primer*. [in English] London: Whitefriars Press, 1964.

Sorkin, M. *Variations on a Theme Park: The New American City and the End of Public Space*. New York: Hill and Wang, 1992.

Speck, Jeff. *Walkable City: How Downtown Can Save America, One Step at a Time*. New York: Farrar, Straus and Giroux, 2012.

Stanilov, Kiril, and Brenda Case Scheer. *Suburban Form: An International Perspective*. New York: Routledge, 2004.

Steadman, Philip. *Building Types and Built Forms*. Kibworth: Matador, 2014.

Storring, Nate. *Placemaking and the Evolution of Innovation Districts*. New York: Project for Public Spaces, 2019.

Stroope, Samuel, Aaron B. Franzen, Charles M. Tolbert, and F. Carson Mencken. "College Graduates, Local Retailers, and Community Belonging in the United States." *Sociological Spectrum* 34, no. 2 (2014): 143–62.

Taubman, A. Alfred. *Threshold Resistance: The Extraordinary Career of a Luxury Retailing Pioneer.* [in English] New York: Collins, 2007.

Turley, L. W., and R. E. Milliman. "Atmospheric Effects on Shopping Behavior: A Review of the Experimental Evidence." *Journal of Business Research* 49, no. 2 (2000): 193–211.

Ulden, Eric van, Daniel Heussen, and Sander van der Ham. *De Stoep: Ontmoetingen Tussen Huis En Straat.* [in Dutch] Rotterdam: 010 Publishers, 2015.

Van Nes, A., and M. J. J. López. *Micro Scale Spatial Relationships in Urban Studies: The Relationship Between Private and Public Space and Its Impact on Street Life.* Proceedings of the 6th International Space Syntax Symposium, Istanbul, 2007.

Von Thünen, Johann Heinrich. *Der Isolirte Staat in Beziehung Auf Landwirtschaft Und Nationalökonomie.* Vol. 1. Berlin: Wiegant, Hempel & Parey, 1875.

Wagenaar, Cor. *Town Planning in the Netherlands since 1800: Responses to Enlightenment Ideas and Geopolitical Realities.* [in English] Rotterdam: 010 Publishers, 2011.

Wagner, Julie, Bruce Katz, and Thomas Osha. "The Evolution of Innovation Districts." Washington, DC and Lugano: Global Institute on Innovation Districts, 2019.

Whitehand, J. W. R. "Urban Fringe Belts: Development of an Idea." *Planning perspectives* 3, no. 1 (1988): 47–58.

Whyte, W. H. *City: Rediscovering the Center.* 1st ed. New York: Doubleday, 1988.

———. *The Social Life of Small Urban Spaces.* Washington, DC: Conservation Foundation, 1980.

Willis, Carol. *Form Follows Finance: Skyscrapers and Skylines in New York and Chicago.* [in English] New York: Princeton Architectural Press, 1995.

Yerkes, R. M., Dodson, J. D. "The Relation of Strength of Stimulus to Rapidity of Habit-Formation." *Journal of comparative neurology and psychology* 18 (1908): 459–82.

Yin, R. K. "Case Study Research." *Design and methods* 5 (1994).

Zukin, Sharon, Philip Kasinitz, and Xiangming Chen. *Global Cities, Local Streets: Everyday Diversity from New York to Shanghai.* [in English] New York and London: Routledge, 2016.

2 DETROIT
EYE-LEVEL DEATH AND RESURRECTION

Figure 2.0 The Millender Center in Detroit.[1]
DOI: 10.4324/9781003041887-2

Of all the four cities we study, downtown Detroit presents us with the greatest eye-level challenges, but also with the greatest rebirth of street-level architecture. Known the world over as the poster child for urban decline, the familiar imagery of Detroit includes crumbling architecture, crime, and vacancy. At the heart of the Motor City, downtown Detroit presents us with a different narrative – certainly one of decline, but also of contrast. At eye level, downtown's most central streets have become a regional hub for sidewalk life, with interactive storefronts welcoming passersby to dinner, drinks, and unique merchandise. Only a block away, pedestrians are confronted with a far more familiar image of architectural hostility, vacancy, and car-dominated land use. This chapter describes how more than a century of social, economic, professional, and cultural tensions have created this fascinating contrast. Detroit serves not only as a warning to architectural and urban erosion, but also as a hopeful beacon to the value of a fine-grained relationship between buildings and public space. Its downtown presents new ideas and trends that await many other cities on either end of the Atlantic – for better and for worse.

Introduction

Despite Detroit's early settlement by French colonists in the 1700s, much of downtown Detroit's street and block structure as it is seen today was shaped by a judge in the early 19th century, following a tragic fire in 1805, inspired by the baroque plan for Washington, D.C.[2] The city's first commercial heart lined the shores of the Detroit River, the city's lifeline to the Great Lakes and the East Coast for the first half of the 19th century. Economic growth soon brought diverse immigration, including Detroit's first major African American settlement east of downtown. By the late 1830s, Detroit built its first railway lines into the growing Michigan hinterland, which began to shift the commercial core further inland and fostered a railroad industry that laid the groundwork for Detroit's later dominance in automobile construction (Figure 2.1).[3]

Accelerating industrial growth by the late 19th century yielded Detroit's first department stores, theaters, and office skyscrapers downtown, bolstered by innovations in steel frame construction and elevators.[4] Urban growth began to stratify wealth north and west of downtown, concentrating poverty and minorities to the east. The rise of streetcars by the late 19th century exacerbated Detroit's segregation, setting up a divide that lasted well into the next century.[5] Detroit's transition from a provincial trade city to an industrial powerhouse by the turn of the 20th century, due to the rise of automobile manufacturing, further accelerated its outward growth. As new factories in search of cheap and rail-connected land sprouted suburban worker settlements, a new symbiosis emerged between miles of single-family housing and

Figure 2.1a–b The fruits of rapid growth: Detroit's new 1871 City Hall dwarfs its predecessor on the other end of Campus Martius square (a). However, growth in Detroit mostly went outward, not upward. A 1889 lithograph shows the smokestacks of industry and transportation miles outside downtown (b).
Sources: Image (a) courtesy of the Burton Historical Collection, Detroit Public Library. Image (b) by Calvert Lithography, courtesy of Library of Congress Geography and Map Division.

an increasingly dense, streetcar-connected commercial downtown that remained Detroit's office, retail, and entertainment heart. A new wave of department stores and offices bolstered downtown's sidewalk life as much as it enlivened the city's skyline. Yet nearby, housing conditions began to deteriorate, especially on the East End where African Americans were forced to settle into increasingly crowded and dilapidated conditions.[6]

While today we think of Detroit as being remarkable for its urban decline, it was its rapid growth and development at the turn of the 20th century that initially put the city on the map. Amidst a city of more than half a million inhabitants and producing a quarter billion dollars' worth of cars every year, downtown was clearly in a state of transition in 1911.[7] As Figure 2.2 demonstrates with a map of street-level frontage interactivity, Detroit's downtown architectural experience

DETROIT – EYE-LEVEL DEATH AND RESURRECTION   23

Figure 2.2   Frontage interactivity in downtown Detroit in 1911.
Source: Diagram by Conrad Kickert, 2021.

at eye level was incredibly vibrant and diverse. A central core of department stores and adjoining retailers (1) radiates out into mostly continuous retail corridors along Detroit's radial avenues (2) – and business was only growing.[8] Just around the corner, thousands of densely built up residential buildings surrounded downtown, interspersed with a fine-grained pattern of corner shops, bars, and restaurants (3). Detroit's Eastern Market on the northeast corner of the map (4) had already grown to become a hub of both retail and wholesale activity in Michigan, increasingly taking over the market activity at the heart of downtown (5).[9] Yet, we can also see the first sign of downtown Detroit's pattern of obsolescence along the waterfront, where the city's former water-based commercial vibrancy only remained as relatively inactive warehousing, wholesale, and manufacturing frontages (6). These buildings would slowly creep into waterfront neighborhoods over the next decades, starting a 'zone of transition' that would increasingly sever the downtown from its residential hinterland.

1911–1937

A visitor to downtown Detroit in 1911 would hardly recognize the same places by 1937, as the city's core skyline and streetscape nearly completely transformed – for the better, at first. As car manufacturing continued to ramp up, downtown Detroit was booming with construction of skyscrapers for financial offices, department stores for shopping, and a new high-rise district of hotels and offices further inland. A visitor to Detroit noted in 1913 that "there is not another city in the United States . . . where building operations are being conducted on such a proportionate scale as they are here".[10] For almost two decades, downtown growth added to street-level vibrancy, as offices, hotels, and dwellings catered to passersby and tenants alike with profitable storefronts.[11] A growing real estate empire west of downtown hinged on a symbiotic skyward growth of hotel rooms and offices atop a solid retail district that could rival New York's Fifth Avenue. This yielded a series of large buildings that enlivened and gave new purpose to the sidewalks they lined.[12] The primary retail street of the city, Woodward Avenue, solidified its hegemony with ever-larger and more opulent department stores and other retail palaces, vying for the attention of passersby with lavishly decorated display windows and new shopping arcades.[13] Detroit's leading department stores grew their downtown premises in a battle for the Detroit consumer, usurping entire city blocks with lavish multistory buildings. During the 1910s and 1920s, Detroit's three largest department stores increased their footprint between five and tenfold; their sales skyrocketed even further. Hudson's department store led the pack by the late 1920s with a nearly two million square feet (200,000 square meters), 17-story department store – the world's tallest, only rivalled by Macy's in New York by size.[14]

At the same time that retail was expanding, Detroit's nightlife similarly flourished. Tens of thousands of new theater seats were added during the 1910s and 1920s, – all despite a 1920 national alcohol prohibition.[15] Skyscraper construction in Detroit's financial district was already noteworthy during the 1910s, but only accelerated during the following decade with the completion of several high-profile office buildings. As one building after the other vied for prominence on the skyline, their street-level relationship with downtown became increasingly ambivalent, as financial institutions began to commission more introverted buildings in search of a dependable and secure image (Figure 2.3).[16] While impressive to behold, downtown Detroit's office construction significantly lagged behind larger cities like Chicago and New York, ranking last among American's large cities – and many never reached full occupancy. This tepid growth mostly reflected industrialists' reluctance to invest and conduct their financial business downtown.[17] In fact, Detroit's largest early 20th-century office building was constructed for the newly formed General Motors headquarters in a 'New Center' three miles north of downtown – right amongst its growing inland empire of factories.[18]

Detroit's explosive mixture of suburbanizing jobs and population, automobile dominance, and inner city slum formation first became apparent downtown. When the *New York Times* visited "Detroit the Dynamic" in 1927, it found a prosperous city, but without a "general stampede

Figure 2.3a–b Skyscraper growth created some of Detroit's most impressive Art Deco architecture, but skyward prowess decreasingly coincided with street-level interactivity. Whereas the 1908 Ford Building contains active storefronts (a), the 1929 Guardian Building internalizes its activity (b).
Source: Both images by Conrad Kickert.

toward a centralized workshop district", its jobs and population rather dispersing "as a city on wheels must".[19] The dwellings left behind by suburbanizing residents and jobs were increasingly subdivided into rooming houses for transient workers and African Americans with no other choice of housing. The resulting "score of massive houses in varying stages of unkemptness" surrounding downtown by the 1910s had spiraled into "almost intolerable" conditions by the late 1920s, yet housing and zoning regulations were rejected by downtown business interests, politicians, and voters as obstructions to growth. Instead, early city plans focused on aesthetic improvements, and they often remained unbuilt.[20]

Planners were more successful in tackling Detroit's growing traffic problems, often to the detriment of street-level frontage interactivity. Rather than meaningfully improving public transportation, the city opted to plan for a program of road widenings. Furthermore, a 'traffic belt' of widened roads was proposed around the downtown, running right through downtown's oldest surrounding neighborhoods. These street-widening projects were supported by downtown businesses and approved in several referenda. The city bought thousands of mixed-use buildings along one side of Detroit's main arterials to widen streets, paid for by the remaining businesses on the other side of the street under the premise that wider streets were good for business.[21] Within years, it became clear this had been a false assumption. The widenings scarred miles of formerly vibrant urban retail frontages with demolitions and business failures. Flooding from newly widened streets onto the nation's busiest intersections, cars soon began to erode the downtown landscape with car dealerships, repair shops, and gas stations – but especially with parking lots. In the 1910s, a car parts salesman started a modest off-street parking lot as a side business, which grew into an empire of dozens of lots by the 1920s, virtually encircling downtown.[22] Unhindered by zoning restrictions, other landowners soon took notice, tearing down hundreds of buildings to create more than a million square feet (100,000 square meters) of parking by the end of the decade. When the lights went out in Depression-struck Detroit and its downtown in the 1930s, car parking remained among the only viable land use option among vacant offices and department stores. For the first time in its history, downtown had begun to shrink, especially in its already beleaguered peripheral blocks.

Within three short decades in the early 20th century, Detroit's downtown grew, found its limits to growth, and began to contract. Figure 2.4 shows the uneven outcomes

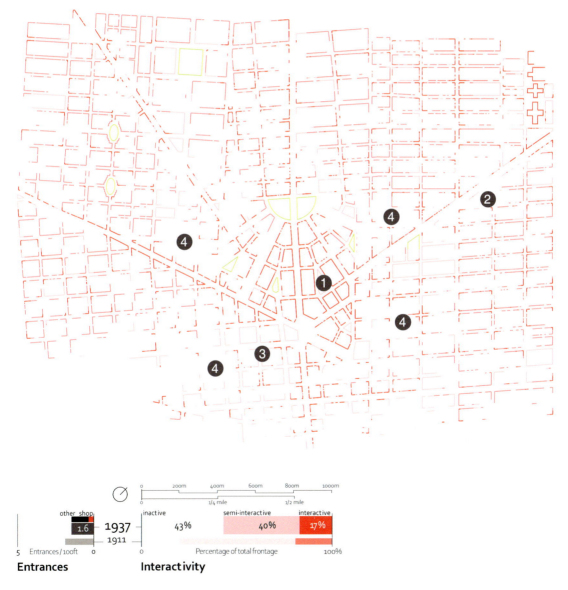

Figure 2.4 Frontage interactivity in downtown Detroit in 1937.
Source: Diagram by Conrad Kickert, 2021.

of this rollercoaster of transformation at eye level. We can clearly distinguish a solid core of department stores and surrounding retailers (1), yet we can also see the first signs of serious storefront erosion along peripheral streets – especially those hit by widenings (2). We can see the growth of a financial district of office skyscrapers (3), but we can also see that for every tower or retail palace that went up, a nearby block was cleared for parking lots (4). Parking and deteriorating dwellings grew to surround the entire downtown area into a 'twilight' zone neither residential or commercial; not walkable, nor truly accessible to cars either. What remained was a "creeping paralysis that gradually is encircling the downtown business district".[23] The negative effects of car parking were especially apparent at eye level as they broke up and dissolved otherwise viable retail districts in the periphery. As Detroit planners described "block after block of store frontage deteriorated because no prospective shoppers live nearby and no space is available to park the cars of those who might stop and shop as they passed".[24] Over the next decades, new parking lots in the fringe would be at the root of downtown's problems, but also the root of its modern renewal – for better or worse.

1937–1961

The Depression hit Detroit hard, but nowhere harder than in its downtown. In the downtown core, department stores were gutted by double-digit sales losses, and offices reeled from equally significant vacancy rates. A few blocks away, unpaved parking lots had multiplied so rapidly they were starting to throw up dust storms, and lots were beginning to chip away at the heart of downtown itself. Where some Detroiters saw self-modernization in the parking lots, most saw a battle for survival.[25] Further afield, Detroit's oldest neighborhoods were impacted by a lack of maintenance both of buildings and streets, the latter an outcome of targeted city budget cuts and federal redlining. Newly widened roads leading to downtown had decimated neighborhood businesses, and nearly instantly filled with new traffic jams.[26] The continuing segregation and concentration of African Americans amplified the overcrowding of the downtown-adjacent Black Bottom neighborhood, and a wave of incoming African American workers during World War II only exacerbated untenable housing conditions and racial prejudice. Amidst the city's worst housing stock, African Americans, shunned from downtown establishments, established a thriving retail and entertainment scene along Black Bottom's main streets, soon named Paradise Valley.[27] Furthermore, Detroit's ongoing suburbanization began to erode more than just the residential base for downtown, as new centers throughout the region replicated downtown's retail and office functions by the early 1940s, followed by manufacturing during the 1950s.[28]

By the end of World War II, downtown business interests and city leaders understood the urgency of threats to downtown. The following decades marked a shift in the forces shaping downtown, as cooling market conditions made way for stronger public interventions. A key term in this shift was 'blight', denoting poor physical and social conditions, but especially the tax burden of these conditions and their ability to spread throughout the city.[29] The term became crucial in garnering business and political support to target neighborhoods around the urban core for urban renewal in the postwar decades. As a result, Detroit's first zoning passed in the early 1940s, followed by a 'blight committee' that soon called for a master plan to bring back a middle-class and business-friendly order to the inner city, emulating the suburbs that threatened it.[30] The Black Bottom neighborhood was chosen to pilot this approach, transforming the heart of African American Detroit over nearly two decades into Lafayette Park, an orderly and modern layout of low-rise town houses and apartment buildings in a green setting – mostly occupied by white residents. The historic yet struggling downtown riverfront was similarly transformed into a modern civic center, part of the city's first comprehensive masterplan in 1951.[31] Urban freeways formed another pillar of Detroit's postwar inner-city renewal to bolster downtown. Initial routes drawn in 1930 crystallized into a citywide network plan by the 1940s and construction ramped up in the 1950s with local, state, and federal support – often through African American districts without the political clout to halt construction.[32]

The modernist renewal of downtown shifted up a gear under planner and architect Charles Blessing, hired in 1952 as director of Detroit's City Plan Commission. Like his contemporaries in Birmingham and Vancouver, Blessing's vision on urban renewal was clear, suggesting "we may now consider downtown Detroit as almost raw land".[33] In the span of just a few years, Blessing refocused and created downtown visions to fit the automobile age, re-planning downtown into nothing short of a modernist 'New City'.[34] Building upon the visions of the blight committee and city leaders, Blessing organized his downtown renewal plans into distinct rings, each with their own goals and approach.[35] The heart of downtown was to be mostly retained and pedestrianized, surrounded by a ring of parking, followed by a ring of complete clearance and renewal in Detroit's oldest neighborhoods to make way for infrastructure, modern housing, and industry (Figure 2.5). While downtown retailers opposed pedestrianization, Blessing's parking ambitions did materialize through public and private efforts. As legal challenges prevented public garages from containing street-level storefronts and private operators usually built open lots, the deterioration of downtown's pedestrian experience only accelerated.[36]

Blessing's most radical renewal took place in Detroit's downtown-adjacent neighborhoods, which he considered a mixture of "blighted and obsolete

DETROIT – EYE-LEVEL DEATH AND RESURRECTION

Figure 2.5a–b Blessing in front of his New City model, with a gleaming mayor Louis Miriani in the background. New buildings in white covered most of Detroit's inner city amidst ample car infrastructure (a). The reality of Detroit's modern visions: demolition without reconstruction (b).
Source: Image (a) by Joe Clark, Life, August 25, 1958. Image (b) of Black Bottom from Detroit Housing Commission, Slum Clearance and Public Housing in Detroit (Detroit: Detroit Housing Commission, 1953), 9.

structures" whose ongoing socioeconomic deterioration increasingly threatened downtown businesses.[37] Here, he foresaw and oversaw the further construction of Detroit's highway ring around downtown, as well as a slew of clearance and urban renewal projects bankrolled by growing federal urban renewal subsidies. Right north of downtown, two public housing sites were constructed to alleviate skyrocketing housing pressures for displaced African Americans. The western side of downtown, which had grown to house Detroit's transient and homeless population was cleared to become a downtown gateway.[38] Further west, the fine-grained homes and storefronts of the historic Corktown neighborhood were to be razed for an industrial area in an effort to retain rapidly suburbanizing manufacturers and wholesalers. Contrary to the largely African American Black Bottom neighborhood, Corktown residents successfully opposed the plans, ultimately preventing at least some of their implementation.[39] As Corktown was partially spared, a new expressway drove the final nail into Black Bottom by razing its main business street.[40]

By the end of the 1950s, the outlines of Blessing's renewal plans toward a downtown befitting the Motor City began to take shape. As a giant model of Blessing's vision made national headlines and wowed Detroiters in Hudson's downtown department store, the reality at eye level proved to be more sobering.[41] Blessing's modernization visions prompted some building activity, especially at the heart of downtown, but new buildings rarely made downtown's streets more vibrant. Scores of historic storefronts and fine-grained built fabric were replaced by aloof office lobbies, car parking ramps, and a riverfront convention center – an 'arena for the auto age' that replaced one of Detroit's oldest streets with a freeway passage and surrounded itself with blank walls.[42] Even more worrying, many renewal sites remained undeveloped after they were cleared, as market demand for new downtown development began to drop – a problem that plagued many other American cities.[43] Renewal efforts hurt downtown business activity more than they helped, as downtown department stores and offices departed for Detroit's rapidly growing suburbs. Public opposition grew stronger and more organized, and politicians were starting to notice.[44]

Figure 2.6 demonstrates the extent to which downtown Detroit had eroded at eye level over the past decades. Almost the entire ring of fine-grained neighborhoods around downtown Detroit has been replaced with an inactive mixture of infrastructure and urban clearance. To the west of downtown, a freeway had been finished (1), and to the east, Black Bottom's entire main street had been cleared for another imminent freeway (2). The rest of the former heart of African American Detroit had transformed into the Lafayette Park development (3), a modernist enclave with less permeable urban fabric and far less interactive frontages. Furthermore, land clearance in Corktown (4) and various downtown development sites (5) were carving out further vacant lots and blocks – often never to be built. Amidst these modernist dreams, downtown continued to modernize by giving up more and more peripheral buildings to open parking lots and introverted parking garages (6). The end result: an unprecedented eye-level erosion of frontage interactivity and entrances, paired with the only actual decline in floorspace in downtown Detroit's history thus far.[45] Fortunately, the modern bulldozer would soon grind to a halt, but not before leaving a permanent scar on Detroit, its downtown, and its society.

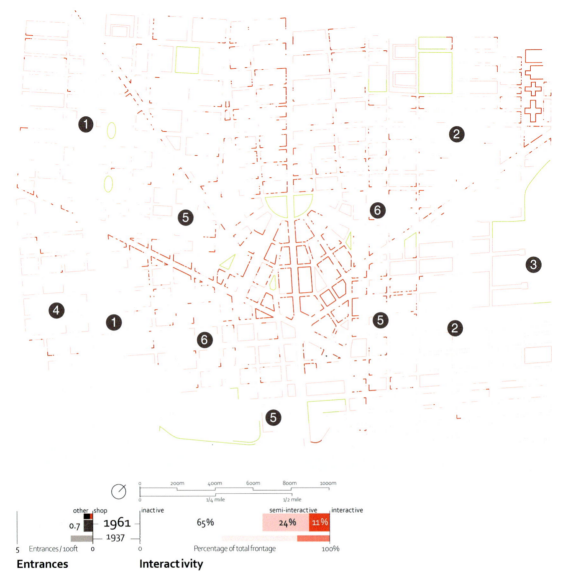

Figure 2.6 Downtown Detroit's blocks, buildings, parcels, open spaces, parks, and rivers in 1961.

1961–1988

By the early 1960s, with urban renewal in full swing in downtown Detroit, signs of discontent began to grow. While planners were keen to note their national recognition, fueling "the biggest [downtown] building boom since the '20s" and improving Detroit's fiscal situation with clear-and-renew schemes like Lafayette Park, discontent with Detroit's renewal paradigm grew and political and business support waned.[46] On the ground, urban renewal dreams were often unable to spur private market interest for rebuilding, as downtown Detroit was increasingly eclipsed by suburban business parks and shopping malls. Instead of new construction, many renewal areas only sprouted tumble weeds.[47] Fearing they would be cleared next, many downtown-adjacent building owners stopped already minimal investments in their properties, exacerbating inner city decline.[48] Blessing's visions could not even materialize at the heart of downtown, where Detroit's historic city hall was torn down for "the demands of progress" – a parking garage below a windswept plaza, across from a cleared retail block that remained vacant for nearly four decades.[49] Those projects that were finished, such as the completed downtown freeway ring and the introverted offices and parking garages that filled some renewal sites, increasingly reflected defensibility, if not outright hostility, for remaining pedestrian passersby – a reflection of the spiraling socioeconomic conditions of Detroit's inner city.[50] Hemorrhaging middle class residents and jobs for decades, Detroit's overall population and job base had shrunk since the 1950s, especially hurting the social and economic prospects of inner-city neighborhoods and their increasingly African American residents.

Business leaders and politicians increasingly took their hands off the postwar renewal machine, realizing that Blessing's modernism failed to stem Detroit's accelerating social and economic decline. Instead, plans only seemed to exacerbate the plight of mostly African American inner-city neighborhoods and residents to accommodate the cars, offices, and homes of a white middle-class clientele that had set its sights elsewhere decades ago.[51] Yet, the real nail in the coffin of urban renewal did not come from politicians, but from citizens. Aggravated by police brutality but frustrated by poverty, appalling housing conditions, segregation and a lack of job prospects, Detroit's (mostly African American) inner-city residents decided they had enough on a hot summer night in 1967. Subsequent mass civil disorder left dozens deceased, hundreds wounded, and acres of burned rubble. The damage made it all too clear that deeply segregated and rapidly declining Detroit could not be salvaged by physical interventions alone. In the years following the 1967 civil disorder, white flight intensified, crime spiked, and downtown decline of sales and office jobs accelerated. Detroit's reputation was shattered, dwindling from a place of opportunity to "Problem Town, USA".[52] At the same time the city was running out of funds to stem its decline the physical way they knew how, especially as federal funding for urban renewal was cut off in the early 1970s. Historian Robert Conot described the result for Detroit: "Twilight was settling upon the city; the twilight of an eclipse."[53]

Indeed, the forces shaping downtown Detroit and its street-level architecture after 1967 shifted drastically from public to private plans; mostly smaller, and certainly less coherent. Elected in 1974, Detroit's first African American mayor Coleman Young dismantled the modernist planning apparatus that had razed the Black Bottom neighborhood he grew up in, instead building a network of agencies to shape the city through discrete dealmaking.[54] Like his predecessors, Coleman Young continued to focus on downtown redevelopment, spending his dwindling resources on high-profile projects that showed the world Detroit wasn't going down without a fight. At the vanguard of this new paradigm was the Renaissance Center, a massive multi-block office, hotel, and retail complex built on Detroit's riverfront by a philanthropic organization spearheaded by Henry Ford II (Figure 2.7). Ford commissioned architect John Portman to design a city-within-a-city, promising to revitalize not only the physical conditions but also the image of downtown Detroit. From a distance, the Center did indeed add dynamism to Detroit's skyline, its 70-story hotel tower briefly the tallest in the world. From the inside, the Center offered a splendid space for shoppers, workers, and tourists in a series of atria. But at eye level, the

(a)

(b)

Figure 2.7a–b Artist rendering for Renaissance Center with downtown in the background (a). Reality proved harsher, as entire historic blocks lay fallow throughout downtown (b).
Source: Image (a) from Americal Development Corporation, Traugott Schmidt & Sons, a Melieu of Entertainment Experiences! (Detroit: Americal Development Corporation, 1974). Image (b) courtesy of Library of Congress, from Historic American Buildings Survey, HABS MICH, 82-DETRO, 58–1.

Center earned scorn among Detroiters and international architects for hiding its front door behind car parking ramps, and shielding itself from the rest of downtown with a 25-foot concrete berm – a defense against Detroit's urban disorder, as later conceded by architect Portman.[55] The Renaissance Center marked the dawn of what urban scholar Nan Ellin coined 'postmodern urbanism', whose focus on security, control and privatization would deteriorate the relation between buildings and public space, between white-collar downtown workers and the decaying city that surrounds them.[56] Within years, the Renaissance Center eroded its direct surroundings with more parking lots, and drew the last tenants and customers out of downtown Detroit's many struggling office towers and department stores.[57]

Unfortunately, the introversion and parasitism of the Renaissance Center soon became the norm for downtown Detroit development, reflecting its struggles with rising crime and declining business activity to draw from. Learning from the bridges that connected the Renaissance Center to a surrounding constellation of parking garages, as well as from Minneapolis' system of raised pedestrian walks, Detroit began to build its own 'skyway' system in the 1970s.[58] Yet the main system taking remaining Detroiters off downtown sidewalks would become the above-grade People Mover. Originally intended to serve as the hub of a never-built regional transit system, the People Mover was proposed in 1976 and completed in the mid-1980s after significant political battles and construction problems. Today it moves only a fraction of its originally projected ridership. Furthermore, its short loop shaves mere minutes over a walk along downtown's own sidewalks, pointlessly hurting business viability by sidelining "the random strolling that lies at the heart of the dynamics of urban street life. The best people movers are attractive sidewalks."[59]

Mayor Young started a Downtown Development Agency in 1976, benefiting from his federal connections to fund a bevy of projects. Unfortunately, these public efforts remained scattered, hardly making a dent in countering a market that had lost its pulse. Street renovations and the construction of a historic trolley line failed to move the needle; plans to pedestrianize Woodward Avenue dwindled to a transit mall whose remaining storefront businesses emptied out within years. A riverfront plaza with a privately donated fountain was cut off from the rest of the city by nine lanes of traffic. Highly subsidized downtown apartments faced the street with multistory parking garages. A 'festival marketplace' transforming a former alleyway into a secured and historicized mixture of shopping and entertainment failed within a matter of years, as suburban customers were increasingly fearful of entering downtown Detroit altogether. This fear also prompted the failure of the shops at the base of the Renaissance Center within years after opening, nearly bankrupting the entire complex in the early 1980s.[60] Further inland, Hudson's retrenched its 17 sales floors to only three; nearby department stores closed and were demolished altogether. Plans to construct a downtown shopping mall that contained Hudson's and another anchor wavered when other retailers refused to sign up and loans dried up; it died when a deep recession hit Detroit in the 1980s. In 1983, Hudson's closed Detroit's last remaining department store, taking a final wave of nearby retailers in its wake. By the mid-1980s, most storefronts in downtown Detroit had fallen vacant.[61]

The periphery of downtown fared even worse. The remaining historic urban fabric to the north of downtown absorbed displaced transients and concentrated a citywide drug crisis into one of Detroit's highest crime areas. Planners decided to concentrate gas stations, car workshops, and drive-throughs along the radial avenues leading outside of downtown, killing off any remaining pedestrian-oriented storefronts. Relaxed zoning allowed light manufacturing and wholesaling to take up their vacant buildings. By the 1980s, downtown's formerly lively walk-up streets had devolved into a muddle of asphalt, billboards, warehouses, and ragweed.[62] Even the still-lively Eastern Market turned toward wholesaling, clearing its surroundings for industrial warehousing.[63] Amidst this erosion, parking lots still thrived, and federal and county governments built two downtown prisons.[64] A large regional utility company saw opportunity in the decline of downtown's periphery and bought up entire blocks west of downtown, only to fill them with an introverted office campus lined by parking structures and blank office walls.[65] Grassroots efforts to revitalize specific downtown streets mostly remained a drop in the bucket, and besides a vague document in the mid-1980s, the city refused to draft a masterplan for turning the tide.[66]

A grand grassroots plan to revitalize the struggling area north of Grand Circus Park never materialized, but a private owner was holding on to the nearby Fox theater with the intention of creating an entertainment district. Struggling Brush Park was designated a historic district, but its decline continued unabated. Neighboring Cass Park had deteriorated from a Skid Row outpost into one of the highest crime areas in the city. Meanwhile, parking attrition continued unabatedly, as one Detroiter commented: "It seems like the whole downtown area is becoming a parking lot for the Renaissance Center."[67] As the last remaining ground-floor merchants were struggling to survive along Detroit's struggling sidewalks by the late 1980s, white collar office workers increasingly traversed downtown above street level in publicly subsidized yet privately secured skywalks or the People Mover.[68]

More than 20 years after the 1967 civil disorder, downtown Detroit had seemingly reached a low point (Figure 2.8). The tail end of Blessing's New City had cut into downtown's periphery in the form of cleared land and the downtown freeway ring (1) – rightfully declared by Detroit journalist George Cantor as "the automobile's final revenge on the city".[69] The freeways had replaced the city's formerly grand radials, which had declined into "a long trail of steel gates . . . and neglected, vacant store fronts" (2).[70] Indeed, almost no interactive frontages remained in the entire periphery of downtown, usurped by freeways, vacancy, parking, and fear. Even the heart of downtown Detroit had withered, as Coleman Young's high-profile projects to spur downtown investments (3) proved unable to swim against a citywide tide of decline and decentralization.[71] Circled by a practically empty People Mover, downtown Detroit's most central streets were lined with a fearsome mixture of boarded-up storefronts, defensive architecture, and parking ramps. Upstairs, offices and hotels had emptied out. The

Figure 2.8 Downtown Detroit's interactivity in 1988.
Source: Diagram by Conrad Kickert, 2021.

peripheral rot that had started in the 1960s had finally made its way into the heart of downtown, destroying any continuous interactive frontages – let alone storefronts (4). Ultimately, Young's grand visions without a grand plan had prompted little spin-off beyond their own perimeter – if anything, introverted projects like the Renaissance Center (5) and various downtown apartment buildings had only further deactivated sidewalks.[72] More than three-quarters of downtown was inactive at eye level, and only a handful of building entrances remained. As even the city's planning director resignedly admitted downtown's eclipse in the 1980s, its mean streets featured in the international blockbuster movie *RoboCop* as a warning of obsolescence and danger. Scribbled atop its screenplay: "The Future left Detroit behind."[73]

1988–2018

By the dawn of the 1990s, downtown Detroit had reached its nadir. Most of the downtown storefronts lay vacant, below dozens of vacant skyscrapers holding more than seven million square feet (700,000 square meters) of emptiness. Upon another visit to downtown in 1990, the *New York Times* commented that "Detroit today is a genuinely fearsome-looking place. Worst of all is the downtown. . . . Entire skyscrapers – hotels, office buildings and apartment houses – are vacant and decaying; you can walk a downtown block during business hours without passing a living soul."[74] Among a lack of demand, high taxation, and high demolition costs, renovating downtown buildings was as unfeasible as demolishing them, leaving only the twilight of neglect. A 1992 masterplan perpetuated Coleman Young's paradigm of flexible, silver-bullet dealmaking that had failed to yield significant revitalization. In a four-page special, the Detroit News lamented his legacy: a combination of defensive architecture, car dependence, and laissez-faire planning that had resulted in an unexciting, unwalkable, and downright unsafe downtown streetscape.[75]

Amidst the crumbling terracotta of empty offices and desolate sidewalks, green shoots would begin to appear. A new mayoral regime rebuilt the city's planning apparatus, benefiting from an uptick in the regional economy. As downtowns were rediscovered nationwide as unique historical destinations to live, work, and play, Detroit would slowly catch up with this trend – with entertainment emerging as the first wave of a larger downtown reinvention. By the late 1980s, techno musicians discovered downtown Detroit as an underground destination, invigorating downtown clubs to levels not seen since the Motown heydays of the 1960s. Eastern Market and the Greektown entertainment district – a one-block stretch of ethnically themed bars and restaurants – began to draw in larger crowds as well.[76] Pizza magnate and sports club owner Michael Ilitch bought the ailing Fox and Palms Theaters north of downtown, renovated the buildings and relocated his corporate headquarters. Over the following years, Ilitch transformed the entire northern downtown into an entertainment district, squarely aimed at a suburban clientele to enjoy Detroit in security and comfort, introducing a new scale of development to downtown – and a new break between buildings and public space. Desperate for downtown development, the city supported Ilitch's transformation with tax breaks, subsidies, and by strong-arming land and building sales. Taking a page out of the playbook of the utility company that had bought up the western part of downtown, Ilitch grew his holdings into an entire neighborhood, controlling its mixture of bars, restaurants, and sports stadiums – effectively turning the northern part of downtown into a car-oriented leisure district, from which downtown Detroit only served as a background during games.[77]

Casinos were also added to the mix. Swayed by city leaders' promises to use casino revenue to thwart Detroit's declining tax base, Detroiters approved the construction of three downtown mega-casinos. After land speculation left a devastating trail of failed sites through the downtown and the riverfront, the casinos landed on the fringes of downtown, taking up dozens of cleared freeway-adjacent blocks with massive parking garages and introverted gambling halls, wrapped by a mixture of lawns, driveways, neon, and blank walls. The casinos would mark a new era of architecture for downtown Detroit's periphery, in which automobile accessibility and garish iconography trumped human scale and interaction – an ironically postmodern conclusion to Charles Blessing's modernist playbook.[78]

(a)

(b)

Figure 2.9a–b The end of the 20th century saw a growing dichotomy between pedestrian-oriented construction at the heart of downtown (a) and car-oriented architecture for entertainment at the periphery (b). *Source: Both images by Conrad Kickert, 2018.*

The heart of downtown saw a very different dynamic by the end of the 20th century (Figure 2.9). Frustrated by decades of decline and embarrassed by widely published skyscraper vacancy, Detroit's mayor convened a group of business leaders to revitalize the vacant skyscrapers at the heart of downtown, with the nearly two million square foot vacant shell of Hudson's department store at its core. After commissioning Toronto urban designer Ken Greenberg to draft a plan for downtown as a series of 'urban villages', the Greater Downtown Partnership began to quietly buy up strategic vacant properties to prevent speculation.[79] The Partnership understood that downtown revitalization hinged on much more than streetscape or cosmetic improvements, and focused on renovating or constructing new buildings to bring life to downtown's desolate sidewalks. It also understood it had to act as active developers in an otherwise stagnant market.[80] The Partnership's vision culminated into a multi-block development scheme that included replacing the vacant Hudson's building with a new office building. Unlike the shopping mall proposal of two decades prior, this plan followed through – at least partially. Hudson's vandalized remains were imploded in a highly televised 1998 event, but its site did not materialize beyond an underground parking garage. However, two adjacent blocks, part of the same proposal, did see a large new office building and parking garage, with new active storefronts on at least one side of their blocks. In front of these buildings, Detroit's central Campus Martius square was redesigned into an attractive green plaza with year-round programming, funded by a nonprofit organization.[81] On the riverfront, the Renaissance Center was bought up by General Motors for pennies on the dollar in 1996, and refurbished to connect better with its surroundings, including a Winter Garden toward the river and a proper unbarricaded front door toward downtown – the first breaches of the fortress. Further inland, two historic hotels were renovated and reopened with significant public subsidies; they addressed the street with vibrant new restaurants and restored lobbies. Even the neighborhoods around downtown saw their first reinvestments, either through federal programs or bottom-up initiatives.[82]

Together, these new developments achieved spin-off not seen since the 1970s, convincing a growing cohort of Detroiters and developers that downtown was uniquely worth living, staying, playing, and investing in. In the early 2000s, the first vacant office buildings and retail stores were beginning to transform into loft apartments, hotels, and night clubs.[83] Increasingly, private investors understood that underneath downtown's crumbling terracotta and concrete lay gold. Increasingly, downtown's past, embodied in its impressive building stock that comprised some of the region's last remaining walkable urbanism, became an asset rather than a liability. Especially mortgage banker and sports team owner Dan Gilbert unsentimentally understood the value of downtown's unique heritage as a destination, not just for suburban visitors but his envisioned Creative Class workforce. After moving his headquarters right to Campus Martius in 2011, Gilbert bought up more than 100 downtown buildings in a self-described "skyscraper sale".[84] Buying, financing, developing, and operating his own holdings, Gilbert changed the downtown landscape in a matter of years. As the city gladly stepped aside, Gilbert and other downtown owners commissioned various plans and designs to transform downtown into a "great urban neighborhood . . . where people will choose to live, work, shop, and play" – repositioning downtown as a self-sufficient entity looking to attract a global elite of young professionals, rather than as the hub of a still-struggling city.[85] Gilbert and his company have helped finance a streetcar line that connects downtown to other thriving parts of the city, and they operate safety and maintenance crews downtown. The increasing contrast between the manicured, privately policed spaces of Gilbert's "Detroit 2.0" and the ongoing socioeconomic decline of the rest of the city raises questions on the role, representation,

and connection of downtown to Detroit, exacerbated by continuing auto-oriented development that cuts off the downtown fringe.[86]

By 2018, downtown Detroit became an island of prosperity for a targeted few, amidst an ocean of decline in the rest of the city. We see the separation between a thriving core and a struggling periphery even within the downtown itself at eye level (Figure 2.10). The core of downtown has rebound somewhat from its nadir in the late 1980s, with the region's hippest bars, restaurants, and retailers at the foot of repurposed office buildings and unique dwellings (1). On an ironically blank slate, new storefronts cater to the 21st-century experience economy, spilling over onto sidewalks with lively patios – improving eye-level interactivity for the first time since 1929 (1). Nevertheless, even in Detroit's most central streets, new storefronts remain interspersed with vacant neighbors and dotted with parking lots, which become more numerous and deleterious the further out we move (2). The periphery of downtown remains an inhospitable hodgepodge of parking lots – still taking up about a third of all downtown land – parking garages (3), vacant buildings (4), and freeway infrastructure (5). Multi-block casinos (6), sports stadiums (7), and office campuses (8) only exacerbated the erosion of downtown at eye level. One can now walk entire blocks without any eye-level activity or any doorway. While downtown is now connected to a new streetcar line and has become more vibrant at its core, it remains inherently car-oriented and insular. Plans to remove parts of the freeway ring around downtown Detroit may physically reconnect downtown to its surroundings, but social and cultural connections may still be a long way ahead.

Conclusion

After decades of steep decline, downtown Detroit is entering an era of rebirth. Shuttered storefronts and vacant skyscrapers have made way for the city's hottest destinations. After decades of quiet, downtown's core streets are abuzz with chatter, laughter, traffic horns, and streetcar bells. Yet, only a block away from the bright lights, downtown's periphery remains hostile to pedestrians. This downtown landscape of contrasts is the result of strong tensions – between downtown's past, present, and future; its own people; automobiles and pedestrians; public and private control; but mostly, between dreams and reality. Frequently out of step, these tensions have shaped downtown Detroit and the architecture within it from a close-knit, pedestrian-oriented urban fabric in 1911, largely toward eye-level erosion, introversion, and consolidation.

The biggest and most detrimental tension that has shaped downtown Detroit and its eye-level experience takes place between the city's past, present, and future. Nowhere is Detroit's fascination with the future more

Figure 2.10 Interactivity in downtown Detroit in 2018.
Source: Diagram by Conrad Kickert, 2021.

apparent than in downtown – the one place Detroit couldn't simply erase its past. From an impediment to progress in its feverish early 20th-century growth, to an embarrassing testament to the city's decline in subsequent decades, the built heritage of the city had not received much appreciation by Detroiters until its recent rediscovery as an attractor for young professionals in the 2010s. The demolition of historic buildings has always been a centerpiece to downtown's transformation, but where clearance and demolition usually made way for progress until 1929, destruction was hardly followed by meaningful improvements in the decades that followed. Between the Depression and the peak of urban renewal in the late 1960s, demolition often preceded vacancy or parking; in later years, it was followed by the construction of larger, more introverted architecture, often meant for cars rather than people (Figure 2.11). Detroit's volatile and manufacturing-based economy and segregated society also obstructed long-term investments in downtown architecture. Detroit's financial district paled in comparison with larger American cities; its housing and commercial building stock was often rapidly built for short-term profit, and by the end of World War II, downtown's economic hegemony had effectively been surpassed by new suburban frontiers. Most projects have since struggled to overcome downtown's lack of economic demand, from renewal dreams that did not make it past the clearance stage, to the disastrous demolition of

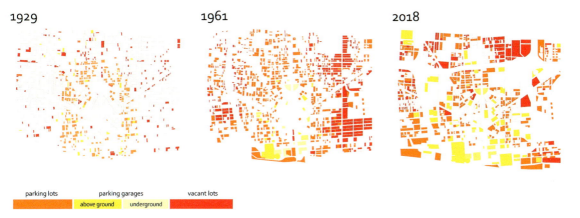

Figure 2.11 Since 1929, parking has multiplied from a ring around downtown into the dominant downtown land use today.
Source: Diagram by Conrad Kickert, 2021.

African American neighborhoods, to Coleman Young's shotgun projects that failed to generate spin-off. Only by redefining downtown as its own district with their own money, have Dan Gilbert and a handful of other developers been able to bring life back to some storefronts and skyscrapers alike – without connecting downtown to its still-declining urban environment.

Even more volatile than Detroit's economy has been its society, with great repercussions on its downtown architecture. As an early 20th-century boomtown, downtown was where Detroit experienced its first growing pains as it crammed newcomers in overcrowded housing, which increasingly flared racial tensions. Intolerance between classes and races only mounted over time, and downtown destinations tended to shun lower-income and non-white Detroiters. While the bulk of the devastating 1943 and 1967 civil disorder did not take place downtown, its repercussions certainly did, and downtown often served as an involuntary backdrop to violence. White flight not only accelerated the decline of downtown street-level business activity, it eroded remaining trust in the safety of public space from the 1970s onward. The architecture from this era onward reflects a deep-rooted fear of crime and disorder, with most buildings presenting themselves to the street through secured lobbies, parking ramps, and blank walls. Coveted white-collar office workers who remained in downtown would be siphoned off the street into overhead walkways and the People Mover system. Most street-level business activity would be internalized into controlled environments like the Renaissance Center, leaving remaining street-level retailers to ensure the security of their business by barricading shop windows and minimizing the number of entrances. Fear and built form have come to mutually reinforce themselves, reflecting Detroit's ongoing class and race segregation and harming the revitalization of street life by failing to address public space in an open and positive manner. Recent downtown revitalization has broken this cycle visually, but not socially.

Burdened by amnesia and internal volatility, downtown Detroit was practically defenseless against its own technological creation – the private automobile. Amidst the cradle of American car production, downtown faced the constant threat of suburbanization as the automobile middle class replaced downtown's function in suburban homes, malls, and Edge Cities. It also suffered from the attempts to reshape downtown's urban fabric and architecture to accommodate a technology it wasn't originally built for. The result has been a rapid and self-perpetuating erosion of widened streets and parking lots from the 1910s onward, spiraling into a circle of parked cars that cut off downtown from its surroundings at eye level by the end of the 1920s. Even at the peak of downtown's growth in the 1920s, for every skyscraper going up, a built block of urban fabric on the periphery came down for parking. Especially storefronts suffered from the interruption of continuous retail districts by new roads, parking lots, and garages, accelerating their decline first in the periphery of downtown, then at its heart. Unfortunately, much of this obliteration was fueled by government policies, welcoming cars for their riddance of historical 'obsolescence'. Architects added fuel to the fire by designing buildings for passing cars rather than pedestrians and hiding buildings behind garages and open parking lots. By the time that more than half of downtown land served cars rather than people and even parking lots fell vacant in the 1970s, it was too late to turn the tide. While the heart of downtown is returning to people-centric architecture, frontages, and public space, on the whole most of downtown Detroit's periphery is as car-dependent and inactive as its suburban adversaries.

How could one expect architects and urban designers to be able to counter these forces that eroded eye-level interactivity? After all, downtown has been mostly shaped by private forces that eluded design professionals and public organizations. Its growth was one of capital accumulation, consolidating hundreds of small retailers into a nearly two million square foot department store and dozens of smaller banks into the skyscrapers of the financial district. And when downtown declined, land and building consolidation grew even faster, further eroding the fine-grained connection between buildings and public space. Public policies often only accelerated this process. The city was glad to see its peripheral buildings cleared for parking by the 1930s, and today's multi-block stadiums and mega-casinos greatly benefited from 1950s land clearance and eminent domain. As a result, most downtown land and buildings are currently controlled by only a handful of organizations – privately planned, designed, managed, and policed.[87] Public policies typically prioritized traffic and profit over people, and didn't understand that without market demand, revitalization dreams rarely materialized. The road widening of the 1920s killed most businesses in the periphery of downtown; 1930s redlining killed the neighborhoods that fed these businesses; 1950s urban renewal cleared up the remains, only to remain unfilled for years or decades; Young's 1970s and 1980s downtown projects made headlines but hardly turned heads; the downtown reinvention of the 1990s brought peripheral megastructures and downtown demolition. Only in the 21st century did we see a renewed focus on downtown's unique built heritage and high quality public space – but these opportunities have been mostly leveraged by private rather than public stakeholders.

It would be arrogant to state that the planning and design professions alone could have changed downtown's tide. Professionals made their fair share of mistakes, yet they neither had the tools nor the means to counter the cultural, social, economic, and technological threats to vital street life in downtown Detroit. Downtown simply couldn't build its way out of the downward spiral the city was in. The unbreakable bond between public space, architecture, and society was both reflected in the street-level vitality of downtown's early 20th-century boom years, as silence, danger, and eye-level defensiveness that followed downtown's demise. On the other hand, it would be too easy, if not defeatist, to state that no planning or design interventions could have prevented downtown's eye-level downfall. Especially at the building ensemble level, the collective benefits of fine-grained, continuous, and interactive frontages could have been protected better. When the downtown periphery showed its first parking-induced cracks in the 1930s, policies could have maintained pockets of interactive frontages rather than let erosion reach downtown itself in the following decades. Only by the 21st century, the understanding that building back interactive architecture required a vision beyond the project site returned to downtown, and has been a success at its core. This is the scale we know as urban design.

Notes

1 Image by author, 2018.

2 A more extensive, albeit more general history of downtown Detroit has been published by Conrad Kickert as *Dream City – Creation, Destruction, and Reinvention in downtown Detroit* (Cambridge, MA: MIT Press, 2019). David Lee Poremba, *Detroit in Its World Setting: A Three Hundred Year Chronology, 1701–2001*, Great Lakes Books (Detroit: Wayne State University Press, 2001), 90. L. E. McMahon and Alice I. Bourquin, "Detroit's Evolution of an Expressway System," *Landscape Architecture* 44, no. 1 (1953).

3 Robert E. Conot, *American Odyssey* (New York: Morrow, 1974); George Byron Catlin, *The Story of Detroit* (Detroit: The Detroit News, 1923); Silas Farmer, *History of Detroit and Wayne County and Early Michigan*, 3rd ed. (Detroit: Pub. by S. Farmer & co., for Munsell & co., New York, 1890).

4 Farmer, *History of Detroit and Wayne County and Early Michigan*, 459–63.

5 David M. Katzman, *Before the Ghetto: Black Detroit in the Nineteenth Century*, Blacks in the New World. (Urbana: University of Illinois Press, 1975).; Conrad Kickert, *Dream City: Creation, Destruction, and Reinvention in Downtown Detroit* (Cambridge, MA: MIT Press, 2019), Chapter 2.

6 On theaters, see e.g. Michael Hauser and Marianne Weldon, *Detroit's Downtown Movie Palaces*, Images of America (Charleston, SC: Arcadia Pub., 2006).; on retailing, see Michael Hauser and Marianne Weldon, *Hudson's: Detroit's Legendary Department Store*, Images of America (Charleston, SC: Arcadia, 2004); Jean Maddern Pitrone, *Hudson's: Hub of America's Heartland* (West Bloomfield, MI: Altwerger and Mandel Pub. Co., 1991). See also Kickert, *Dream City: Creation, Destruction, and Reinvention in Downtown Detroit*, Chapter 2.

7 R. L. Polk & Company, *Detroit City Directory*, eds. R. L. Polk and Company (Detroit: R. L. Polk & Company, 1911), introduction, pp. 6–10.

8 "Brushaber's New Store to Be Forerunner of Business Extension of Michigan Avenue," *Detroit Free Press*, May 13, 1910.

9 Randall Fogelman and Lisa E. Rush, *Detroit's Eastern Market*, Images of America (Charleston, SC: Arcadia Publishing, 2013).

10 "Is Detroit Prosperous?" *Detroit Free Press*, October 12, 1913.

11 Ground floor retail was among the most profitable real estate in any downtown skyscraper: Carol Willis, *Form Follows Finance: Skyscrapers and Skylines in New York and Chicago* (New York, NY: Princeton Architectural Press, 1995).

12 "Boulevard's Growth Is the Result of a Farsighted Program," *Detroit Saturday Night*, April 21, 1923.

"Book Building," *Detroit Saturday Night*, December 30, 1916. The plans were only partially realized.

13 *Lower Woodward Avenue Historic District Final Report*. City of Detroit (Detroit, 1999).

14 Conrad Kickert, "The Other Side of Shopping Centres: Retail Transformation in Downtown Detroit and the Hague," in *The Shopping Centre*, eds. Janina Gosseye and Tom Avermaete. (TU Delft, Faculty of Architecture and the Built Environment, Netherlands, 2015).

15 Hauser and Weldon, *Detroit's Downtown Movie Palaces*; Poremba, *Detroit in Its World Setting: A Three Hundred Year Chronology, 1701–2001*.

16 This image did not last when the Union Trust declared bankruptcy in the 1929 stock market crash. James W. Tottis, *The Guardian Building: Cathedral of Finance* (Detroit, MI: Wayne State University Press, 2008).

17 Carl S. Wells, *Proposals for Downtown Detroit*, (Washington, DC: Urban Land Institute, 1942); Kickert, *Dream City: Creation, Destruction, and Reinvention in Downtown Detroit*, 87; W. Hawkins Ferry, *The Buildings of Detroit; a History* (Detroit: Wayne State University Press, 1968), 365.

18 "Durant Tells Gigantic Aims of Expansion," *Detroit Free Press*, April 4, 1919; "G. M. C. Occupies New Building," *Detroit Free Press*, November 25, 1920; Randall Fogelman, *Detroit's New Center* (Mount Pleasant, SC: Arcadia Publishing, 2004).

19 R. L. Duffus, "Our Changing Cities: Dynamic Detroit," *New York Times*, April 10, 1927. A similar description of the city's growth was given in the Detroit News that same year: "The City – What Lies Behind Veil That Conceals Its Future?" *Detroit News*, 1927. Almost 60,000 acres of new subdivisions were built around Detroit during the 1920s, prompting Detroit's oldest district to lose population for the first time; Kickert, *Dream City: Creation, Destruction, and Reinvention in Downtown Detroit*, 78–79.

20 First quote from "Passing of Fort Street West," *Detroit Free Press*, November 9, 1913. Second quote by the city itself, in City Plan Commission, *Annual Report* (Detroit: City of Detroit, 1928), 14. See also: Edward H. Bennett and Cass Gilbert, *Preliminary Plan of Detroit*, eds. City Plan and Improvement Commission (Detroit: City of Detroit, 1915); Martin S. Hayden, *Detroit's Master Plan*, ed. The Detroit News (Detroit 1947). It would take until the 1940s to finally draft an accepted zoning plan. On early plans for the esthetic improvement of downtown see Kickert, *Dream City: Creation, Destruction, and Reinvention in Downtown Detroit*, 90–91.

21 Charles K. Hyde, "Planning a Transportation System for Metropolitan Detroit in the Age of the Automobile: The Triumph of the Expressway," *Michigan Historical Review* 32, no. 1 (2006).

Car vehicle registrations skyrocketed during the 1920s: R. L. Polk & Company, *Detroit City Directory* (Detroit: R. L. Polk & Company, 1921); Duffus, "Our Changing Cities: Dynamic Detroit." Meanwhile, transit ridership to downtown fell: Sidney D. Waldon, "Superhighways and Regional Planning," in *Planning Problems of Town, City and Region* (Washington, DC: William F. Fell, 1927).

22 John A. Jakle and Keith A. Sculle, *Lots of Parking: Land Use in a Car Culture* (Charlottesville: University of Virginia Press, 2004); E. J. Beck, "Runs 23 Parking Lots in Downtown Detroit and Watches over Them with a Spy Glass," *The Detroit News*, September 20, 1928; E. J. Beck, "Auto Parking a Big Industry," ibid., April 28, 1929. Car registration increased nearly tenfold between 1917 and 1926 alone from 38,000 to 350,000: Company, "Detroit City Directory."; Duffus, "Our Changing Cities: Dynamic Detroit."

23 Mentioned as one of Detroit's ills by ULI special representative Carl S. Wells, "Downtown Detroit Plan Published," *Detroit Free Press*, June 28, 1942. Second quote by James Steep in James B. Steep, "Traffic Troubles Pare Property Values, Expert Declares," *Detroit News*, October 8, 1939.

24 Hayden, "Detroit's Master Plan," 8.

25 "Downtown Dust Storms," *The Detroit News*, June 2, 1938. On modernization versus survival, see Kickert, *Dream City: Creation, Destruction, and Reinvention in Downtown Detroit*, 123.

26 *Dream City: Creation, Destruction, and Reinvention in Downtown Detroit*, 108–9. On federal redlining policy: Richard Rothstein, *The Color of Law: A Forgotten History of How Our Government Segregated America* (New York; London: Liveright Publishing, 2017).

27 Kickert, *Dream City: Creation, Destruction, and Reinvention in Downtown Detroit*, 125–26. The extent of poor housing conditions were demonstrated by Detroit's Real Property Survey published in 1939, showing dilapidation, lack of plumbing, and racial segregation: Detroit Bureau of Governmental Research, *Real Property Survey* (Detroit: Works Projects Administration, 1939).

28 Downtown visitor numbers decreased 16% between 1925 and 1940. See Wells, "Proposals for Downtown Detroit." On suburbanization in the 1950s, see Kickert, *Dream City: Creation, Destruction, and Reinvention in Downtown Detroit*, 147–49.

29 For a more detailed exploration of blight, see Robert M. Fogelson, *Downtown: Its Rise and Fall, 1880–1950* (New Haven: Yale University Press, 2001), Chapter 7: "inventing blight."

30 On zoning, see Hayden, "Detroit's Master Plan," 6. On the Blight Committee, see June Manning Thomas, *Redevelopment and Race: Planning*

a Finer City in Postwar Detroit, Creating the North American Landscape (Baltimore: Johns Hopkins University Press, 1997), 38. Downtown business leaders understood that downtown was unlikely to grow by the 1930s, flipping their stance on public intervention: Kickert, *Dream City: Creation, Destruction, and Reinvention in Downtown Detroit*, 131.

31 Initially called the Gratiot Project, Lafayette Park faced significant delays in clearing and redeveloping the site and displaced thousands of African Americans: *Dream City: Creation, Destruction, and Reinvention in Downtown Detroit*, 133, 157–58. On the civic center and masterplan, see ibid., 138–41; City Plan Commission, *Detroit Master Plan* (Detroit: City Plan Commission, 1951).

32 Public transportation was part of infrastructure plans, but consistently failed to materialize. Detroit's final streetcar ran in 1956 Kickert, *Dream City: Creation, Destruction, and Reinvention in Downtown Detroit*, 134–38, 162–64. Ominously, the mayor at the time confessed he didn't know whether the freeways would save downtown by connecting it better, or ultimately destroy the city in their path: *Federal Aid for Post-War Highway Construction*, ed. U.S. House commitee on Roads (Washington, DC: U.S. Government Printing Office, 1944), 764–68.

33 William Harlan Hale, "Detroit: How to Save a Great City from Itself," *The Reporter*, October 31, 1957, 29.

34 John M. Carlisle, "Billion Dollar Boom Downtown," *Detroit News*, April 1, 1957.

35 The pedestrianization failed due to opposition by local retailers. City Plan Commission, *Central Business District Study: Land Use, Trafficways and Transit*, Master Plan Technical Report (Detroit: City Plan Commission, 1956).

36 Joseph N. Hartmann, "City Finds Gold Underground in Grand Circus Park Garage," *Detroit News*, December 5, 1960; J. D. McGillis, "Detroit That Makes Many Motorcars Must Also Park Them," *Traffic Quarterly* 10, no. 3 (1956): 313.

37 City Plan Commission, *Economic Analysis of the Central Business District Fringe* (Detroit: City Plan Commission, 1957).

38 The housing projects did little to alleviate African Americans' pressure for housing. On downtown renewal, see June Manning Thomas, "Seeking a Finer Detroit," in *Planning the Twentieth-Century American City*, eds. Mary Corbin Sies and Christopher Silver (Baltimore: Johns Hopkins University Press, 1996); Thomas, *Redevelopment and Race: Planning a Finer City in Postwar Detroit*. On the West Side "Skid Row," see Kickert, *Dream City: Creation, Destruction, and Reinvention in Downtown Detroit*, 158–61, 165, 176, 183.

39 Detroit City Plan Commission, *Industrial Development; West Side Industrial District* (Detroit: Detroit City Plan Commission, 1958).

40 John Frederick Cohassey, *Down on Hastings Street: A Study of Social and Cultural Changes in a Detroit Community 1941–1955* (Detroit: Wayne State University, 1993). Meanwhile, transit ridership plummeted and Detroit's last streetcar ran in 1956: Department of Transportation, *Detroit Central Business District Cordon Count 1966–1974* (Detroit: Department of Transportation, 1974).

41 "Dramatic Rise for Big Construction: A Strong Sign of Recovery," *LIFE*, August 25, 1958. The $250,000 model was supported by the Detroit Tomorrow Committee and local businesses: Kickert, *Dream City: Creation, Destruction, and Reinvention in Downtown Detroit*, 152.

42 "Arena for the Auto Age," *Architectural Forum* 113 (1960).

43 Federal subsidies could only pay for clearance, not for rebuilding. Fogelson, *Downtown: Its Rise and Fall, 1880–1950*; Alison Isenberg, *Downtown America: A History of the Place and the People Who Made It* (Chicago: University of Chicago Press, 2004).

44 The number of downtown visitors continued to decline between 1950 and 1960, without an end in sight: Transportation, "Detroit Central Business District Cordon Count 1966–1974." On opposition, see Thomas, "Seeking a Finer Detroit."

45 See Kickert, *Dream City: Creation, Destruction, and Reinvention in Downtown Detroit*, 276, figure 14.6.

46 Quote from Frank Beckman, "Detroit – Biggest Boom since'20s," *Detroit Free Press Sunday Magazine*, February 17, 1963. On fiscal improvements from urban renewal, see Housing Commission, *Urban Renewal and Tax Revenue: Detroit's Success Story* (Detroit: Housing Commission, 1960). On national recognition, see Thomas, *Redevelopment and Race: Planning a Finer City in Postwar Detroit*, 103–4. On discontent, see ibid., 122–24.

47 John Gill, "Wild 'Shrubs' Landscape Empty Lots," *Detroit News*, 1963.

48 Jerome Aumente, "A New Blueprint for Change," ibid., August 14, 1966, 42.

49 Quote from Carl Konzelman, "Detroit Deepling Committed to Meeting the Challenge of Decay," *Detroit News*, October 12, 1962. Retail sales steeply dropped in the 1960s due to suburbanizing wealth and the inability of downtown retailers to cater to Detroit's growing African American clientele: Kickert, *Dream City: Creation, Destruction, and Reinvention in Downtown Detroit*, 176–77.

50 On this architectural hostility and inner-city socioeconomic conditions, see *Dream City: Creation, Destruction, and Reinvention in Downtown Detroit*, 180–83.

51 Michael Maidenberg, "10 Painful Years of 'Urban Renewal': What It Means When You Live There," *Detroit Free Press*, March 1, 1970.

52 Susan McBee, "Detroit, Problem Town U.S.A., Grows Older, Poorer, Tougher," *Boston Globe*, 4 March, 1973.

53 Conot, *American Odyssey*, 616.

54 On the restructuring of the planning department, including the departure of Charles Blessing, see Thomas, *Redevelopment and Race: Planning a Finer City in Postwar Detroit*, 145–47.

55 Kickert, *Dream City: Creation, Destruction, and Reinvention in Downtown Detroit*, 197–200.

56 Nan Ellin, *Postmodern Urbanism* (Cambridge, MA: Blackwell, 1996).

57 Parasitic acquisition of tenants had started before the Renaissance Center's completion: Peter Gavrilovich, "Marketing a Renaissance – Problem: Take 39 Floors X 4 and Fill . . ." *Detroit Free Press*, August 22, 1976.

58 Gerald Storch, "What's up for Detroit? It Could Be Pedestrians," *Detroit News*, December 28, 1975. Earlier proposals included Blessing's vision for the separation of pedestrians and traffic, as outlined in John F. Nehman, "Elevated Woodward Mall Eyed," ibid., March 25, 1965.

59 Quote from Jay Carr, "Rencen, Don't Turn Your Back on Old Detroit," ibid., March 20, 1977. For the original proposal, see Southeastern Michigan Transportation Authority, *Proposal: Downtown People Mover Detroit, Michigan* (Detroit: Southeastern Michigan Transportation Authority, 1976). See also Kickert, *Dream City: Creation, Destruction, and Reinvention in Downtown Detroit*, 201–2, 214–18, 228, 231–32, 279.

60 On the Downtown Development Agency and its projects, see *Dream City: Creation, Destruction, and Reinvention in Downtown Detroit*, 212–21.

On the festival marketplace, see Corporation, "Traugott Schmidt & Sons, a Melieu of Entertainment Experiences!" On fear of entering downtown, see Michigan Citizens Research Council of, *Police Precinct One in Downtown Detroit: A Survey of Trends in Crime, Economic Activity, and Public Attitudes*, Its Report, No. 258 (Detroit: The Council, 1979).

61 Kickert, *Dream City: Creation, Destruction, and Reinvention in Downtown Detroit*, 217–21. Downtown sales had nearly halved between 1963 and 1977, as sourced from the US Census of Business 1963 and 1977. Visitor numbers dropped by a third between 1960 and 1974: Transportation, "Detroit Central Business District Cordon Count 1966–1974."

62 Don Ball, "Big Victory against Detroit Blight," *Detroit News*, May 12, 1970.

63 Paul Gainor, "The Eastern Market Getting a New Look," ibid., September 12, 1976.

64 Christopher Willcox, "Millions to Save Downtown Ok'd," ibid., May 18, 1978; "Compromise Site for New County Jail," *Detroit Monitor*, February 15, 1978.

65 Raymond Curtis Miller, *The Force of Energy: A Business History of the Detroit Edison Company* (East Lansing, MI: Michigan State University Press, 1971).

66 Don Tschirhart, "Downtown 'Blueprint' Unveiled," *Detroit News*, December 15, 1983; Rick Ratliff, "Without Wide Support, Plan Only Blueprint of a Dream," *Detroit Free Press*, June 22, 1985; Thomas, *Redevelopment and Race: Planning a Finer City in Postwar Detroit*, 189–93.

67 "Grand Circus Park Area Revitalization Plan Announced," *Detroit Monitor*, November 8, 1979; Chauncey Bailey, "Preserving History," *Detroit News*, February 10, 1983; Rick Ratliff, "An Old Area, a New Dream," *Detroit Free Press*, April 12, 1984. A major issue was that parking would take over-assessed vacant downtown buildings off the tax rolls, making their demolition as attractive as during the Depression. Thomas C. Fox, "Parking Woes Grow Along with Rencen," *Detroit Free Press*, September 25, 1978; Thomas C. Fox, "Need for Parking Gobbling Dozens of City's Buildings," *Detroit Free Press*, January 29, 1978.

68 Robert E. Roach, "A Lift for Pedestrians," *Detroit News*, May 20, 1980.

69 George Cantor, "Grand River Makes It Hard to Praise Detroit," *The Detroit News*, December 9, 1984.

70 James Tittsworth, "Seedy Woodward Fighting for Comeback," ibid., January 30, 1978.

71 John McCarthy, "Revitalization of the Core City: The Case of Detroit," *Cities* 14, no. 1 (1997): 4–5.

72 Robert H. Giles, "Detroit: A 20-Year Search for Renaissance," *Detroit News*, June 28, 1987.

73 Betsey Hansell and Rick Ratliff, "A History of Sprawl, an Eclipsed Downtown," *Detroit Free Press*, December 11, 1983; Oliver Joy, "Robocop Creator: Detroit Shows the Film's Fictional Future Is Upon Us," *CNN*, July 25, 2013.

74 Ze'ev Chafets, "The Tragedy of Detroit," *New York Times*, July 29, 1990. On vacancy, see David Barkholz, "Downtown Lost 18,500 Jobs in'80s: Semcog," *Crain's Detroit Business*, July 23, 1990. "Empty Hulks Scar Detroit," *Crain's Detroit Business*, May 21–27, 1990.

75 "Downtown Outlook – Can the People of the Motor City Learn to Walk Again?" *Detroit News*, July 26, 1990.

76 Kickert, *Dream City: Creation, Destruction, and Reinvention in Downtown Detroit*, 224.

77 "What a View! Tigers Offer First Glimpse Inside Park," *Detroit News*, March 19, 1999.

78 Kickert, *Dream City: Creation, Destruction, and Reinvention in Downtown Detroit*, 236–66.

79 Jon Pepper, "Power Elite Designing a New Downtown," *Detroit News and Free Press*, March 10, 1996; John Gallagher, "Planner Envisions (Just One) Downtown – Greenberg Enjoys Support Unseen since the '60s," *Metro Times*, June 10, 1997.

80 For commentary on looking beyond design into development, see Lynn Waldsmith, "Facelift Urged for Woodward," *Detroit News*, November 11, 1994; John Gallagher, "Hopes Blossom on Downtown's Woodward Ave.," *Detroit Free Press*, January 5, 2000.

81 The Compuware Building as it was called initially struggled to find tenants: Daniel G. Fricker, "Campus Martius Still Lacks Tenants – Confidence Remains High Despite Development's Slow Start," ibid., April 13. On Campus Martius, see Laura Berman, "Vision, Past Make Detroit Tale of 2 Cities," *The Detroit News*, April 24, 2012; Conrad Kickert, "What's in Store: Prospects and Challenges for American Street-Level Commerce," *Journal of Urban Design* (2019): 253.

82 R. J. King, "Rencen Upgrade to Glitter," *Detroit News*, December 21, 1997; Louis Aguilar, "Restored Fort Shelby Hotel Opens," ibid., December 16, 2008; Louis Aguilar, Susan Whitall, and Maureen Feighan, "Restored Book Cadillac Hotel Reopens with Glitz, Glamour and Memories," ibid., October 26; Kickert, *Dream City: Creation, Destruction, and Reinvention in Downtown Detroit*, 244.

83 R. J. King, "New Developments Bring Lower Woodward to Life," *Detroit News*, January 4, 2000; Gallagher, "Hopes Blossom on Downtown's Woodward Ave."

84 Louis Aguilar and Lauren Abel-Razzaq, "Five Years, 78 Properties Later – Dan Gilbert's 'Detroit 2.0' Plan Still Going Strong," *The Detroit News*, August 18, 2015. On the Creative Class, see R. L. Florida, *The Rise of the Creative Class: And How It's Transforming Work, Leisure, Community and Everyday Life* (New York: Basic Books, 2002).

85 Opportunity Detroit, Project for Public Spaces, and Dhive Detroit, *A Placemaking Vision for Downtown Detroit* (Detroit: Private Report, 2013).

86 Quote from David Segal, "A Missionary's Quest to Remake Motor City," *New York Times*, April 13, 2013. See also Kickert, *Dream City: Creation, Destruction, and Reinvention in Downtown Detroit*, 257–63.

87 See Kickert, *Dream City: Creation, Destruction, and Reinvention in Downtown Detroit*, 284, figure 14.11.

3 BIRMINGHAM
THE CONCRETE COLLAR UNLEASHED

Figure 3.0　Birmingham's skyline.[1]

DOI: 10.4324/9781003041887-3

Birmingham is the second city of the United Kingdom after London, known for the drastic and ongoing transformation of its urban core. More than perhaps any other British city, Birmingham has reinvented its core over the 20th century to reflect its social, economic, technological, and cultural forces. In some ways, the city had little other choice. At the heart of the Midlands region, which has struggled from a post-industrial transition since the 1970s, Birmingham seeks to reposition its urban core for a new economy – while repairing the damage done by previous efforts to propel its core into the future. Specifically, the city has gained notoriety for its planning and architectural mistakes of the mid-20th century, which include one of Britain's most infamous urban freeways cutting off the urban core from its surroundings through sprawling car ramps, dangerous pedestrian tunnels, and surrounding brutalist architecture. However, the city is increasingly becoming known for its efforts to overcome these mistakes through another unprecedented urban core overhaul, as described by the British Observer newspaper: "A major city – sequentially industrialized, motorized, traumatized, demonized, stigmatized, de-industrialized – is now being reinvented."[2] Like The Hague and Detroit, Birmingham's decline and rebirth represent many of the typical urban interventions conducted in urban cores nationally – albeit amplified. This chapter describes Birmingham as this amplified reflection of the British urban core condition and transformation.

Pre-1911

Growing slowly over thousands of years, Birmingham was propelled in the 18th and early 19th centuries from a regional market hub to become "the first manufacturing town in the world".[3] Fueled by rapid innovation, the city's web of small workshops in metal, jewelry, and guns had grown south of the urban core along the Rea River valley into "a huge forge, a vast shop" as witnessed by Alexis de Tocqueville in 1835.[4] By the late 19th century, many workshops began to specialize in steel and motor manufacturing, establishing Birmingham as a key automotive center. Like in Detroit, manufacturing growth in Birmingham moved outward toward larger suburban locations along new canals, railroads, and highways, yet many of the smaller workshops in the urban core still house manufacturers today.[5] The city's manufacturing growth attracted immense immigration from surrounding regions and countries; many factory workers moved into a ring of back-to-back and tunnelback houses that ringed the pre-industrial core of Birmingham by the 19th century without much regulatory oversight.[6] At the same time, the growth of the city began to push out residents in the urban core for civic developments like an 1830 town hall and 1870 Council House along an enlarged central square in the 1880s, but also commercial developments like new banks, offices, and exhibition spaces like the Exchange Building and Bingley Hall.[7] Railways also impacted the urban fabric of Birmingham's core, as new lines and stations like New Street replaced entire blocks of historic fabric. The construction of Snow Hill Station along with a series of shopping arcades on top of an open-cut railway tunnel through the heart of Birmingham was even considered "the first great work of slum-clearance to be done in Birmingham".[8] Nearby, a late 19th-century land lease expiration prompted the transformation of the northwest side of Birmingham's urban core toward a new district of prestigious offices and banks.[9]

Before 1911, the most significant transformation of Birmingham's urban core came from government action rather than the railways, private projects, or land leases; the intent of the government was to propel Birmingham to a global city – and make some money at it. Using an 1875 national dwelling act, progressive mayor Joseph Chamberlain proposed to build "a great street, as broad as a Parisian Boulevard" through the heart of Birmingham's core, with the city purchasing land and leasing it back to developers for 75 years (Figure 3.1).[10] In

(a)

(b)

Figure 3.1a–b Slum conditions in Birmingham 'courts' (a) prompted the regulation to create Corporation Street, as shown in 1902 (b).
Source: Both images courtesy of Birmingham Museum and Art Gallery. Image (a) accession number 2002 v5; image (b) accession number 1995 V632.722.

the following decades, Chamberlain replaced an 93-acre area of "bowing roofs, tottering chimneys, tumbledown and often disused shopping" with Corporation Street to improve Birmingham's image and to generate public lease and tax revenue by actively recruiting retailers to make Birmingham "the retail shop of the whole of the midland counties of England".[11] His plans were on trend, as the motley open air marketplaces and "the finest Market Hall in England" built in the 1830s around the historic Bull Ring began to make way for a northward thrust of increasingly elaborate shops in subsequent decades, followed by a wave of new shopping arcades.[12] By the turn of the 20th century, Corporation Street had firmly established itself among Birmingham's key civic and retail streets, "without precedent for the boldness and extent in the whole country".[13] Riding a wave of progressive governance and private thought leadership, Birmingham became known as the "Best Governed City in the World", complete with a growing planning apparatus that would transform the city and its suburb in the decades to follow.[14]

By 1911, Birmingham's urban core (Figure 3.2) contained a lively mixture of centuries-old retail streets (1) radiating out into a fine-grained urban fabric of

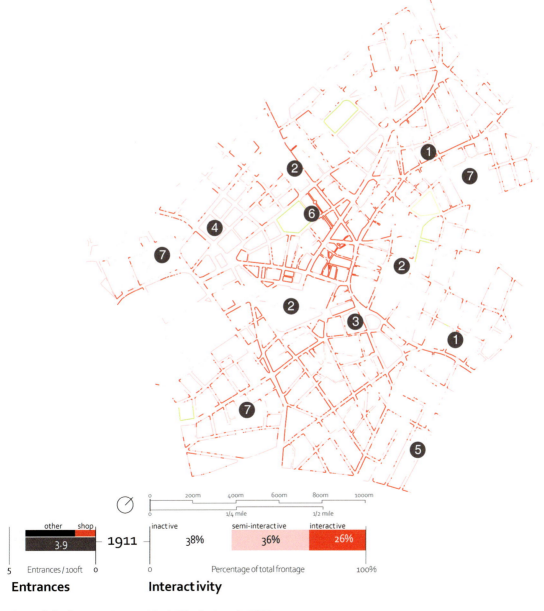

Figure 3.2 Frontage interactivity in Birmingham in 1911.
Source: Diagram by Conrad Kickert, 2021.

stores, pubs, dwellings, workshops and offices. The city's railway stations (2) brought customers and commuters from around the region to Birmingham's markets (3), offices (4), and the workshop district around the River Rea (5). Yet behind its eye-level vibrancy, the medieval core struggled to keep up with the city's explosive growth into a hub of the Industrial Revolution. Away from the plate glass glamour of Corporation Street and the city's arcades (6) lay "a jumble of mean streets, huddled terraces, and dark, insanitary and badly ventilated courts" (7).[15] Traditionally a regional market town, Birmingham's core streets buckled under the weight of industrial-era traffic growth, and its housing conditions worsened to the point where many "dwelling houses and workshops were not even structurally separate, and in many a court the huddled buildings, half-dwelling house, half-factory, sprawled in squalor".[16] Despite the city's much-touted improvements in some areas, the urban core's ongoing deterioration created what historian Gordon Cherry coined "a city of bits and pieces" without a clear identity, let alone one befitting a growing metropolis.[17] Thus begins a century-long struggle for Birmingham's urban core to keep up with the city's breakneck transformations.

1911–1938

In many ways, Birmingham simply did not have the time to care about its haphazard housing conditions, nor its jumbled urban core – it was busy growing into the industrial heart of the British Empire. After consistent double-digit population growth in the 19th century and the early 20th century, Birmingham reached a million inhabitants by 1931.[18] Similarly, Birmingham's manufacturing output continued to grow at a steady pace – even during several recessions during the 1920s and 1930s.[19] Reflecting the city's growth, the urban core of Birmingham increasingly grew into a commercial, retail, and entertainment center during the early 20th century.[20] While the historic Bull Ring remained "the most colourful and exciting corner of Birmingham", department store growth and the popularity of the new Corporation Street increasingly pulled retail northward.[21] Birmingham's core became the city's entertainment hub with the construction of thousands of new theater and cinema seats, fueling a thriving nearby pub scene.[22]

As in previous decades, core growth came at a cost. While commercial growth and still-thriving workshops pushed residents out of the core, those who remained lived in Birmingham's worst housing conditions.[23] Industrial powerhouses like Liverpool and Manchester had cleared most of their back-to-back dwellings by the early 20th century. However, in Birmingham, hundreds of thousands of residents continued to live in substandard structures for decades to follow. While many back-to-back homes were updated with modern plumbing, their number would only decrease by 11% between the 1910s and the late 1930s, as city council mostly focused on building new working-class homes on the outskirts of town.[24] With urban growth also came increasing traffic congestion. After municipalizing streetcars in 1911, the city initially expanded routes, but soon began to replace them with buses – especially in Birmingham's growing ring of low-density suburbs.[25] Factory workers mainly arrived to work by transit well into the 1930s, but soon mirrored Detroiters in their embrace of their own main product, the automobile.[26] Inspired by Vienna's Ringstrasse, Birmingham public officials proposed a "kind of loop" around the urban core as well as various road widenings and civic buildings throughout the city in an ambitious 1917 plan. While the plan was adopted, difficulties purchasing land and the tail end of World War I stopped its progress. Meanwhile, congestion only increased as the number of registered cars in Birmingham grew by 40% in the 1930s alone (Figure 3.3).[27] Traffic lights, Britain's first one-way street system, and parking management had little effect.[28]

Birmingham embraced planning to battle the dual challenge of slum formation and congestion. Benefiting from its tradition of progressive public leadership with private support over previous decades, Birmingham was the first city to use Britain's 1909 Planning Act to set up a 'Town Planning Committee' with ambitious proposals for urban redevelopment and regional growth. A decade later, more than half of Britain's nationally reviewed planning schemes came from Birmingham.[29] While planners mostly focused on laying out suburban estates, a late 1910s civic center plan on the west side of the urban core prompted land clearance for a Hall of Memory in the mid-1920s. However, subsequent design competition for a fully-fledged civic center failed, yielding only a pared-down ensemble of offices and civic buildings a decade later.[30] By the mid-1930s, Birmingham shifted its planning paradigm from esthetic quarreling to pragmatic power, bolstered by new nationally enabled powers of slum clearance and eminent domain, and the hiring of a city engineer who would gladly use these powers: Herbert Manzoni.[31] As the city had run out of land to grow, Manzoni would redraw the map of Birmingham in the decades to follow, based on an agenda of radical redevelopment.[32]

When he arrived in Birmingham in the 1930s, Manzoni found a city and a core he deemed to have "little of real worth in [its] architecture. Its replacement should be an improvement."[33] At the time, many could agree. Around the corner of new department stores drawing "metropolitan crowds" (1) and stately offices (2) where novelist John Priestley praised "you could imagine yourself in the second City of England", the fringe of Birmingham's heart continued to fray.[34] The west side civic center (3) and new colleges and civic buildings on the east side of the urban core (4), coupled with electrification,

Figure 3.3a–b Unbuilt proposal for a municipal building by William Haywood in 1917, which was to anchor a new civic center (a). As plans for the civic center faltered, congestion in the urban core increased, as depicted in a traffic jam on Corporation Street in 1935 (b).
Source: Top image from Haywood, The Development of Birmingham – an Essay, 90. Bottom image by unknown author in 1935, from the collection of Geoff Dowling via Flickr.

industrial innovation, and suburbanization improved core pollution and overcrowding. However, most of the core building stock continued to deteriorate.[35] The city's health department deemed thousands of homes in the core unfit for habitation, scattered between a jumble of workshops and congested streets (5).[36] Figure 3.4 shows how the eye-level experience of the urban core hardly changed between 1911 and 1937, except for a slight thinning out of peripheral retailers and a subsequent decrease in the number of street-level entrances. After decades of focusing on building new suburbs and leaving urban core redevelopment to an incrementalism that simply could not keep up with the pressure of a growing metropolis, Birmingham's planners would soon become far more involved in the fate of the urban core.

1937–1961

While Birmingham's feverish population growth of the early 20th century eventually slowed, the city's economic growth remained relatively steadfast during the Depression and blossomed due to World War II manufacturing growth.[37] Unfortunately, Birmingham's wartime industrial prowess made it a leading target for German air raids, which damaged more than 5,000 homes and several key central sites like the Market Hall, one of the city's most central retail blocks, a leading theater and the roof of New Street station. Nevertheless, Birmingham's urban core had remained far more intact than cities like Coventry, Liverpool, or London, even prompting the national government to deny initial rebuilding grants in the city.[38] This funding denial initially stalled Manzoni's expanding renewal visions, many of which had been drafted in the late 1930s. These included clearing a large part of the eastern urban core and a 1939 expansion of Birmingham's inner ring road proposal from two decades prior.[39] But ultimately, the air raids would clear the way for renewal by opening land and minds to a new era of Modern planning.[40] Even before the war had ended, in 1943, Birmingham adopted an overall framework for their urban core that mainly hinged on Manzoni's 1939 inner ring road trajectory.

The dominant role of the inner ring in the urban plan had several reasons. Birmingham wanted to accommodate motorized traffic in its urban core as much as possible; the city saw the inner ring road as "indispensable . . . when traffic once again resumes a normal basis".[41] The inner ring plans were widely supported by public and private leadership. Unanimously, Birmingham's political parties approved making way for the city's own product – the private automobile. Birmingham's powerful Chamber of Commerce desired new infrastructure to transport supplies and goods between the city's fine-grained network of manufacturers. Last but not least, the wider roads were also seen to improve the traffic flow for the city and regional bus networks.[42] Beyond infrastructure, the city also understood that new road construction could

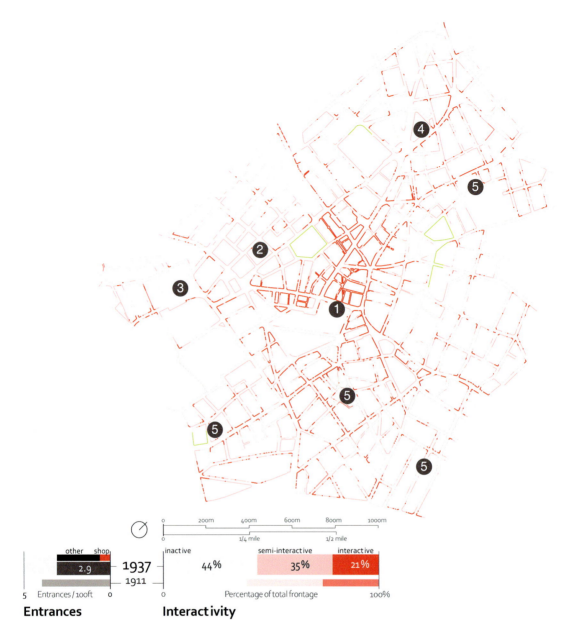

Figure 3.4 Frontage interactivity in Birmingham in 1937.
Source: Diagram by Conrad Kickert, 2021.

also be immensely profitable, learning from Corporation Street's 19th-century success in boosting the city's image, but also its land lease and tax revenues. Like with Corporation Street, the city would own any land on and around the inner ring road and lease it back to building developers, allowing it to simultaneously control and benefit from any urban core improvements.[43] For this very reason, Manzoni argued to keep planning controls along the new inner ring as flexible as possible to maximize development potential and interest. Together with its existing land holdings along Corporation Street, the city would control much of its core land to simultaneously benefit from envisioned postwar commercial growth, boost revenues, and raise Birmingham's image as Britain's motor city.[44] Eager to hit the ground running as World War II was winding down, Birmingham approved a more detailed version of the inner ring road scheme in 1944, which successfully traversed through higher governmental layers in the following years.[45]

With the dust of World War II barely settled, Birmingham saw a glimpse of its postwar future, an almost complete urban core overhaul fueled by economic growth, pro-development leadership, and national government support, with architect, engineer, and de-facto planner

Herbert Manzoni at the helm.[46] The inner ring was just the start. Manzoni's respect and connections with London lawmakers enabled him to expand national legislation and funding from just war damage reconstruction to fixing the still-worsening building conditions in and around the urban core.[47] Coined a 'sea of slumdom' by city leaders, the small homes, shops, and workplaces of more than 100,000 people were to be completely cleared, rearranged, and even renamed as 'new towns' of modern slabs and towers in a green setting. Armed with nationally enabled powers of compulsory purchase, but lacking any funding or even a detailed plan for renewal, the city nevertheless began to buy up entire historic neighborhoods in preparation for their ultimate demolition, effectively becoming "a slum landlord virtually overnight".[48] Slowly, plans began to materialize for these sites, which increasingly adopted high-rise towers to efficiently accommodate population growth in a city that had run out of land.[49] Yet, like in The Hague, significant postwar restrictions on labor, building materials, and funding would delay Birmingham's ambitious plans for its self-reinvention until well into the 1950s, leaving the urban core and many of its surrounding neighborhoods and business streets in limbo for more than a decade.[50]

Nevertheless, the urban core did get a taste of what was to come in its most central and highly valued retail blocks. Owning the land on a key war-damaged retail corner, the city sought to maximize its lease and tax revenues by allowing a developer free reign to build a massive and rather underwhelming mixed-use complex of shops and offices – a more introverted caricature of the site's former elaborate network of Victorian shopping arcades.[51] Nearby, the expiration of land leases on Corporation Street fueled a similar round of replacing original Victorian stores and civic buildings with anonymous retail architecture.[52] Many more followed, as the city held back on detailed plans or design guidelines for core sites, instead often consolidating smaller parcels in central blocks to invite more lucrative tenders for large commercial complexes (Figure 3.5).[53] When the national government finally began to release funding for the inner ring construction in 1957, the city's opportunism would truly begin to leave a trace on the urban core.[54] Just a year prior, a Birmingham delegation had visited a range of American cities to understand large-scale urban renewal, returning with a stronger conviction than ever before that Birmingham's future was one on rubber wheels. Retiring its last original streetcar in 1953, the city squarely envisioned an inner ring and parking system to allow businesses and suburban consumers and commuters to "[bring] their cars into the City".[55]

The tone was set in the 1950s for a toxic mixture of engineering-led, laissez-faire redevelopment of Birmingham's urban core in the following decade, in which traffic and cash flow trumped architectural quality and the eye-level experience.[56] While Manzoni's

Figure 3.5a–b The fine-grained urban fabric and storefronts of Smallbrook Street in 1951 (a) were replaced in the late 1950s by Smallbrook Queensway, the first portion of the inner ring (b). The renewal signified a leap from pedestrian to automobile scale, while the 760-foot Ringway Centre still defined the curving ringway on the right of the image.
Source: Image (a) from 1951, author unknown, source Louise Derrick via Pinterest. Image (b) 1963 by John Ball.

initial drawings for an inner ring presumed a relatively continuous, if large-scale urban fabric surrounding newly built roads, he increasingly relinquished this esthetic control. By the late 1950s, he openly acknowledged his inner ring scheme was an "engineer's solution . . . not an architect's", giving developers free reign to devise buildings that would not last longer than a few decades before they would be obsolete.[57] The first section of the inner ring opened in 1960 as a curious hybrid between a traditional urban boulevard and the grade-separated highway ring that would circle the urban core in following phases.[58] After accumulating three large sites along this ring road section, a developer constructed the 760-foot long Ringway Centre, a horizontal slab of storefronts with upstairs offices, and a hotel and more offices to the north. Replacing hundreds of historic buildings and their frontages with Britain's longest continuous retail building signified an architectural leap from the pedestrian to the automobile scale, and pedestrians crossing the new

48 BIRMINGHAM – THE CONCRETE COLLAR UNLEASHED

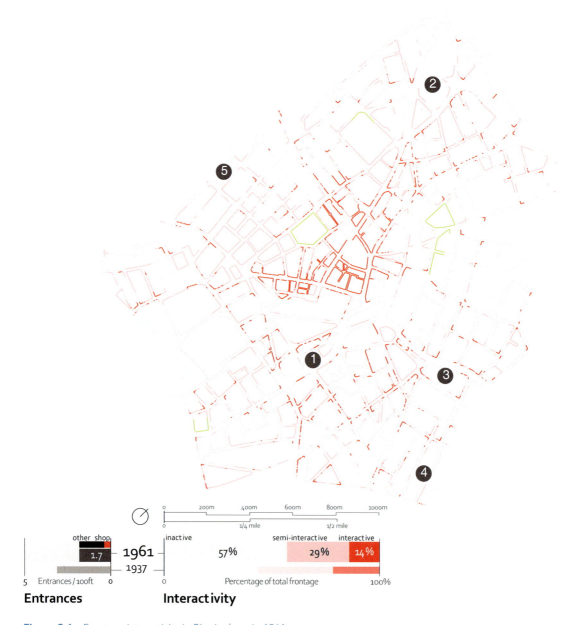

Figure 3.6 Frontage interactivity in Birmingham in 1961.
Source: Diagram by Conrad Kickert, 2021.

inner ring were forced to descend into Britain's first pedestrian tunnel – allegedly for their safety, but mostly not to "interfere with the free flow of traffic".[59] Eye-level matters were only about to get worse, as Manzoni was already envisioning the next decade of ring expansion: a fully grade-separated freeway, inspired by America.[60]

The first signs of the inner ring became visible in Birmingham by the late 1950s. A 1959 series of promotional articles on urban renewal by the city promised a wholesale reinvention of the urban core into 'The New Birmingham'. Yet the first signs of the touted 'Clean Sweep to a City of the Future' did not look too promising. Pedestrians funneled into a maze of tunnels and ramps certainly wouldn't agree with the city's boosterism but, more importantly, neither could Birmingham's businesses.[61] The inner ring promise to unlock Birmingham's oldest neighborhoods for urban core commercial expansion failed to launch, as core retailers and theaters snubbed new inner ring road parcels and peripheral businesses faltered when the new ring cut them off from the action in the urban core. Instead of an economic boom, many businesses simply decided to follow Birmingham's population growth into the suburbs.[62] Figure 3.6 shows the eye-level result of the growing schism between central consolidation and peripheral decline, with the first trace of the inner ring (1). The technocratic renewal of Birmingham had clearly begun to deteriorate its core eye-level experience, replacing fine-grained urban fabric with concrete hulks of infrastructure and commerce aiming to "catch the eye of the automobile citizen", surrounded by peripheral vacancy.[63] Besides the inner ring, Birmingham planners also cleared peripheral dwellings and businesses with a technical college campus on the northeastern side of the urban core (2) and road widening on the southern side of the urban core (3).[64] Small central workshops resisted city pressure to move toward the suburbs, many staying in the southern part of the urban core (4) or moving to new central 'flatted factories' (5), a vertical replication of their fine-grained symbiosis of proximity.[65] Like many of its British peers, the engineer and developer-led renewal of Birmingham's urban core was only getting started.[66]

1961–1988

As national funding skyrocketed during the 1960s for urban road construction, Birmingham took the crown for the pace and extent of its automobile-led renewal. By this decade, the city's mixture of drastic infrastructure construction and laissez-faire entrepreneurship to attract surrounding new development began to pay off. Birmingham surpassed its British and European peers in the pace of new construction during the 1960s, helped by a national property boom and pent-up demand for new development in the growing city's core.[67] Newly cleared land along the inner ring and expiring land leases along Corporation Street unlocked a wave of new office and retail development, and new inner ring sections increasingly comprised fully grade-separated fly-overs, underpasses, and pedestrian tunnels propagated by architects and national regulators.[68] Unhindered by a masterplan or any serious architectural guidance, feverish new urban core development gave Birmingham "an almost transatlantic Modernity" over the span of just a decade.[69] While making for splashy magazine covers and a novel windshield experience, neither the feverish inner ring construction nor the projects it unlocked resonated well with pedestrians, who saw swaths of historic urban fabric making way for a 'concrete collar' of speeding cars, surrounded by parking garages and other introverted, if not outright hostile, architecture. Below the surface of professional praise, a "deep, underlying resentment" against core renewal soon brewed among Birmingham residents.[70]

A large part of this resentment came from the downright disappointing eye-level experience of the New Birmingham. Many residents missed Birmingham's fraying but fine-grained blend of dwellings, workshops, shops, and pubs as they navigated the city's new concrete archipelago of sterile commercial developments amidst a

(a)

(b)

Figure 3.7 The Bull Ring market hall and street vending in 1958 (a) was replaced by a far larger, more introverted shopping mall that embraced a new inner ring and delegated pedestrians to a network of tunnels (b).
Source: Image (a) by D. J. Norton, July 1958. Image (b) of the Bull Ring by John Ball in 1966.

brutalist sea of tarmac, tin, and tunnels. One of the projects that aroused this public sense of loss and hostility the most was the 1964 Bull Ring shopping mall (Figure 3.7), named after the lively, if downtrodden historic marketplace and hillside commercial district it replaced. Even after its central Market Hall suffered severe bomb damage during World War II, the Bull Ring district remained a "cheap and vigorous mixture of barrow boys and shops, the most celebrated of old Birmingham's street markets".[71] Strategically located within Birmingham's retail and rail station structure, and tragically located on the future path of the inner ring, the city cleared the Bull Ring for its signature blend of car infrastructure and lucrative development opportunities.[72] The winning development bid weaved the new Rotunda office tower with inner ring viaducts down the Bull Ring hill toward a multistory indoor mall and open-air marketplace on top of parking and a bus station.[73] The Bull Ring's lack of atmosphere soon resulted in its commercial failure; architecturally, the building was an outright disaster. Designed as a "town within a city", the introverted mall funneled pedestrians through dimly lit pedestrian tunnels and oft-broken escalators into a confusing array of shapeless and aimless spaces – an experience historian Gordon Cherry ascribed to "'functional' architecture where people came second".[74]

The Bull Ring was only one of many architectural disappointments in Birmingham's 1960s urban core building boom. On the air rights above the nearby New Street Station, a developer constructed another shopping mall with parking and offices on top, a dark and introverted welcome to more than two million monthly passengers.[75] Next door, a 22-story residential tower was but one of 400 high-rises constructed throughout Birmingham, a dwelling type propagated by city architect Shepard Fidler and national builders, but reviled by residents.[76] Besides tearing up entire inner city neighborhoods, Birmingham's tower-in-the-park urban renewal would soon lead to significant social and safety issues.[77] Within the city's retail core, block-sized developments demolished and inverted historic retail blocks into self-contained 'precincts', funneling pedestrians away from public streets into mall-like environments, topped by office slabs and parking garages.[78] The wholesale function of the now-demolished Bull Ring area was reshaped into a multi-block complex of halls and distribution lots, disrupting the fine-grained urban fabric and vibrant sidewalks of the southern urban core.[79] To the west, another half-finished round of designs for the civic center yielded a disjointed landscape of vacant lots, introverted apartment and office towers and a new theater without a proper front door. A new central library carried pedestrians over a massive inner ring interchange, yet its half-finished, brutalist design prompted the Prince of Wales to deride it as a place where "books were incinerated, not borrowed".[80] To the east, the city college expanded into a walkable campus with an unfortunate introversion that reflected and exacerbated its disintegrated surroundings.[81]

As the dust of Birmingham's feverish renewal began to settle by the end of the 1960s, the music stopped. After a series of economic and political stutters, the city entered a steady spiral of deindustrialization which erased around 200,000 manufacturing jobs in the 1970s alone – and service jobs would not fill the entire gap.[82] Birmingham's subsequent post-industrial struggle became most visible in its central districts, which contained the first plants to close and the city's oldest housing stock. A growing cohort of immigrants from the British Commonwealth, who were shunned from newly built public housing, brought diversity and new life into Birmingham's central neighborhoods. However, this also continued concentrated poverty, segregation, and unemployment as the middle class increasingly suburbanized.[83] As Birmingham lost population and wealth, it soon became clear that the city's postwar focus on quantity over quality had yielded an oversupply of underwhelming office and commercial space.[84] Key retailers and entertainment venues in the urban core began to shut their doors by the late 1960s, prompting debates on the merits of Birmingham's infrastructure and development-led renewal.[85] Architectural disappointment was soon joined by increasing opposition to Birmingham's

road construction ambitions. Instead of bolstering the city's image and economy, roads like the inner ring had only fueled further gridlock, pollution, and pedestrian unsafety. On a walk along the newly opened inner ring in 1971, an alderman confessed: "The whole concept [of the Inner Ring] was wrong", passing a market trader who complained "Birmingham has been built by the car for the car . . . people feel insignificant."[86]

Amidst growing public and political disenchantment over the results of its postwar renewal, Birmingham's planning paradigm slowly began to shift during the 1970s. Only a year after the inner ring opened, the city pedestrianized the first streets in the urban core, and a final piece of core road construction was dropped.[87] A few years later, the first proposals emerged to remove the "depths of despair" that tunneled pedestrians under the inner ring.[88] High-profile demolitions like the historic Snow Hill station in the late 1960s also fueled Birmingham's preservation movement. Bolstered by stronger national preservation laws, public campaigns were able to stop subsequent demolitions of key landmarks, instead choosing to preserve historical districts like the Jewellery Quarter and Colmore Row.[89] Bit by bit, Birmingham's planning apparatus transitioned from its postwar engineer-led tradition toward a more diversified team of planners, architects, and landscape architects. The paradigm shift yielded the city's first 'structure plan' in 1973 that emphasized public transportation and pedestrianization, followed almost a decade later by an urban core plan that further emphasized pedestrianization and the creation of distinct districts.[90]

As Birmingham stumbled into the 1980s, it had become clear what damage the city had inflicted on its urban core. Instead of paving the way for economic growth, the inner ring and its adjacent development had cut off the city's already-struggling commercial heart from the rest of the city during the 1960s, leaving its most central blocks gasping for air in the following decades.[91] Figure 3.8 demonstrates the sad outcome of this process, as almost two-thirds of the eye-level experience of central Birmingham had become completely inactive by 1988 – "a non-place, bounded by motorways", as an urban designer described it.[92] Not only were the new parts of the inner ring itself mostly inactive (1) – save for the internalized commerce of the Bull Ring (2) and the first inner ring portion built by the early 1960s (3) – the ring had killed off most of the remaining commercial activity and fine-grained dwellings of its surrounding streets (3) as well. The number of entrances had plummeted by over half since the 1930s, with retail entrances leading the fray. Even at the height of their power during the 1960s, Birmingham's postwar coalition of engineers, developers, and politicians had not been able to build a better urban core for Birmingham. Ultimately, their preference for speed and profits over quality had yielded a disjointed landscape in which pedestrians lost to cars, preservation

BIRMINGHAM – THE CONCRETE COLLAR UNLEASHED 51

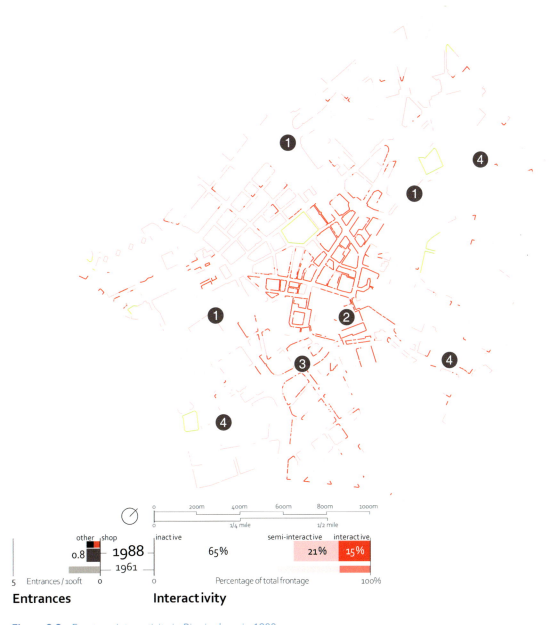

Figure 3.8 Frontage interactivity in Birmingham in 1988.
Source: Diagram by Conrad Kickert, 2021.

lost to progress, and dreams lost to reality.[93] Amidst a post-industrial city losing population, jobs and hope, an urban core struggled with disillusionment and confusion. How to emerge?

1988 to now

As job and population losses mounted during the 1980s, the decline of Birmingham's urban core accelerated. The city's pride in prioritizing pragmatism over esthetics or experience in the name of growth clearly wasn't working.

The city's oldest neighborhoods were caught up in a spiral of racial segregation and socioeconomic decline, prompting several major civil disorders between 1981 and 1991.[94] By 1988, half of the city's unpopular modern housing towers already needed renovation.[95] At the heart stood an unloved urban core, mockingly described by architectural critic Jonathan Meades as mostly comprising "Birmingham's predominant land use: wasteland, car parks, car lots".[96] Urban core retailers suffered from the opening of Europe's largest out-of-town shopping mall west of Birmingham in 1985, despite several core mall projects during the 1980s.[97] Yet green shoots were starting to appear. The city's rough transition from a manufacturing to a service economy boosted core office construction, and significant European Union grants began to transform the city into a convention hub.[98] City leaders began to realize that to keep up with its revitalizing British and European peer cities, Birmingham had to brush off its Spartan image to become a more attractive place to visit, live, work, and invest. The time was right for another urban core reinvention.

A major impetus behind this reinvention was the Highbury Initiative in 1988, a workshop with a delegation of 80 leading urbanists from Europe, Japan, and North America to rethink a more human-centered future for Birmingham's urban core. Deriding Birmingham and its core as "addicted to instant success . . . confusing, incoherent and monotone", delegates suggested a complete overhaul of the urban core aimed at accommodating the human experience and environmental quality, rather than cars and elusive economic efficiency. Birmingham's core public spaces should become far more pedestrian friendly, surrounded by an inner ring rebuilt as a tree-lined surface boulevard, its traffic delegated to a larger ring road that defined a new, expanded urban core. While the workshop only took one weekend, it would shape the design and development agenda for Birmingham for decades to follow.[99] As a result, existing pedestrian efforts were accelerated across the urban core, bolstered by newly redesigned, high-quality public squares like Victoria Square.[100] Pedestrian tunnels were slowly removed for at-grade intersections, slowly chipping away at the inner ring's free traffic flow to turn it into a more 'people-friendly' boulevard. While the northern and western side of the urban core kept the inner ring as a grade-separated arterial, the ring on southern and eastern sides has been largely erased for a finer-grained block pattern, and even completely closed to cars underneath the Bull Ring.[101] Just over two decades after its completion, the inner ring had already started to fade from the Birmingham landscape. Instead, public transportation blossomed with the reopening of a rail line and the electrification of another, the construction of a light rail line and bus only lanes, and plans to refurbish key railway stations.[102]

The infrastructural paradigm shift accompanied a similar shift in thinking about new development from quantity to quality. A 1990 urban design framework, since overseen by a dedicated team of urban designers, has guided new development to respond to the street via interactive frontages, human-scaled development, and protected viewsheds – although prioritization of development revenue and job generation over enforcing eye-level design quality continues to be a struggle.[103] Taming the inner ring also unlocked a wave of new developments in the periphery of Birmingham's urban core. European funding enabled Birmingham to finally complete its Civic Center with the International Convention Center, a large and somewhat introverted block of almost a dozen convention halls and a symphony orchestra hall, which has spurred nearby hotel development and a newly refurbished entertainment district and arena along its historic canals.[104] On the other side of the Civic Center, Birmingham replaced its postwar library on top of the inner ring with a new mixed-use development and Europe's largest regional library, a landmark project that propelled Birmingham's image of rebirth.[105] To the south, a developer reinvented a former post office as a high-end retail mall, two hotels, bars, restaurants, apartments, and the regional headquarters of the BBC, connecting the urban core under the inner ring to another canal-side renovation.[106]

On the southern end of the inner ring, the closure of Birmingham's first inner ring pedestrian tunnel invigorated the transformation of Hurst Street into the Chinese Quarter, one of several areas in the urban core that received a rebranding, public space investments, and subsequent private growth.[107] Nevertheless, the remainders of the inner ring continued to isolate and stifle the success of new theater and entertainment developments aimed to draw leisure visitors from the urban core and its railway station.[108] Further down Hurst Street, a cluster of historically LGBT-friendly bars gave rise to the 'Gay Village', which now features in Birmingham policy and travel guides.[109] While these developments have ignited nearby residential development, a significant part of the southern urban core remains as small-scale workshops. Urban policy has aimed to protect these small industries since the 1990s, as they have been coined "one of the most exciting parts of the city, [with] authenticity, grit, great buildings". However, these policies have been unable to stem the ongoing decline of small industrial activity, and efforts to bring in the creative sector have yet to reach a critical mass amidst a sea of industrial vacancy and dereliction.[110] To the east of the urban core, two universities have grown their campuses and spun off a science park, connecting to a downgraded inner ring and a renovated canal. These efforts grew into the Eastside regeneration by the late 1990s, which now include a new city park and educational and arts center Millennium point. Parts of the eastern inner ring have been removed to make way for offices, dwellings, and a hotel, impressive skyline additions that unfortunately have yet to translate into eye-level excitement.[111]

Less than four decades after its original opening, the Bull Ring mall was slated to be replaced with a multi-block successor in the 1990s, but public outcry over another "huge aircraft carrier settled on the streetscape of the city" would significantly change the course of the project.[112] Action group Birmingham for People proposed a more permeable, traditional urban plan for the Bull Ring replacement that included closing the inner ring, premised on the belief that "in the street, in the square, or in the market, we are citizens; in the mall, we are consumers".[113] Ultimately, the Bull Ring has been replaced a hybrid enclosed mall with an open-air pathway, traversing a mostly closed inner ring to a new square around a historic church, and anchored by a futuristically designed Selfridges department store (Figure 3.9). The mall has become a prominent feature in Birmingham's rebranding from a production to a consumption hub, yet at eye level, its introversion remains a compromise between pedestrian permeability and consumer containment.[114]

While Birmingham's most recent developments have gone a long way to address the city's pedestrian-hostile history, they struggle to shake off the structural issues of land consolidation, privatization, and incoherence that have plagued the city for most of the 20th century. Birmingham has codified its urban character, public space, and urban design guidelines in the 2011 "Big City Plan", yet large singular projects continue to trump design scrutiny and more incremental transformation.[115] Several high-profile projects continue to raise debates over balancing private development and public benefits, which include high quality architecture and public space. The former wholesale markets on south of the urban core are to be replaced with nothing short of "a city-changing scheme", which has raised opposition for its lack of green space, its overconfidence on retail, and its bland replacement of Birmingham's last remaining central open-air markets.[116] A high-speed rail line is about to link Birmingham's urban core to London in less than an hour, yet developers and governments still struggle to balance viability and eye-level excitement, leaving a swaths of land around the new high-speed rail station waiting in twilight.[117] Figure 3.10 demonstrates the double-edged outcomes of nearly three decades of urban core reinvention. While the new Bullring (1), International Conference Center (2), University Campus (3), Chinese Quarter (4) and Gay Village (5) redevelopments have breached the stranglehold of the inner ring, and while pedestrianization and arts-led redevelopment are gathering pace, many other peripheral streets remain mostly inactive at eye-level (6), awaiting their moment to become part of the urban core renaissance. Transit improvements move forward at an agonizing pace, and many inner ring sections still remain (7). Furthermore, the institutional persistence to reinvent the urban core through oversized, introverted developments (8) continue to plague prospects for eye-level quality and vibrancy.[118]

Conclusion

Birmingham exemplifies how a thirst for urban core reinvention can overlook the timeless qualities of eye-level experience. More than a century of feverish renewal demonstrates a city in search of growth and recognition, first molding its modernization toward European splendor in the 1910s, then following American exemplars of modern dynamism in the 1950s, before rediscovering the more continental European concept of urban renaissance in the 1980s – but always looking for the next big thing. As the workshop of Britain, Birmingham had little time for perceived frivolities like esthetics or monumentality. Beyond war damage, decades of engineer and

Figure 3.9a–b New projects like the subtly renamed Bullring shopping mall and its iconic Selfridges department store have added architectural flair to the urban core of Birmingham (a). Nevertheless, many streets in Birmingham's urban core remain hostile to pedestrians – especially at eye level (b).
Source: Image (a) by Martin Pettitt via Flickr, CC-by-2.0. Image (b) by Conrad Kickert, 2017.

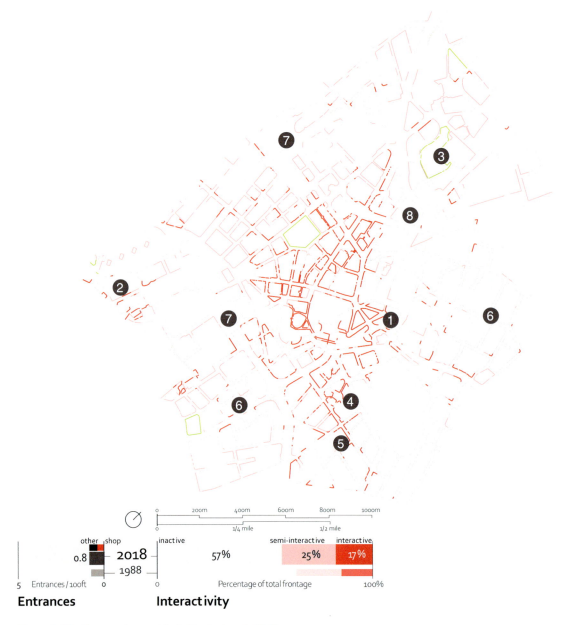

Figure 3.10 Frontage interactivity in Birmingham in 2018.
Source: Diagram by Conrad Kickert, 2021.

developer-led postwar renewal has yielded a landscape of architectural and urban disillusionment. However, it took more than just a lack of civic pride or professional oversight to devolve the urban core's most defining challenge, the inner ring, from a 1917 blend of civic grandeur and traffic ingenuity into today's nightmare of tarmac and tunnels. For decades, the city's entangled roles as both regulator and land developer have prioritized short-term lease and tax profits over long-term coherence and urban quality, giving virtually free reign for the low-quality development that amplifies the dread of the inner ring

into Britain's ongoing national butt of jokes. The socio-economic decline of Midlands region only added to the insurmountable challenge to maintain eye-level excitement in the urban core, as public ambitions rarely equaled private market enthusiasm.

The city has come to understand its past mistakes and has aimed for a more pedestrian-friendly future since the 1980s, investing in higher quality public spaces and taming portions of the inner ring. Yet planners and politicians remain tempted – if not forced – to follow a format of large, high-profile developments that promise growth but often underdeliver on street-level quality. Lacking Vancouver's level of market pressure or The Hague's culture of strong design governance, Birmingham still struggles to demand higher-quality development that engages passersby at eye level as much as the city's skyline ambitions. Despite strong urban design guidelines to ensure high-quality urbanism and architecture, the enchantment of silver bullet projects continue to pierce planners' and politicians' armor – despite a track record of internalizing life (and profits) at the expense of surrounding streets. The future will judge whether Birmingham leaders will look down from their upward gaze toward skyline novelty to discover the city's age-old motto 'Forward' has been right in front of them all along – at eye level.

Notes

1 Image by Photoeverywhere (Travel Stock Photos), license CC-BY-2.0.
2 Stephen Bayley, "It's All Change in the Second City . . . Again," *Observer*, June 29, 2008.
3 Statement by Arthur Young in 1791, in Gordon Emanuel Cherry, *Birmingham: A Study in Geography, History, and Planning* (Chichester, West Sussex, England and New York: J. Wiley, 1994), 35.
4 Asa Briggs, "Social History since 1815," in *A History of the County of Warwick. Volume Vii: The City of Birmingham*, ed. William Brewer Stephens (Oxford: Oxford University Press, 1964), 223; Cherry, *Birmingham: A Study in Geography, History, and Planning*, 41.
5 Anthony Sutcliffe and Roger Smith, *History of Birmingham. Vol. 3–1939–1970* (London: Oxford University Press for Birmingham City Council, 1974), 5–8, 158; Cherry, *Birmingham: A Study in Geography, History, and Planning*, 35, 49, 129, 231.
6 Sutcliffe and Smith, *History of Birmingham. Vol. 3–1939–1970*, 9–10; Gordon Emanuel Cherry, *Factors in the Origins of Town Planning in Britain: The Example of Birmingham, 1905–14* (Birmingham: Centre for Urban and Regional Studies, University of Birmingham, 1975), 8.
7 On urban core crowding and residential displacement, see Cherry, *Factors in the Origins of Town Planning in Britain: The Example of Birmingham, 1905–14*, 5; *Birmingham: A Study in Geography, History, and Planning*, 67; Asa Briggs, *History of Birmingham, Volume Ii* (Oxford: Oxford University Press, 1952), 140. On civic construction and commercial growth, see Christopher Upton, *A History of Birmingham* (Chichester, Sussex: Phillimore, 1993), 125, 79, 202; Briggs, *History of Birmingham, Volume Ii*, 18.
8 Quote from Briggs, *History of Birmingham, Volume Ii*, 12; Christopher Gill, *History of Birmingham, Volume I* (Oxford: Oxford University Press, 1952), 339. See also Cherry, *Birmingham: A Study in Geography,*

History, and Planning, 85; Upton, *A History of Birmingham*, 185.
9 Land leases are common in the United Kingdom; expiration can prompt the renewal of buildings on the land as well: Cherry, *Birmingham: A Study in Geography, History, and Planning*, 85; Briggs, *History of Birmingham, Volume Ii*, 12; Andy Foster, *Birmingham* (New Haven: Yale University Press, 2005), 129.
10 Eric Hopkins, *Birmingham: The Making of the Second City, 1850–1939* (Stroud: Tempus, 2001), 56; Upton, *A History of Birmingham*, 152; Briggs, *History of Birmingham, Volume Ii*, 81–82. The city had experience with smaller road widenings and cuts: ibid., 12–13; Cherry, *Birmingham: A Study in Geography, History, and Planning*, 53.
11 First quote by Chairman of Improvement Committee set up by Chamberlain, Hopkins, *Birmingham: The Making of the Second City, 1850–1939*, 57. Second quote from City of Birmingham, *Proceedings for the Adoption by the Council of a Scheme for Improvement of the Borough*, October 1875, 19. See also Upton, *A History of Birmingham*, 153, 85; Birmingham Mail of April 22, 1922 in Briggs, *History of Birmingham, Volume Ii*; Deborah Parsons, "Shopping for the Future – the Re-Enchantment of Birmingham's Urban Space," in *Remaking Birmingham: The Visual Culture of Urban Regeneration*, ed. Liam Kennedy (London: Routledge, 2004), 27. Existing residents were barely compensated to relocate: Hopkins, *Birmingham: The Making of the Second City, 1850–1939*, 58; Briggs, *History of Birmingham, Volume Ii*, 82–83.
12 Cherry, *Birmingham: A Study in Geography, History, and Planning*, 56; Briggs, *History of Birmingham, Volume Ii*, 13–14, 325; Hopkins, *Birmingham: The Making of the Second City, 1850–1939*, 44; Upton, *A History of Birmingham*, 185.
13 Quote from P. J. Larkham and Bournville Village Trust, *When We Build Again* (London: Routledge, 2013), 6. Construction took between 1878 and 1903, so as not to flood the market with new leasable land. The street was extended after 1903. The street's financing was controversial; it only turned a profit for the city by 1937. Other than John Bright Street, many other proposals by Chamberlain faltered. Upton, *A History of Birmingham*, 153–55; Cherry, *Birmingham: A Study in Geography, History, and Planning*, 80, 85; Briggs, *History of Birmingham, Volume Ii*, 19–21, 81, 130.
14 Quote from J. Ralph in an 1890 issue of Harper's Magazine in Hopkins, *Birmingham: The Making of the Second City, 1850–1939*, 49. On progressive governance, see ibid., 62; Cherry, *Birmingham: A Study in Geography, History, and Planning*, 77; Briggs, *History of Birmingham, Volume Ii*, 96.

Birmingham's industrialist Cadbury Brothers built an innovate garden suburb and started the Bournville Trust to propel planning research: ibid., 158; Cherry, *Factors in the Origins of Town Planning in Britain: The Example of Birmingham, 1905–14*, 4–5. On Birmingham's growing planning apparatus, site visits to Austria and Germany, and the role of planning pioneer J. S. Nettlefold, see ibid., 8, 17–18; Cherry, *Birmingham: A Study in Geography, History, and Planning*, 234; Briggs, *History of Birmingham, Volume Ii*, 162.

15 Quote from around 1913 by the Bournville Trust in Larkham and Trust, *When We Build Again*, 15.

16 Ibid., 18.

17 Cherry, *Birmingham: A Study in Geography, History, and Planning*, 86.

18 Part of Birmingham's population growth came from amalgamating nearby municipalities. Hopkins, *Birmingham: The Making of the Second City, 1850–1939*, 61; Larkham and Trust, *When We Build Again*, 42; Upton, *A History of Birmingham*, 203.

19 Briggs, *History of Birmingham, Volume Ii*, 200, 80, 82, 86–87; Cherry, *Birmingham: A Study in Geography, History, and Planning*, 127; Hopkins, *Birmingham: The Making of the Second City, 1850–1939*, 143–45.

20 Briggs, *History of Birmingham, Volume Ii*, 302–3, 12.

21 Quote from Hopkins, *Birmingham: The Making of the Second City, 1850–1939*, 127. See also Cherry, *Birmingham: A Study in Geography, History, and Planning*, 132; Briggs, *History of Birmingham, Volume Ii*, 325.

22 On cinemas and theaters, see Briggs, *History of Birmingham, Volume Ii*, 315; Hopkins, *Birmingham: The Making of the Second City, 1850–1939*, 125; Upton, *A History of Birmingham*, 132. Urban core pub growth prompted the municipality to consolidate and suburbanize pubs: Sutcliffe and Smith, *History of Birmingham. Vol. 3–1939–1970*, 254–55; Briggs, *History of Birmingham, Volume Ii*, 307.

23 Briggs, *History of Birmingham, Volume Ii*, 302; Larkham and Trust, *When We Build Again*, 33.

24 Larkham and Trust, *When We Build Again*, 31; Hopkins, *Birmingham: The Making of the Second City, 1850–1939*, 64, 153; Sutcliffe and Smith, *History of Birmingham. Vol. 3–1939–1970*, 9–10. A major housing shortage after World War I halted the demolition and replacement of back-to-backs: Upton, *A History of Birmingham*, 195. On the suburban council houses and their lack of amenities, see Cherry, *Birmingham: A Study in Geography, History, and Planning*, 114, 235; Hopkins, *Birmingham: The Making of the Second City, 1850–1939*, 154; Sutcliffe and Smith, *History of Birmingham. Vol. 3–1939–1970*, 10–13. On the remaining urban core dwelling conditions, see ibid., 11; Hopkins, *Birmingham: The*

Making of the Second City, 1850–1939, 166; Briggs, *History of Birmingham, Volume Ii*, 303.

25 Briggs, *History of Birmingham, Volume Ii*, 96–97; Hopkins, *Birmingham: The Making of the Second City, 1850–1939*, 159; Cherry, *Birmingham: A Study in Geography, History, and Planning*, 132; Sutcliffe and Smith, *History of Birmingham. Vol. 3–1939–1970*, 412. The national Royal Commission on Transport considered trams "in a state of obsolescence" by 1931, but the city only reluctantly removed them, as they continued to turn a profit: Briggs, *History of Birmingham, Volume Ii*, 249.

26 A 1937 census at the Austin factory noted over 50% of employees used transit to arrive at work: Briggs, *History of Birmingham, Volume Ii*, 326.

27 On the 1917 plan, see Cherry, *Birmingham: A Study in Geography, History, and Planning*, 131, 201; Sutcliffe and Smith, *History of Birmingham. Vol. 3–1939–1970*, 399–400; Herbert Manzoni, "The Development of Town Planning in Birmingham," in *History of Birmingham Seminar no. 2* (Birmingham, UK: University of Birmingham, 1968); William Haywood, *The Development of Birmingham – an Essay* (Birmingham: Kynoch Ltd., 1917). On a 1910 visit by officials to Vienna that inspired the 1917 plan, see John C. Holliday and Neville Borg, *City Centre Redevelopment: A Study of British City Centre Planning and Case Studies of Five English City Centres* (London: C. Knight, 1973), 51. On growing congestion, see Sutcliffe and Smith, *History of Birmingham. Vol. 3–1939–1970*, 400, note 5.

28 *History of Birmingham. Vol. 3–1939–1970*, 400; Hopkins, *Birmingham: The Making of the Second City, 1850–1939*, 159; Upton, *A History of Birmingham*, 202; Briggs, *History of Birmingham, Volume Ii*, 255, 357.

29 Briggs, *History of Birmingham, Volume Ii*, 157, 62; Cherry, *Birmingham: A Study in Geography, History, and Planning*, 107, 11; Cherry, *Factors in the Origins of Town Planning in Britain: The Example of Birmingham, 1905–14*, 20. Birmingham's first comprehensive urban plan was adopted in 1912: Briggs, *History of Birmingham, Volume Ii*, 355. On Birmingham's prior institutional planning tradition, see Cherry, *Birmingham: A Study in Geography, History, and Planning*, 132, 49; Larkham and Trust, *When We Build Again*, X.

30 On suburban planning priorities, see Sutcliffe and Smith, *History of Birmingham. Vol. 3–1939–1970*, 427; Hopkins, *Birmingham: The Making of the Second City, 1850–1939*, 165. On the Civic Center, see Upton, *A History of Birmingham*, 195; Briggs, *History of Birmingham, Volume Ii*, 277, 358; Cherry, *Birmingham: A Study in Geography, History, and Planning*, 132, 215; Larkham and Trust, *When We Build Again*, X.

31 Larkham and Trust, *When We Build Again*, X; Cherry, *Birmingham: A Study in Geography, History, and Planning*, 124. Slum clearance became possible through the National Housing Act of 1935 and a new Corporation Act in 1936, which Manzoni credited with starting "the idea of redevelopment in Birmingham": Herbert Manzoni, "Redevelopment of Blighted Areas in Birmingham," *Journal of the Town Planning Institute* 41, no. 3 (1955); Briggs, *History of Birmingham, Volume Ii*, 235.

32 Sutcliffe and Smith, *History of Birmingham. Vol. 3–1939–1970*, 469.

33 Foster, *Birmingham.*, citing Manzoni 1957, but providing no further reference.

34 Quotes from J. B. Priestley, *English Journey* (New York; London: Harper & Brothers, 1934), 78–80, 84; Hopkins, *Birmingham: The Making of the Second City, 1850–1939*, 163–64.

35 Cherry, *Birmingham: A Study in Geography, History, and Planning*, 132; Briggs, *History of Birmingham, Volume Ii*, 304, 27–28.

36 *History of Birmingham, Volume Ii*, 298; Hopkins, *Birmingham: The Making of the Second City, 1850–1939*, 153.

37 Upton, *A History of Birmingham*, 197, 203; Cherry, *Birmingham: A Study in Geography, History, and Planning*, 135; Sutcliffe and Smith, *History of Birmingham. Vol. 3–1939–1070*, 158.

38 On the bombings, see Larkham and Trust, *When We Build Again*, 55, Cherry, *Birmingham: A Study in Geography, History, and Planning*, 137, 139; Upton, *A History of Birmingham*, 199. The bombed retail block hosted a temporary circus, earning it the nickname "Big Top." On the denied building grants, see Sutcliffe and Smith, *History of Birmingham. Vol. 3–1939–1970*, 442–43; Larkham and Trust, *When We Build Again*, Xi.

39 On the eastern core plan, see Sutcliffe and Smith, *History of Birmingham. Vol. 3–1939–1970*, 469; Briggs, *History of Birmingham, Volume II*, 304; Larkham and Trust, *When We Build Again*, xii. On the inner ring proposal, see Sutcliffe and Smith, *History of Birmingham. Vol. 3–1939–1970*, 442.

40 Planners openly described wartime damage as an opportunity for renewal. See e.g. Ralph Tubbs, *Living in Cities* (Harmondsworth; Middlesex: Penguin Books, 1942), viii; Larkham and Trust, *When We Build Again*. Commenting on the wartime damage in a 1941 interview with a local newspaper, Manzoni urged Birmingham to use the wartime raids as an "opportunity to carry out the plans we have already": ibid., xii. See also Public Works Committee minutes in Sutcliffe and Smith, *History of Birmingham. Vol. 3–1939–1970*, 401. Besides city officials, conceptual input on Birmingham's wartime urban renewal and planning came from various publications from the Bournville Village Trust: Larkham and Trust, *When We Build Again*.

41 Quote from the Public Works Department, overseen by Manzoni in Upton, *A History of Birmingham*, 200.

42 Cherry, *Birmingham: A Study in Geography, History, and Planning*, 201; Sutcliffe and Smith, *History of Birmingham. Vol. 3–1939–1970*, 399–401, P404.

43 Ibid., 401.

44 Ibid., 401, 442; Cherry, *Birmingham: A Study in Geography, History, and Planning*, 194. Manzoni had also seen how more detailed plans for the Civic Centre mostly led nowhere: Larkham and Trust, *When We Build Again*, xii.

45 In 1945, city legislation enabled the ring's construction; the following year, the plan was passed with minimal comments by central government: Cherry, *Birmingham: A Study in Geography, History, and Planning*, 148; Sutcliffe and Smith, *History of Birmingham. Vol. 3–1939–1970*, 401–2. By 1947, the central government promised to fund 75% of road construction deemed of national importance. Birmingham saw the leasing of adjacent land as ultimately profitable, but it was unable to front the money to build the inner ring itself. It therefore relied on national funding, arguing that the inner ring was of national industrial interest: ibid., 403–7.

46 Manzoni would ultimately hold several Ministerial committee posts, and boasted of his national influence: Larkham and Trust, *When We Build Again*, xii–xiii. Political changes did not affect Manzoni's power, nor did he suffer from significant professional conflicts that would affect cities like Coventry, Southampton, and Bristol: Cherry, *Birmingham: A Study in Geography, History, and Planning*, 141; Sutcliffe and Smith, *History of Birmingham. Vol. 3–1939–1970*, 429. Manzoni oversaw a formal 'reconstruction committee' with little real influence: Larkham and Trust, *When We Build Again*, xi.

47 Manzoni was appointed to an advisory panel on the issue of urban renewal, which may have significantly shaped the 1944 Town and Country Planning Act's expansion of entitlements to renewal Cherry, *Birmingham: A Study in Geography, History, and Planning*, 14; Sutcliffe and Smith, *History of Birmingham. Vol. 3–1939–1970*, 224–25.

48 The main protest against renewal came from retail businesses: ibid., 225, 427; Cherry, *Birmingham: A Study in Geography, History, and Planning*, 145–46; Upton, *A History of Birmingham*, 203–4. Between 1936 and 1948, Birmingham's number of back-to-back dwellings had only decreased by 25%: ibid., 196; Cherry, *Birmingham: A Study in Geography, History, and Planning*, 141. Minor clearance had occurred in the late 1930s around Gooch Street: ibid., 124. On the renaming and a mid-1950s expansion of the areas, see ibid., 170. Quote from the 1959 "New

Birmingham" series of articles in the Birmingham Mail, in David Adams and Peter Larkham, *The Everyday Experiences of Reconstruction and Regeneration: From Vision to Reality in Birmingham and Coventry* (London: Routledge, 2018), 244.

49 Sutcliffe and Smith, *History of Birmingham. Vol. 3–1939–1970*, 134. While Birmingham politicians and planners initially resisted high-rise housing, the realization that the city had run out of land, a strong agricultural lobby against urban sprawl, and increasing central government support for high-rise construction ultimately changed this standpoint. On the debate of high-rise versus terraced housing, see Cherry, *Birmingham: A Study in Geography, History, and Planning*, 150, 171, 175–76, 235. Birmingham's City architect Sheppard Fidler was instrumental in changing the narrative toward high-rise construction: Upton, *A History of Birmingham*, 204. Partly, city growth would occur in new settlements outside of Birmingham, as stated in the "Conurbation: a planning survey of Birmingham and the Black Country" report in 1948 by the nationally appointed West Midland Group: Cherry, *Birmingham: A Study in Geography, History, and Planning*, 151.

50 Sutcliffe and Smith, *History of Birmingham. Vol. 3–1939–1970*, 472. In 1949, only 270 of the 30,000 homes in the redevelopment districts had been demolished Cherry, *Birmingham: A Study in Geography, History, and Planning*, 146. A required urban development plan in 1952 contained mostly generalities for these central urban redevelopment districts: ibid., 193–94.

51 The site was owned by the city because national legislation placed war-damaged sites under municipal ownership: Sutcliffe and Smith, *History of Birmingham. Vol. 3–1939–1970*, 407. While the site included the city's first true shopping mall and its tallest building thus far, its muted architecture was later derided by architectural historian Nicholaus Pevsner as "a bad joke" in The Architectural Review, Vol cxxi, January–June 1957, 24–25. See also Nikolaus Pevsner and Alexandra Wedgwood, *Warwickshire* (Harmondsworth: Penguin, 1966), 125; Upton, *A History of Birmingham*, 205; Cherry, *Birmingham: A Study in Geography, History, and Planning*, 211.

52 Leases along Corporation Street began to expire in 1957–1958: ibid., 212. Rackham's department store block had a similar program and design to the Big Top site: a large store with an adjoining arcade, topped by an office building. It received similar criticism for its lack of distinctiveness: Sutcliffe and Smith, *History of Birmingham. Vol. 3–1939–1970*, 466.

53 Upton, *A History of Birmingham*, 205; Cherry, *Birmingham: A Study in Geography, History, and Planning*, 6.

54 Sutcliffe and Smith, *History of Birmingham. Vol. 3–1939–1970*, 407. The central government had higher-priority rebuilding projects elsewhere during the late 1940s and early 1950s, but changed tracks when it envisioned Birmingham at the nexus of an envisioned national motorway system: ibid., 405, 472; Cherry, *Birmingham: A Study in Geography, History, and Planning*, 148–49. Prior to the inner ring, the government had provided funding to widen a downtown-adjacent radial trunk route: ibid., 201; Sutcliffe and Smith, *History of Birmingham. Vol. 3–1939–1970*, 403.

55 Sutcliffe and Smith, *History of Birmingham. Vol. 3–1939–1970*, 409–10; Upton, *A History of Birmingham*, 201. Transit passenger numbers began a steady decline by the late 1950s, and several revival attempts failed: Sutcliffe and Smith, *History of Birmingham. Vol. 3–1939–1970*, 405–6, 413–14.

56 Cherry, *Birmingham: A Study in Geography, History, and Planning*, 212. The city consolidated cleared sites to make them more attractive to developers: Sutcliffe and Smith, *History of Birmingham. Vol. 3–1939–1970*, 444, 464.

57 Upton, *A History of Birmingham*, 20; Matthew Parker, *Making the City Mobile: The Place of the Motor Car in the Planning of Post-War Birmingham, C. 1945–1973* (Leicester: University of Leicester, 2015).

58 Sutcliffe and Smith, *History of Birmingham. Vol. 3–1939–1970*, 408; Upton, *A History of Birmingham*, 200.

59 Quote from Public Works Committee *Inner Ring Road Scheme* document, in Parker, *Making the City Mobile: The Place of the Motor Car in the Planning of Post-War Birmingham, C. 1945–1973*, 71. The tunnel was lined with shops and showcase windows to make the crossing experience somewhat more pleasant. On infrastructure, see also ibid., 72–74; Upton, *A History of Birmingham*, 200–1. Local architect James Roberts designed both the long southern frontage and the northern hotel: Cherry, *Birmingham: A Study in Geography, History, and Planning*, 211. Only three bids were received for the inner ring site, as department stores hesitated to move their premises outward: Sutcliffe and Smith, *History of Birmingham. Vol. 3–1939–1970*, 443.

60 On the 1960 opening: Cherry, *Birmingham: A Study in Geography, History, and Planning*, 201; Upton, *A History of Birmingham*, 201. On the inner ring design shift toward grade separation: Sutcliffe and Smith, *History of Birmingham. Vol. 3–1939–1970*, 408–9.

61 Frank Price wrote a series of articles, which appeared in undated issues of the Birmingham Mail in 1959, and was later bound as "The New Birmingham." See also Parker, *Making the City Mobile: The Place of the Motor Car in the Planning of Post-War Birmingham, C. 1945–1973*, 192; Upton, *A History of Birmingham*,

203; Adams and Larkham, *The Everyday Experiences of Reconstruction and Regeneration: From Vision to Reality in Birmingham and Coventry*, footnote 17.

62 The city planned a "Theatre-land" along the Hurst Street intersection with the new inner ring, to no avail: Sutcliffe and Smith, *History of Birmingham. Vol. 3–1939–1970*, 304. Theaters also hesitated to locate along and beyond the ring road due to the saturation of the theater market, as the city had a relatively small middle class and long work hours, and suffered from competition of nearby cities: ibid., 292–94, 331. See also Upton, *A History of Birmingham*, 131–33. Birmingham actively pursued to move pubs from the urban core to underserved suburbs through their licensing policy. Furthermore, the city had far fewer pubs per capita than the national average: ibid., 254–55. On suburbanization, see also Larkham and Trust, *When We Build Again*, xx.

63 T. Bendixson, "Las Vegas of the Midlands," *Guardian*, December 20, 1969, describes Smallbrook Ringway as the Las Vegas "Strip" of the United Kingdom: Parker, *Making the City Mobile: The Place of the Motor Car in the Planning of Post-War Birmingham, C. 1945–1973*, 69.

64 The Central Technical College became the University of Aston in 1964: Sutcliffe and Smith, *History of Birmingham. Vol. 3–1939–1970*, 353.

65 These workshops did diminish in number, but remained a key element of the Birmingham industrial economy well into the 1960s: ibid., 129, 139, 157–58; Cherry, *Birmingham: A Study in Geography, History, and Planning*, 157–58.

66 Ibid., 234, P201. Frustration with the low architectural quality of new construction grew by the mid-1950s: Sutcliffe and Smith, *History of Birmingham. Vol. 3–1939–1970*, 429. Birmingham only appointed a city architect in 1952; Sheppard Fidler initially held little power over central projects. To compare Birmingham's engineer-led renewal to other British cities, see John R. Gold, *The Practice of Modernism: Modern Architects and Urban Transformation, 1954–1972* (London and New York: Routledge, 2007), 69.

67 Cherry, *Birmingham: A Study in Geography, History, and Planning*; Sutcliffe and Smith, *History of Birmingham. Vol. 3–1939–1970*, 232.

68 The transition toward an urban freeway for the inner ring was propagated by architects and national policies. For example, architect Ian Nairn attributed pedestrian congestion along the initial inner ring stretch to the storefronts along the road: Ian Nairn, "Birmingham: Liverpool: Manchester," *Architectural Review* cxxviii, no. July–December (1960). Architect Leslie Ginsburg similarly criticized frontage development: Leslie B. Ginsburg, "The Birmingham Ring Road: Town Planning or Road Building?" *Architect's Journal* cxxx, no. 3363

(1959). Both articles featured in Sutcliffe and Smith, *History of Birmingham. Vol. 3–1939–1970*, 447. Most importantly, city architect Sheppard Fidler strongly opposed buildings lining the inner ring road. Government regulations also suggested full separation between pedestrians and traffic, inspired by Colin Buchanan, *Traffic in Towns*, Penguin Book (Harmondsworth, England: Penguin Books, 1963). See also Adams and Larkham, *The Everyday Experiences of Reconstruction and Regeneration: From Vision to Reality in Birmingham and Coventry*, 248; Peter J. Larkham, "Replanning Post-War Birmingham: Process, Product and Legacy," *Architectura: Zeitschrift fur Geschichte der Baukunst* 46, no. 1 (2018); Cherry, *Birmingham: A Study in Geography, History, and Planning*, 201. Already by the end of World War II, the national government discouraged having storefronts along new road construction. On regulation and spending, see Parker, *Making the City Mobile: The Place of the Motor Car in the Planning of Post-War Birmingham, C. 1945–1973*, 79. Manzoni did warn the grade-separated inner ring would take up too much space, which would "diminish very severely the economic value of the centre for whose benefit the road was being constructed." He retired in 1964, when the inner ring construction as still underway: Sutcliffe and Smith, *History of Birmingham. Vol. 3–1939–1970*, 409. By 1967 Birmingham had accumulated debt for road building at twice the national average pace, except for London: ibid., 399. Meanwhile, transit ridership had decreased by almost 40% between 1950 and 1968, despite attempts to invest in suburban train services: ibid., 414–15.

69 Quote from Sutcliffe and Smith, *History of Birmingham. Vol. 3–1939–1970*, 468. See also ibid., 169, 409, 447–48; Cherry, *Birmingham: A Study in Geography, History, and Planning*, 159, 201; Upton, *A History of Birmingham*, 201.

70 This warning came from former Mayor Norman Tiptaft, in *Daily Telegraph, 23 November 1960*. See also Peter Shapely, "The Entrepreneurial City: The Role of Local Government and City-Centre Redevelopment in Post-War Industrial English Cities," *Twentieth Century British History* 22, no. 4 (2011): 518.

71 Quote from Oliver Marriott, *The Property Boom* (London: Hamish Hamilton, 1967), 222–23. In Cherry, *Birmingham: A Study in Geography, History, and Planning*, 214. On the history of the Bull Ring, see also Upton, *A History of Birmingham*, 180–83.

72 The same year the Market Hall was bombed, Manzoni had drawn plans for its retention in the middle of the inner ring. In later schemes, the Hall was removed to consolidate three interlinked sites for better development potential: ibid., 183; Cherry,

Birmingham: A Study in Geography, History, and Planning, 212–13.

73   On the initial bid process, which switched from J.L.G. Investments to John Laing & Sons but retained design elements: ibid., Sutcliffe and Smith, *History of Birmingham. Vol. 3–1939–1970*, 444–46.

74   Cherry, *Birmingham: A Study in Geography, History, and Planning*, 214; Upton, *A History of Birmingham*, 184–85. Real estate expert Oliver Marriott ascribed the architectural failure to "a restrictive brief": Marriott, *The Property Boom*, 227.

75   Like to Bull Ring, this mall was also a commercial failure, and had to be relaunched in the mid-1980s as the Pallasades: Upton, *A History of Birmingham*, 187. The concept was envisioned during World War 2 by the Bournville Trust: Larkham and Trust, *When We Build Again*, 41.

76   Upton, *A History of Birmingham*, 205; Cherry, *Birmingham: A Study in Geography, History, and Planning*, 214, 235. Fidler's support for high-rise flats resonated with planners as the city had run out of land, but a housing manager admitted that at least 80% of their residents did not like living in them. By the early 1970s, the high-rise building era was over: Sutcliffe and Smith, *History of Birmingham. Vol. 3–1939–1970*, 430–40. Fidler had resigned by 1964: Cherry, *Birmingham: A Study in Geography, History, and Planning*, 179.

77   Ibid., 169–73. Demolition and renewal speed increased markedly after 1966: Sutcliffe and Smith, *History of Birmingham. Vol. 3–1939–1970*, 232; Upton, *A History of Birmingham*, 204.

78   Cherry, *Birmingham: A Study in Geography, History, and Planning*, 214.

79   Ibid., 195–96; Sutcliffe and Smith, *History of Birmingham. Vol. 3–1939–1970*, 455–57; Upton, *A History of Birmingham*, 213.

80   Quote from ibid., 206. On the Civic Centre and library, see ibid., 205–6; Cherry, *Birmingham: A Study in Geography, History, and Planning*, 216–17; Sutcliffe and Smith, *History of Birmingham. Vol. 3–1939–1970*, 452, 454–55; Parker, *Making the City Mobile: The Place of the Motor Car in the Planning of Post-War Birmingham, C. 1945–1973*, 79. Proposals for a new convention center in the Civic Centre initially materialized outside the city in the 1970s, supported by European subsidies: Upton, *A History of Birmingham*, 211; Cherry, *Birmingham: A Study in Geography, History, and Planning*, 163, P217–18.

81   Ibid., 196–97; Sutcliffe and Smith, *History of Birmingham. Vol. 3–1939–1970*, 354; Upton, *A History of Birmingham*, 163.

82   On the decline of Birmingham in the 1970s, see ibid., 210; Cherry, *Birmingham: A Study in Geography, History, and Planning*, 159–61; Sutcliffe and Smith,

History of Birmingham. Vol. 3–1939–1970, 470; Simon Gunn, "Ring Road: Birmingham and the Collapse of the Motor City Ideal in 1970s Britain," *The Historical Journal* 61, no. 1 (2018): 246. By 1965, the national Labour government banned new office construction in Birmingham, but loosened these restrictions again in 1967. Meanwhile, the city began to sell rather than lease cleared land, which did incite more development: Sutcliffe and Smith, *History of Birmingham. Vol. 3–1939–1970*, 446–47.

83   Ibid., 477–78; Cherry, *Birmingham: A Study in Geography, History, and Planning*, 157, P162, 187, 204–7.

84   Ibid., 217; Sutcliffe and Smith, *History of Birmingham. Vol. 3–1939–1970*, 466. Between 1939 and the end of 1963, 700,000 square feet of retail space and 2.3 million square feet of office space had been added: M. B. Stedman and P. A. Wood, "Urban Renewal in Birmingham: An Interim Report," *Geography* 50, no. 1 (1965). On growing disenchantment with 1960s construction, see Cherry, *Birmingham: A Study in Geography, History, and Planning*, 217–19.

85   On the retail and entertainment closures, see Upton, *A History of Birmingham*, 186; Parsons, "Shopping for the Future – the Re-Enchantment of Birmingham's Urban Space," 28.; Sutcliffe and Smith, *History of Birmingham. Vol. 3–1939–1970*, 296. The number of pubs in Birmingham had also steadily declined over the past decades: ibid., 254–55.

86   Birmingham Mail, 26 March 1971, in Gunn, "Ring Road: Birmingham and the Collapse of the Motor City Ideal in 1970s Britain," 240.

87   Ibid., 241; Upton, *A History of Birmingham*, 214; Cherry, *Birmingham: A Study in Geography, History, and Planning*, 220. Citizens strongly supported pedestrianization in a local survey: Gunn, "Ring Road: Birmingham and the Collapse of the Motor City Ideal in 1970s Britain," 240. Sheppard Fidler was another major proponent: Sutcliffe and Smith, *History of Birmingham. Vol. 3–1939–1970*, 447–48. On dropping the Colmore Row widening, see Larkham, "Replanning Post-War Birmingham: Process, Product and Legacy," 11.

88   This quote is from the title of an article in the Birmingham Post, 28 June 1977, in Gunn, "Ring Road: Birmingham and the Collapse of the Motor City Ideal in 1970s Britain," 243–44.

89   The Snow Hill station demolition coincided with the closure of its railway line: Cherry, *Birmingham: A Study in Geography, History, and Planning*, 197–98, 214; Adams and Larkham, *The Everyday Experiences of Reconstruction and Regeneration: From Vision to Reality in Birmingham and Coventry*, 248; Upton, *A History of Birmingham*, 202. Preservation also affected the areas around the urban core: older warehouse and residential districts were designated as 'improvement

areas' where buildings were refurbished rather than demolished: Cherry, *Birmingham: A Study in Geography, History, and Planning*, 188, 208.

90 Birmingham City Council, *Structure Plan – Written Statement*, ed. City Planning (Birmingham, UK: Birmingham City Council, 1973). In Gunn, "Ring Road: Birmingham and the Collapse of the Motor City Ideal in 1970s Britain," 248; Parker, *Making the City Mobile: The Place of the Motor Car in the Planning of Post-War Birmingham, C. 1945–1973*, 152. The plan attracted little public interest, a sign of disillusionment: Cherry, *Birmingham: A Study in Geography, History, and Planning*, 197 On the changing planning apparatus, see ibid., 200; Sutcliffe and Smith, *History of Birmingham. Vol. 3–1939–1970*, 441. On the 1984 "Central Area Local Plan," see Cherry, *Birmingham: A Study in Geography, History, and Planning*, 220.

91 On the enabling role of Birmingham and other industrial cities during the 1950s and 1960s, see Shapely, "The Entrepreneurial City: The Role of Local Government and City-Centre Redevelopment in Post-War Industrial English Cities."

92 John Chatwin, "Brindleyplace," *Urban Design Quarterly*, no. 62 (1997).

93 On the underlying political and institutional power dynamic, see Larkham, "Replanning Post-War Birmingham: Process, Product and Legacy," 22–23.; Cherry, *Birmingham: A Study in Geography, History, and Planning*, 199–200, 215, 220.

94 Ibid., 165, 205–6; Sutcliffe and Smith, *History of Birmingham. Vol. 3–1939–1970*, 209, 374–77; Upton, *A History of Birmingham*, 206–9. See also Bishop's Council of the Diocese of Birmingham, *Faith in the City of Birmingham* (Exeter: The Paternoster Press, 1985).

95 Many towers were ultimately demolished: Upton, *A History of Birmingham*, 213.

96 Comment from a 1998 BBC documentary: Jonathan Meades: "Birmingham, Heart Bypass" (BBC, 1998). On commentary on Birmingham in the 1980s, see also Liam Kennedy, *Remaking Birmingham: The Visual Culture of Urban Regeneration* (London: Routledge, 2004).

97 On the 1.7 million square foot Merry Hill Centre, see P. J. Larkham and T. Westlake, "Retail Change and Retail Planning in the West Midlands," in *Managing a Conurbation: Birmingham and Its Region*, eds. A. J. Gerrard and T. R. Slater (Studley: Brewin, 1996), 203–13; Upton, *A History of Birmingham*, 187; Cherry, *Birmingham: A Study in Geography, History, and Planning*, 221–22. The 1989 City Centre Review saw out-of-town retail as a threat, as retail demand had stagnated: Graham Shaylor and Strategic Planning, *1989 Birmingham City Centre Review*, ed. Planning Division (Birmingham, UK: Graham Shaylor and Strategic Planning, 1989), 4, 11.

98 On the economic transition from manufacturing to service industries, see ibid., 4–5; Cherry, *Birmingham: A Study in Geography, History, and Planning*, 165. On office development, see ibid., 220–21. The European subsidies recognized Birmingham's stagnation: Upton, *A History of Birmingham*, 213.

99 Two Highbury members received commissions to study further pedestrianization and urban design guidelines, which were completed in subsequent years: Joe Holyoak, "Birmingham: Translating Ambition into Quality," in *Urban Design and the British Urban Renaissance*, ed. John Punter (London and New York: Routledge, 2009), 36.; Cherry, *Birmingham: A Study in Geography, History, and Planning*, 222; Shaylor and Planning, "1989 Birmingham City Centre Review," 18. While transformational, the Highbury Initiative was prefaced by a 1984 Central Area Local Plan and 1987 City Centre Urban Design Strategy: Upton, *A History of Birmingham*, 213–14; Geoff Wright, "Urban Design 12 Years On: The Birmingham Experience," *Built Environment* 25, no. 4 (1999).

100 Birmingham City Council, *The Birmingham Plan – Unitary Development Plan* (Birmingham, UK: Birmingham City Council, 1993).; Upton, *A History of Birmingham*, 201, 202, 214.

101 Quote from Francis Tibbalds et al., *City Centre Design Strategy*, ed. Birmingham Urban Design Studies (Birmingham, UK: Government Document, 1990), 1–2. See also Upton, *A History of Birmingham*, 201, 213; Council, "The Birmingham Plan – Unitary Development Plan," 146–53. On the tunnel removals, see Upton, *A History of Birmingham*, 200–1. The Bull Ring traffic closure was initiated by local activists and approved by politicians in the 1990s: Joe Holyoak, "Street, Subway and Mall – Spatial Politics in the Bull Ring," in *Remaking Birmingham: The Visual Culture of Urban Regeneration*, ed. Liam Kennedy (London: Routledge, 2004).

102 Tibbalds et al., *City Centre Design Strategy*, 10–11; Shaylor and Planning, "1989 Birmingham City Centre Review," 17–18; Upton, *A History of Birmingham*, 201.

103 On the 1990 "City Centre Design Strategy" see Holyoak, "Birmingham: Translating Ambition into Quality." The strategy specifically stated that buildings must be "richer, more colourful, and more attractive to look at [than their postwar predecessors], especially at street level, close to eye level": Tibbalds et al., *City Centre Design Strategy*, 2. (report, p2). The Birmingham Urban Design Studies of which this strategy was part was integrated in "The Birmingham Plan" of 1993. On the merits, leadership and caveats of Birmingham's urban design regulation in the 1990s and 2000s, see Holyoak, "Birmingham: Translating Ambition into Quality."

104 Shaylor and Planning, "1989 Birmingham City Centre Review," 20.; Cherry, *Birmingham: A Study in Geography, History, and Planning*, 218–19; Upton, *A History of Birmingham*, 213–14; Tim Hall, "Public Art, Civic Identity, and the New Birmingham," in *Remaking Birmingham: The Visual Culture of Urban Regeneration*, ed. Liam Kennedy (London: Routledge, 2004). The economic benefits of the ICC, especially for poorer Birmingham residents, are contested: Holyoak, "Birmingham: Translating Ambition into Quality," 35–36.

105 Ibid., 43–44.

106 Ibid., 48.

107 Shaylor and Planning, "1989 Birmingham City Centre Review," 21; Council, "The Birmingham Plan – Unitary Development Plan," 146, 56–57. On the different quarters with townscape plans, see Tibbalds et al., *City Centre Design Strategy*, Chapter 8. Birmingham for People leader Joe Holyoak warns that quarters can caricaturize the layered character of districts into imposed themes: Holyoak, "Birmingham: Translating Ambition into Quality," 40.

108 Council, "The Birmingham Plan – Unitary Development Plan," 157; Upton, *A History of Birmingham*, 187; Cherry, *Birmingham: A Study in Geography, History, and Planning*, 222.

109 Council, *Birmingham Big City Plan – City Centre Masterplan*, ed. Development Directorate (Birmingham, UK: Council, 2011), 59–66.

110 Quote from Prof. Michael Parkinson's draft document for the Big City Plan, in Holyoak, "Birmingham: Translating Ambition into Quality," 47. See also Council, "The Birmingham Plan – Unitary Development Plan," 154, 157.

111 Holyoak, "Birmingham: Translating Ambition into Quality," 46–47. The area's redevelopment suffered from a rather vague master plan, and continuing uncertainty around development proposals such as a new library and a new railway station. See also Council, "The Birmingham Plan – Unitary Development Plan," 158; Cherry, *Birmingham: A Study in Geography, History, and Planning*, 208.

112 Quote from mall architects Chapman Taylor in Birmingham Post, 10 March 1988, in Holyoak, "Street, Subway and Mall – Spatial Politics in the Bull Ring," 18.

113 Quote from ibid., 23. See also Larkham and Westlake, "Retail Change and Retail Planning in the West Midlands," 208–13; Shaylor and Planning, "1989 Birmingham City Centre Review," 13; Council, "The Birmingham Plan – Unitary Development Plan," 1464; Cherry, *Birmingham: A Study in Geography, History, and Planning*, 222–23; Upton, *A History of Birmingham*, 205; Holyoak, "Birmingham: Translating Ambition into Quality," 37.

114 John Emery, "Bullring: A Case Study of Retail-Led Urban Renewal and Its Contribution to City Centre Regeneration," *Journal of Retail & Leisure Property* 5, no. 2 (2006); Parsons, "Shopping for the Future – the Re-Enchantment of Birmingham's Urban Space," 31; Larkham and Westlake, "Retail Change and Retail Planning in the West Midlands," 211. The leader of Birmingham for People is critical of the new Bull Ring's impermeability, lack of mixed use, and surrounding blank walls, which ignore the city's own urban design guidance: Holyoak, "Street, Subway and Mall – Spatial Politics in the Bull Ring," 37–38.

115 Council, *Birmingham Big City Plan – City Centre Masterplan*. See also Bayley, "It's All Change in the Second City . . . Again."

116 Quote from Dan Labbad, CEO of Landlease Europe, the Smithfield developer, in Carl Jackson, "This is how old wholesale markets will be transformed into housing and leisure attractions" BirminghamLive, 9 january 2019. Criticism in Graham Yound, "Bull Ring Market May Only Have One Year Left Claims Boss of Europe's Oldest Veg Supplier," *BirminghamLive*, February 6, 2020.

117 For example, see Carl Jackson, "Martineau Galleries to Transform Birmingham Crime-Zone to become 'Front Door' for HS2," *BirminghamLive*, October 10, 2019. See also DTZ, *Birmingham City Centre Retail Assessment* (Birmingham: DTZ, 2013).

118 Holyoak, "Birmingham: Translating Ambition into Quality," 50; Phil Jones, "Different but the Same? Post-War Slum Clearance and Contemporary Regeneration in Birmingham, Uk," *City* 12, no. 3 (2008).

4 THE HAGUE
THE LAYERED CITY AT EYE LEVEL

Figure 4.0 The Hague's Grote Markt.
DOI: 10.4324/9781003041887-4

The Hague is known across the Netherlands and the world as a center of public and legal power. As the seat of the Dutch government, the economic base of The Hague focuses on public agencies, their private industry suppliers, and a growing network of international NGOs.[1] While a strong governmental presence has given the city a reputation for dullness, The Hague's 'inner city' – the Dutch rough equivalent of an American downtown – has won national awards for its high-quality public space, excellent retail offering, and increasingly vibrant night life.[2] Almost fully built out and between the North Sea and surrounding municipalities, The Hague's urban core has among the highest densities of dwellings, offices, and commerce in the country. Furthermore, The Hague features a wide range of typical urban interventions that have occurred in many Dutch cities over the past century, making it a stereotype of typical downtown transformation in the Netherlands – a country known for strong governmental planning and cutting-edge urbanism and architecture.[3] Forces from land consolidation and traffic interventions to radical urban renewal and subsequent repair have shaped the inner city of The Hague as a laboratory of urban transformation, resulting in an urban landscape with a rich, layered history.[4] This chapter will describe how these various forces and responses have transformed The Hague's inner city and its eye-level experience.

Pre-1911

The Hague originally grew as the residence of the Dutch aristocracy from the 13th century onward; it is traditionally regarded as 'neutral ground' that serves as the ideal seat of a relatively modest centralized government amidst rivalling trade cities like Amsterdam and Rotterdam. The Hague initially grew as a village of servants and aristocrats that were attracted by the wealth of a Count and his recreational mansion that was built next to a spring-fed Court Pond – the start of a long-standing duality between the governing and the governed that is still apparent in The Hague's urban form today. While the relatively leafy and open northern part of the inner city was built on higher sandy soil for The Hague's growing concentration of aristocratic and institutional powers, the western and southern parts on lower peat grounds contained a dense network of streets and canals to house servants and suppliers to these powers. After a devastating occupation by Spanish troops during the 16th century, The Hague was allowed to build a modest ring canal system in the following century, accompanied by a Baroque urban extension with canals to the west of the city. Yet a lack of growth in The Hague – and for that matter, the country as a whole – meant that these extensions remained unfilled until well into the 19th century.[5]

As The Hague grew as the administrative center of a growing country and colonial empire brought scores of newcomers, its population tripled between 1850 and 1900 alone.[6] The city grew beyond the canal ring to house population growth, two railway stations, and accompanying commercial activity. Many poorer residents and newcomers, however, would be housed in increasingly cramped and unhygienic quarters within the canal ring.[7] To make way for a new streetcar system and other traffic growth, many canals were filled in and traffic 'breakthroughs' cut new streets through The Hague's dense historic fabric. Amidst increasingly crowded streets, the Passage shopping arcade was constructed in the late 19th century as a haven of tranquility and gentility for The Hague's growing bourgeoisie. This development was followed by countless retail palaces that in turn transformed the city's center into a cosmopolitan commercial hub.[8] At the close of the 19th century, urban chronicler Johan Gram described the eye-level experience of this new hub as "the heart of the flaneur-world", lined with exciting window displays to appease to The Hague's growing wealth. Yet, this grandeur was only blocks away from a maze of narrow streets and canals lined with a mixture of shops, street vendors, small factories, and some of the city's worst housing conditions, as the city had grown to more than a quarter million inhabitants by 1911 (Figure 4.1).[9]

(a)

(b)

Figure 4.1a–b An evening stroll through the Passage arcade (a), and a mixture of housing, vending and manufacturing at the Voldersgracht one block to the south (b). Source: Image (a): hand-colored and altered postcard by W. de Haan, published by Morks & Geuze, Utrecht, ca. 1905, courtesy of The Hague municipal archives, ID 0.54732. Image (b): hand-colored postcard, author unknown, ca. 1900, courtesy of The Hague municipal archives, ID 0.74478.

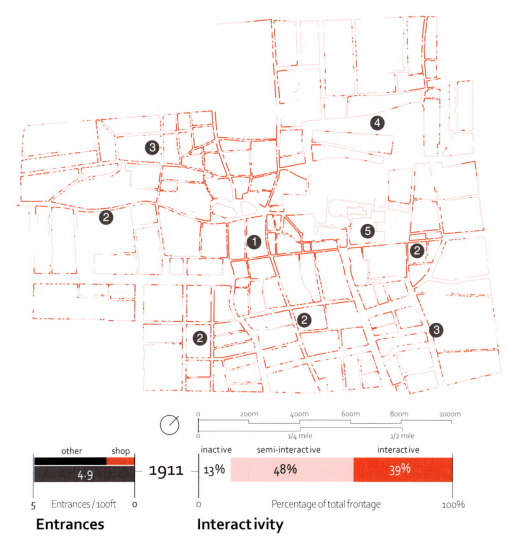

Figure 4.2 The Hague's inner-city interactivity in 1911.
Source: Diagram by Conrad Kickert, 2021.

While socioeconomically uneven, the physical manifestation of The Hague's rapid inner-city growth and transformation was surprisingly interactive at eye level, as the map of 1911 demonstrates (Figure 4.2). Central department stores and boutiques presented a solid core of storefronts (1), offering an "unrivaled overview of all sorts of tasteful shop windows in all sorts of styles and fantasies, [and] of coquetting appearances behind high mirror windows, in other words, the most curious attempts to draw the attention from the public".[10] Storefronts had risen above mere conduits for inciting purchases, instead stirring a wider excitement for urban life among The Hague's high society, becoming part of the city's consumer culture. Business owners understood that their storefronts added eye-level interest for passersby beyond esthetics: "Even if beautifully laid out, a street or canal without shops only has a short [span of] attractiveness."[11]

Beyond the glamour of The Hague's central storefronts, interactive frontages permeated into a more mundane fine-grained network of mixed-use inner-city streets (2). Often selling from their workshops or even their living rooms, a motley mixture of artisans, secondhand vendors, grocers, butchers, and bars blended production, consumption, and living along lively yet run-down streets. Streets and districts would specialize in producing, importing, and selling specific items such as textiles and books, but also fish and vegetables – often reflecting centuries-long symbiotic and regulatory concentrations.[12]

In The Hague's poorer districts, even residential streets contained a wide variety of street-level businesses (3) – far more than the other three cities studied in this book. Only in the city's highest-class residential streets had the Dutch aristocracy removed themselves from the bustle and perceived immorality of street-level business activity in opulent yet aloof mansions behind large stoops and raised entrances (4). A growing number of introverted administrative offices for governments and private businesses added further distance between the city's economy and its eye-level interactivity (5). The city's concentration of power hence began to solidify an "air of solid comfort and quiet opulence", with an eye-level inactivity "wholly different from the commercial prosperity associated with the chief cities of other European countries".[13] The balance between The Hague's staid center of power and buzzing working-class districts would begin to tip over the next decades.

1911–1937

While The Hague's streets were certainly teeming with life by 1911, the city's continued rapid growth called for drastic transformations to its urban core. Mere blocks away from upscale stores and mansions, slum conditions were worsening in many parts of the inner city.[14] Besides their physical deterioration, the social and economic conditions in these neighborhoods were similarly deemed marginal, even morally unfit. Along the same street, you could find secondhand goods, dog grooming, writing services, birds, horse meat, chimney sweepers, clothing, and groceries – a vibrant mixture, yet altogether economically unviable for its purveyors. A journalist explains: "Everywhere, something was for sale . . . one would sell to the other and that's how they survived."[15] While a 1901 national housing act aimed to improve these slum conditions, regulations proved fruitless in the inner city. Like many other cities, true urban transformation came on wheels, with the rapid growth of streetcar traffic and the first automobiles threatening to jam The Hague's medieval urban fabric.[16] Learning from earlier projects, the city effectively killed two birds with one stone by cutting new roads through the city's worst slum areas. Instead of widening existing streets as was done in Detroit, The Hague deliberately chose to create a new network of wider streets to create an entire new image of "a modern city, ready for all traffic", with an inner city ready to serve as the business core of a rapidly growing metropolitan area.[17] Devised as a Gesamtkunstwerk of traffic engineering and architecture by nationally renowned architect Berlage, the city purchased or condemned land to make way for new 60-foot streets, lined by relatively narrow parcels to be resold for new development. Slow land acquisition and hefty debates on their harm to the historic character of the medieval core would delay the new road cuts well into the 1920s.[18]

Besides accommodating The Hague's rapid growth in streetcar traffic and the city's first automobiles, these new road's mostly contributed to the inner city's eye-level experience by introducing a new scale and style of development. The Amsterdam-based Bijenkorf department store (Figure 4.3) built a block-long brick expressionist

Figure 4.3a–b The Bijenkorf department store with vacant land behind it in 1935 (a), and a rendering of the Torengarage with its showroom (b).
Source: Image (a): Weenenk & Snel, Utrecht 1935, courtesy of The Hague municipal archives, ID: 0.24768. Image (b): Dienst voor de Stadsontwikkeling, 1951; courtesy of The Hague municipal archives, ID: 0.69720.

"fairytale palace" that lured "the shopping pedestrian by its exterior appearance, walking past its endless range of window displays".[19] The largest department store in the country at its opening dwarfed its local competitors, making "the already difficult struggle for survival for many shop owners much harder".[20] Next door, the local newspaper built another block-long headquarters office building, lined by display windows that offered passersby a glimpse of ever-moving printing presses, later accompanied by the city's first news ticker tape.[21] Other office buildings would soon follow during the 1920s, although unlike North American downtowns, skyscrapers never took hold, as many offices decided to disperse throughout the city.[22] The first dedicated parking garage in the Netherlands was built along a new inner-city street, a "house for your automobile" complete with a relatively transparent street-level automobile showroom and service station – yet still replacing dozens of smaller storefronts, workshops, and dwellings.[23] While parked cars took over public squares elsewhere in the inner city, they did not yet lead to significant demolition of buildings for off-street lots like in

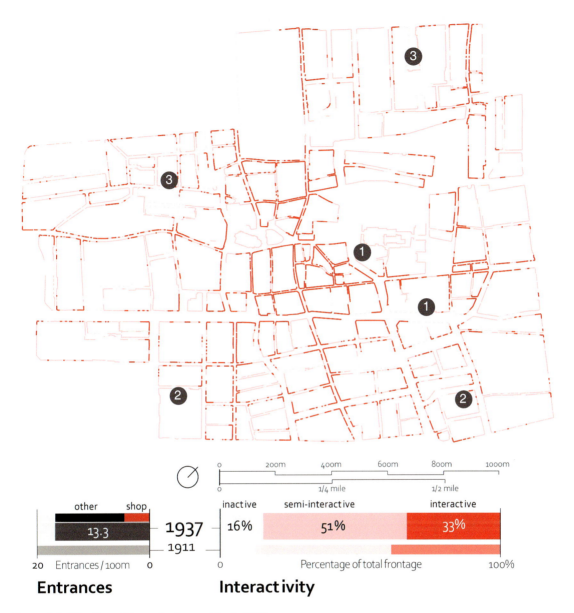

Figure 4.4 The Hague's inner-city interactivity in 1937. *Diagram by Conrad Kickert, 2021.*

North America – partially because the city maintained tight control of parking and land use regulation, and partially because car ownership and use was still relatively modest.[24] Nevertheless, the newly cut streets almost instantly clogged with car traffic, and many aligning parcels wouldn't be sold for decades due to their odd sizes, failed plans for a new city hall, and the onset of the Depression.[25]

While the Depression treaded relatively lightly in The Hague's government-oriented economy, the 1930s did strongly affect the eye-level inner city economy. After a warning by The Hague's chamber of commerce that small retailers in the inner-city periphery would be pushed out of business by larger central competitors, a city survey found that The Hague's sheer number of small shops far exceeded their owners' capacity to make a living. Furthermore, reflecting the views of its elite, the city considered these smaller businesses a visual and social blight to their surroundings. The city hence recommended to weed out small businesses to ensure the viability of larger remaining retailers and the appearance of city streets.[26] This process ultimately took hold in 1937 through a national licensing policy that especially curbed the number of smaller retailers – a regulation that would reverberate through The Hague's inner-city periphery in the decades to follow.[27]

Between 1911 and 1937, the relative homogeneous eye-level interactivity began to separate (Figure 4.4).

While new city streets (1) had cut their way through the city's dense medieval fabric to make way for a new era of department stores and offices, they had also left significant vacant lots waiting for post-Depression development, giving "some parts of the old inner city the impression of a war ruin" according to a local journalist.[28] Furthermore, the new streets introduced an architectural leap in scale that not only decreased granularity along their frontages, whose businesses also threatened to outcompete struggling fringe stores and workshops. While these smaller businesses would arguably have met their economic demise anyway in the fever of 20th-century creative destruction, the effects of their closure could readily be felt in The Hague's inner-city fringes, where storefronts made way for dwellings and small workshops with far less physical and visual interactivity (2). Furthermore, the first small urban renewal projects on the western and northern edge of the city (3) replaced fine-grained, albeit run-down urban fabric with larger buildings that contained a fraction of the displaced businesses, entrances, and frontage interactivity – a process that would truly take hold in the following decades.

1937–1961

Like in most of the other cities studied in this book, the late 1930s into the early 1960s marked an era of paradigm shifts over the role, structure, and architecture of the urban core – rather than direct action. The Hague's initial steps toward renewal through street breakthroughs had been "only a very partial success". New streets simply filled with more traffic, while many adjacent parcels remained devoid of development for decades. Frustrating citizens and leaders alike, the early 20th-century plans largely failed to alleviate some of the city's worst slum conditions.[29] In frustration with the city's inaction, business leaders set up an organization to 'renew' or 'sanitize' the inner city in 1939, proposing to clear and reconstruct struggling canal dwellings, businesses, and workshops in The Hague's southeastern urban core into a new district of large-scale offices, department stores, and apartment buildings. Their plans ultimately faltered due to the onset of World War II; however, the leap in scale to renew an entire district, the focus on the southeastern core, and the clever terminology of 'sanitization' to reflect a hygienic, almost medical procedure to bring order to perceived inner-city chaos certainly planted a seed in the minds of citizens and planners.[30]

Although The Hague's inner city was able to avoid major war damage, the city as a whole had greatly suffered from German-built beach defense works, forced evacuations of entire districts, exploding missile launch sites, and an allied bombing error, altogether obliterating 8,000 homes and leaving 27,000 residents and the national government scrambling to find a space to live and work. A postwar baby boom only exacerbated The Hague's housing crisis, which forced the city, well into the 1960s, to prioritize rehousing its citizens over any lofty inner-city renewal.

At the same time, the city faced pressures from a rapidly growing postwar national government apparatus, growing traffic congestion, and ongoing marginalization of small inner-city businesses.[31] As a result, by the late 1940s, city council commissioned architect Dudok to draft an inner-city and citywide plan for The Hague. Dudok proposed new suburbs to the west to alleviate The Hague's housing shortage, as well as a citywide network of wide traffic arteries, partly to be cut through the inner city, and a national government district to replace the southeastern inner city. Like his predecessors, Dudok's inner-city plans faltered due to political and institutional opposition. However, he set another milestone in the political and professional mindset toward large-scale inner-city traffic interventions and office and infrastructure construction.[32] A subsequent attempt at a radial city plan by the newly established Department of Rebuilding and City Development proposed neatly separated inner-city zones for offices, retail, and traffic, with a small historic core of retail and monuments surrounded by a ring of office and apartment towers along a freeway-like ring road (Figure 4.5).[33] More than 1,200 acres of inner-city land

(a)

(b)

Figure 4.5a–b Image of The Hague as a fast-growing city: grade-separated traffic, wide vistas, and modern office buildings (a). The reality of this vision: demolition without new construction (b).
Source: Image (a) from Stadsontwikkeling and Municiteit, Den Haag, Snel Groeiende Stad, 28. Image (b) of the Zuilingstraat by Dienst Stedelijke Ontwikkeling, 1961, courtesy of The Hague Municipal Archives, ID. 2.05402.

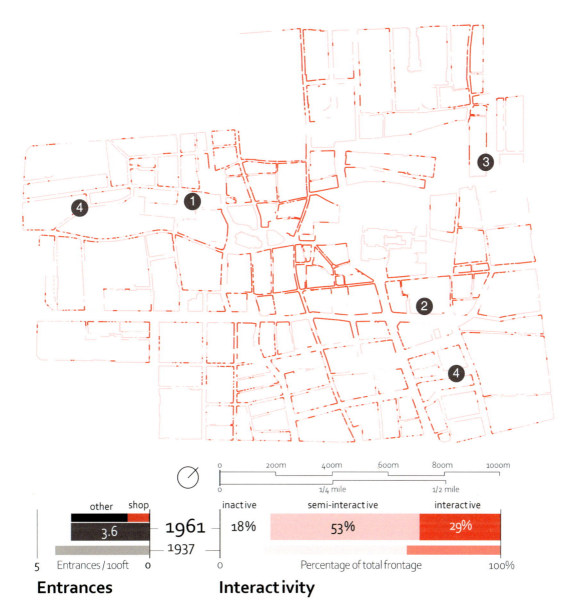

Figure 4.6 The Hague's inner city interactivity in 1961.
Source: Diagram by Conrad Kickert, 2021.

was to be cleared of homes and their "very poor [and] anti-social elements" to build to and for a "higher level", most saliently to make way for a 180-foot-wide inner ring – a seemingly technocratic yet highly traffic-led and moralistic rhetoric reminiscent of the other cities in this book.[34] Like with Dudok, continued opposition and the ongoing postwar housing crisis would kill this plan, yet not its ultimate renewal ambitions.[35]

Few drastic changes to The Hague's inner-city form took place between 1937 and 1961, as the city's modern visions lacked the resources necessary for implementation (Figure 4.6). The city had started to purchase some buildings on the path to its proposed inner ring road, mostly on the western end of the inner city (1). Haphazard construction filled in some of the gaps around the new streets of the 1920s (2), and even the odd war damage was slow to be filled with new construction, like the introverted American Embassy building designed by Marcel Breuer in the 1950s (3). Certainly, these larger interventions decreased the interaction and number of entrances in the city. However, the inner city mostly changed at eye level through a "quiet renewal" of retail businesses, as the government-regulated decline of small retailers continued to erode the interactivity of frontages in The Hague's inner-city fringe (4).[36] Most frontages along peripheral streets had become occupied by small wholesalers and workshops, replaced by ground-floor dwellings, or fell vacant altogether. The ongoing economic marginalization of the inner-city fringe would only incite more drastic physical consequences in the decades to follow.

1961–1988

Following two decades of postwar scarcity, by the 1960s national support and a thriving economy increasingly allowed planners, architects, and developers to implement their modernist inner-city visions. As the postwar housing shortage eased, planners could refocus on the growing need for building national government offices, addressing slums and traffic congestion, and the increasing threat of suburbanization. After a population peak in 1957, The Hague began to lose wealthy residents to neighboring municipalities and government-planned new towns. Additionally, suburban shopping malls were beginning to threaten downtown's retail viability.[37] In an effort to attract the increasingly automobile middle class, inner-city department stores remodeled to add parking lots and garages, including a parking deck remodeled on top of the Netherlands' largest department store in 1962.[38] Mere blocks away, the commercial might of these auto-oriented retail palaces exacerbated the decline of the inner city fringe, which had spiraled into a landscape of boarded-up storefronts "slums and vacant lots".[39] Whether through core modernization or fringe marginalization, the inner city experience at eye level began a decades-long downward spiral.

Urban plans were little relief, as they struggled to emerge from their postwar stalemate. A 1962 proposal to clear and renew the western portion of the inner city stalled due to a lack of private developer interest, and the cleared land was haphazardly filled with apartment slabs that turned away from the street.[40] The long-desired renewal of the southeastern part of the inner city turned a new page when a private developer purchased most of the land in this district to build a megastructure of leisure, shops, and parking topped by a nearly 500-foot office tower. After two rejected proposals, only one isolated office tower materialized, the start of an unfortunate trend of half-finished renewal projects in this area.[41] A subsequent city-led plan for a megastructure that would "cut away the sick peel around the old urban core and replace it with . . . the new The Hague" only yielded two isolated national ministry office towers surrounded by a moat and parking garages – an eye-level blight that survived well into the 2000s.[42]

Facing skyrocketing car ownership rates during the 1960s, the city doubled down on its radical 1950s infrastructure plans for an inner ring road. Inner-city retailers lobbied the city to pedestrianize some of its central streets to create "an oasis of peace" for shoppers.[43]

(a)

(b)

Figure 4.7a–b "Impression of The Hague as a growing service center" from the 1970 draft master plan: towers, traffic, and nary a pedestrian in sight (a). The far more prosaic inner-city result: a purgatory patchwork of introverted towers, blight, and vacancy (b).
Source: Image (a) by M. Toner in 1970 Master Plan. Caption from this plan, in Haagse Stedebouw: Mijn Ervaringen in De Jaren 1946–1983, 77. Image (b) of Hekkelaan in 1979 by Dienst Stedelijke Ontwikkeling, courtesy of The Hague Municipal Archives, ID: 0.27241.

Yet only blocks away, peripheral urban fabric was dismissed as "obstructions to the ever-busying traffic", and was cleared or condemned to make way for an inner ring road the city couldn't even afford to build.[44] The result was a ring of planners' blight, trapped in the twilight between lofty modern dreams and harsh fiscal reality. The Hague's planners, emboldened by growing national resources for urban renewal, drafted its most radical inner-city master plan yet in 1970 (Figure 4.7); which was ultimately not even considered by city council.[45] Fueled by increasing public and professional protest, the time had come for a radical rethink on the inner city, its economy and its eye-level experience.[46]

The first signs of this paradigm shift were hopeful. Public participation, social planning, and historic preservation gained momentum, responding to the trauma of ruthless clearance and physical determinism.[47] However, a 'schizophrenic' battle in the city's planning department between the old and new guard ultimately resulted in the unfortunate, though truncated, construction of a portion of the inner ring freeway in the southeastern part of the inner city. This construction was 'poisonous' enough to damage the vitality of the remaining blocks that surrounded it.[48] Despite city council protests, several blocks in the western inner city were cleared for a modern hospital structure devoid of context and street-level interactivity.[49] As planners and politicians fought, the inner city suffered from the resulting limbo and half-built dreams. By the mid-1970s the national government and the economy receded and inner-city office vacancy tripled. Most commuters arrived by car, drowning out transit and pedestrian life; inner-city residents continued to flee; and scores of shuttered storefronts forced the city to support their transformation into dwellings and workshops.[50] Daytime exhaust fumes made way for a nighttime ghost town, devoid of eyes on the street and leisure options.[51]

It would take political action to break the stalemate. After a successful plea to refocus inner-city visions from offices and traffic toward humanly scaled construction "for people", local activist Adri Duivesteijn became alderman in 1980.[52] He managed to demolish part of the recently completed inner-city ring, abandon further inner-city road plans in lieu of traffic improvements further afield, and focus on healing the 'holes' of planning blight with more than 2,000 homes in the years to follow – often designed by well-known architects.[53] After a false start with another round of introverted architecture in the now mostly cleared southeastern inner city, Duivesteijn solidified his humanistic architectural vision by the mid-1980s.[54] Envisioning architecture as a "cultural activity", he specifically reasoned from the eye-level experience. Duivesteijn and his contemporaries condemned postwar urban renewal as comprising monotonous "non-architecture", its introversion as creating street-level "dead spots . . . which invite unwanted behavior . . . and promote the alienation of children and adults with their environment" – also a reference to growing crime in the inner city.[55]

Instead, Duivesteijn's proposed inner city urban renewal propagated a diverse and human-scaled architecture that would fit within the specific culture and needs of a district and its residents. This vision was especially successful in housing renewal projects, which enabled a sharp rise in inner-city population from 1980 onward, moving into award-winning projects by local, national, and international designers supported by increasingly generous national funding.[56] Yet inner-city retail continued to struggle. Partially, this was due to ongoing consolidation of retailers, solidifying The Hague's most central streets for successful chain and department stores, but emptying out remaining storefronts along struggling peripheral streets.[57] Partially, retailers struggled to adapt to changing consumer tastes, which increasingly sought a holistic consumer experience beyond merely making a targeted purchase. While The Hague's inner city offered the most retail floor space of any Dutch city in the 1980s, visitors complained of its lack of upkeep and atmosphere, including cultural and leisure uses like theaters, bars, and restaurants. The opening of new midblock arcades to add more sales square footage hardly alleviated this issue; they soon faltered.[58] It would take another decade for the city to successfully address the pedestrian and consumer experience of its core.

The modernist urban renewal dreams of the 1940s and 1950s had firmly landed between 1961 and 1988 (Figure 4.8), leaving a trail of eye-level destruction (Figure 4.9). A toxic mixture of planners' blight, clearance, and introverted new construction had especially left its mark in the periphery of the inner city, with entire blocks replaced by large infrastructural projects and offices in the east of the city (1), and housing, parking, and a hospital (2) in the west. Furthermore, some crucial parcels in the city still laid vacant, hopefully awaiting a more enlightened redevelopment (3). There was a clear distinction between the eye-level granularity and interactivity of new construction before the 1970s, exemplified by the introverted ministerial office complex in the eastern inner city (4), and afterwards, exemplified by the fine-grained Katerstraat redevelopment (5) and a new covered market (6).[59] Nevertheless, retail erosion continued its decades-long path through The Hague's peripheral retail streets (7).

1988–2018

At the end of the 1980s, The Hague knew it had to change its attitude and approach toward its urban core to stay relevant as the heart of a growing region amidst increasing competition for residents, jobs, and shoppers. Dull during the daytime and dead at night, The Hague's downtown had suffered from decades of false priorities of quantity over quality, offices over residents, traffic over people, and, most importantly, an unachievable future over a crumbling past. The positive momentum started in the 1970s officially materialized in inner-city policy by the late 1980s, which envisioned the urban core as The Hague's 'living room' and cultural heart by bolstering its historic and current identity, adding more residents, and especially by drastically improving the quality of its public spaces.[60] Planners understood that the inner city was about more than just shopping, acknowledging that its framework of retail streets was simply oversized, re-concentrating retailers to a solid core while repurposing peripheral streets for dwellings, workshops and offices – land uses they also sought to include upstairs in more central blocks.[61]

The key to The Hague's inner-city renewal since the 1980s has been its drastically upgraded public spaces,

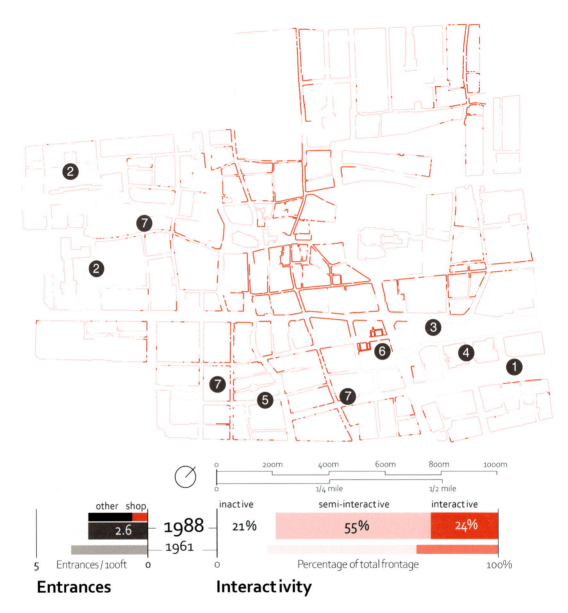

Figure 4.8 The Hague's frontage interactivity in 1988.
Source: Diagram by Conrad Kickert, 2021.

the result of a landmark policy The Healthy Core[62] in 1988 that re-envisioned the urban core as a mostly car-free zone for strolling, shopping, socialization, and leisure activities (Figure 4.10). Inspired by the success of Barcelona's public space-led urban revitalization in the 1980s and bolstered by national government policy, The Hague's improvement of public spaces recognized the experiential quality of the inner city, choreographing public space to connect and distinguish unique 'atmospheres'. Most car traffic was rerouted outside the urban core, with the controversial inner ring diluted into a simple signage system for motorists to reach the nearest available parking garage – which were increasingly constructed below ground.[63] The newly renovated public spaces catalyzed the city as a leisure destination, as the spaces became popular spots for impromptu meetings, cafe patios, and open-air festivals. To facilitate the growing night life in the inner city's without disturbing residents, bars and restaurants were concentrated around several squares, where establishments could open their premises and patios at later hours. The Hague's ubiquitous nighttime shutters were replaced to give afterhours visitors a safer, more positive experience. Within a few years, inner city car commuters fell by half, visitors increased by half, and sales rose even more.[64]

(a)

(b)

Figure 4.9a–b Closed shutters after business hours on the Vlamingstraat (a), parked cars and vacant land in the former Spui district (b).
Source: Image (a) by Bert Mellink for Dienst Stedelijke Ontwikkeling in 1991, ID: imf10119. Image (b) Turfmarkt/Houtmarkt by Dienst Stadsontwikkeling February 14, 1984, ID: 2.01765. Both images courtesy of The Hague municipal archives.

(a)

(b)

Figure 4.10a–b With parking now underground, the Plein square has transformed from a parking lot in the 1950s (a) to one of The Hague's prime leisure spots today (b).
Source: Image (a) by Stokvis in 1957, courtesy of The Hague municipal archives, ID: 0.56187. Image (b) by author, summer 2012.

The inner-city public space improvements accompanied a leap in the scale of new developments, yet even new multi-block buildings engaged far better at eye level with passersby than their modern-era predecessors (Figure 4.11). Rather than keeping pedestrians out, new buildings welcomed them in through a diversity of indoor and outdoor public spaces in a who's who of contemporary starchitecture. A renovation of the House of Representatives by architect Pi de Bruijn in 1992 offered an originally envisioned passageway through the Dutch heart of democracy.[65] A glass-covered Bernard Tschumi-designed extension of The Hague's original Passage shopping arcade has become one of the city's busiest pedestrian corridors, topped with a multistory hotel. Below runs a Rem Koolhaas-designed streetcar tunnel, the centerpiece of an inner-city modal shift toward transit.[66] Nearby, an 800-foot-long Richard Meijer-designed City Hall and central library complex completed in 1995 not only engages with passersby through interactive storefronts along its perimeter but welcomes them to traverse the building through an 11-story atrium that contains city services, stores, and a restaurant.[67] The building connects the historic urban core to a 'new center' that has arisen from the ashes of the cleared southeastern inner city. An existing modern office building was wrapped into a neo-traditional mixed-use district of dwellings, private and government offices, stores, and restaurants designed by postmodern architect Rob Krier, blending high development density with eye-level interaction and humanly scaled architecture.[68] Repairing nearby postwar planning mistakes, a nearby ministerial complex has been partially repurposed as an apartment tower with ground-floor retail and a university campus, next to a former housing complex replaced by government offices and luxury apartments that similarly offer street-level businesses.

Figure 4.11 Contemporary urban 'bricolage' in The Hague: a street cut through the historic inner city in the 1920s has been pedestrianized, leading past centuries-old buildings toward a skyline built only over the past few years. Bricolage refers to Colin Koetter Fred Rowe, *Collage City* (Cambridge, MA: MIT Press, 1978).
Source: Image by Conrad Kickert, 2021.

The Hague's new development ambitions certainly came at a price, as the city briefly entered receivership in 1995 due to its star-studded renewal fever.[69] Aligning with national neoliberal policy, inner-city renewal has become an express collaboration between public and private partners in more recent decades. In collaboration with local retailers and the Chamber of Commerce, The Hague set up an Inner City agency in 1992, which would release plans for inner-city development in the decades to follow. In its focus to attract highly educated residents from the Netherlands and abroad, the city understood the value of a lively and distinct urban core. Inner-city policy increasingly focused on its internal diversity of identities, from the northern grandeur of its historic government buildings and aristocratic mansions to its eastern New Center modernity and its increasingly multicultural southern portion. While northern retail streets were targeted toward The Hague's elite, a southern inner-city district was branded as The Hague's Chinatown, with the local Chinese community sponsoring two gates.[70] As visitor numbers, sales, and evaluations improved over the years, The Hague's inner city won the Best Inner City 2013–2015 award, specifically for its significant development from a monofunctional retail core to a multifunctional 'destination' that combines leisure, work, culture, events, housing, and an increasing student scene.[71] While the inner-city skyline continues to add office space and dwellings amidst record market pressure, architectural quality continues to improve due to strict esthetic controls, and the city aims to become the "best shopping city of the Netherlands", the inner-city eye-level future has become less certain as unprecedented challenges to central retailers now threaten to mirror decades-long peripheral storefront struggles.[72] Change remains a constant.

The Hague's inner-city eye-level experience has notably improved since the late 1980s, as interactivity and the number of entrances has increased (Figure 4.12). The city's core blocks have only solidified their strength as a regional and national consumption hub through its upgraded public spaces and new connections (1). The amount of frontage taken up by commerce has actually increased somewhat since 1988, although the fate of The Hague's retail anchors remains unclear in the current commercial revolution. Furthermore, the inner-city periphery has continued to shed retail business, albeit slower than before. Indeed, the most notable eye-level improvements occurred in the periphery over the past decades, as ill-conceived postwar renewal efforts – both built and unbuilt – have largely been replaced with new architecture that respects the passerby with finer-grained, more interactive frontages. Introverted postwar architecture in the southeastern core has been replaced with an interactive pedestrian route (2), and vacant lots have been filled with Krier's new eastern district (3). Throughout the downtown, smaller projects have added new humanly scaled architecture and public space (4). Ranging from modest infill projects to grandiose landmarks, the inner city has become a heterotopia of architectural styles – a layered landscape of past ideals and present struggles and successes that may feel incoherent to some, "the city's greatest quality" to others.[73]

Conclusion

In an urban bricolage almost unparalleled in any Dutch city, The Hague's inner city now reflects the thinking of every decade of its growth, decline, and rebirth. Generations of architects, urban designers, developers, politicians, but also activists, storefront businesses, residents, and even graffiti artists have each contributed their viewpoints and actions into a layered patchwork of ideals and unrealized dreams. While an outsider may only recognize incoherence between the bricolage of styles, functions, and spaces that resulted, we can clearly recognize consistent forces that have shaped The Hague's inner city at eye level.

Compared to the other cities in this book, The Hague's efforts to preserve the relevance and the building stock of its urban core stands out. From the first major street cuts in the early 20th century to the most radical rebuilding plans from the 1940s to the 1970s, The Hague has tried to balance preservation and progress, as residents and politicians widely regarded historic buildings and cityscapes as significant and worth protecting. This hinged on a common belief that the inner city should remain the functional and cultural heart of the growing metropolitan region. Even in the inner city's darkest days, businesses continued to invest and expand their core premises. Governments played their part to ensure The Hague's

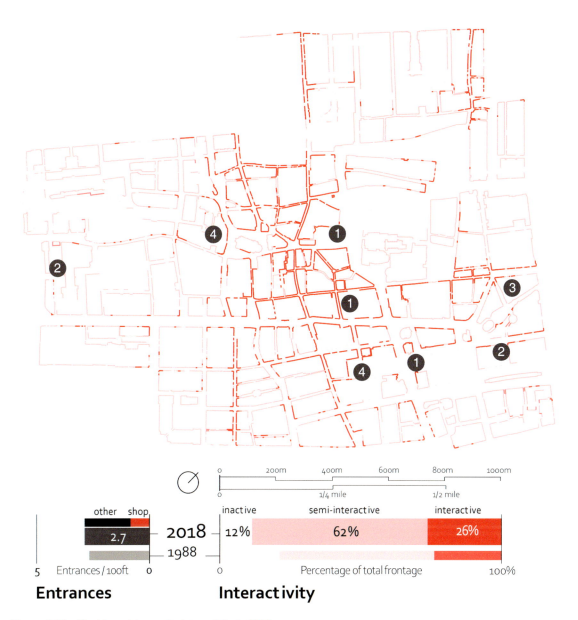

Figure 4.12 The Hague's inner-city interactivity in 2018.
Source: Diagram by Conrad Kickert, 2021.

inner-city hegemony, from national and regional policies to protect urban commerce and offices to significant investments in inner-city developments, public space, and centralizing public transportation. And although they had vastly different viewpoints on the inner city's future, local politicians never questioned its importance.

Like the other cities in this book, The Hague's eye-level transformation has vastly differed between different parts of its urban core. A centuries-long tradition of class division resulted in a stark division between a largely protected aristocratic northern half of the inner city and a working-class southern half of the inner city, where eye-level transformations have been far more drastic.

The Hague's elite considered the motley mixture of small dwellings, workshops, storefronts, and vendors in the southern inner city morally inferior, equating diversity with deprivation. Their renewal plans subsequently sought to bring a new order, separating not only land uses but neighbors, cultures, and the street-level relationship between buildings and public space. The result is an almost wholesale demolition of vast parts of the inner city to make way for The Hague's growing metropolitan ambition – an exciting skyline that may still bore us at eye level. Ironically, those mixed-use streets that survived the public bulldozer have now become among the city's most prized places to live, work, and play.

Nevertheless, we cannot ignore that the economy of The Hague's working-class streets had no choice but to adapt. While exciting at eye level, their medieval blend of consumption, production, and living hinged on an unsustainable economic model. Single ownership, low volume production and sales, hard (family) labor, below-poverty level wages, and a lack of outlook for growth was unhealthy for residents and proved ultimately unable to face increasingly sophisticated competition. The grand department stores along The Hague's new streets of the 1920s notably killed their smaller competitors, as did consumer cooperatives and supermarkets in the decades that followed. City and national policies exacerbated this purge of small retailers, partially for moral reasons, but mostly to protect the economy and citizen well-being.[74] Small inner-city workshops suffered a similar fate, as its craftsmen moved out to larger premises outside the city, or were superseded by those who did. The decline of the southeastern inner city started when its canals were filled in, gravely disrupting its traditional mixture between wholesale trade and small manufacturing, to ultimately be replaced by a new service economy encased in office towers.[75]

Technology proved a major factor in the changing fate of the inner city, as even its most central streets transformed from places of socialization and cultural and economic exchange to spaces for traffic, first in streetcars, then in moving and parking cars. For decades, The Hague sought to adapt its inner-city urban form to the ever-increasing needs of traffic by demolishing or condemning thousands of buildings for parking, road widening, and ultimately an urban freeway. The city only understood by the 1980s that it had to reverse course, matching traffic to fit its remaining urban form. As cars and streetcars move underground, the city's public spaces have been returned to its citizens once again to enjoy – a smart move, as visitor numbers and appreciation has risen.[76]

Where does this leave The Hague's street-level architecture? For much of the past century, often beyond the power of the traditional design and building professions. Whether modest, modern, or monumental, architects, urban designers, and even developers did provide the imaginaries for inner-city futures. However, over the past century the realization of these visions were beholden to the changing economic, technological, and cultural landscape of The Hague's inner city, and visions only succeeded if they aligned with these waves of change. The city's new streets of the 1920s simply responded to the rise of traffic, in turn enabling the rise of new retail, office, and parking formats that materialized as The Hague's first major modern buildings. As architects and planners drafted grand plans for urban modernization during the 1940s and 1950s, housing, material, and funding shortages hamstrung their visions until the following decade. Even then, the grand visions of the 1960s and 1970s mostly stranded into singular, introverted buildings – a fortunate dwindling of potential district-wide disasters at eye level.

Slowly, professionals began to counteract the myriad forces of street-level deactivation with increasing public support. Political opposition stalled The Hague's modern bulldozer before it could reach full speed, refocusing designers and developers toward a more humanistic – if still sweeping – urbanism and architecture from the 1980s onward. While led by some of the world's foremost architects and urbanists, The Hague's subsequent return to an architecture of trust and interactivity at eye level reflected a strong cultural and political shift toward dense yet livable urban areas. The city's current symbiosis between the skyline and the street has therefore been the result of a successful interplay between politicians, professionals, and the public.

Notes

1 The Hague's key private headquarters often have public roots or ties, such as telecommunications and insurance companies and Royal Dutch Shell. Dienst Stedelijke Ontwikkeling, *De Staat Van De Haagse Economie* (The Hague: Dienst Stedelijke Ontwikkeling, 2007).

2 Rather than referring to its entire urban area, the Dutch 'inner city' is defined by being within (former) fortifications.

3 On designation methodology, see Neil Brenner, "Stereotypes, Archetypes, and Prototypes: Three Uses of Superlatives in Contemporary Urban Studies," *City & Community* 2, no. 3 (2003); Robert A. Beauregard, "City of Superlatives," ibid.

4 J. G. Smit and E. Beukers, *Den Haag: Geschiedenis Van De Stad* (Zwolle: Waanders, 2004). The importance of layered history for urban places is explored in A. V. Moudon, *Built for Change: Neighborhood Architecture in San Francisco* (Cambridge, MA: MIT Press, 1986).

5 R. A. F. Smook, *Binnensteden Veranderen: Atlas Van Het Ruimtelijk Veranderingsproces Van Nederlandse Binnensteden in De Laatste Anderhalve Eeuw* (Zutphen: De Walburg Pers, 1984); Smit and Beukers, *Den Haag: Geschiedenis Van De Stad*.

6 P. R. D. Stokvis, *De Wording Van Modern Den Haag: De Stad En Haar Bevolking Van De Franse Tijd Tot De Eerste Wereldoorlog* (Zwolle: Waanders, 1987), 146.

7 Cees Boekraad and Joos Aerts, "Berlage En De Lotgevallen Van De 'Schone Stad' – Den Haag in De Jaren 1900–1934," in *Het Veranderend Stadsbeeld Van Den Haag*, ed. Victor Freijser (Zwolle: Waanders, 1991), 17; Auke van der Woud, *Koninkrijk Vol Sloppen: Achterbuurten En Vuil in De Negentiende Eeuw* (Amsterdam: Bert Bakker, 2010); Michelle Provoost, "De Grenzen Van De Metropool – Den Haag in De Jaren 1950–1970," in *Het Veranderend Stadsbeeld Van Den Haag*, ed. Victor Freijser (Zwolle: Waanders, 1991), 36–37.

8 On traffic improvements, see Monique van Veen and Henk Ambachtsheer, *"Een Simpele Verkeersverbeetering": De Geschiedenis Van De Grote Marktstraat En Omgeving* (Den Haag: Gemeente Den Haag, dienst Stedelijke Ontwikkeling, 2005), 30–34. On commercial and retail construction, see ibid.; Coos Vereniging Passage Belangen Versteeg, *Passage 100 Jaar* (Den Haag: Vereniging Passage Belangen, 1985); Rolf de Booij, *De Haagse Passage: Geschiedenis Van Een Nieuw Winkelfenomeen* ('s-Hertogenbosch: Wolfaert, 2011); Jan Hein Furnée, "Om Te Winkelen, Zoo Als Het in De Residentie Heet'. Consumptiecultuur En Stedelijke Ruimte in Den Haag, 1850–1890'," *Jaarboek voor Vrouwengeschiedenis* (2002): 28–55.

9 Quote from J. Gram, *'S Gravenhage in Onzen Tijd* (Beijers, 1893), 26.

10 Johan Gram, *'S-Gravenhage Voorheen En Thans* ('s-Gravenhage: Couvée, 1905), 84.

11 C. M. M. van den Berg, "Etalagewedstrijd Boekhorststraat," *De handeldrijvende middenstand* 5, no. 17 (1910).

12 On the Dutch history of urban retailing, see Clé Lesger, *Het Winkellandschap Van Amsterdam. Stedelijke Structuur En Winkelbedrijf in De Vroegmoderne En Moderne Tijd, 1550–2000* (Hilversum: Uitgeverij Verloren, 2013).

13 Unknown author, *Guide to the Hague* (Zeist: Meindert Boogaerdt Jr., 1911).

14 A vivid description of slum housing conditions was presented in "Hoe Arm Den Haag Woont," *De Stedelijke Courant*, November 24, 1908.

15 "Nieuwe Verkeerswegen in Den Haag – Prinsegracht – Noordwal," *Haagsche Schouw*, March 20, 1925. See also I. B. van Creveld, *De Verdwenen Buurt: Drie Eeuwen Centrum Van Joods Den Haag* ('s-Gravenhage: De Walburg Pers, 1989). "Hoe Arm Den Haag Woont."

16 While The Hague's automobile ownership was far below Detroit's levels during the first counts in the 1920s, so was the available space to accommodate cars. Gemeentebestuur, "Enige Grondslagen Voor De Stedebouwkundige Ontwikkeling Van 'S-Gravenhage," (The Hague: Hega, 1948).image 89 Veen and Ambachtsheer, *"Een Simpele Verkeersverbeetering": De Geschiedenis Van De Grote Marktstraat En Omgeving*, 60.

17 Quote from Herman Poot, "De Doorbraken in De Binnenstad: Hoe Uit De Oude Stad Een Moderne Groeit," *'s-Gravenhage in beeld*, April 26, 1929. See also I. A. Lindo, *De Openbare Werken Van 'S-Gravenhage, 1890–1918: Uitgegeven Ter Gelegenheid Van Het Aftreden Van Den Heer I.A. Lindo Als Directeur Der Gemeentewerken Op 1 Juli 1918* (The Hague: Mouton, 1918), 40.

18 Poot, "De Doorbraken in De Binnenstad: Hoe Uit De Oude Stad Een Moderne Groeit"; K. G. Valentijn

19 Dick Rouwenhorst, *'S-Gravenhage 1840–1940: "100 Jaar Haagse Stadsontwikkeling"* ('s-Gravenhage: Gemeente 's-Gravenhage, Afd. Verkeer en Vervoer, Openbare Werken en Monumentenzorg (VOM), 1988), 25. Boekraad and Aerts, "Berlage En De Lotgevallen Van De 'Schone Stad' – Den Haag in De Jaren 1900–1934," 83–84.

20 Chief urban planner P. Bakker Schut in ibid., 13.

21 Veen and Ambachtsheer, *"Een Simpele Verkeersverbeetering": De Geschiedenis Van De Grote Marktstraat En Omgeving*, 85–86.

22 Christiaan Vaillant, "De Haagse Architectuur En Stedebouw in De Periode 1900–1940," in *Gids Van De Moderne Architectuur in Den Haag – Guide to Modern Architecture in the Hague*, eds. Cees van Boven, Victor Freijser, and Christiaan Vaillant (The Hague: Ulysses, 1997).

23 Unknown author, *Iets Nieuws Onder De Zon Is De Torengarage* (The Hague: S. Viskoper, 1930).

24 P. Bakker Schut, "De Binnenstad Van Den Haag Als Parkeer-Ruimte," *Wegen* 11, no. 9 (1935).

25 Veen and Ambachtsheer, *"Een Simpele Verkeersverbeetering": De Geschiedenis Van De Grote Marktstraat En Omgeving*, 92–93; A. H. Wegerif and Stichting Saneering Binnenstad, *Plan Tot Verbetering Van Het Stadsgedeelte Tusschen Spui En Zwarteweg* (The Hague: NV Drukkerij Trio, 1941). The number of vehicles on some of The Hague's most central streets had increased up to twentyfold between 1912 and 1937: Boekraad and Aerts, "Berlage En De Lotgevallen Van De 'Schone Stad' – Den Haag in De Jaren 1900–1934," 53; Gemeentebestuur, "Enige Grondslagen Voor De Stedebouwkundige Ontwikkeling Van 'S-Gravenhage," 275.

26 More than half of the shops were smaller than 500 square feet (50 square meters), and almost a fifth were not located in a retail building – mostly illegally: P. Bakker Schut, *Rapport Betreffende Winkeltelling 1935* (The Hague: Dienst der Stadsontwikkeling en Volkshuisvesting, 1936); P. Bakker Schut, *De Ontwikkeling Van Het Bedrijfsleven in Het Gebied Van De Kamer Van Koophandel En Fabrieken Voor 'S-Gravenhage* (The Hague: P. Bakker Schut, 1932).

27 The policies were the Vestigingswet Kleinbedrijf 1937 (establishment law small business 1937) and the Besluit Algemeen Vestigingsverbod Kleinbedrijf 1941 (decree general ban on establishment small business 1941).

28 Herman Poot, "De Verruiming Der Binnenstad," *'s-Gravenhage in beeld*, April 12, 1929.

29 Quote by Kamer van Koophandel en Fabrieken voor Zuid-Holland, *Rapport Van De Commissie*

Tot Voorbereiding Van Herbouw En Herstel Van 'S-Gravenhage (The Hague: N.V. boek- en kunstdrukkerij v/h Mouton & Co., 1945), 26. Car ownership had almost doubled between 1928 and 1939, and due to suburbanization, traffic continued to grow: Boekraad and Aerts, "Berlage En De Lotgevallen Van De 'Schone Stad' – Den Haag in De Jaren 1900–1934," 52–53.

30 The organization was named "Stichting Saneering Binnenstad," directly translated as Foundation Sanitization Inner City": "Saneering Binnenstad – De Acte Van Oprichting Gepasseerd," *Het Vaderland*, December 28, 1939. Nederlandsche Maatschappij voor Nijverheid en Handel – Departement 's-Gravenhage, *Rapport over De Saneering Van De Binnenstad Van 'S-Gravenhage in Het Bijzonder Van Het Spui En Omgeving* (The Hague: Self-published report, 1939); Stichting saneering binnenstad 's-Gravenhage, *Plan Tot Verbetering Van Het Stadsgedeelte Tusschen Spui En Zwarteweg* (The Hague: N.V. Drukkerij Trio, 1941).

31 Zuid-Holland, *Rapport Van De Commissie Tot Voorbereiding Van Herbouw En Herstel Van 'S-Gravenhage.*
Irene van Huik, "'Ingebed in Het Zo Karakteristieke Groen' – Dudok En Den Haag in De Jaren 1930–1950," in *Het Veranderend Stadsbeeld Van Den Haag*, ed. Victor Freijser (Zwolle: Waanders, 1991), 113; F. van der Sluijs, *Haagse Stedebouw: Mijn Ervaringen in De Jaren 1946–1983* (Utrecht: Matrijs, 1989). Gemeentebestuur, "Enige Grondslagen Voor De Stedebouwkundige Ontwikkeling Van 'S-Gravenhage."

32 Huik, "'Ingebed in Het Zo Karakteristieke Groen' – Dudok En Den Haag in De Jaren 1930–1950," 123–24. Ibid., 124–29; Sluijs, *Haagse Stedebouw: Mijn Ervaringen in De Jaren 1946–1983*, 30–31.

33 Dienst van de Wederopbouw en de Stadsontwikkeling and Afdeling Publiciteit, *Den Haag, Snel Groeiende Stad* (The Hague: Dienst van de Wederopbouw en de Stadsontwikkeling and Afdeling Publiciteit, 1957); F. Bakker Schut, "Sanering en Reconstructie in de Grote Stad," *Bestuurswetenschappen* 9 ["Slum Clearance and Renewal in The Hague," *Building Trade*; "Renewal and Reconstruction in the Big City," *Management Science* no. 2 (1955): 153–68].

34 Quote on residents by journalist J. Groenendaal, "Houdt Het Hart Van Onzen Steden Jong!" *Vrijheid en Democratie*, May 14, 1960; second quote by planning director Bakker Schut December 14, 1957, file 365 archief Urban Development in Michelle Provoost, *De Grenzen Van De Metropool: Stadsontwikkeling in Den Haag 1950–1970* (Dissertation, Rijksuniversiteit Groningen 1989), 32.

35 Sluijs, *Haagse Stedebouw: Mijn Ervaringen in De Jaren 1946–1983*, 45–55; Provoost, *De Grenzen Van De Metropool: Stadsontwikkeling in Den Haag 1950–1970*, 50–51.

36 David Kooijman D. C. Krabben Erwin van der Evers, *Planning Van Winkels En Winkelgebieden in Nederland* (Den Haag: Sdu Uitgevers, 2011), 40–43.

37 Kamer van Koophandel en Fabrieken – afdeling 's-Gravenhage, *Het Parkeerprobleem in De Haagse Binnenstad in Verband Met Het Verkeersvraagstuk* (The Hague: Government Report, 1961), 11.

38 "Binnenstad Gezelliger Om Te Winkelen," *Haagsche Courant*, June 23, 1962; "Stadscentrum Mag Geen Dode Wijk Worden Door Concurrentie Van De Winkelcentra," *Haagsche Courant*, March 22, 1962. "Gebouwenarchipel Verenigd," *Het Binnenhof*, May 13, 1961.

39 "Den Haag Maakt Van Binnenstad Een Smeerboel," *Haagsche Courant*, October 26, 1966.

40 Provoost, *De Grenzen Van De Metropool: Stadsontwikkeling in Den Haag 1950–1970*, 36–39; Sluijs, *Haagse Stedebouw: Mijn Ervaringen in De Jaren 1946–1983*, 157.

41 Rudie van Meyer Theo Meurs, *De Zwolsman-Connection: Een Meester-Speculant En Zijn Christen-Democratische Vrinden* (Amsterdam: Weekbladpers, 1977), 50–52. Sluijs, *Haagse Stedebouw: Mijn Ervaringen in De Jaren 1946–1983*, 146. See also Tim Verlaan, *De Ruimtemakers: Projectontwikkelaars En De Nederlandse Binnenstad 1950–1980* (Nijmegen: Vantilt, 2017).

42 First quote from Afdeling voorlichting en congreszaken, *De Nieuwe Hout 'S-Gravenhage* (The Hague: Government Report, 1970). Second quote from architectural critic Vincent van Rossem in Robbert Hekkema Herma Meijer Anne-Ruth Roos, *Bouwen Voor De Macht: Den Haag* (Amsterdam: Stichting Kunst & Onderwijs, 1997), 10. See also Provoost, *De Grenzen Van De Metropool – Den Haag in De Jaren 1950–1970*, 165–70.

43 "Paleispromenade Nu Bekroond," *Haagsche Courant*, November 24, 1966. Quote from Afdeling Voorlichting en Congreszaken, *Promenades in 'S-Gravenhage* (The Hague: Afdeling Voorlichting en Congreszaken, 1969), 2.

44 Educatieve Dienst, *Den Haag – Vandaag, Gisteren En in De Toekomst*, ed. Dienst voor Schone Kunsten der gemeente 's-Gravenhage (The Hague: Government Report, 1964), 8.

45 Dienst Stadsontwikkeling en Volkshuisvesting, *Structuurplan Voor 'S-Gravenhage* (The Hague: Dienst Stadsontwikkeling en Volkshuisvesting, 1970); Provoost, *De Grenzen Van De Metropool – Den Haag in De Jaren 1950–1970.*

46 Rainer Bullhorst, "De Jaren Zeventig in De Haagse Stedebouw," in *Gids Van De Moderne Architectuur in Den Haag – Guide to Modern Architecture in the Hague*, eds. Cees van Boven, Victor Freijser, and

Christiaan Vaillant (The Hague: Ulysses, 1997). See also Casper Versteeg Coos Haagsche Courant Postmaa, *Den Haag Op Z'n Smalst: Teloorgang Van Een Hofstad* (Den Haag: Haagsche Courant, 1979). For a surprised reaction of the master plan's creator, see Sluijs, *Haagse Stedebouw: Mijn Ervaringen in De Jaren 1946–1983*, 71.

47 Leo Oorschot, *Conflicten over Haagse Stadsbeelden* (Delft: TU Delft, 2014), 391–95; M. J. E. Blauw, *Ruimte Maken Voor Den Haag: Schetsen Uit Een Kleine Eeuw Uitbreiden En Inschikken* (Den Haag: Dienst Stedelijke Ontwikkeling gemeente Den Haag, 2008), 81; Sluijs, *Haagse Stedebouw: Mijn Ervaringen in De Jaren 1946–1983*, 135–37.

48 Oorschot, *Conflicten over Haagse Stadsbeelden*, 342–44. Richard Kleinegris, "Democratisering Van De Stedebouw – Den Haag in De Jaren 1970–1980," in *Het Veranderend Stadsbeeld Van Den Haag*, ed. Victor Freijser (Zwolle: Waanders, 1991); Postmaa, *Den Haag Op Z'n Smalst: Teloorgang Van Een Hofstad*.

49 Sluijs, *Haagse Stedebouw: Mijn Ervaringen in De Jaren 1946–1983*, 159; Joop Niesten, "Nieuw Westeinde Ziekenhuis Den Haag," *Cobouw magazine* 6 (1980).

50 Dienst voor de Stadsontwikkeling, *Haagse Aanloopstraten Met Een Winkelfunctie* (The Hague: Dienst voor de Stadsontwikkeling, 1980).

51 Gemeentesecretarie, *Manual Binnenstad* (The Hague: Gemeentesecretarie, 1976).

52 A. Th. Duivesteijn and J. J. ten Velden, "Aanval Op Cityvorming Den Haag," *Plan* 3 (1980). Another key activist group "Dooievaar" comprised many design professionals and proved highly influential in shifting the public debate on urban renewal: Tim Verlaan, "Mobilization of the Masses: Dutch Planners, Local Politics, and the Threat of the Motor Age 1960–1980," *Journal of Urban History* 47, no. 1 (2021).

53 Sluijs, *Haagse Stedebouw: Mijn Ervaringen in De Jaren 1946–1983*, 159; Oorschot, *Conflicten over Haagse Stadsbeelden*, 415.

54 Kleinegris, "Democratisering Van De Stedebouw – Den Haag in De Jaren 1970–1980," 215.

55 First quote from Adri Overduin Henk Rook G. J. de Duivesteijn, *Stadsvernieuwing Als Kulturele Aktiviteit* ('s-Gravenhage: Gemeentemuseum [etc.], 1985). Second quote from Joris Molenaar, "Architectuurklimaat Na 1980," in *Gids Van De Moderne Architectuur in Den Haag – Guide to Modern Architecture in the Hague*, eds. Cees van Boven, Victor Freijser, and Christiaan Vaillant (The Hague: Ulysses, 1997), 31. Third quote from A. A. Hebly Hebly and Theunissen, *Bouwen in De Stad: Stedebouwkundige & Architektonische Aspekten Van De Stadsvernieuwing in Den Haag* ('s-Gravenhage: Project Organisatie Stadsvernieuwing, 1989).

56 Victor Freijser and Ruud Ridderhof, "Stedelijke Vernieuwing Door Architectonische Vormgeving – Den Haag in De Jaren 1980–1990," in *Het Veranderend Stadsbeeld Van Den Haag*, ed. Victor Freijser (Zwolle: Waanders, 1991); Molenaar, "Architectuurklimaat Na 1980," 31. P. Almekinders, *Bevolkingsveranderingen in De Binnenstad Van Den Haag* (Utrecht: Rijksuniversiteit te Utrecht – Faculteit der Ruimtelijke Wetenschappen, 1989).

57 Werkgroep lange termijn stadsvernieuwing, *Stadsvernieuwing in Perspectief* (The Hague: Werkgroep lange termijn stadsvernieuwing, 1986), 55–60. For a street-level perspective of the shuttering of retailers, see Wijkberaad Westeinde-Kortenbosch, *De Toekomst Die Ons Toekomt* (The Hague: Wijkberaad Westeinde-Kortenbosch, 1980), 7–8; Dienst voor de Stadsontwikkeling, *Knelpuntennota Centrum-West* (The Hague: Dienst voor de Stadsontwikkeling, 1980).

58 Stadsontwikkeling, *Haagse Aanloopstraten Met Een Winkelfunctie*, 14–16; Centraal Instituut voor het Midden- en Kleinbedrijf and Stichting Binnenstad Den Haag, *De Binnenstad Van Den Haag – Kansrijke Strategieën Ter Verbetering Van Het Binnenstedelijk Milieu* (The Hague: Centraal Instituut voor het Midden- en Kleinbedrijf and Stichting Binnenstad Den Haag, 1985). Evers, *Planning Van Winkels En Winkelgebieden in Nederland*, 45–46, 119. For an example arcade, see Makelaars A. Nadorp en Zoon BV, *Pasadenha Den Haag* (The Hague: Self-published Brochure, 1975).

59 See also Architext-Haarlem, *De Katerstraat: Voorbeeld Van Haagse Stadsvernieuwing* (Haarlem: Architext-Haarlem, 1987).

60 For an early outline of this policy paradigm shift, see G. P. H. Brokx and A. Th. van Delden, *Hart Voor Den Haag* (The Hague: Gemeentedrukkerij, 1987).

61 Afdeling Economische Zaken, *Winkelen in De Haagse Kern*, ed. Dienst Stadsontwikkeling (The Hague: Afdeling Economische Zaken, 1988); Dienst Bouwen en Wonen, *Evaluatie Wonen Boven Winkels: Met Het Oog Op De Toekomst* (The Hague: Dienst Bouwen en Wonen, 1991).

62 Translated from "De Kern Gezond," which also refers to the superlative "very healthy."

63 Oorschot, *Conflicten over Haagse Stadsbeelden*, 471–74; Dienst Stadsontwikkeling, *De Kern Gezond – Plan Voor De Herinrichting Van De Openbare Ruimte in De Haagse Binnenstad* (The Hague: Dienst Stadsontwikkeling, 1988), 19–26. It would take until 2009 to complete the rerouting of car traffic around the inner city due to strong opposition from adjacent neighborhoods. Gemeente Den Haag, *Verkeerscirculatieplan* (The Hague: Gemeente Den Haag, 2009).

64 V. Kompier and L. van der Meij, *Nota Horeca Binnenstad* (The Hague: Stichting binnenstadsmanagement, 1994); V. Kompier and L. van der Meij, *Den Haag Grijpt Zijn Kansen* (The Hague: Stichting binnenstadsmanagement, 1995).

65 The passageway has since unfortunately shuttered due to security concerns: Oorschot, *Conflicten over Haagse Stadsbeelden*, 427–31.

66 Veen and Ambachtsheer, *"Een Simpele Verkeersverbeetering": De Geschiedenis Van De Grote Marktstraat En Omgeving*, 120–34; Gonda Mellink Bert Buursma, *Architectuurgids Den Haag* (Rotterdam: Uitgeverij 010, 2011).

67 Significant controversy surrounding city hall hinged on the financial burden to the city and political infighting on the designer selection. Hans Schmit, "Den Haag Schept Een Binnenstad," *Trouw* (1995); Veen and Ambachtsheer, *"Een Simpele Verkeersverbeetering": De Geschiedenis Van De Grote Marktstraat En Omgeving*, 109–16.

68 Oorschot, *Conflicten over Haagse Stadsbeelden*, 512–14; Den Haag Nieuw Centrum, *The New the Hague Centre: 'More Than Five Billion Guilders'* (The Hague: Den Haag Nieuw Centrum, 1999).

69 Aukje van Roessel, "Den Haag Wacht in Spanning Op Artikel 12-Status," *Volkskrant* 1995.

70 Oorschot, *Conflicten over Haagse Stadsbeelden*, 553–56; Bureau Binnenstad Den Haag, *Binnenstad Buitengewoon!* (The Hague: Bureau Binnenstad

Den Haag, 2001); Bureau Binnenstad and CityWorks, *Naar Een Complete Haagse Binnenstad! Binnenstadsplan Den Haag 2010–2020* (The Hague: Bureau Binnenstad and CityWorks, 2010).

71 Platform binnenstadsmanagement, *Juryrapport Beste Binnenstad 2013–2015* (Boxtel: Self-published Report, 2014).

72 Interview with Martijn van Dam, senior policy advisor retail at the City of The Hague July 18, 2013. Official city policy in Afdeling Economie, *Detailhandel in Den Haag – Maak Het Nieuwe Mogelijk, Behoud Het Goede*, ed. Dienst Stedelijke Ontwikkeling (The Hague: Afdeling Economie, 2005).

73 Oorschot, *Conflicten over Haagse Stadsbeelden*, 629.

74 This process was worsened by the fact that the downtown population and hence the local customer base was also rapidly shrinking. More on this process in: Gerard Koning Josee Rutte, *Zelfbediening in Nederland: Geschiedenis Van De Supermarkttoekomst* (Baarn: De Prom, 1998).

75 Gerda van Mast Michiel van der Beek, *Van Ambachtelijk Tot Ambtelijk: Het Spuikwartier Door De Eeuwen Heen* ('s-Gravenhage: Staatsuitgeverij, 1978).

76 Binnenstad and CityWorks, *Naar Een Complete Haagse Binnenstad! Binnenstadsplan Den Haag 2010–2020*; binnenstadsmanagement, *Juryrapport Beste Binnenstad 2013–2015*.

5 VANCOUVER
THE FRONTAGE FORMULA

Figure 5.0   Vancouver's waterfront, a mixture of low and high-rise living.[1]

DOI: 10.4324/9781003041887-5

Topping global lists for livability, Vancouver has become an international exemplar for good urbanism. Much of Vancouver's praise comes from its stunning natural setting between the Pacific Ocean and the North Shore Mountains, its downtown scenically wedged on a peninsula between Burrard Inlet and False Creek. An image search for Vancouver invariably yields a modern if undistinguished skyline set amidst a stunning natural backdrop, which has prompted the city's mockery as a "setting in search of a city". Besides the vistas, we truly experience Vancouver's livability much closer at eye level, where high-quality street-level architecture serves, acknowledges, and excites pedestrian passersby.[2] Especially in its downtown area, decades of collaboration between planners, designers, developers, and public participation have resulted in a careful balance between high densities and lively streets, a unique blend of Le Corbusier's towers-in-the-park with Jane Jacobs' dreams of fine-grained urbanism.[3] Uniquely, Vancouver's eye-level excitement does not just hail from cosmopolitan storefronts, but from entire new districts with convivial, almost pastoral streets of carefully designed town houses, which domesticate a more familiar urbanism of high-rise apartment and office towers. This combined vertical prowess and street-level intricacy house more than 100,000 people in Canada's highest-density environment, almost unbeknownst to those walking through Vancouver's leafy downtown streets and well-designed parks and waterfront trail system.[4] This balance between density and street-level intensity has been so successful that its underlying political and professional process has been coined with its own noun 'Vancouverism', which has since been largely reduced to a formal archetype replicated as far as Dubai.[5] This chapter explores how downtown Vancouver was able to diverge from a familiar 20th-century North American narrative of growth and decline into a global exemplar for balancing growth with human-centered architecture and urban design.

Before 1911

Named after a British captain who visited the area in the late 18th century, Vancouver is a relatively young city that first truly prospered as the western terminus of the Canadian Pacific Railroad (CPR) a century later.[6] Vancouver's relatively long peninsula shoreline wedged between Burrard Inlet and False Creek offered CPR plenty of space for ship docking and transferring goods, and the federal government and local landowners further supported the arrival of the railroad. Any pre-railroad settlements almost cathartically burned to the ground in 1886 to make way for Vancouver's first transcontinental train arrival the next year – the start of an inseparable relationship between the city and its rail connections for almost a century to follow.[7] CPR redefined the city not just by connecting it to the

rest of the world but by actively developing a hotel, opera house, various banks, and department stores around its terminus station at the foot of Granville Street, west of the existing commercial heart.[8] As the first trains rolled into the city, Vancouver attracted scores of real estate speculators that foresaw the potential of Canada's western capital. Understanding the symbiosis between rail connections and growth, Vancouver developers built new neighborhoods along a rapidly expanding streetcar system.[9] CPR's new commercial cluster around its railway station soon served the West End, an airy hinterland of executive mansions and denser middle-class housing anchored by Stanley Park in 1888.[10] Directly to the east, the gridded remnants of Vancouver's pre-railroad Gastown settlement struggled to keep up with CPR's prowess, growing eastward into a working-class downtown and neighborhood for dock and mill workers with a wealth of ethnic backgrounds, including Vancouver's first Chinese immigrants. Commonly discriminated against, the Chinese soon organized commercial and cultural activities in their own Chinatown.[11]

The Klondike gold rush and the growth of agricultural, mining and lumber output of Vancouver's hinterland of British Columbia drastically increased the city's port activity to become Canada's largest Pacific gateway by the turn of the 20th century.[12] Boasting more than 20,000 residents by 1897, Vancouver's eastern and western downtowns grew together into a single U-shaped circuit of smaller and larger stores, warehouses, and cultural venues, surrounded by increasingly feverish construction and land speculation. Large department store openings continued to shift Vancouver's commercial center of gravity westward, aligning with the continued concentration of wealth in the West End.[13] Beyond the bustle of downtown, eye-level architecture and public life soon began to differ between both sides of the city. While grandiose and pastoral, the West End mansions fueled a neighborly symbiosis of "wooden trimmings and verandahs", where "visitors came and sat and talked", although the city's elite began to move southward into newer, fashionable suburbs (Figure 5.1).[14] Conversely, Vancouver's East End increasingly densified and diversified into a feverish mix of living, working, recreation, and shopping at the heart of a city whose population tripled between 1901 and 1911 alone.[15]

The eye-level manifestation of this growth and stratification can be clearly seen in the 1911 map of Vancouver (Figure 5.2). While the mostly residential West End still contained vacant 60-foot-wide parcels housing the city's most opulent mansions (1), other parcels have been split to house smaller middle-class dwellings (2). CPR's push to propel Granville Street as Vancouver's commercial heart had clearly paid off, as the street contained over a mile of fine-grained retail businesses (3), culminating in a northern hub of commerce, culture, and transportation. In the most central blocks of this western business district, narrower parcels had already begun to consolidate into larger office

(a)

(b)

Figure 5.1a–b West End mansions in 1906 (a) compared to a more modest, denser, mixed-use, and mixed-ethnicity street scene in the East End that same year (b). Source: Image (a) of Burnaby Street from 1906 by Philip Timms, courtesy of Vancouver Public Library, ID: 5266. Image (b) of Dupont Street, later Pender Street in Chinatown attributed to Philip T. Timms, courtesy of Vancouver Archives, ID: AM336-S3-3-: CVA 677–530.

and retail buildings (4). In the eastern business district, a network of east-west streets brought a mixture of retailers, services, bars, and restaurants into the dense East End (5). A north-south Main Street dominated this side of Vancouver, soon bolstered by new railway connections (6). The U-shaped pattern of interactive retail frontages between the West and East End cores anchored their respective residential districts, with dwellings especially crowded in with commercial and industrial uses in the East End. The waterfront revealed Vancouver's frontier roots with a motley mixture of rail yards, mills, factories, and ramshackle accommodation for transients and day laborers (7), creating a noisy barrier to nature that would last well into the 20th century.[16]

1911–1937

By the 1910s, Vancouver's promise to become 'The London of the Pacific' was coming true, as population, industrial output, and port activity skyrocketed, and the city became a preferred location for Canadian west coast headquarters. Vancouver's outward "battle waged against forests and stumps by the makers of homes" had long passed downtown, where an upward battle for the skyline began to be waged. On their way to a growing hinterland of suburbs, Vancouver's electric streetcars rumbled past vibrant department stores, busy shoreline warehouses and factories, and glistening offices – or the brazen steel frames of their ever-taller successors.[17] Despite increasing regulation, banks vied for the skies as the Dominion Trust building became the tallest in the British Empire by 1910, a crown to be taken only a year later by the nearby World Tower. Fueled by foreign capital and the anticipated opening of new shipping routes via the Panama Canal, Vancouver's downtown skyline would blossom over the next decades. While certainly coarsening downtown's architectural grain, these towers welcomed street-level passersby with vibrant retail facades and impressive lobbies.[18]

As the western part of downtown saw skyscraper growth, the East End and its Main Street saw a much-needed boost when the swampy eastern part of False Creek was filled in for railway yards and stations during the 1910s.[19] To counter Vancouver's inevitable growing pains of congestion, pollution, and overcrowding, the Vancouver Parks Board hired British landscape architect and urbanist Thomas Mawson in 1912. Besides improvements for a key park in the city, Mawson envisioned waterfront promenades and a grand boulevard through downtown, culminating with a grand civic center. Mawson's combined this City Beautiful-inspired grandiosity with a distinctly humanist 'Lovable City' that focused on a positive eye-level experience, yet his visions ultimately stranded due to a recession and the onset of World War I.[20]

By the 1920s, Vancouver would prosper from increased shipping, exports, and remaining wartime manufacturing, although these space-hungry activities began to shift outward. Instead, downtown growth mostly came in the form of central skyscrapers and densification, fueled by a growing service and tourist industry.[21] As if "rising from the sea . . . touched in gold", Art Deco skyscrapers like the Marine Building and the new Hotel Vancouver especially redefined the western part of downtown's skyline, while welcoming street-level passersby through grand lobbies and street-level storefronts (Figure 5.3). Like in most other cities, Vancouver's continuing symbiosis between vertical growth and street-level engagement was fueled by the profitability of downtown retail space, which benefited from a growing hinterland and new nearby department stores.[22]

Nearby, the West End was beginning to transform from the home of Vancouver's elite into an apartment district. Wealthy mansions were subdivided into rooming houses or replaced by a range of apartment buildings, from swanky 'mansion flats' to modest walkups. This

Figure 5.2 Frontage interactivity in Vancouver in 1911.
Source: Diagram by Conrad Kickert, 2021.

transition marked a demographic shift and added to the neighborhood's density, transforming the odd corner store to merge into fledgling retail strips.[23] Like in other cities, suburbanization came with inner city traffic congestion, especially as streetcar ridership had already peaked by the mid-1910s and car ownership skyrocketed from the following decade onward. Besides traffic jams, cars left their urban mark with early parking lots, traffic lights and gas stations, creating the first signs of a ring of eye-level inactivity around downtown. Vancouver didn't

Figure 5.3 Vertical growth mainly occurred in the western end of downtown, with the rise of office skyscrapers and the first apartment buildings.
Source: Image by J. S. Matthews ca. 1929; courtesy of Vancouver Archives, ID: AM54-S4-: Van Sc N63.

were replaced with a fully-fledged business district with a vibrant retail core anchored by large department stores and surrounded by office skyscrapers (1), mostly replacing existing housing. Especially the western side of the downtown core became much larger, serving a rapidly growing metropolitan population (2). As the quiet residential streets of the West End intensified into a mixture of apartment buildings and street-level retail, they began to mirror the existing eye-level vibrancy of the East End – albeit grander and more orderly (3). The car had also clearly arrived in Vancouver, with the imminent opening of a new bridge across the Burrard Inlet in 1938. Like in Detroit, downtown Vancouver also saw the first erosion due to car parking, with garages and open lots emerging in lower-priced fringe locations (4). Along the Burrard Inlet and False Creek waterfront, Vancouver's mills, warehouses, and rail yards had coalesced into bands of pollution and eye-level inactivity, which would continue to challenge the city for decades to come (5).[27]

1937–1961

Before and during World War II, Vancouver's bustling downtown only intensified in its growth and its challenges. Downtown became increasingly surrounded by polluting waterfront industry and overcrowding led to "slum conditions of the worst kind" in the East End.[28] Significant advertising and the centralizing effect of the remaining streetcar system could maintain downtown's retail core, but the fringes of formerly key retail arteries like Hastings and Granville Street began to empty out in the 1950s.[29]

Nevertheless, surprisingly few downtown developments were achieved in the early postwar era despite support by downtown business interests and the Non-Partisan-Alliance (NPA), which was a technocratic yet development-friendly political party that reigned in Vancouver from the Depression well into the 1960s.[30] The NPA invited Harland Bartholomew back to Vancouver in 1944, but again his suggestions to improve the "barren, awkward, frontier-like appearance" of most of downtown were only partially adopted. The city did embrace his proposal to raise the density limits in the West End again by 70%; this massive increase resulted in the West End becoming one of North America's densest residential neighborhoods, as Vancouverites understood the value of living within walking distance to downtown jobs. Yet Bartholomew's East End suggestions for rehabilitation and conservation – backtracking his previous proposal to replace the neighborhood with industry – fell on deaf ears.[31] Bartholomew's biggest impact came from his recommendation to professionalize the city's planning apparatus with a fully-fledged planning department, to be led by British-born planner-engineer Gerald Sutton Brown.[32] Aligning with Vancouver's pro-development

just need beautification – it needed planning for efficient growth. With the support of local business interest, Vancouver and nearby municipalities commissioned renowned American planner Harland Bartholomew to create the area's first metropolitan plan. From his familiar North American template, Bartholomew recommended a mixture of road widenings and new road construction, but also zoning, parks, and a new civic center. While many of his proposals went unheeded, his plan to allow denser apartment construction in the West End was eagerly accepted and fueled a veritable building boom in subsequent decades. His proposal to transform the East End's motley mixture of small homes, stores, and workshops into an industrial district was far less fortunate, as it accelerated the district's decline by prompting widespread public and private disinvestment.[24] His radical transformation proposal not only reflected the East End's continuing issue of overcrowding but also the area's common negative association as Vancouver's 'Sin City', rife with prostitution, opium dens, and gambling – often associated with the area's Chinese population. The Chinese continued to band together in the face of this external hostility, expanding their Chinatown with cultural, educational, health, and commercial amenities with a distinct character.[25] Just like Mawson's proposal, only a small portion of Bartholomew's plan for Vancouver came to fruition due to political handwringing and the onset of the Depression.[26]

After years of waterfront shantytowns and unfinished construction projects, Vancouver slowly began to emerge from the Depression due to an uptick in global shipping and continued growth in the Canadian prairies. Figure 5.4 shows how downtown Vancouver transformed at eye level since 1911. The city's two separate frontier downtowns

Figure 5.4 Frontage interactivity in Vancouver in 1937.
Source: Diagram by Conrad Kickert, 2021.

government and a benevolent Planning Commission, and mostly unhindered by toothless variance, planning, and design advisory boards, Sutton Brown was able to reign with "power verging on the absolute" for decades to come.[33]

Sutton Brown's vision for Vancouver was typically modernist and proved mostly disastrous for the downtown eye-level experience. A 1956 vision for the downtown proclaimed esthetic controls and pedestrian-friendliness, but mostly remained silent on street-level architecture,

Figure 5.5 Due to the 1950s zoning change, West End towers from the 1950s to the 1970s often consolidated several parcels for parking and turned themselves away from the street.
Source: Image of Panorama Place (built in 1965) by Conrad Kickert, 2017.

Figure 5.6 The 1957 redevelopment plan for the East End clears Vancouver's densest residential district for a mixture of apartment towers and slabs amidst undefined green space and expressways.
Source: Image from Planning Department, Vancouver Redevelopment Study (Vancouver: Planning Department, 1957).

in fact condoning the ongoing construction of the Civic Centre, which still contains one of Vancouver's longest stretches of blank walls today.[34] Ratifying Bartholomew's upzoning of the West End, Sutton Brown drafted coarse guidelines that unleashed a new wave of towers that embraced mountain and sea views but denied the street with consolidated blocks, blank walls and parking lots – coined by Australian urbanist Kim Dovey as "density without intensity" (Figure 5.5).[35] Compared to the laissez-faire approach to the West End's densification, city planners became far more involved in the modernization of the East End, which suffered from continued overcrowding and dilapidation despite blossoming Chinatown tourism from the 1930s onward.[36] Local university researchers described widespread patterns of deterioration in the East End in the late 1950s, ranging from poor maintenance and a lack of modern plumbing to residents living over shops – considered a symptom of blight.[37] Vancouver's first urban renewal plan emerged from this study in 1957, proposing to displace more than 10,000 residents and clear and redevelop swaths of the fine-grained East End urban fabric into a landscape of walk-up apartment slabs and towers, undetermined greenery, windowless end walls and parking lots, and a new expressway sought by downtown business interests, suburban developers, and Sutton Brown (Figure 5.6).[38] Despite an outcry from the Chinese community that the plans would uproot Chinatown and its many elderly residents, the plan was craftily adopted in the late 1950s. Even its first phase already displaced more than 3,000 people.[39]

Figure 5.7 demonstrates how downtown Vancouver stood at a turning point by 1961. While downtown population and jobs had continued to grow, especially in the West End, the eye-level interactivity had actually deteriorated. Storefronts continued their shift westward, often haphazardly tacked onto existing West End buildings to serve the neighborhood's growing array of introverted residential towers (1). Conversely, East End retail corridors continued to falter (2), despite blossoming storefronts in Chinatown (3).[40] Perhaps the most worrying downtown eye-level trend was the rapid growth of parking. Between 1947 and 1956 alone, off-street downtown parking spaces had increased by 80%, to almost 15,000, and parking lots had grown from an archipelago into a ring around downtown (4), egged on by plans to consolidate fringe parking.[41] Civic buildings only exacerbate the demise of downtown's fringe (5). While the most radical urban renewal was yet to begin, the "collar of blight" around the downtown core of waterfront industry surrounded by working-class neighborhoods would become the center point of Vancouver's planning debates in the following decades.[42]

1961–1988

By the early 1960s, Vancouver had grown into a sizable city containing some of North America's highest residential densities, a relatively vibrant retail core, and a bustling – if scruffy – industrial waterfront. While West End towers vied for the skies and mountain range views, the central business district's skyline had hardly changed since the end of World War II; its scattering of modest office towers diluted by a growing sea of parking and undermaintained buildings. Fearing to fall into the same trap of decentralization and downtown decline as its peer cities, business interests and planners openly wondered if "downtown Vancouver is too big".[43] In a political effort to 'Get Vancouver Moving' in the 1960s, the city opted to promote new development by hiring an American economic consultant to survey development opportunities, by offering generous development bonuses with few strings attached, and

Figure 5.7 Frontage interactivity in Vancouver in 1961.
Source: Diagram by Conrad Kickert, 2021.

by largely staying out of the way during the development process. Amidst renewed economic growth in the 1960s, development indeed returned to downtown Vancouver. Yet the appalling architectural quality of new buildings soon convinced Vancouverites that growth did not equate to progress, ultimately resulting in an overthrow of Vancouver's business-led development and political paradigm.[44]

Many projects specifically ignited public anger over their lack of regard for historical and natural context, and in particular for their abysmal eye-level experience. But few were as divisive as the Pacific Centre, which replaced dozens of existing small shops with an introverted downtown shopping mall surrounded by wind-swept office plazas and a network of underground retail tunnels that sucked shoppers away from Vancouver's main retail street. Instead of the city council's touted "symbol of confidence for the citizens of Vancouver", the Pacific Centre came to reflect developer excess and planning incompetence; its blank walls were considered an insult to the street; its offices "towers of darkness" replacing coveted sunlight and mountain views with wind tunnels.[45] The residential boom in the West End had added almost 10,000 new residents between 1956 and 1966 alone, yet introverted towers hardly benefited eye-level vibrancy, instead adding congestion and crime to Vancouver's downtown.[46] As projects became bolder, resident pushback intensified. Residents successfully halted a developer proposal for a multi-block series of towers along the West End's northern waterfront, whose inactive parking podium would have simultaneously obliterated mountain views, public waterfront access, and eye-level interactivity.[47] Upstream, a grandiose joint venture between department stores, developers, and the city for a 28-acre mixed-use waterfront office, apartment, and hotel development on top of CPR tracks, parking, and part of the struggling historic Gastown district ultimately withered into a single wind-swept office plaza – not just the results of property rights and financing issues but a sign of changing times.[48]

By the late 1960s, Vancouverites were becoming increasingly vocal on the intransparency of not just new downtown street-level architecture but the process that yielded this architecture. Commenting on a 1969 downtown planning report, the grassroots Citizens Council on Civic Development demanded that "downtown must be planned for people", encouraging a pedestrian-friendly, 24-hour environment with interactive retail frontages.[49] Citizens were increasingly joined by professionals like local architect Wilf Buttjes, who commented on the inactivity of new housing towers and advocated for town houses and ground-floor retail to activate Vancouver's downtown streets.[50] In response to the backroom deals replacing mountain views and street life with tower shadows and blank walls, local journalist and activist Donald Gutstein exasperatedly wondered: "Just who is downtown for anyway?"[51] The response would come from Vancouver's most defining public uprising – not over the next glass tower or concrete megablock, but over its freeway system.

After an initial proclamation on the merit of freeways and a convenient dismissal of transit investments in 1959, Gerald Sutton Brown and his team continued their freeway plans mostly behind closed doors.[52] Fueled by plans for a new downtown Burrard Inlet crossing, more than a hundred planning reports explored a freeway route through downtown, avoiding the holdings of downtown business interests yet cutting right through the heart of Chinatown and the East End (Figure 5.8).[53]

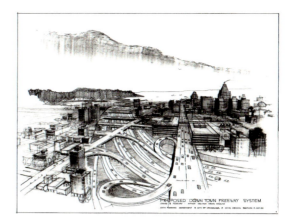

Figure 5.8 A 1960 proposal cuts at least ten freeway lanes through the southwestern downtown periphery toward a third Burrard Inlet crossing.
Source: Image by City Planning department of Vancouver; courtesy of Vancouver Archives.

When plans for an eight-lane downtown freeway were finally released to the public in 1967 as a fait accompli, Vancouverites erupted in anger. After citywide protest and turbulent public meetings, city council caved and voted the freeway plan down – but only for budgetary reasons.[54] Undeterred by this initial setback, an alliance of powerful local business interests, developers, and a mayor dead set on quashing public opposition presented a new round of freeway plans in 1972. Concerted action from East End residents and an increasing loss of public, professional, and business support defeated this second attempt once and for all.[55] As the "most important thing that never happened" to Vancouver, the freeway defeat owed as much to good activism as to bad timing. By the time Vancouver's freeway plans saw the light of day in the late 1960s and early 1970s, Vancouverites could already see their failure in North American and European cities, including several described in this book. Their opposition ensured that Vancouver remained among the only North American metropolises without any major urban freeway.[56] The political shockwaves of the freeway defeat would reverberate at all layers of government in 1972, from Vancouver's pro-freeway mayoral resignation to a landslide election loss for Provincial leadership and a significant reshuffle in federal representation.[57] Instead, The Electors Action Movement (TEAM) rose into power in Vancouver in 1972, emerging from a growing minority, middle-class and counterculture electorate. Providing Vancouver's mayor and the majority of council seats, TEAM soon wiped any remaining freeway plans off the table and replaced Sutton Brown's planning regime with planning director Ray Spaxman, whose focus on participatory, contextual, fine-grained, humanistic urbanism he coined as "neighborliness" – the first seedlings of present-day Vancouverism.[58]

In tune with Vancouver's political sea change, Spaxman effectively turned the city's planning paradigm upside down. Instead of following the wishes of foreign investors and downtown business interests, Spaxman followed the growing body of work by contemporaries like Gordon Cullen, Christopher Alexander, Kevin Lynch, and Ian McHarg that imagined how urban development could attune to human and natural dimensions. Fueled by intensive public participation, Spaxman's vision for Vancouver's urban future prioritized environmental and experiential quality over development quantity. At times, this simply meant simply curbing unchecked growth, as Spaxman abruptly ended the West End's building boom by halving its allowed density.[59] More often, Spaxman leveraged Vancouver's continuing growth pressures, converting its 'currency' of development demand and land value into high-quality design through an elaborate system of zoning rights and bonuses – effectively starting a public-private partnership between developers and planners. Spaxman permitted developers to build more only if they met the discretionary oversight of an Urban Design Panel and the public. This process boosted city power, promoted innovation, and went a long way to convince growth-averse Vancouverites that new development could improve the city.[60]

In downtown, a 1975 plan replaced building allowances with a set of discretionary guidelines for new development; the guidelines hinged on contextual and human-scaled development in eight character areas – including three new office areas.[61] Spaxman translated his concept of "neighborliness" into effective rules for eye-level excitement, eliminating open parking lots and blank walls while promoting façade articulation, public parks and plazas, and interactive street-level uses such as retail and community amenities. Frontage interactivity guidelines prominently featured in the plans that also encouraged residential development to ensure a 24-hour city, repurposed streets for transit and pedestrians, and protected mountain range viewsheds.[62] However, requiring a continuous 'streetwall' of active retail uses for new office developments and maintaining retail continuity along main downtown corridors proved a bridge too far, as newly mandated street-level storefronts simply couldn't find enough tenants.[63] Nevertheless, Spaxman understood the true power of urban designers lay in shaping the city from the bottom up through a fine-tuned design guideline apparatus.[64] Blueprint urbanism made way for a "pattern language" of small-scaled behavior settings and designs, a paradigm devised by American architect Christopher Alexander, which successfully underpinned a development just south of downtown and made its way into Spaxman's guideline vocabulary.[65]

Besides controlling the quality of new private development, Spaxman and the TEAM administration also focused on improving the quality of public space. Vancouver's main downtown retail street was pedestrianized to revitalize the "roughest main drag" of Canada, although it continued to struggle with crime and homelessness issues shifting from the East End, which saw its first brittle waves of gentrification after it was designated a historic district. There, Gastown was preserved into a tourist destination, complete with cobblestone streets.[66] Spaxman's streetscape improvement plans and design guidelines along key downtown streets hinged on developer cooperation, which resulted in the same scattered pattern of oft-hidden plazas that plagued similar public-private partnerships in cities like New York.[67] Rapid transit failed to launch despite regional planning efforts, which would however ensure that downtown-adjacent neighborhoods like the West End remained attractive to downtown workers looking to escape grisly commutes – in spite of the district's continuing congestion and crime struggles.[68] As the city improved the district's street-level experience through traffic calming and crime prevention, architectural innovation truly marked the West End's next chapter. A new wave of architects began to challenge Spaxman's density crackdown by the 1980s, designing contextual combinations of high-rise towers with retail and residential podiums that ensured street-level excitement.[69] Increasingly, these luxury developments targeted Asian homebuyers and investors, as foreign unrest and Canada's welcoming investment and immigration policy increasingly drew Vancouver into the Pacific Rim. As Asian capital mainly sought residential investments, Vancouver's skyline increasingly shifted from the relatively stagnant downtown office market toward high-density residential areas in its fringe.[70] A key moment in this shift occurred when the site of Expo 86, a world exposition on former rail yards on the downtown shore of False Creek, was sold to a Hong Kong developer – starting a development and design process that would again shift the city's architectural and urban paradigm.[71]

While Vancouverites' victories against developer excess and freeway construction at least prevented the downtown from eroding much further at eye level between 1961 and 1988, it hardly resulted in a new pattern of interactive frontages (Figure 5.9). Gastown's preservation efforts (1) and the West End's residential growth (2) had resulted in more street-level retail activity, but new buildings often presented blank walls, and parking and architectural erosion hardly slowed down. The southeast side of downtown remained a wasteland of modernist institutional buildings, stadiums, bridges, and parking lots (3), and the former site of Expo 86 along False Creek still awaited its final purpose (4). Rather than heralding a new era of human-scaled architecture, Spaxman's new planning paradigm suffered from an economic slump in the 1970s and early 1980s, which prevented its guidelines from influencing many new developments.[72] Only when development activity picked up in the late 1980s would Vancouverites be forced to reckon and ultimately reconcile

VANCOUVER – THE FRONTAGE FORMULA 91

Figure 5.9 Frontage interactivity in Vancouver in 1988.
Source: Diagram by Conrad Kickert, 2021.

the dichotomies between their dream of human-scaled urbanism in balance with nature and the growth of urban density and foreign investment.[73] This reckoning was to launch Vancouver as an international exemplar for urban design in the following decades.

1988 to now

As Expo 86 had showcased the city's potential to the world, Asian investment continued to ramp up, and a new service economy boomed downtown, nearly two decades of taming density in the Spaxman and TEAM era came to an end in the late 1980s. Agreeing with Vancouver architect that "we have to grow up", Vancouverites reelected the pro-business NPA party, although they certainly hadn't forgotten the ills of overdevelopment.[74] Instead, citizens and planners opted for a carefully controlled balance of vertical growth and street-level design quality, which has become known as Vancouverism.

Compared to a glut of new downtown office space in the early 1990s, development demand for high-rise, luxury condominiums continued to rise – especially among Asian investors, who often bought up all units in new Vancouver developments within hours of sales opening.[75] Planners soon reallocated almost seven million square feet (700,000 square meters) of unused office zoning allocation toward new residential development capacity, which Vancouver's new planning director Larry Beasley coined a "living first" strategy. Beyond downtown and the still-popular West End, residential development pressure also spilled into new areas for growth, most notably along Vancouver's waterfront.[76] Understanding Spaxman's mantra that "the tender at play was density", Beasley successfully leveraged Vancouver's unprecedented development pressure into high-quality design and new public spaces through public input, a system of development contributions, and a revamped system of discretionary design control.[77] Beasley was fully aware that he would never be able to convince Vancouverites to embrace density without ensuring that high-density development would help their everyday environment by providing safe and vibrant streets, new walkable destinations, and much-needed park space and waterfront access.[78] He updated Spaxman's design guidelines, learning from ongoing research on public space by urbanists William Whyte and Christopher Alexander; the West End architectural experiments that combined dwelling towers and interactive frontages; and research on the value of safety, territoriality, and street-level interactivity for high-density family housing by his colleague Ann McAfee. Responding to the political and market shifts since Spaxman, Beasley turned his predecessor's restrictive design guideline apparatus into a more collaborative model that hinged on providing certainty for developers, engendering public support for large-scale developments, and safeguarding design quality.[79]

Beasley's Vancouverist approach to balancing density and street-level quality has become known among professionals especially for its formal manifestation of slender towers on a podium of town houses and retailers. While the tower-podium model has evolved into a visual caricature of the far more complex context and process of Vancouverism, it indeed provides significant benefits for developers, residents, and passersby alike. As architectural historian Robert Walsh argues, this formal archetype had been long in the making in Vancouver and beyond, yet it matured in the city's 200 hectares of waterfront megaprojects – most notably, in the former Expo 86 site north of False Creek. After a false start in the late 1980s, developer liaison and architect Stanley Kwok started a collaboration with city planners to simultaneously develop urban design principles and guidelines for the site, while enacting them in actual development.[80] Collaborative work sessions yielded North False Creek, which extended Vancouver's street grid into coherent blocks that fronted a continuous waterfront park. Most importantly for street-level architecture, it introduced Vancouverism's formal tower-podium model to balance between Kwok's quest for high-rise towers with natural views with planners' desires for affordable housing, park space, and street-level interaction. Towers were not just placed on a retail podium, but mostly on and next to 'enclaves' of street-facing town houses that interacted with the sidewalk through street-level entrances and intricate public-private transitions like porches, stoops, bay windows, balconies, and front yards. This ensured a varied eye-level experience between shops and restaurants along the waterfront and key intersections, as well as fine-grained housing that interacted with passersby in side streets.[81] North False Creek's successful tower-podium model was soon replicated in another waterfront 'megaproject' Coal Harbour, and became a staple in city design guidelines for nearly three dozen downtown development areas, such as Downtown South (Figure 5.10).[82]

The makeup of Vancouverism's podiums are especially relevant for the city at eye level. Vancouver's design guidelines for downtown development mandate sufficient retail to ensure that daily items can be purchased within walking distance from new homes. Local clusters of grocers and pharmacists and 'third places' like coffee shops and restaurants permeate new neighborhoods, while regional retailers and nighttime activity remains concentrated along key streets to bolster their existing retailers and keep noise away from residents (Figure 5.11). Retail guidelines limit frontage width to prevent blank walls; mandate sidewalk setbacks to allow patio seating; and hide larger retailers above, below, or behind finer-grained stores and town homes.[83] Street-level retail is also interspersed with developer-subsidized community services like schools, daycares, and cultural centers.[84] But the distinguishing eye-level element of Vancouverism is not the storefront but the fine-grained, street-accessible town houses that "domesticate the high-density residential streetscape", and have become "perhaps one of the most essential contributions to the day-to-day livability of Vancouver" according to planning director Larry Beasley.[85] The town houses provide more than just a family-friendly place to live downtown: they provide eyes on the street for safety (a lesson learned from Jane Jacobs) and ensure eye-level permeability, sociability, and resident expression – enforced by detailed design guidelines, which we will discuss further in Chapter 9. While developers were initially wary that the town

Figure 5.11 Subtle grade changes and town houses with front yards 'domesticate' the high-density development of North False Creek.
Source: Image by Conrad Kickert, 2021.

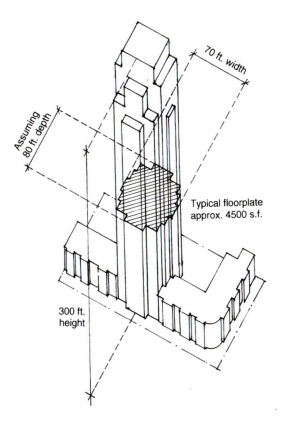

Figure 5.10 Urban design guidelines like the Downtown South guidelines from 1991 mandate towers to be placed on a fine-grained podium that relates to the street.
Source: Planning Department, Downtown South Guidelines (Excluding Granville Street) (Vancouver: Planning Department, 1991).

houses wouldn't sell, they actually proved very popular with buyers, relieving developers of oversupplying street-level retail and community amenities.[86]

Compared to Vancouver's successful urban design in large waterfront projects, the improvements of the downtown core have been more muted since the 1980s. While Vancouver's relative lack of road and rapid transit investments have boosted the attractiveness of living close to downtown and lowered the number of people driving into downtown, the pedestrian quality of downtown's public spaces is mostly unremarkable except for bonus-incentivized office plazas and modest sidewalk investments.[87] After another pedestrian makeover in the 1990s due to ongoing business stagnation and crime, the number of visitors has risen modestly. Similarly, other downtown retail streets have received some pedestrian improvements.[88] On the eastern side of downtown, Chinatown's public space and preservation continues to struggle in the face of ongoing drug abuse, crime, homelessness, and mental and physical health issues. As the 'biggest black eye' of Vancouver's downtown revitalization, the East End has become a poster child for Vancouverism's flip side of increasing income inequality, public austerity, housing unaffordability, and displacement of social issues.[89] While preservation in Chinatown has struggled, repurposed warehouses in the south of downtown have become a hub for Vancouver's creative and dining scene.[90] Public investments in large civic infrastructure like the 1995 Vancouver Public Library has resonated with Vancouverites, but subsequent nearby developments have not improved the character of the library's struggling surroundings.[91] Furthermore, in many smaller downtown projects, Vancouverism has often been reduced to its formalist caricature, resulting in monotonous design – albeit with interactive frontages.[92]

Today, the downtown peninsula of Vancouver is more exciting at eye-level than ever before – a feat compared to many of our other case study cities. Figure 5.12 shows a city that excites downtown pedestrians at eye-level with more storefronts, more fine-grained dwellings, and more interactive office lobbies. New megaprojects like North False Creek (1) and Coal Harbour (2) have turned formerly vacant waterfronts into vibrant new districts. The preservation of warehouses south of downtown in Yaletown has revitalized its eye-level experience (3). Large swaths of inactive frontages are rare and often in progress of remediation, like downtown's last former industrial land in Northeast False Creek (4).[93] Even otherwise inactive uses like the Vancouver Convention Centre's new West Building interacts and intermingles surprisingly well with surrounding public spaces, which was partially the result of active planning intervention (5).[94] Downtown Vancouver's high level of frontage interactivity reflects the influx of tens of thousands of residents and jobs, hundreds of new high-rises, and especially billions of investment dollars into Vancouver's

Figure 5.12 Frontage interactivity in Vancouver in 2018.
Source: Diagram by Conrad Kickert, 2021.

downtown peninsula over the past decades.[95] But as we have seen in earlier eras and in other cities, new density does not necessarily relate to eye-level excitement – Vancouver's success has been the result of concerted planning and urban design. We can unfortunately also see the limits of this approach in the ongoing stagnation of the historic East End at eye level (6), where ongoing social issues and a lack of development pressure has failed to set the Vancouver's developer-led eye-level improvement machine in motion.

Conclusion

Vancouver is an exemplar city where through careful design and planning, professionals, politicians, and developers have risen above external forces and built a city "as enthralling as its setting".[96] By harnessing developer's desires for these views to create up-close excitement through high quality, interactive architecture and public space, Vancouver has uniquely balanced density and quality.[97] The city's past explains that this balance was certainly not a force of nature – it required strong political and public support and excellent design strategies in the face of technocrats, shortsighted developers, overzealous traffic engineers, and market instability.

Vancouver's current story of eye-level excitement may read as one written over the past decades by local planners and designers, yet it reflects a much-longer history of successes and failures achieved by a much-larger cast of professionals, politicians, market forces, and the general public. Growing from a ramshackle railroad frontier town by the 19th century, Vancouver already learned about the 'Lovable City' of human-scaled design and planning by the early 20th century, only to act upon this lesson decades later. Meanwhile, Vancouver indulged in a familiar cycle of 20th-century urban trends and ill-fated responses. Economic modernization squeezed and superseded small-scaled urban storefronts, workshops, and offices into a few central blocks of offices and department stores and swaths of suburban sprawl, leaving the downtown fringe to struggle for its survival. The growth of car traffic compounded this peripheral struggle through jammed streets, parking lots and conniving freeway plans. Economic inequality and anti-Chinese discrimination prompted slum formation and resultant radical renewal plans. Mid-century political and developer hubris materialized as soulless office and residential towers that blocked distant mountain views as much as up-close glimpses into windows and doorways.

By the 1970s, Vancouver began to turn the corner toward a more human-centered architecture and urbanism that later become known as Vancouverism. Citizen protests killed the downtown freeways and the technocracy that underpinned it, including decades of virtual free reign by developers and business interest over downtown's streets and its skyline. From then on, citizens and planners controlled development as "a privilege conferred by the community and not a fundamental right", leveraging Vancouver's ongoing high-growth pressure into public amenities and qualities it otherwise couldn't afford, such as high-quality public space and public architecture, parks, waterfront trails, and fine-grained retail and community spaces.[98] Modernist blueprint planning and design was replaced with research-based urban design guidelines, which unleashed a wave of new high-density developments that pleased Vancouverites with sought-after public waterfront access and eye-level design quality, while satisfying developers' desires to quench Pacific thirst for luxury housing.[99]

We can also see the limits of this seeming symbiosis among public, private, and professional dreams. Since a creative outburst of waterfront projects in the 1980s and 1990s, Vancouverism has increasingly become distilled into a teal-glass formula for luxury living that reflects architectural mediocrity, conspicuous consumption, and a lack of affordability – pricing out low-income and middle-class residents, but even much-desired creative industries. Also, acquiring street-level urban amenities and public space improvements mostly from new development contributions has left existing downtown neighborhoods by the wayside.[100] Away from luxury high-rises and the pastiche of Gastown's cobblestone streets, the desolate streets and ongoing socioeconomic decline of the East End presents the dark flipside of Vancouver's boom. One can also question whether Vancouverism is easily applicable to other cities, especially if they lack the unique political and natural context of Vancouver – let alone its red-hot market. We can also wonder if these carefully designed buildings and public spaces are flexible enough to withstand the test of rapidly changing times for street-level uses and users.[101] Yet, we cannot deny the merits of Vancouverism. Especially at eye level, lofty architectural ideals matter less than lively storefronts, stoops, and front yards, which Larry Beasley rightfully ascribes to careful design guidance beyond merely extraverted inhabitation by residents and businesses.[102] As a new generation of planners, designers, and architects aims to blend in sustainability with Vancouver's reputation for livability, we can expect to see Vancouver remain at the vanguard of urban design – albeit at a premium.[103]

Notes

1 Image by author, 2017.
2 Lance Berelowitz, "From Factor 15 to Feu D'artifice: The Nature of Public Space in Vancouver," *a/r/c: Architecture Research Criticism* 1, no. 5 (1997).
3 Robert M. Walsh, "The Origins of Vancouverism: A Historical Inquiry into the Architecture and Urban Form of Vancouver, British Columbia" (PhD Thesis, University of Michigan, 2013), 666.
4 Vancouver is the only Canadian city that has grown and become denser since 1980: ibid., 2. See also Larry Beasley and Frances Bula, *Vancouverism* (Vancouver: On Point Press, 2019), 14–15, 26; John Punter, *The Vancouver Achievement – Urban Planning and Design* (Vancouver: UBC Press, 2003), xvi–xxv, 3–12, 347.
5 Walsh, "The Origins of Vancouverism: A Historical Inquiry into the Architecture and Urban Form of Vancouver, British Columbia," 6, 36–39; Beasley and Bula, *Vancouverism*, 38.

6 On the settlement of Vancouver, see Patricia E. Roy, *Vancouver* (Toronto: Lorimer, 1980), 11. The original settlement of Granville is still visible as skewed blocks in Vancouver's urban fabric, now known as the Granville townsite or Gastown Derek Hayes, *Historical Atlas of Vancouver and the Lower Fraser Valley* (Vancouver: Douglas & McIntyre, 2007), 33; Roy, *Vancouver*, 12. On the West End and its grid, see Walsh, "The Origins of Vancouverism: A Historical Inquiry into the Architecture and Urban Form of Vancouver, British Columbia," 154–55; Hayes, "Historical Atlas of Vancouver and the Lower Fraser Valley," 50–51.

7 The name Vancouver was devised by a CPR executive to market the settlement. "Historical Atlas of Vancouver and the Lower Fraser Valley," 48–52; Donald Gutstein, *Vancouver Ltd* (Toronto: J. Lorimer, 1975), 11–15; Walsh, "The Origins of Vancouverism: A Historical Inquiry into the Architecture and Urban Form of Vancouver, British Columbia," 154–55; Roy, *Vancouver*, 12–14; Graeme Wynn and Timothy Oke, *Vancouver and Its Region* (Vancouver: UBC Press, 1992), 117; Hayes, "Historical Atlas of Vancouver and the Lower Fraser Valley," 48–51; Gutstein, *Vancouver Ltd.*, 11; Walsh, "The Origins of Vancouverism: A Historical Inquiry into the Architecture and Urban Form of Vancouver, British Columbia," 154–55.

8 Gutstein, *Vancouver Ltd.*, 14; Wynn and Oke, *Vancouver and Its Region*, 87, 162 East of Granville, the province and land speculators started their own settlements, which form the base of the East End: Hayes, "Historical Atlas of Vancouver and the Lower Fraser Valley," 51.

9 Roy, *Vancouver*, 19; Hayes, "Historical Atlas of Vancouver and the Lower Fraser Valley," 76 Vancouver's largest property owner and richest resident by the late 1880s was the co-founder of the BC Electric Railway, Vancouver's largest streetcar operator: Gutstein, *Vancouver Ltd.*, 63. This company would usurp all other streetcar and interurban railways by the 1890s. For more on Vancouver's early streetcar system growth, see Punter, *The Vancouver Achievement – Urban Planning and Design*, 5; Hayes, "Historical Atlas of Vancouver and the Lower Fraser Valley," 56, 64–66; Wynn and Oke, *Vancouver and Its Region*, 72.

10 Roy, *Vancouver*, 29–30; Wynn and Oke, *Vancouver and Its Region*, 87; Walsh, "The Origins of Vancouverism: A Historical Inquiry into the Architecture and Urban Form of Vancouver, British Columbia," 156; Beasley and Bula, *Vancouverism*, 17.

11 Gutstein, *Vancouver Ltd.*, 63; Roy, *Vancouver*, 30; Walsh, "The Origins of Vancouverism: A Historical Inquiry into the Architecture and Urban Form of Vancouver, British Columbia," 106–7; Wynn and

Oke, *Vancouver and Its Region*, 89. The Chinese had been part of Vancouver's ethnic fabric since its onset, having worked on the CPR railroad and working in local manufacturing. Anti-Chinese sentiments frequently flared over racial and wage disparities: Walsh, "The Origins of Vancouverism: A Historical Inquiry into the Architecture and Urban Form of Vancouver, British Columbia," 211. On Chinatown, see also Wynn and Oke, *Vancouver and Its Region*, 135.

12 On the recession and the subsequent Klondike gold rush, see Hayes, "Historical Atlas of Vancouver and the Lower Fraser Valley," 56; Gutstein, *Vancouver Ltd.*, 63–64; Roy, *Vancouver*, 51. Vancouver aggressively advertised itself as a port city to fuel economic growth: Wynn and Oke, *Vancouver and Its Region*, 107.

13 Roy, *Vancouver*, 39, 51, 72; Wynn and Oke, *Vancouver and Its Region*, 92; Gutstein, *Vancouver Ltd.*, 64.

14 A recollection of Ethel Wilson's character Aunt Topaz in her classic 1949 novel *The Innocent Traveller*: Wynn and Oke, *Vancouver and Its Region*, 129. On the southern suburbanization, see ibid., 89, 130–32.

15 Gutstein, *Vancouver Ltd.*, 63–64; Hayes, "Historical Atlas of Vancouver and the Lower Fraser Valley," 76.

16 On Vancouver's highly variable building conditions in 1911, see Beasley and Bula, *Vancouverism*, 16; Walsh, "The Origins of Vancouverism: A Historical Inquiry into the Architecture and Urban Form of Vancouver, British Columbia," 48.

17 The quotation is from observer Frank Yeigh in "Through the heart of Canada" in 1911: Wynn and Oke, *Vancouver and Its Region*, 71. See also ibid., 69, 107–8, 111; Walsh, "The Origins of Vancouverism: A Historical Inquiry into the Architecture and Urban Form of Vancouver, British Columbia," 48, 156; Hayes, "Historical Atlas of Vancouver and the Lower Fraser Valley," 76. Among the most prominent waterfront warehouse districts was Yaletown, just north of False Creek: Roy, *Vancouver*, 72.

18 Walsh, *Origins of Vancouverism*, 48–49; Gutstein, *Vancouver Ltd.*, 64–65, Roy, *Vancouver*, 51, 72; Wynn and Oke, *Vancouver and Its Region*, 88–89.

19 East False Creek was donated by the city to a railway company in return for new infrastructure, a new terminus station and surrounding development: Hayes, *Historical Atlas of Vancouver*, 56, 73, 100–2; Wynn and Oke, *Vancouver and Its Region*, 108, 162–66.

20 Wynn and Oke, *Vancouver and Its Region*, 95–108, 117, 119–21; Walsh, *Origins of Vancouverism*, 43, 67, 76–79, 83–85, 95–97, 102–3; Gutstein, *Vancouver Ltd.*, 65–66; Roy, *Vancouver*, 87–88. Mawson's mostly esthetic visions were supplanted by his effective successor Thomas Adams' focus on efficiency: Wynn and Oke, *Vancouver and Its Region*, 122.

21 Gutstein, *Vancouver Ltd.*, 66, Roy, *Vancouver*, 88; Wynn and Oke, *Vancouver and Its Region*, 109–10; Walsh, *Origins of Vancouverism,* 106, 118–19.

22 Quote from Roy, *Vancouver*, 103. See also ibid., 92.

23 Beasley, *Vancouverism*, 15, 18–19; Gutstein, *Vancouver Ltd.*, 66; Walsh, *Origins of Vancouverism*, 156–57; Roy, *Vancouver*, 73. The exodus of the West End elite started in earnest in the late 1900s. By 1913, 50 apartment blocks had already been constructed in the neighborhood. By 1927, only a fifth of Vancouver's elite listed in the *Vancouver Social and Club Register* lived in the West End: Wynn and Oke, *Vancouver and Its Region*, 133 As suburbanization became accessible to a larger cohort of Vancouverites, the city amalgamated with its key suburbs by the late 1920s – an act of fiscal foresight that benefited Birmingham, but eluded Detroit during the same era.

24 Walsh, *Origins of Vancouverism,* 118–19, 130, 209; Wynn and Oke, *Vancouver and Its Region*, 128.

25 Roy, *Vancouver*, 28; Wynn and Oke, *Vancouver and Its Region*, 136–40. On Chinese immigration and anti-Chinese sentiment, see Walsh, *Origins of Vancouverism*, 211–13; Wynn and Oke, *Vancouver and Its Region*, 130, 137.

26 Walsh, *Origins of Vancouverism,* 79, 103, 114, 120–21; Wynn and Oke, *Vancouver and Its Region*, 128. On the Depression, see Roy, *Vancouver*, 92, 103; Gutstein, *Vancouver Ltd.*, 66–67, 139; Wynn and Oke, *Vancouver and Its Region*, 115; Walsh, *Origins of Vancouverism*, 121–22; Roy, *Vancouver*, 110.

27 Roy, *Vancouver*, 93; Wynn and Oke, *Vancouver and Its Region*, 164.

28 Gutstein, *Vancouver Ltd.*, 67; Roy, *Vancouver*, 93, 135, 140; Wynn and Oke, *Vancouver and Its Region*, 164; Hayes, *Historical Atlas of Vancouver,* 129; Walsh, *Origins of Vancouverism*, 122; Punter, *The Vancouver Achievement*, 8. Proposals in the 1950s fruitlessly sought to fill in False Creek for a much narrower canal to free up land for development: Hayes, *Historical Atlas of Vancouver,* 103.

29 Gutstein, *Vancouver Ltd.*, 68–69; Wynn and Oke, *Vancouver and Its Region*, 206–7.

30 For more information on the NPA, see Beasley, *Vancouverism*, 27–28; Gutstein, *Vancouver Ltd.*, 139; Punter, *The Vancouver Achievement*, 13–14; Walsh, *Origins of Vancouverism,* 124. Downtown business interests formed a lobbying alliance in 1946: Hayes, *Historical Atlas of Vancouver,* 64–66, 144; Roy, *Vancouver*, 146–47, Punter, *The Vancouver Achievement,* 19.

31 Quote from 1947 report "Preliminary Report upon the City's Appearance: Vancouver British Columbia (Harland Bartholomew and Associates, September 1947, p. 11; Walsh, *Origins of Vancouverism,* 125–28, Beasley, *Vancouverism*, 23–24. On the East End, see Walsh, *Origins of Vancouverism,* 132–35.

32 Bartholomew was terminated before he could finish his report in 1949. Other refused proposals by Bartholomew include a revised downtown Civic Center and a point-to-point urban freeway that led from downtown to New Westminster: Walsh, *Origins of Vancouverism,* 115, 117, 136–40; Beasley, *Vancouverism* 24; Harland Bartholomew and Associates, *A Preliminary Report Upon the Downtown Business District* (St Louis, MO: Vancouver Town Planning Commission, 1945). The freeway proposal was much smaller than the successors of the 1950s and 1960s, yet he can still be ascribed to have introduced the concept: *MacDonald 2008 paper on Vancouver planning*. On Sutton Brown, see Walsh, *Origins of Vancouverism,* 145–46; Gutstein, *Vancouver Ltd.*, 144–45.

33 Quote from Donald Gutstein, "Vancouver," in *City Politics in Canada*, eds. Warren Magnusson and Andrew Sancton (Toronto: University of Toronto Press, 1983), 199. On the postwar planning apparatus' organization, see: Punter, *The Vancouver Achievement*, 18, Gutstein, *Vancouver Ltd.*, 144–45. Sutton Brown benefited from the Canadian cultural and political adoption of stronger bureaucracies, placing more power in the hands of planners: Beasley, *Vancouverism*, 25. Sutton Brown switched from Director of Planning to City Manager in 1963, which only solidified his grip on planning matters: ibid., 24, Walsh, *Origins of Vancouverism,* 152. A predecessor to the design panels was the Architectural Board of Control established in 1936, which had proven similarly ineffective: Roy, *Vancouver*, 108.

34 Technical Planning Board, "Downtown Vancouver 1955–1976," in *City of Vancouver Development Plan* (Vancouver: City Council of Vancouver, 1956). The report was not officially adopted.

35 Kim Dovey and Felicity Symons, "Density without Intensity and What to Do About It: Reassembling Public/Private Interfaces in Melbourne's Southbank Hinterland," *Australian Planner* 51, no. 1 (2014); Beasley, *Vancouverism*, 19–21, 25–26; Walsh, *Origins of Vancouverism*, 157–60; Roy, *Vancouver*, 142; Punter, *The Vancouver Achievement*, 18–19. Ultimately 181 high-rise residential towers were built in the West End between 1956 and 1973: Walsh, *Origins of Vancouverism,* 164, 167–69, 175–76. The NPA government rejected planners' pleas for reducing density in the West End Zoning: Punter, *The Vancouver Achievement*, 18–20, Gutstein, *Vancouver Ltd.*, 98–99.

36 Wynn and Oke, *Vancouver and Its Region*, 141; Roy, *Vancouver*, 137, Walsh, *Origins of Vancouverism,* 213.

37 Beasley, *Vancouverism*, 29, Walsh, *Origins of Vancouverism,* 136, 216–19. Interestingly, the team concluded the "blight-core of False Creek" fared even worse: Roy, *Vancouver*, 144.

38 Department, "Vancouver Redevelopment Study"; Walsh, *Origins of Vancouverism,* 221–22, 228, 231–34; Roy, *Vancouver,* 144; Wynn and Oke, *Vancouver and Its Region,* 260; Walsh, *Origins of Vancouverism,* 231; Gutstein, *Vancouver Ltd.,* 144, 162; Beasley, *Vancouverism,* 28.

39 Roy, *Vancouver,* 144; Gutstein, *Vancouver Ltd.,* 158; Beasley, *Vancouverism,* 29; *Origins of Vancouverism,* 234.

40 Board, "Downtown Vancouver 1955–1976," 23–30, including maps.

41 Ibid., 12–13. The West End's parking supply would similarly grow to over 10,000 spots by the mid-1960s, mostly through the sea of lots surrounding new residential high-rises: Transportation Engineering Branch, *1965 West End Parking Study* (Vancouver: City Engineering Department, 1965). However, a 1961 zoning draft abolished minimum parking requirements and strongly restricted parking maximums along core streets. It also had detailed language on retail frontage requirements, and set out corridors that would undergo design panel scrutiny. Technical Planning Board, *A Zoning Plan for the Downtown Area – Draft* (Vancouver: Technical Planning Board, 1961).

42 Term from City Planning Department, *Redevelopment in Downtown Vancouver* (Vancouver: Downtown Redevelopment Advisory Board, 1961). The Downtown Redevelopment Advisory Board consisted of downtown business and professional interests.

43 Ibid., 12. In 1961, downtown Vancouver more than double the regional retail sales than Toronto, and far higher than most American cities: Planning Department, *Downtown Vancouver – Part 1 – Present Conditions* (Vancouver: Planning Department, 1968).

44 Quote from Mayor William Rathie's 1962 campaign: Wynn and Oke, *Vancouver and Its Region,* 199. See also Roy, *Vancouver,* 129, 134, 140, 147; Punter, *The Vancouver Achievement,* 21–22. City Council hired American economic consultant Larry Smith to recommend a downtown development program in 1963. He recommended freeways, downtown housing, and public land assembly for large-scale private development: Gutstein, *Vancouver Ltd.,* 69–71.

45 The project was inspired by Montreal's Place Ville Marie, prompted by looming retail suburbanization, designed by mall architect Victor Gruen, and enabled by city land assembly. Gutstein, *Vancouver Ltd.,* 29, 69–71. See also Punter, *The Vancouver Achievement,* 21–22. The public backlash against the Pacific Centre high-rises would influence subsequent office developments: Roy, *Vancouver,* 146–48. Downtown's regional retail sales market share had dropped precipitously between 1951 and 1966, even though

sales themselves had risen: Hedlin Menzies & Associates Ltd., *Downtown Vancouver 1969 – an Economic Study* (Vancouver: Hedlin Menzies & Associates Ltd., 1970).

46 Beasley, *Vancouverism,* 21–22, 26–28. Geographer and planner Walter Hardwick ascribed criticism on the West End's density to a suburban mindset: Walter G. Hardwick, *Vancouver* (Don Mills: Collier-Macmillan Canada, 1974), 202–3. See also Walsh, *Origins of Vancouverism,* 199–202, 369–70; Beasley, *Vancouverism,* 276; Roy, *Vancouver,* 144.

47 Gutstein, *Vancouver Ltd.,* 76–79, 166; Walsh, *Origins of Vancouverism,* 297–308; Punter, *The Vancouver Achievement,* 22.

48 One of the lead developers was Marathon, CPR's real estate arm. The development consortium also included Grosvenor-Laing, the largest developer in downtown Birmingham, England at the time: Gutstein, *Vancouver Ltd.,* 17, 154, 162; Punter, *The Vancouver Achievement,* 25; Walsh, *Origins of Vancouverism,* 308–12; Roy, *Vancouver,* 148–50. Despite merchant attempts to preserve and spruce up the area, a city planner derided Gastown as a district of "especially old men" living in cheap hotels and rooming houses by the mid-1960s: Vancouver Planning Department, *Downtown East Side: A Preliminary Study* (Vancouver: City of Vancouver, 1965), 21; Walsh, *Origins of Vancouverism,* 314–18; Punter, *The Vancouver Achievement,* 25.

49 Citizens Council on Civic Development, *Downtown Vancouver – Part 1 – the Issues* (Vancouver: Citizens Council on Civic Development, 1969).

50 George Peloquin and Stan Shillington, "West End Future Lies in Its Heart," *The Vancouver Sun,* September 23, 1968.

51 Gutstein, *Vancouver Ltd.,* 20.

52 Gutstein, *Vancouver Ltd.,* 154–55, 162; Walsh, *Origins of Vancouverism,* 251; Hayes, *Historical Atlas of Vancouver,* 155; Technical Committee for Metropolitan Highway Planning, "Freeways with Rapid Transit," in *A study on highway planning* (Vancouver: Metropolitan Vancouver, 1959); Walsh, *Origins of Vancouverism,* 249, 251, 266; Roy, *Vancouver,* 150. On the transit study, see Gutstein, *Vancouver Ltd.,* 154.

53 On the East End renewal, see Hayes, *Historical Atlas of Vancouver,* 154; Gutstein, *Vancouver Ltd.,* 154, 157–58; Walsh, *Origins of Vancouverism,* 235, 240. Vancouver planners tried to demonstrate that East End housing conditions were beyond repair, for example in their 1964 propaganda film "To Build a Better City": Walsh, *Origins of Vancouverism,* 227.

54 The only remainders of this first battle are two viaducts across North False Creek: Beasley, *Vancouverism,* 29, 143–44; Hayes, *Historical Atlas of Vancouver,* 156–57; Punter, *The Vancouver Achievement,* 24; Walsh, *Origins*

of Vancouverism, 128, 251. Mayor Tom Campbell was especially divisive in the freeway debates: ibid., 254; Roy, *Vancouver*, 154.

55 Hayes, *Historical Atlas of Vancouver,* 156–58; Beasley, *Vancouverism*, 29–30; Punter, *The Vancouver Achievement,* 24; Roy, *Vancouver*, 150; Walsh, *Origins of Vancouverism,* 260–63; Gutstein, *Vancouver Ltd.,* 162–66; Wynn and Oke, *Vancouver and Its Region,* 259–60. By 1972, even many planners and the Downtown Business Association favored transit over the freeways, often prompted by widespread public outrage: Punter, *The Vancouver Achievement,* 25; Walsh, *Origins of Vancouverism,* 263; Hayes, *Historical Atlas of Vancouver,* 158. On the East End activism, see Walsh, *Origins of Vancouverism,* 241–43; Punter, *The Vancouver Achievement,* 23.

56 Quote from Tyler Stiem, "Vancouver Dumps Its Freeway Plan for a More Beautiful Future (Story of Cities #38)," *The Guardian*, May 9, 2016; Walsh, *Origins of Vancouverism,* 246–47, 268, 274, 397; Beasley, *Vancouverism*, 30; Gutstein, *Vancouver Ltd.,* 154, 165; Wynn and Oke, *Vancouver and Its Region,* 259; V. Setty Pendakur, *Cities, Citizens & Freeways* (Vancouver: Transportation Development Agency, 1972).

57 Campbell's loss also coincided with accusations of murky development deals: Punter, *The Vancouver Achievement,* 23–25; Hayes, *Historical Atlas of Vancouver,* 158; Gutstein, *Vancouver Ltd.,* 140.

58 Roy, *Vancouver*, 157; Wynn and Oke, *Vancouver and Its Region,* 261; Beasley, *Vancouverism*, 29–31, 40, 47–48, 240, 272–73; Walsh, *Origins of Vancouverism,* 197, 263, 397–400; Punter, *The Vancouver Achievement,* 14, 17, 26–29.

59 Walsh, *Origins of Vancouverism,* 50, 197, 678, 681; Beasley, *Vancouverism*, 30–31, 280. The West End rezoning met relatively little resistance, as developers anticipated transit construction that would make connect more homes to downtown, and a slowdown in office demand reflected in lower anticipated West End housing demand: Gutstein, *Vancouver Ltd.,* 102.

60 Beasley, *Vancouverism*, 328–37. Discretionary zoning was recommended by external consultants to amend the by-right development system downtown. It was later expanded to other parts of the city: Punter, *The Vancouver Achievement,* 27–30.

61 Gutstein, *Vancouver Ltd.,* 55, 146; Beasley, *Vancouverism,* 47; Punter, *The Vancouver Achievement,* 28–29, 58, 62–64; Wynn and Oke, *Vancouver and Its Region,* 208–9. The 1975 downtown plan was inspired by an iterative feedback loop between pre-Spaxman planners and citizen input, for example producing Planning Department, *A Proposal for Downtown Development* (Vancouver: Planning Department, 1973).

62 City Planning Department, *Downtown Guidelines (Iii) Character Areas* (Vancouver: City of Vancouver, 1975); ibid.; The downtown guidelines were amended in 1977 and 1985. See also Beasley, *Vancouverism*, 147, 191–92.

63 Punter, *The Vancouver Achievement,* 58, 63; Beasley, *Vancouverism,* 241.

64 Punter, *The Vancouver Achievement,* 70–73.

65 On the development south of downtown in South False Creek, see Wynn and Oke, *Vancouver and Its Region,* 209, 213; Hayes, *Historical Atlas of Vancouver,* 103, 168; Punter, *The Vancouver Achievement,* 8; Roy, *Vancouver*, 134–37; Walsh, *Origins of Vancouverism,* 321–28, 346, 371, 390–405; City of Vancouver, *Official Development Plan for False Creek* (Vancouver: City of Vancouver, 1974). A post-occupancy evaluation revealed the successful use of a pattern language: Jacqueline Vischer, "False Creek: Decline and Rebirth," *The Canadian Architect* July (1980): 50; Walsh, *Origins of Vancouverism,* 407–27, 440–41; Beasley, *Vancouverism*, 180–81. North False Creek developed later due to disagreements between the city and Marathon: Gutstein, *Vancouver Ltd.,* 84.

66 Granville Street pedestrianization had been dreamt up by planners since the 1950s. The mall was modeled after the Nicollet Mall in Minneapolis: Punter, *The Vancouver Achievement,* 27; Roy, *Vancouver*, 148; R. E. Kalapinski, *A Survey of the Granville Mall – Retail Sales – Phase Ii* (Vancouver: Social Planning Department, 1975); M. E. Turner and A. V. Gray, *Granville Mall – Preliminary Impact Study* (Vancouver: AVG Management Science Ltd., 1974). On the East End in the 1970s, see Roy, *Vancouver*, 150, 162; Walsh, *Origins of Vancouverism,* 259; Wynn and Oke, *Vancouver and Its Region,* 260–61; Punter, *The Vancouver Achievement,* 52–55; Beasley, *Vancouverism*, 285–86. Besides Gastown and Chinatown, Granville Island south of downtown was redeveloped as a themed retail and entertainment destination: ibid., 147–48, 183. Historic preservation in Vancouver had a slow start: 77.

67 Punter, *The Vancouver Achievement,* 74. See also: W. H. Whyte, *The Social Life of Small Urban Spaces* (Washington, DC: Conservation Foundation, 1980); William Hollingsworth Whyte, *City: Rediscovering the Center*, 1st Anchor Books ed. (New York: Doubleday, 1990).

68 Punter, *The Vancouver Achievement,* 9, 19, 61; Gutstein, *Vancouver Ltd.,* 91–98; Roy, *Vancouver*, 159.

69 Beasley, *Vancouverism*, 147–48; Walsh, *Origins of Vancouverism,* 200–1, 400, 437–53, 466–72.

70 Wynn and Oke, *Vancouver and Its Region*, 187, 194, 199, 254; Punter, *The Vancouver Achievement,* 9, 19, 58–61, 73–80, 85; Walsh, *Origins of Vancouverism,* 481–82; Beasley, *Vancouverism,* 241. Asian investment in Vancouver real estate was already significant

in previous decades, albeit at a lower profile: Roy, *Vancouver*, 148.

71 The developer appointed architect Stanley Kwok to lead the project; he had served as the prior Provincial site owner's president: Punter, *The Vancouver Achievement*, 187–89. Before the Province bought the site for Expo 86, CPR's Marathon had fruitlessly tried to build a residential site: Walsh, *Origins of Vancouverism*, 358–60, 495–548; Hayes, *Historical Atlas of Vancouver*, 160; Wynn and Oke, *Vancouver and Its Region*, 221; Punter, *The Vancouver Achievement*, 187, 190–94. Tensions rose between Vancouver and the Province over the displacement of low-income East End residents due to the influx of Expo 86 tourists, exacerbated by a federal and provincial move away from social housing: Wynn and Oke, *Vancouver and Its Region*, 237–39; Beasley, *Vancouverism*, 186–90.

72 See Walsh, *Origins of Vancouverism*, 495, 682 and figure 11.4 on a notable slump in high-rise construction during the Spaxman era.

73 Wynn and Oke, *Vancouver and Its Region*, 235; Punter, *The Vancouver Achievement*, 14.

74 Quote from Wynn and Oke, *Vancouver and Its Region*, 234. On Vancouver's downtown growth, see ibid., 229; Beasley, *Vancouverism*, 50.

75 On office oversupply between 1989 and 1992, see Wynn and Oke, *Vancouver and Its Region*, 218–21; Punter, *The Vancouver Achievement*, 258, 61. On the other hand, condominium median prices rose 44% in real terms between 1986 and 1996, coinciding with (often Asian) interest in Vancouver residential real estate: Punter, *The Vancouver Achievement*, 61, 86, 98; Walsh, *Origins of Vancouverism*, 573–76. The "Condo-Mania" hurt housing affordability, and conversions of Single Room Occupancy hotels pushed out lower-income residents: Punter, *The Vancouver Achievement*, 94, 259.

76 Quote from Beasley, *Vancouverism*, 83. See also ibid., 48, 50–51, 111, 147, 179–80, 192. Like in the West End in previous decades, the need for downtown housing was also prompted by a continuing lack of rapid transit investment; ibid., 118–19; Walsh, *Origins of Vancouverism*, 482–86, 579–81; Punter, *The Vancouver Achievement*, 233, 242–44; Planning Department, *Central Area Plan – Goals and Land Use Policy* (Vancouver: Planning Department, 1991).

77 Quote from Beasley, *Vancouverism*, 94. Beasley had been on Spaxman's planning team since 1976, focusing on downtown. On Beasley, see: ibid., 31, 48, Walsh, *Origins of Vancouverism*, 577, 581–82; Punter, *The Vancouver Achievement*, 109. The NPA had returned to power in 1986, which soon prompted the resignation of Ray Spaxman. The NPA was far more amenable to development than their predecessors, reflecting Vancouverites' (slow) embrace of growth

due to high-quality examples of dense development: Walsh, *Origins of Vancouverism*, 564–66. On Beasley's system of development contributions and permitting, see: Beasley, *Vancouverism*, 329–39; Walsh, *Origins of Vancouverism*, 582–84; Punter, *The Vancouver Achievement*, 108, 368–70. On his organizational update of the Spaxman planning apparatus, including the Urban Design Panel, see: ibid., 58, 337.

78 Beasley, *Vancouverism*, 95–100.

79 Punter, *The Vancouver Achievement*, 88, 92, 107; Walsh, *Origins of Vancouverism*, 591, 592. These guidelines were inspired by Herman Hertzberger, Laila Ghaït, and Ina Rike, *Lessons for Students in Architecture* (Rotterdam: Uitgeverij 010, 1991); Christopher Alexander, Sara Ishikawa, and Murray Silverstein, *A Pattern Language: Towns, Buildings, Construction* (New York: Oxford University Press, 1977); Whyte, *City: Rediscovering the Center*. Developers pay to set up a collaborative urban design team with the city to go through the permitting process: Punter, *The Vancouver Achievement*, 238. On Ann McAfee's research work, see: ibid., 95; Ann McAfee, "Housing Families at High Density," *Urban Forum* 4, no. 3 (1978). The work was translated into Japanese, and fed into City Planning Department, *High-Density Housing for Families with Children – Guidelines* (Vancouver: City Planning Department, 1992).

80 The Provincial sale of the North False Creek lands was competitive; to win the bid Kwok initially proposed a disconnected scheme on behalf of the developer, which raised citizen protest. Later news on murky sale conditions added fuel to the fire: Walsh, *Origins of Vancouverism*, 549–61; Beasley, *Vancouverism*, 51, 113.

81 The initial development plan for North False Creek was approved in 1990, but further collaboration took until 1993 for the first building completion. Besides architecture, the allocation of affordable housing, community amenities and park space were major topics: Punter, *The Vancouver Achievement*, 196–205, 233, 236; Walsh, *Origins of Vancouverism*, 561–63, 586, 598, 601–10; Beasley, *Vancouverism*, 192–93, 184.

82 Punter, *The Vancouver Achievement*, 216; Walsh, *Origins of Vancouverism*, 576, 627. One the Downtown South design guidelines, see Punter, *The Vancouver Achievement*, 98–104; Planning Department, *Downtown South Guidelines (Excluding Granville Street)* (Vancouver: Planning Department, 1991).

83 Beasley, *Vancouverism*, 114–32, 255. An example of big-box retail integrated into a street-facing block is Costco's integration in the 'Spectrum' development – which does still have one blank service street: Walsh, *Origins of Vancouverism*, 621–22.

84 Often, these noncommercial uses have struggled to meet outsize resident demand. Beasley, *Vancouverism*, 115, 121, 134.

85 Quotes from ibid., 244, 257.

86 Ibid., 242–44, 257–59; Walsh, *Origins of Vancouverism*, 670. A study that proves the eye-level effectiveness of Vancouver's townhouses: Elizabeth Macdonald, "Street-Facing Dwelling Units and Livability: The Impacts of Emerging Building Types in Vancouver's New High-Density Residential Neighbourhoods," *Journal of Urban Design* 10, no. 1 (2005). On the townhouses' street-level safety benefits, see: Beasley, *Vancouverism*, 281–82. A one-meter (3.3-foot) grade change was deemed so important that universal access had to be provided through a back door: ibid., 271.

87 Ibid., 155–57; Punter, *The Vancouver Achievement*, 286, 368. On infrastructure, see also ibid., 245, 284–85; Beasley, *Vancouverism*, 148–59, 255. Regionally, see ibid., 81–83; Hayes, *Historical Atlas of Vancouver*, 167. On Vancouver's proposed 2040 infrastructure, see City of Vancouver, *Transportation 2040* (Vancouver: City of Vancouver, 2012); Beasley, *Vancouverism*, 164.

88 Punter, *The Vancouver Achievement*, 252–55, 285. A critical note on Granville Street's over-sanitized redevelopment: Robin Ward, "Architecture Centre Preserves Past the Right Way," *Vancouver Sun*, April 15, 1998.

89 Quote from Beasley, *Vancouverism*, 230. An early activist group was the Downtown Eastside Residents Association (DERA) in the 1973: Punter, *The Vancouver Achievement*, 96–97. On the East End decline since the 1980s, see ibid., 276–83; Beasley, *Vancouverism*, 132, 230–32; Walsh, *Origins of Vancouverism*, 132.

90 On Yaletown and its relation to the creative economy, see Punter, *The Vancouver Achievement*, 251; T. A. Hutton, "Spatiality, Built Form, and Creative Industry Development in the Inner City," *Environment and Planning A* 38, no. 10 (2006). On Vancouver's various preservation programs, see: Beasley, *Vancouverism*, 285–91. On Victory Square, see Punter, *The Vancouver Achievement*, 271–75.

91 The library was the largest capital project ever undertaken by the City of Vancouver: ibid., 262–67.

92 Walsh, *Origins of Vancouverism*, 638, 655–58; Punter, *The Vancouver Achievement*, 362.

93 City of Vancouver, *Northeast False Creek Plan* (Vancouver: City of Vancouver, 2018).

94 Beasley, *Vancouverism*, 273.

95 Between 1988 and 2012, more than 300 new high-rises have been constructed in downtown, including more than 200 residential towers: Walsh, *Origins of Vancouverism*, 573.

96 Ibid., 84.

97 Beasley, *Vancouverism*, 15, 53–78, 99.

98 Ibid., 235.

99 Walsh, *Origins of Vancouverism*, 650–51.

100 On architectural homogeneity, see Beasley, *Vancouverism*, 84, 283, 292–93; Punter, *The Vancouver Achievement*, 345; Walsh, *Origins of Vancouverism*, 683. On lack of affordability, see Beasley, *Vancouverism*, 135–36, 193, 200, 224–27. On conspicuous consumption, see Punter, *The Vancouver Achievement*, 226–27; Walsh, *Origins of Vancouverism*, 567. On downtown public space, see Beasley, *Vancouverism*, 376.

101 Ibid., 38, 236–39, 299; Walsh, *Origins of Vancouverism*, 663–66, 684.

102 Beasley states: "Through Vancouverism, we have left behind the notion that the accidental city is the only city that we can ever hope to achieve": ibid., 300.

103 Ibid., 49–50.

6 THE FRONTAGE ECOSYSTEM

Figure 6.0 The relation between buildings and public space in The Hague in 2018.

DOI: 10.4324/9781003041887-6

The four urban cores described in the previous chapters have faced remarkably similar challenges over the past century: a mixture of socioeconomic attrition, an older building stock, the pressure of automobility, and the need to accommodate increasing commercial and institutional functions. The political and professional responses have also been quite similar, such as constructing taller and larger buildings, making room for moving and parked cars, and modernizing urban districts, reaching a crescendo in the mid-20th century. Where we see divergent paths, we can often trace differing cultural views toward urban cores and their eye-level architecture, which in turn influenced political and professional decisions. From the embrace of private enterprise to the belief in strong governance, to the conviction in progress and obsolescence versus a desire to preserve a collective memory – these urban cores and their buildings have been strongly shaped by what their societies expected to give and receive from them.

These drastic histories especially played out at eye-level. After studying over a century of urban change, can we recognize the forces, processes, and trends that affect street-level architecture? This chapter synthesizes the key lessons from our case study cities, dissecting street-level architecture as an ecosystem that has been disrupted by a self-reinforcing set of social, economic, technological, and architectural forces and processes. Once we understand these forces and processes, we know what to target in our strategies toward a better relationship between buildings and public space.

Street-level erosion

As the previous chapters have clearly demonstrated, street-level architecture has deactivated over the past century in every city and in every dimension. Figure 6.1 compares frontage interactivity in all case study cities and clearly demonstrates a downward trend. Yet the figure also shows the starkly different trajectory between the cases. Birmingham and Detroit represent two cities that have lost most of their interactivity over the past century; in contrast, The Hague and Vancouver are two cities that have been able to maintain much of their interaction between buildings and public spaces. Vancouver has even added interactive frontages since the mid-20th century as its population and economy grew. In every city, we can also see that the decline of interactivity has mostly halted since the 1980s – marking a turning point in the way planners, designers, and decision makers viewed cities. The same holds true for the number of entrances to buildings from streets, which Figure 6.2 shows has declined in all cities. Again, the decline is more pronounced in Birmingham and Detroit, which have especially erased entrances (and buildings) around major urban renewal and infrastructure projects, as well as experienced growing vacancy. One can walk entire blocks in both cities without being able to enter a single building – let alone a street-level business. Conversely, The Hague and Vancouver have maintained a solid pattern of retail and non-retail entrances, although Vancouver's lofty residential streets have always had fewer entrances than The Hague's narrow streets and buildings. And again in these cities, entrance erosion has stabilized or even reversed since the 1980s.

Of course, what we see at eye level reflects a variety of processes. Spatially, the deactivation of a frontage might be the result of replacing an interactive frontage with a less active one; the replacement of an entire building with a larger, less-interactive one; or even the demolition of an interactive building without any replacement. Contrary to most discourse on our changing urban cores, this deactivation is not simply the result of aloof architecture or automobile attrition. There is a far more complex dynamic at play that certainly includes the way our buildings are designed, but also reflects a complete change in the way we use and imagine our urban cores and their buildings. Understanding the interplay between form, function, and meaning as an ecosystem is key to improving our cities at eye level. This chapter will therefore uncover these forces in the next two sections.

Evolution: economic and technological change

More than anything, our frontages needed to adapt to vastly different roles over the past century. Most of these roles reflect the changing use of ground floors. This use tends to go beyond the purview of designers, instead reflecting the everyday desire and activities of tenants and passersby – the street-level economy. No matter how transparent, fine-grained, or inviting we design a frontage to be, it needs an interactive use and inhabitant to make it come to life. It should come as no surprise that these uses and their interactivity have vastly changed over the past century. The fine-grained ecosystem of production, consumption, and living of the early 20th century has been carefully dissected, stratified, enlarged, moved indoors, and sometimes even moved out of urban cores. The transactions between buyers, sellers, producers, and dwellers no longer takes place on the sidewalk but inside office buildings, apartments, and enclosed malls – prompting a loss of 'transactional value' for frontages, one that British architect MacCormac already lamented decades ago.[1] Furthermore, new technology has vastly impacted the fine-grained use of frontages. We are familiar with the negative impacts of cars on our cities at eye level, but think of the devastating impact of home refrigeration in the 1930s on corner stores, or the current impact of e-commerce on retail. All these economic and technological evolutions have impacted the way we use cities, their buildings, and their streets.

THE FRONTAGE ECOSYSTEM   105

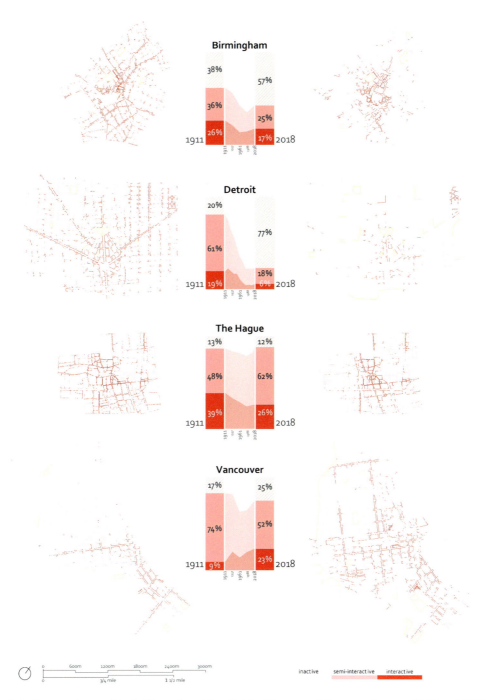

Figure 6.1 Frontage interactivity in Birmingham, Detroit, The Hague, and Vancouver between 1911 and 2018.
Source: Diagram by Conrad Kickert, 2021.

Economic and technological evolution have especially impacted how we have utilized our urban ground floors over the past century. For The Hague and Detroit, detailed data was available to show the exact functions that ground floors had over this time period. Figure 6.3 shows how both cities have each shifted their ground-floor use significantly, but also how both cities have taken vastly different paths in this shift. While each urban core lost many ground-floor storefronts, The Hague has retained street-level dwellers and workers, while Detroit shows a near-complete exodus of any interactive street-level functions, with downtown now mostly accommodating cars at eye level, or simply nothing at all. While Detroit serves as an amplification of the economic and technological pressures facing a declining downtown, its dynamics ring true in most other cities. Studying the

106 THE FRONTAGE ECOSYSTEM

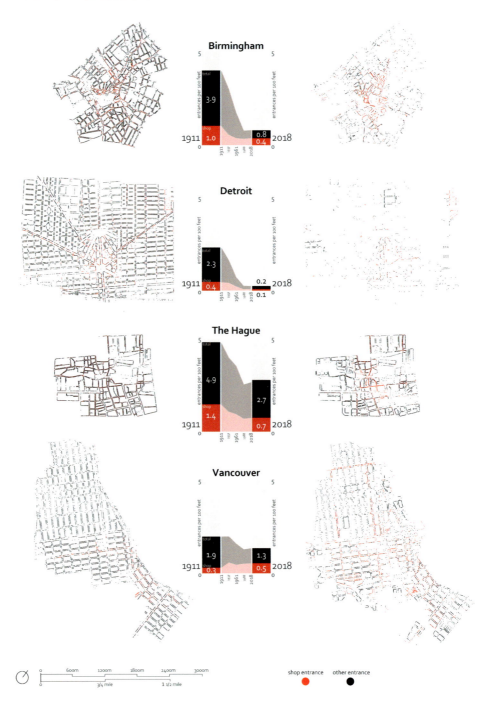

Figure 6.2 Entrances per 100-meter frontage in Birmingham, Detroit, The Hague, and Vancouver in 1911 and 2018. *Source: Diagram by Conrad Kickert, 2021.*

changing use of both cities in more detail reveals what is plaguing our urban cores in general.

Let's start with the most visible and widely discussed economic shift at eye level: the disappearance of commercial storefronts. Whether through suburban competition, internalization into shopping malls, or simply through the rapidly changing retail economy, all cities but Vancouver have seen a significant decrease in street-level retailers over the past century. As a young city, Vancouver only saw an increase as its population and downtown job base skyrocket. Regional, but especially national, governments have the most power to alter the pathway of urban retail decline. The centralizing retail policies of the Netherlands mitigated the loss of storefronts in The Hague's urban core by restricting large out-of-town stores and ensuring that the urban core

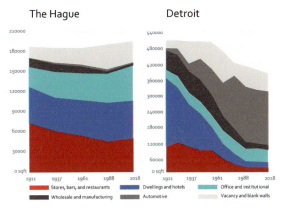

Figure 6.3 Key frontage use categories in Detroit and The Hague between 1911 and 2018.
Source: Diagram by Conrad Kickert, 2021.

Figure 6.4a–b Closed storefronts abound in our urban cores, reflecting the changing retail economy.
Source: Image (a): vacant storefront on Woodward Avenue, Detroit. Image by author, 2012. Image (b), vacant storefront on Wagenstraat, The Hague. Image by author, 2014.

remained economically vibrant, populated, and accessible by transit and infrastructure investments. Yet, The Hague's number of core retailers still declined by nearly half over the past century, especially due to early 20th-century Dutch policies to outlaw small independent retailers. Downtown Vancouver's retail growth benefited from the city growing around it, but suburban shopping mall competition certainly hindered downtown retail during the mid-20th century. Birmingham, but especially Detroit, illustrates what happens when regional and national policies fail to protect urban retail – and by extension, urban life in general. Birmingham's core retailers reeled from ill-conceived mid-century urban renewal, followed by the rise of significant suburban mall competition and urban socioeconomic decline during the 1970s and 1980s, only to rebound with significant public investment in core public spaces and private investment in core malls. Downtown Detroit never saw similar counter-efforts come to fruition, and the city's well-documented spiral of socioeconomic decline and suburban exodus is reflected in a nearly 90% decline of downtown retailers over the past century (Figure 6.4). The result is clearly visible at eye-level, The Hague and Vancouver remain regional shopping and entertainment destinations with block after block of solid storefronts, while in contrast Birmingham's retail core has significantly shrunk, and downtown Detroit's storefronts are only narrowly avoiding near extinction due to recent private investments.

However, no government policy or private plan can counteract the inevitable – the number of storefronts, especially in cities, have been on the decline across the Atlantic since records began early in the 20th century. Envisioning a fine-grained pattern of independent, small retailers denies more than a century of social and economic change that has seen mass-market success benefit fewer, larger retailers, many of whom are in turn succumbing to e-commerce competition. The rise of urban leisure and the experience economy has the potential to stem some of the decline of storefront commerce, as bars, restaurants, and coffee shops have taken our urban cores by storm over the past decades (Figure 6.5). As urban cores have turned into places to have a good time, the leisure economy should be carefully orchestrated to support vibrant street-level architecture rather than internalized into controlled complexes. While the following chapter will discuss these trends in more detail, we can expect the overall pool of interactive storefronts to continue to decline, making plans and designs for more street-level commerce increasingly tenuous.

Around the corner from the buzz of storefronts, we often find quieter residential streets, which are actually the most prominent street-level uses in our cities and even their cores. As the following chapters will describe, a social and vibrant residential frontage can be just as exciting at eye level as any storefront could be. Yet, in

(a)  (b)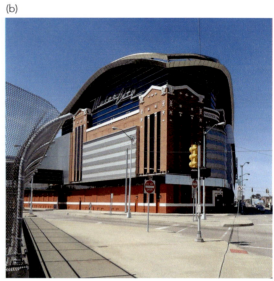

Figure 6.5a–b The leisure economy comes to urban cores in many different forms, from extraverted patios (a) to introverted casino complexes (b).
Source: Image (a) by Conrad Kickert, 2012. Image (b) by Conrad Kickert, 2014.

our case study urban cores, street-level dwellings have dwindled, sometimes giving way to more interactive storefronts, but usually to larger office frontages and less interactive parking lots, infrastructure, or blank walls – or even vacancy, as in the case of Detroit. This loss of core domesticity has two main underlying reasons. First, homes have relatively low land values compared to commercial functions, and therefore easily give way to these higher-and-better uses such as storefronts, but also to offices, unless prevented by zoning. For example, downtown Detroit, unobstructed by any policy, replaced most of its historic homes for offices, department stores, or parking by the first part of the 20th century. Second, homes in urban cores are naturally among the oldest in each city. They have frequently struggled to offer modern, clean, safe, and healthy living environments, which attracted the interest of planners over the course of the century. When Detroit's planning efforts ramped up in the mid-20th century, entire central residential districts were swept aside for freeways, parking lots, and new construction. Similarly, Vancouver's East End was partially razed for infrastructure and modern housing, and many West End mansions were equally replaced by successive waves of ever-taller apartment buildings and office towers, lined by street-level retailers or parking. Birmingham and The Hague were no less aggressive in razing and replacing their oldest housing stock in the name of public welfare and private development. With the exception of Vancouver, all case study cities saw a very significant decline in the number of downtown residents over the past century – more than two-thirds in The Hague and Detroit alone.[2]

Offices have become of the fastest growing street-level tenants during the 20th century. Reflecting the rapid growth of urban industrial and knowledge production, office complexes had begun to replace finer-grained core fabric by the previous century, but growth really took off during the first decades of the 20th century (Figure 6.6). During these decades, North American skyscrapers were usually built on top of lucrative retail frontage, but by the mid-20th century, corporate power had surpassed retail rents to take over the city at eye level with purpose-built lobbies.[3] While central office growth was less pronounced in European cities like The Hague and Birmingham, offices have traditionally taken up entire buildings, including rather institutional ground floors that did not interact with streets. The mid-20th century growth of offices in European urban cores continued this rather introverted trend. For example, the growth of the national government apparatus prompted an office boom in The Hague's urban core that the city is still looking to heal today (more about this later in this chapter). Office growth in urban cores follow simple land economics, easily pushing aside dwellings with lower land values. Yet the same economic processes now prompt increasing office conversions into residential space as we enter a new era of hybrid work in the 21st century. Besides offices, institutions like churches, libraries, and schools are a key part of our cities at eye level. However, many of these institutions have disappeared over recent decades, as residents and public and private funding receded.

Figure 6.3 also shows that our urban cores hold significant amounts of manufacturing and wholesaling frontages, which add to the economic base of urban cores yet often struggle to interact with public space.

Figure 6.6a–b Office lobbies and frontages have sprouted throughout urban cores, generally decreasing interactivity between buildings and public space. Many of these offices were built over the past decades as modernization projects. Source: Image (a) of Birmingham by Conrad Kickert, 2017. Image (b) of Detroit by Conrad Kickert, 2014.

These uses have significantly declined in all cities over the past century but Birmingham – which has decided to protect its core manufacturers. While central streets used to contain a motley hybrid between production and consumption a century ago, their separation has usually meant a departure of manufacturers, egged on by local governments and developers keen to repurpose prime central land. Beyond zoning out factories, Detroit and Vancouver actively cleared their waterfront industries for civic centers and high-rise dwellings. The Hague similarly cleared its western factories for new housing and parks. However, urban production is making a bit of a comeback with the rise of artisanal production, including in former vacant storefronts. As Chapter 8 will describe, these new urban makerspaces tend to interact far more with passersby than their predecessors.

While manufacturing and wholesaling has mostly left urban cores, the crown for deactivation the eye-level experience has been taken by technology, in the form of moving, parking, fueling, selling, and repairing cars. As Detroit and Birmingham demonstrate, cars can take over cities promptly and completely, and as The Hague and Vancouver demonstrate, battling the rise of cars is a tough task. Notwithstanding the occasional parking garage, street widening, and even urban freeway slip-up, these two cities have been able to minimize the space for cars at eye-level, sometimes burying them below ground and hiding them behind more active buildings, but mostly just limiting their role in the urban core. After very similar public uprisings against auto-centric urbanism during the 1970s, The Hague and Vancouver realized their core public spaces – and the buildings that line them – should be built around pedestrians, bicycles, and transit rather than cars. In subsequent decades, a combination of infrastructure investments, centralizing planning policies, and design guidelines and reviews minimized the role of cars at eye level. Today, both urban cores barely contain visible freeway and parking infrastructure – and are even removing existing auto-oriented mistakes from the past.

Conversely, Birmingham and Detroit have largely surrendered their urban cores to cars, befitting their roles as global automotive manufacturing hubs. From the earliest parking lots, repair shops, and garages in the 1910s, downtown Detroit was cut off from its surroundings by a veritable ring of parked cars by the end of the 1920s, amplified by devastating street widenings in the 1930s. As car parking spread throughout downtown, other land uses became less desirable, creating a self-reinforcing phenomenon that will feature later in this chapter. By the mid-20th century, moving and parked cars took up over half of downtown Detroit's land; then state-sponsored freeway construction prompted another leap. Unstoppable automobile erosion of the urban fabric was only reinforced by car-centric architecture: beyond parking garages, most buildings adopted the scale of the car in what architect Jan Gehl coins "35 mile per hour [50 kilometer/hour] architecture".[4] Even in downtown Detroit's current renaissance, more than three-quarters

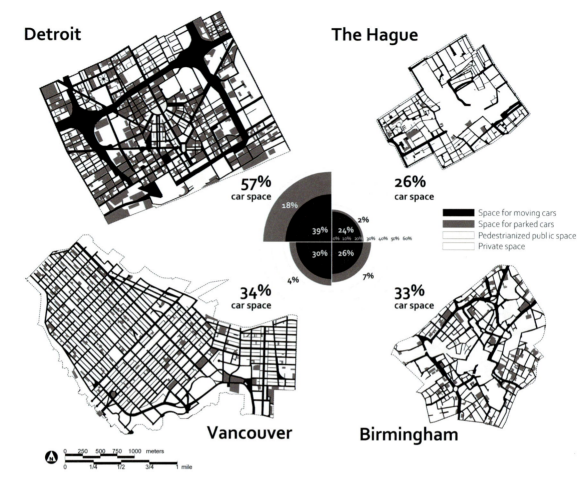

Figure 6.7 Space dedicated to moving and parked cars in Detroit, The Hague, Vancouver, and Birmingham. *Source: Diagram by Conrad Kickert, 2021.*

of new construction will hold cars, not people. Only now, Detroit is considering demolishing some of its excess downtown freeway infrastructure. Conversely, Birmingham's mid-20th-century freeway dreams had already cooled during the 1970s, and the city removed large portions of its 'concrete collar' from the 1980s onward.

While most other frontage use shifts were mainly economically driven, the automobile takeover of the city at eye level has been mostly technological, and clearly fell in the realm of decision makers, engineers, and designers – professionals that can also turn the tide. The power of these professionals to surrender or reconquer urban cores from cars can be seen in Figure 6.7, which demonstrates how downtown Detroit has more than half of its space dedicated to moving or parked cars, compared to around a third in Vancouver and Birmingham and a quarter in The Hague.

A final type of street-level use has gained unfortunate prominence over the past century: no use at all. Vacant lots, vacant buildings, fences, and blank walls have always been a part of our urban core experience, for example in The Hague's fenced parks and church yards, but they often signal deeper underlying issues of distrust and decline. Nowhere have vacant buildings and lots proliferated as much as in Detroit, first as an inevitable part of early 20th-century growth, then as a holdover for large-scale urban renewal during the mid-20th century, but then as a permanent reminder of decline from the late 20th century onward. Even today, vacant buildings and land represent more than 15% of downtown Detroit at eye level. But we see vacancy in other cities as well; sometimes in the hopeful scaffolding around new construction, but often in the shuttered storefronts of struggling peripheral retail corridors or in the distrustful moats around modern construction. While vacant land and vacant buildings reflect an elusive dynamic of urban, regional, and even national growth and decline, blank walls can be battled more directly. We will return to this issue later in this chapter and in our book.

Consolidation

Besides changing the way we use our most central buildings and their street-level frontages, we have also radically increased their size. Regardless of how we use them, our most central buildings have become larger and taller over the past century, while interacting less with the street – a paradoxical process Australian urbanist Kim Dovey has coined *density without intensity*.[5] While urban planners and designers can take part of the blame for this, like with changing ground-floor uses, our larger buildings mostly reflect land economics. When central land becomes more valuable and development pressure increases, viable development depends on density, which tends to prompt land consolidation. From optimized floorplates and taller building technology such as steel frames and elevators to regulations on sunlight and setbacks – each push for larger parcels to maximize the amount of development on expensive urban land.[6] Similarly, retail operations benefit from larger-scale floorplates, as they can offer more merchandise and other services to customers. As a result, the average size of a retail establishment has grown precipitously over the past century.[7]

The resulting larger parcels and floorplates rarely keep pace with the interactivity and number of entrances of the smaller, fine-grained parcels they consolidate. Whether it takes up a corner or an entire block, whether a two-story walkup or a 70-story skyscraper – most buildings have only one front door to the street (or less than a handful for larger public buildings and department stores). Furthermore, taller buildings amplify pressures on their frontage to welcome more than just pedestrians, but also to accommodate cars, deliveries, and garbage hauling. Taller, newer buildings also increasingly incorporate more technological and logistical space that presents itself as blank walls than their smaller, historic neighbors. We hence enter a paradoxical spiral in which more pressure on urban land and higher density actually *decreases* building interactivity with public space.

From downtown Detroit's commercial blocks of the early 19th century to Birmingham's Corporation Street construction and The Hague's traffic breakthroughs – land consolidation for larger buildings started long before our case studies began in 1911. The following century simply continued this pattern of consolidation and accumulation of land and capital, as private developers bought up and cleared entire blocks of smaller buildings to construct office skyscrapers or retail palaces. While density and land values skyrocket as a result, the number of entrances actually often dwindles as fine-grained urbanism of small mixed-use dwellings and shops makes way for grander buildings with centralized lobbies or limited entryways. Government interventions even allowed for the consolidation of entire districts toward one development parcel, for example in Detroit's Renaissance Center, The Hague's eastern urban core, or Birmingham's Bullring. More about this process later.

We see how the cycle of added density, land consolidation, and decreasing street-level interaction

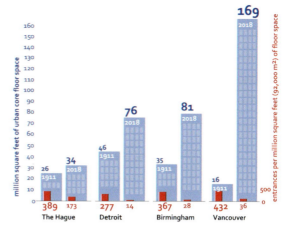

Figure 6.8 As density increased in our urban cores over the past century, entrance intensity decreased. *Source: Diagram by Conrad Kickert, 2021.*

occurs when we compare The Hague's ability to maintain most of its original two-to-four story mixed-use fabric with other urban cores that have seen significant growth and consolidation. Even The Hague saw its entrances per square foot of built floorspace decrease by more than 55%, but in all other case studies, entrances per square foot decreased by *more than 90%* (Figure 6.8).

The most central blocks in Detroit and The Hague illustrate at the architectural level how this process of densification, consolidation, and deactivation has taken place over the past century. As both cities grew, their central blocks became the territory of a handful of large department stores, which replaced dozens, if not hundreds of smaller retailers, usurping entire city blocks in their path to growth and prosperity. The multistory department stores drastically increased the density of these blocks, but the interactivity and the amount of entrances between buildings and public space actually decreased. Furthermore, as dozens of retailers made way for less than a handful of large retailers, the economic resilience of these central blocks decreased. As the tide turned for department stores due to surrounding socioeconomic decline and the obsolescence of their business model, these blocks turned from urban assets to liabilities. The limited flexibility of department store buildings to turn back to other uses prompted either drastic retrofits (in The Hague) or full-blown demolition (in Detroit). In both cities, central blocks are still recovering from this cycle of land and capital accumulation, coined by urbanist Jane Jacobs as "the self-destruction of diversity".[8]

Detailed maps of the ground floors of Detroit and The Hague's central blocks, assembled from insurance mapping, building plans, permit applications, and other historical records, demonstrate this process (Figure 6.9). By 1911, The Hague's central blocks contained a mixture

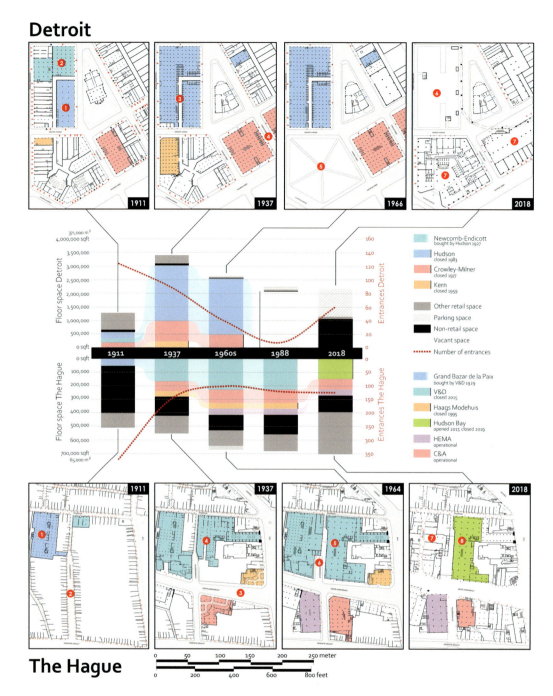

Figure 6.9 Key retailers took up increasing space in The Hague and Detroit's most central retail blocks before they retrenched or collapsed. Both in times of growth and of decline, the number of entrances decreased.
Source: Diagram by Conrad Kickert, 2021.

of mainstay retailers along a key east-west corridor anchored by the Grand Bazar de la Paix department store (1), around the corner from a district of small-scaled, often Jewish retailers, manufacturers and residents along a former canal (2). A nearby branch of the national department store chain V&D greatly expanded its holdings over the next decades, ultimately buying out the Grand Bazar to expand to a newly opened traffic artery (3) by the late 1920s, which in turn spawned new chain and department store construction by the late 1930s. V&D became one of the biggest winners of this race toward growth (4). Many new storefronts adopted a hybrid approach between indoors and outdoors, displaying their merchandise in a combination of well-lit storefronts and

Figure 6.10a–c V&D's new department store was the largest in the Netherlands when opening in the 1960s (a). However, its construction turned the former heart of The Hague's Jewish business district (b) into a blank service alley (c).
Source: Image (a) by Dienst Stadsontwikkeling en Volkshuisvesting, 1964. Image courtesy of The Hague municipal archives, ID 0.24883. Image (b) by Dienst Stadsontwikkeling, circa 1915. Image courtesy of The Hague municipal archives, ID 0.74462. Image (c) by Paul Lunenburg at Dienst Stedelijke Ontwikkeling, circa 2001. Image courtesy of The Hague municipal archives, ID imf-9501.

kiosks, which served as evening outings at a time that TV was not yet widespread. We can see these as the corner 'mazes' in the 1937 plan. Unfortunately, these display routes were removed within a few decades due to safety concerns, greatly diminishing the articulation of facades.

From the late 1920s onward, V&D's consolidated department store spanned two entire urban blocks on either end of the main artery of the former Jewish business district. As new construction made V&D the largest department store in the Netherlands in the early 1960s (5), this artery mostly lost its function amidst the prowess of more than 20,000 square meter store. Customers could park on a new roof deck or enter the store through a few key entrances, but they no longer had a reason to traverse what had essentially become a blank, inhospitable service alley (6; Figure 6.10). For decades, V&D's multi-block

Figure 6.11a–b Hudson's block in Detroit: from America's tallest department store (a) to a hole in the ground, currently under reconstruction (b).
Source: Image (a) postcard with unknown author, circa 1930s. Image (b) by gab482 via Flickr, CC-BY-2.0.

behemoth remained a regional shopping anchor, until department stores increasingly fell out of favor by the early 21st century. V&D relinquished its western block for the construction of a Tschumi-designed shopping arcade in the late 2000s (7), and the store went bankrupt in 2015. A 2018 revival of the store by Canadian Hudson Bay was short-lived, and the V&D building is still only partially occupied in 2021 (8).

The dramatic rise and fall of The Hague's department stores is highly similar to Detroit's core blocks, where Hudson's department store also bought out early competitor Newcomb-Endicott in the late 1920s to consume the city's prime retail block. By the late 1920s, Hudson's department store had become America's tallest and second-largest retail palace, holding nearly 200,000 square meters in 17 floors of merchandise, including its own hospital, library, and telephone exchange (3). Nearby retailers had expanded their premises by leaps and bounds during the roaring 20s as well, including Crowley-Milner's premises that spanned two city blocks (4). As downtown Detroit's tide turned by the 1940s and 1950s, department stores were among the first to retrench. One by one, stores either closed their downtown premises or went out of business altogether. One of the first to fail was Kern's department store in 1959, whose building fell to the urban renewal axe in the 1960s, leaving an empty lot for decades to follow (5). Crowley-Milner's store was demolished without replacement in 1977, and Hudson closed its downtown store in 1983, leaving it vacant and pilfered until its implosion in 1998 for a project that didn't materialize. By 2018, Hudson's site remained vacant but for an underground parking garage (6), although the other department stores were ultimately replaced by a multi-block office building and parking garage with only a fraction of the interactivity of decades prior (7). As of 2022, the Hudson's site is under construction to become one of Detroit's tallest skyscrapers atop a retail base (Figure 6.11).

As these examples show, land consolidation and coarser urban fabric increases the chance that buildings turn themselves away from public space for a variety of reasons. As mentioned, logistics access plays a role, as does an increasing focus on car accessibility. A coarser architectural grain can hence turn entire streets into blank alleyways, as both The Hague and Detroit's central blocks have shown. Consolidation also decreases entropy and increases risk. As entire districts are owned and operated by only a few entities, the failure of these entities can have massive consequences: Hudson's failure caused a block-sized gap in downtown Detroit for nearly four decades, and V&D's failure has significantly upended the street-level experience and retail dynamics of The Hague's urban core. And the larger the failure, the harder it is to find a proper replacement.

Introversion

The increasing scale of public buildings was not just the outcome of land economics but of a deteriorating attitude to public space and public life among decision makers, developers, and designers over the past half century. Higher density and bigger buildings mean bigger risks for fewer owners, which have subsequently maximized their ability to control economic or social externalities and potential failure – usually with little success and to the detriment of street-level architecture. As dozens or hundreds of smaller buildings by a variety of smaller owners were swept up into one complex owned by one entity, the exterior public life that these smaller buildings

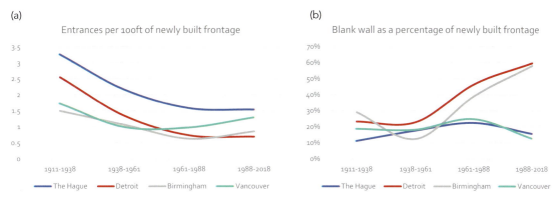

Figure 6.12a–b New construction has become more introverted over the past century, although tides are turning in some cities.
Source: Graph by Conrad Kickert, 2021.

harbored increasingly internalized into controlled environments. Residential streets moved into the apartment lobby; home-based ideation moved into the office cubicle; and street-level retail moved into the internalized shopping mall. As scholar Nan Ellin describes in her work on the postmodern city, this reflects a cycle of privatization in which "form follows fear", a process through which buildings seek to internalize reward (such as well-paying renters, eager customers, and a positive corporate image) and minimize risk (such as crime or vacancy).[9] The rise of automobiles and modern and postmodern architecture has dovetailed well with the desires of developers and governments for a 'bigness' that internalized the functions of urban life.[10]

The amount of introverted architecture built in our case study cities clearly illustrates how risk-averse we have become over the past century. Figure 6.12 illustrates how new construction in each era has added fewer entrances to our urban cores, which reflects land consolidation. However, the figure also shows that new construction has increasingly surrounded itself with blank walls at street-level, which urbanist William Whyte aptly recognized as signs of distrust that "proclaim the power of the institution and the inconsequence of the individual, whom they are clearly meant to intimidate".[11] Part of the graph represents the propensity of modernist architecture and urbanism toward acontextualism, as witnessed by a peak of blank walls between 1961 and 1988, which represents the most drastic postwar renewal period in most cities. Yet the connection between architecture, trust, and society becomes even more tangible when we recognize that Detroit and Birmingham still surround most new construction with blank walls, which may reflect their ongoing socioeconomic struggles more than renewed insights on architecture and urban design. Conversely, The Hague and Vancouver's hard-fought urban design policies and active interventions began to turn the tide away from introverted architecture from the 1980s onward. The success in these cities was not just formalistic, but understood blank walls as a reflection of interdependent financial, social, technological, and architectural dynamics. The wholesale transformation of two blocks on the periphery of The Hague and Detroit's urban core show just how interrelated these dynamics are. In The Hague's Spuikwartier and Detroit's waterfront, socioeconomic decline, developer distrust, and laissez-faire public policy created the perfect storm of architectural introversion.

The peripheral Spuikwartier district in The Hague has seen one of the most radical downtown transformations in any large Dutch city – to darkness and back (Figure 6.13). By 1911, the district was already in a downward spiral, as it had lost its role as a shipping port due to the removal of canals (1) for hygienic and traffic reasons. While the district's fine-grained urban fabric interacted with passersby with various shops and warehouses, building conditions were dire, especially in courtyard and alleyway housing (2).[12] Starting as early as 1908, the city and various groups attempted to clear the district for a variety of civic and traffic improvements. As plans faltered, buildings continued to deteriorate and street-level businesses departed.

In the mid-1960s, a private developer began to buy up the district in hope of constructing a 140-meter (460 foot) tall, multi-block mixed-use office, hotel, retail, and theater complex. After the national government stopped the project, the developer sold his holdings to a pension fund, which supported another proposal to clear the entire district for high-rise offices and dwellings. In the 1970s, the national government built a vastly downsized version of this ambitious plan as a ministerial complex (3). The design brief for the complex was an architect's worst nightmare: high security requirements, constantly shifting expectations, a location that shifted hundreds of feet

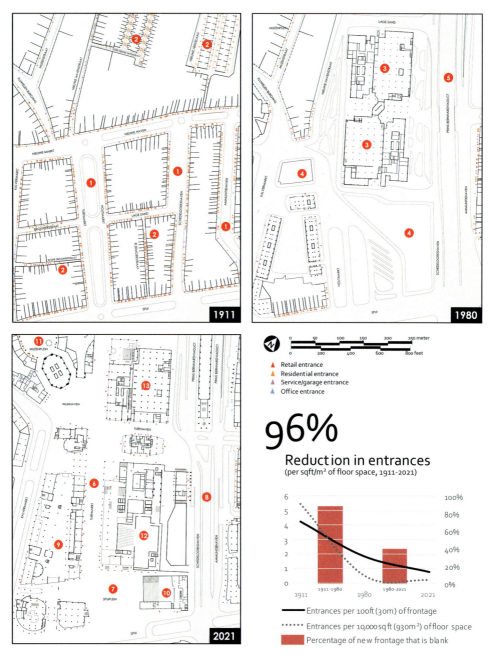

Figure 6.13 The Hague's wholesale transformation of its Spuikwartier from a downtrodden canal district into an insular office and highway hub, back into a vibrant new heart for the city.
Source: Diagram by Conrad Kickert, 2021.

(or meters) at the last minute, and a need for maximal floor space at minimal taxpayer cost. The complex' street-level façade showed the outcomes of this quandary, prioritizing national security over an originally envisioned retail presence, and haphazardly responding to a grim context of cleared land (4) and a newly built urban freeway (5). The resulting fortress was soon recognized as a "meteorite fallen from the sky [with] no visible connection to its environment".[13] By 1980, the Spuikwartier had almost doubled in floor area, but its eye-level vibrancy had all but extinguished.

Over the following decades, the city initiated a series of efforts to make the district more humane, first by improving its public spaces through pedestrianization (6), a new square (7) and the part-removal of the urban freeway (8). Even more importantly, the city incentivized

  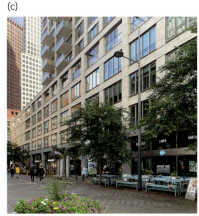

Figure 6.14a–c   A transformation to eye-level inactivity and back: the lively Turfmarkt (a) before demolition for a multi-block ministerial complex with no eye-level interaction (b), which in turn was refurbished into apartments with street-level retail (c). Source: Image (a) from postcard, courtesy of The Hague municipal archives (ID 0.70518). Image (b) by Conrad Kickert, 2012. Image (c) by Conrad Kickert, 2021.

new construction that connected with passersby at eye-level through fine-grained frontages. Among the world's foremost architects constructed new buildings, such as Richard Meier's city hall (9), Carel Weeber's Hotel Central (10), Rob Krier's mixed-use resident district (11), and more recently Jo Coenen's theater complex (12), which replaced a former concert and dance hall that was co-designed by Rem Koolhaas. The ministerial complex has partially been demolished, and partially refurbished into a residential tower fronted by street-level retail and an academic building (13) – a striking return to eye-level interactivity, at least toward its western façade. These recent efforts have successfully mended The Hague's urban core by balancing density with eye-level transparency and vibrancy – even with much larger buildings and fewer connections between architecture and public space than a century ago (Figure 6.14).

Figure 6.15 shows the dramatic history of Detroit's waterfront district as it underwent one of America's most infamous privately financed renewal efforts. Like The Hague's Spuikwartier, Detroit's waterfront has a mixed past of economic obsolescence, failed plans, and building deterioration before major renewal efforts entered the scene. As Detroit's commerce had left behind water transportation in lieu of rail-accessible inland sites, in 1911 the city's waterfront district remained as a hodgepodge of former hotels (1), wholesalers (2), dwellings (3), and small warehouses (4) anchored by a small railway station (5). The next decades mainly saw industrial growth in the area with the construction of new warehouses, car manufacturing, and a massive ten-story flour mill on the waterfront. The city consistently sought to clear its riverfront for a more representative image toward visitors and citizens alike, prompting unrealized plans by designers such as Frederick Law Olmsted and Eliel Saarinen. Instead of their grandiose visions, an underwater car tunnel to Canada just west of the district in 1930 eroded the area with open parking lots and service stations, prompting another wave of fruitless public plans to clear and reimagine the riverfront from the 1940s to the 1960s. Amidst downtown Detroit's feverish postwar renewal, by the early 1970s, the site stood out as anachronistic "wasteland filled with industrial debris and weed-chocked lots".[14]

Interestingly, the true impetus for the riverfront district's renewal came from the aftermath of Detroit's devastating 1967 civil disorder. As part of a corporate group to rebuild post-1967 Detroit, car executive Henry Ford II soon proposed to create a landmark project to prove the city's resilience, and effort "of such scale, of such critical mass, as to have an effect on the whole city". Ford used his corporate might to convince dozens of companies to invest hundreds of millions into a single, massive mixed-use riverfront complex. His consortium hired architect John Portman to design a mixed use "town within a great city", containing more than two million square feet (200,000 square meters) of office space in four 39-story towers (6), the world's then-tallest hotel structure at 73 stories (7) on top of a massive three-story shopping mall aimed toward an upscale suburban clientele. Later unrealized phases would include riverfront residential buildings (8), office expansion, and parking structures.[15] The entire riverfront district was cleared for what became the largest private urban redevelopment project in America when ground was broken in 1973 (see Figure 2.7 for a rendering). When it opened in 1977, the Renaissance Center had introduced a new type of interior public space to the Midwest – an environment in which climate, experience, and public life was optimized. However, it also introduced a new type

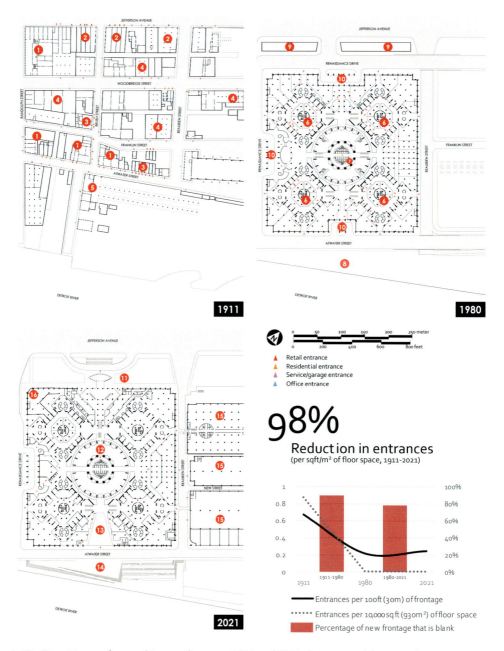

Figure 6.15 Detroit's waterfront architecture between 1911 and 2021 shows consolidation and introversion. *Source: Diagram by Conrad Kickert, 2021.*

of exterior appearance of hostile corporate architecture (Figure 6.16).

Initial media fanfare soon made way for architectural and public dismay at the defensiveness and introversion of the Renaissance Center, which was shielded by a 25-foot berm containing HVAC and other technical systems (9). Furthermore, the building had no proper front door, instead forcing visitors to access the center through parking ramps and garages (10).[16] Locals complained about the "fortress-like berms [which] say the Renaissance Center has chosen not to interact with the streets, but to seal itself off from them", and national architectural commentators including William Whyte commonly cited the center as an example of distrustful architecture.[17] While traffic concerns and technical reasons were publicly cited as the reason for the moats and ramps, architect Portman later admitted in an interview:

> The threat of crime was an important factor. In medieval times they built castles and moats. Society required

Figure 6.16a–b The Renaissance Center offers a year-round interior excitement (a), but its exterior remains forbidding (b). For the front entrance of the Renaissance Center, see Figure 6.6.
Source: Both images by Conrad Kickert, 2014.

protection, that was a fact of life. . . . Likewise today, you have to recognize the real world as it exists. . . . What I have to do is recognize the reality of a situation and seek a solution for that point in time. [The Center needed to] create a desirable option to help stop the outflow to suburbia.[18]

The result is clear in the 1980 map: a building that contained a maze of internal walkways and shops with fewer than a dozen entrances, surrounded by nearly 90% blank walls amidst a sea of highways and car parking. The introverted nature of the Renaissance Center complex cannot be squarely blamed on its design concept, as many parts that would link it to the city were never completed. Like in The Hague's ministerial complex, the center had simply been ripped out of a more contextual plan, with unfinished neighbors accounting for a significant part of its blank walls. The 13-lane widening of Jefferson Avenue that cut off the center from the rest of downtown certainly didn't help either.

The Renaissance Center's introverted architecture did not just alienate passersby. Local journalists called the maze-like interior "forbidding, even oppressive" and visitors frequently lost their way.[19] Office workers felt like "inmates", and the center's retailers fell like dominoes.[20] Furthermore, instead of its promised economic spin-off, the center had mostly taken tenants from other struggling downtown buildings and spawned a ring of parking.[21] The complex was saved from bankruptcy only five years after opening, and received the first in a series of makeovers to open it up to the city. By 1982, the center had received a friendlier front entrance toward downtown, and after another sale for pennies on the dollar to General Motors, SOM architects completed a half-billion-dollar renovation that replaced the berms with a glass front atrium (11), constructed a new interior pathway system (12), and opened the center to the river with an impressive riverfront winter garden (13) and an outdoor plaza (14).[22] Nevertheless, the Renaissance Center remains surrounded by blank walls, parking ramps (15), and open lots, with pedestrians funneled into covered overhead walkways. A significant number of the center's retail units remain vacant, including a short-lived tenant at the front of the complex (16) – the first with an entrance to the street.

The fringe of The Hague and Detroit's urban cores represents more than local conditions – it reflects the struggle of older districts to retain their fine-grained ecology of buildings and street-level uses. Their paradoxical mix of relatively poor building conditions, economic obsolescence, low land values yet central locations made them the ideal sites for modern growth ambitions of larger institutions and corporations. Opening less than a year apart, the public context for The Hague's introverted ministerial complex and Detroit's Renaissance Center reflect a similar, all-too-common urban condition: a mostly derelict district, a desperate city willing to look the other way for design review and land purchase, but, most importantly, a single

Figure 6.17a–b Decision makers and designers are not the only culprits behind barricaded buildings; distrustful tenants may shield themselves from public space as well. A fortified liquor store in downtown Detroit signals distrust (a), as does a fenced-off residential street next to a parking garage in The Hague (b).
Source: Image (a) by Conrad Kickert, 2014. Image (b) courtesy of Google Streetview, 2018.

entity looking to build a self-contained megastructure for reasons of security, image, and control. Whether for national security reasons (in The Hague) or local fear of crime (Detroit), these buildings sought to filter visitors by minimizing permeability and access, create a controlled interior environment at the cost of external connectivity, and preferred logistical efficiency – especially for vehicles – over esthetics and human scale. These conditions and pressures persist in many cities.

Both The Hague and Detroit have learned the hard lessons of architectural introversion for urban life and have taken steps to mitigate their worst offenders. Breaching fortresses is easier said than done, as buildings represent millions in investment. Furthermore, architectural introversion often reflects and reinforces poor public space conditions: The Hague's renovated former ministerial complex still turns itself away from an existing freeway and Detroit's Renaissance Center is still surrounded by blank walls that mostly face parking garages and lots. Introverted architecture literally casts distrust in concrete; the resources spent to repair it may surpass any previous savings, but will definitely pay off in future social and economic vibrancy.

Introverted frontages are not just the reflection of heavy-handed designers or frightened developers – they materialize as tenant decisions before anything else. Beyond the purview of our historical data, we can see in our everyday walks through cities what everyday distrust between street-level tenants and the street looks like. While the Renaissance Center's introversion was a clear target for architecture critics, thousands of store owners across the city had similarly barricaded their premises in what was coined a "post-riot Renaissance" of plywood-clad windows.[23] As The Hague's ministries built a much-maligned moat to protect national security, residents built bars in front of their windows to protect personal security. Metal shutters protecting store windows still remind late night passersby of the potential danger resulting from a lack of residential eyes on the street.[24] When residents don't trust the street, they build chain link fences, shuttered gates, or even makeshift walls to keep passersby off their property (Figure 6.17). It is easy to set a downward cycle in motion, in which a lack of trust in the safety of a public space reflects in fortification, which may actually influence the safety of this space. The conclusion chapter will delve deeper into this cycle, and the role of architecture in breaking it.

Stratification

We have seen how street-level architecture has deactivated due to changing economic, social, and design considerations. But not all frontages have eroded the same way – their fate actually wildly differs depending on their location in the city. Over the past century, we see a growing dichotomy between a vibrant center of interactive storefronts, often bolstered by public policies to improve accessibility, walkability, and subsequent commercial success, surrounded by a beleaguered fringe of vacant storefronts, inactive service alleys, aloof office lobbies, misguided urban renewal, and car infrastructure. In Detroit, this fringe even nearly ate up the entire downtown. Why do we see this stratification?

As in other sections, let's start with storefronts, the most visible sign of street-level interaction. As the total

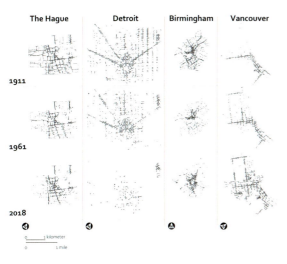

Figure 6.18 Retail storefronts in our four case study cities over the past century.
Source: Diagram by Conrad Kickert, 2021.

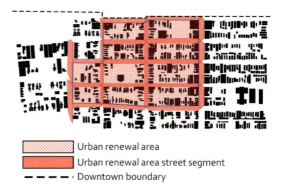

Figure 6.19 Measuring multi-block urban renewal by marking a renewal area with affected street segments. Example from Brewster-Douglas housing project in Detroit; the case study area boundary lies north of the diagram, which is not to scale.
Source: Diagram by Conrad Kickert, 2021.

number of street-level retailers has declined, they have tended to remain only in the most central and well-connected locations, leaving all other streets in the urban core looking for another use. This is due to basic economic processes that have been demonstrated by economists for over a century: most economic activity simply takes place in the most accessible locations. The more people can easily see and access a place, the more vibrant it will be.[25] Our storefronts indeed take up the most central and well-connected streets in our urban cores. In other words, storefronts follow customers. Radiating out from the busiest pedestrian corner in town (known either as the 100% or A1 corner), storefronts spread outward through the urban core along well-connected streets. Except for Detroit's struggling downtown, this axiom has only intensified over the past century: as the pool of retailers shrank, they only remained in the most central and accessible locations (Figure 6.18). While corner stores, bars, and restaurants in peripheral locations suffered from poor accessibility and a dwindling local clientele, central and accessible businesses were able to continue serving a growing regional hinterland. The result is clearly visible in our urban cores: our most central blocks continue to thrive as commercial destinations, but our quieter side streets have lost most of their storefronts. More about the dynamics of this process in the next chapter.[26]

The separation between a highly interactive center and a deactivating fringe goes beyond storefronts. As our previous chapters have shown, the periphery of our urban core generally suffered from far more than just departing retailers. Containing some of the city's oldest housing and street-level businesses, this 'fringe belt' of centuries-old blocks struggled to keep up with modern housing and economic demands.[27] Disinvestment and overcrowding often exacerbated their downward spiral. As we have discussed before, some blocks simply fell to the axe of central business growth. Others were razed for parking lots, especially in our North American cities. By the mid-20th century, the fringe became the target of significant public and private urban renewal efforts. Where central retail streets saw a replacement of smaller premises by larger stores in an evolutionary process, peripheral renewal usually involved wholesale clearance and replacement – as demonstrated in the previous two sections in The Hague and Detroit. In fact, the clearance of inner cities was often at the request of central businesses, which sought nearby space for logistics, parking, and access. At worst, they sought to rid themselves of slums and their – often poor and minority – dwellers, as witnessed by the brutal destruction of Detroit's Black Bottom district and its African American residents at the behest of downtown business interests.[28] Toward the end of the century, some cities saw more privately financed megaprojects such as Detroit's Renaissance Center or Birmingham's recent Smithfield and Eastside redevelopments.

Regardless of whether they were instigated publicly or privately, a significant part of our urban cores have been affected by these large renewal efforts. For example, more than 40% of The Hague's street segments were part of an urban renewal plan over one block in size over the past century, and more than half of Detroit's street segments. Almost all of these larger renewal projects took place in the fringe of their urban cores. And almost all of these severely disrupted the fine-grained ecosystem of street-level architecture in their heavy-handed path. Even with the best intentions to stabilize or improve the vitality of old urban districts, multi-block renewal efforts failed to accomplish either goal at eye level. When we measure just the before-and-after effects of multi-block renewal projects in The Hague and Detroit (Figure 6.19), we see that they decreased frontage interactivity in The Hague over 10% and in Detroit over 27% more than average. The Hague's deliberate effort to 'sanitize' small businesses in their postwar renewal projects even eroded storefronts by almost half more than average. Even after the renewal projects were done, frontages in renewal areas continued to fare more poorly than average over their lifetime.[29]

As we have seen in the previous section for postwar architecture, especially renewal projects implemented after World War II have been detrimental to frontage interactivity and storefronts in particular. And the negative effects of large-scale urban renewal didn't stop at its boundaries, either. As urbanist Jane Jacobs describes, large single-use renewal areas tended to radiate street-level decline outward: "By oversimplifying the use of the city at one place, on a large scale, they tend to simplify the use which people give to adjoining territory too, and this simplification of use (. . .) feeds on itself."[30] Indeed, if we measure a 'border zone' one block out from multi-block renewal areas, we see that these blocks and especially their storefronts have suffered from renewal projects, albeit more strongly in Detroit than in The Hague.

The combination of economic stratification, in which a solid core of retailers is increasingly surrounded and serviced by less-interactive street level uses, exacerbated by harmful renewal efforts have fueled the drastic separation between the urban core and the urban fringe. In a sense, this has created a dichotomy between 'winner and loser' streets, in which some streets have attracted more interactive frontages at the cost of others that have lost their street-level excitement. We can statistically prove this growing dichotomy between interactive and inactive streets with coefficients of interactivity inequality (known as Gini indices), which indeed find a growing separation. Especially Detroit's interactivity has diverged over the past century, as a blend of residential side streets and mixed-use districts have made way for a stark contrast between core storefronts surrounded by a ring of parking and infrastructure.[31]

Another victim in this process of separation is the diversity of frontage uses among streets. Along with zoning, the economic axioms of centrality and connectivity have stratified the fine-grained street-level mixture of dwelling, consumption, and production we saw a century ago toward single uses along entire corridors, which either veer toward interactivity (in the form of storefronts) or inactivity (in the form of offices, dwellings, but mostly parking, infrastructure, and vacancy). When we zoom into retail types, this separation continues. High-rent comparison retailers such as fashion and luxury stores that need to entice a lot of passersby to enter – and can afford the according central rent, especially if they are chains – have pushed out other retailers, leading to a homogenization of main shopping streets toward chain-infested "clone towns".[32] Jane Jacobs describes this process as the "self-destruction of diversity", a process "that operates for a time as a healthy and salutary function, but by failing to modify itself at a critical point becomes a malfunction. The analogy that comes to mind is faulty feedback."[33]

Another statistical index, in this case the Simpson Index of diversity, proves that the use of street-level frontages has indeed become less diverse in The Hague and Detroit over the past century, two cities where data availability enable us to measure frontage use and retail type in more detail.[34] Furthermore, frontage use diversity has decreased the most in the heart and at the edge of each urban core, where we have veered either toward monofunctional retail streets or monofunctional side streets and parking lots. In both cities, areas between overly successful cores and sleepy side streets have fascinatingly been able to retain a mixture of production, consumption, and dwelling, such as Detroit's Corktown and The Hague's and Birmingham's Chinatowns (Figure 6.20). Among the most uniquely vibrant areas in the city, these districts have become regional destinations, yet their street-level diversity remains a fragile balance between the homogenizing failure of vacancy and the homogenizing success of gentrification.

Contagion

We now know that the street-level interaction between buildings and streets has deteriorated over the past centuries, and we have seen the social, economic, technological, and design mechanisms behind this deterioration. One step deeper, we can also see how actual frontage deactivation takes place: it self-accelerates. This is because street-level decline is contagious: vacant storefronts, vacant buildings, and vacant or parking lots drag their direct surroundings along in a downward spiral. We'd rather not live or work next to a vacant lot or a blank wall, and we'd definitely not want to run a business in a vacuum of vacancy. Back to Jane Jacobs, who already recognized when disturbing the ecosystem of fine-grained urban fabric, "a kind of unbuilding, or running-down process is set in motion".[35] With the cards stacked against interactive frontages, it is easy to set this process in motion. And once interactive frontages along a street begin to decline – especially if they hold businesses – this decline will accelerate until a street bottoms out as a shadow of its former self. Three-quarters of Detroit's declining blocks suffered from accelerated decline of frontage interactivity, as did nearly half of The Hague's declining blocks.[36] In Detroit, our case city where vacancy was most prevalent, frontages close to an already vacant frontage were almost twice as likely to also fall vacant over a quarter century.[37] Detroit buildings close to a vacant or parking lot were even more than twice as likely to also be demolished for a vacant or parking lot over the same span of time (Figure 6.21).[38]

More than any other street-level use, businesses are by far the most susceptible to contagious decline. Street-level businesses can only survive in an increasingly

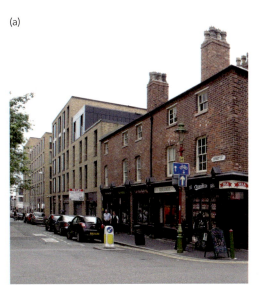

Figure 6.20a–b Street-level diversity in the urban fringe: Hurst Street in Birmingham (a) and the Wagenstraat in The Hague (b) contain bars, restaurants, stores that could not afford high rents, houses of prayer, houses of vice, and both cities' Chinatown.
Source: Image (a) 2009 by Elliott Brown via Flickr, CC-BY-2.0. Image (b) by Conrad Kickert, 2014.

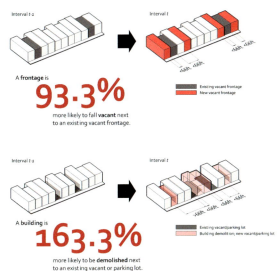

Figure 6.21 Vacancy is highly contagious, as measured in Detroit.
Source: Diagram by Conrad Kickert, 2021.

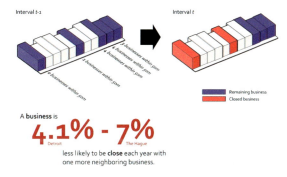

Figure 6.22 Neighboring businesses significantly lower the annual chance a street-level business closes.
Source: Diagram by Conrad Kickert, 2021.

break-neck race against suburban and online competition with the right amount and the right kind of neighbors. More specifically, business streets need to have a continuous critical mass of compatible retailers to remain attractive to customers to visit, and to allow all businesses within to be visible. When closing businesses begin to create gaps in retail streets, the viability of neighboring businesses declines very rapidly. A statistical analysis comparing the annual chance of a business closing to the number of surrounding businesses (within a visible 50-meter or 164-foot radius), we see that the annual risk of closure goes down between 4% and 7% with each additional nearby business (Figure 6.22). In other words, businesses need to stick together and form a critical mass to survive.[39] Comparison shops like fashion, shoe, and art stores are far more sensitive to being part of a critical mass of nearby businesses than 'destination' stores like hardware stores or personal services. Businesses tend to serve as the canary in the coal mine of further decline. As we have seen in our case study cities, they tend to be the first street-level species to vanish when the "close-grained intricacy and compact mutual support" of walkable urbanism is under threat, as Jane Jacobs describes it.[40] The next chapter will discuss strategies to bolster this ecosystem of mutual support to increase retail viability in cities.

Conclusion

The deteriorating relationship between architecture and public space can be attributed to an interconnected trifecta of underlying forces, which set a series of processes in motion. These forces fuel and reinforce one another in a complex dynamic that has stacked the cards against a fine-grained, interactive street-level architecture (Figure 6.23). Architects and urban designers can mitigate some of these forces and processes, directly influence others, yet remain powerless against many.

At the root, the deactivation of our relationship between buildings and public space comes down to three main forces that have impacted our cities for centuries: economic and technological evolution; consolidation of land and buildings; and introversion due to increasing urban control and distrust. These forces connect with each other in many different ways; for example, economic growth has led to the capital accumulation that has fueled land and building consolidation, which has fueled an increasing need to control buildings and districts, which leads to introversion. Feedback loops begin to form: consolidated buildings internalize economic activity, which makes former street-level functions obsolete, which may trigger urban renewal, which in turn consolidates land and buildings.

These underlying forces do not change frontages the same way across cities. We notice that economic evolution has stratified land uses, creating a separation between vibrant cores and inactive fringes at the district level, but even winner-and-loser streets within one block from another, homogenizing each street and district for its 'highest-and-best' use. Sometimes, forces and outcomes reinforce another: introversion creates fortified architecture, which in turn feeds the very unsafety that introversion is looking to protect itself from. At other times, processes simply reinforce themselves, as we have seen with contagious vacancy of buildings, land, and businesses.

With so many cards stacked against the interaction between buildings and public space, it is no wonder that our frontages have lost so much of their excitement over the past century. But now that we know the dynamics of street-level erosion, how can we turn the tide?

The responses of decision makers, designers, and the general public over the past century to street-level deactivation offer us initial clues. First off, we can recognize shared lessons to avoid. A fascination with technology brought unintended consequences such as contagious parking lots and regrettable urban freeways. As e-commerce haunts our storefronts today, we should avoid being blinded again. A belief in universal urban order brought the demolition of entire functioning districts for a universally disappointing esthetic of concrete complexes and aimless asphalt. As megaprojects continue today, we should ask which order we impose, and

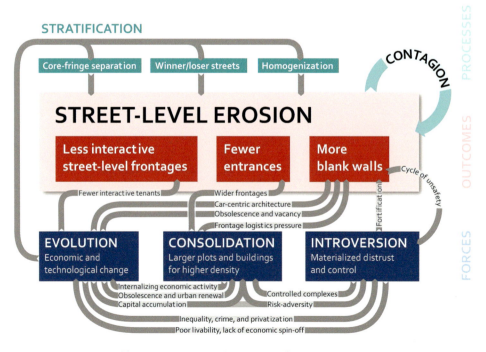

Figure 6.23 The interconnected forces, processes, and outcomes of street-level erosion.
Source: Diagram by Conrad Kickert, 2021.

for whom. A lack of understanding the self-reinforcing street-level ecosystem prompted its demise into vacancy or homogeneity or its replacement. We should harness our understanding of this ecosystem for more sustainable solutions. A lack of interest in listening to and observing people prompted many inhumane interventions without a cause or a future. By the late 1970s, none of our urban cores had been spared these mistakes.

What sets our cities apart today is how they emerged. Here too, we can recognize shared design, planning, and development lessons to pursue a path toward a vibrant city at eye-level. In their own way and at their own pace, all four cities now understand the merit of humanly scaled, walkable urbanism. At the vanguard, The Hague and Vancouver fought back against urban freeway construction and megaprojects that denied street-level intricacy before they could destroy most of their urban cores; Detroit and Birmingham are still recovering from being too late to prevent these mistakes. Each city is investing in pedestrian-oriented public space, and most cities understand the role of interactive street-level architecture to feed their squares and sidewalks. Some have adopted design policies to mandate interactive architecture, and some enforce these policies. Others continue to rely on market forces to reconnect buildings with sidewalks, with mixed success.

The most successful strategies to counter street-level deactivation understand the complex dynamics described in this chapter. They understand that interactive architecture is about more than just transparency, storefronts, or doorways. Successful street-level architecture is not just conceived by professionals, but experienced and shaped every day by tenants and passersby, forming a barometer of a city's social, economic, and cultural health. In other words, they understand frontages as more than just a space, but as a vessel for interactive inhabitation and a connotation of trust – a place. As such, they understand that activating street-level architecture takes more than just well-intended design of singular buildings and frontages – it takes a critical mass of symbiotic space, inhabitation, and trust that can only come from collaborating with a range of different stakeholders beyond architects and urban designers. Designers can turn the levers on many of the forces and processes described in this chapter, but they cannot turn them by themselves. Yet we need to pull all the levers we have to battle the many cards stacked against interactive frontages.

The second part of this book will describe which levers we have to activate and reactivate our urban ground floors. Approaching our frontages not just as designed spaces, but inhabited places that should exude a sense of trust and interaction, the following chapters describe strategies for frontage reactivation categorized by the main inhabitants of frontages: commercial businesses, public amenities, workspaces, and residents. Each inhabitant has their own relationship with the ground floor, the sidewalk, and the city, each of which can be enhanced through various strategies. Each of these strategies understands frontages as an interrelation between their form, their function, and their meaning, both for inhabitants and passersby. Only by comprehending and acting on all three elements of this interrelation can we come to a true architecture of public life.

Notes

1 R. MacCormac, "Urban Reform: Maccormac's Manifesto," *Architects Journal* 15 (1983).

2 Numbers from Dutch and American censuses and various government reports. For more information, see Conrad Kickert, "Active Centers – Interactive Edges" (PhD Thesis, University of Michigan, 2014).

3 "Dream City: Creation, Destruction, and Reinvention in Downtown Detroit," (2019); Carol Willis, *Form Follows Finance: Skyscrapers and Skylines in New York and Chicago* (New York: Princeton Architectural Press, 1995).

4 J. Gehl, "Close Encounters with Buildings," *Urban Design International* 11 (2006).

5 Kim Dovey and Felicity Symons, "Density Without Intensity and What to Do About It: Reassembling Public/Private Interfaces in Melbourne's Southbank Hinterland," *Australian Planner* 51, no. 1 (2014).

6 The process of land consolidation for raising density has been described in New York by architectural historian Carol Willis: Willis, *Form Follows Finance: Skyscrapers and Skylines in New York and Chicago*.

7 See e.g. Conrad Kickert, "Urban Retail," in *A Research Agenda for New Urbanism*, ed. Emily Talen (Cheltenham: Edward Elgar, 2019); David Kooijman D. C. Krabben Erwin van der Evers, *Planning Van Winkels En Winkelgebieden in Nederland* (Den Haag: Sdu Uitgevers, 2011).

8 For more information on these two blocks, see Conrad Kickert, "The Other Side of Shopping Centres: Retail Transformation in Downtown Detroit and the Hague," in *The Shopping Centre*, eds. Janina Gosseye and Tom Avermaete (Conference Proceeding, Delft, Netherlands, 2015).

9 Nan Ellin, *Postmodern Urbanism* (Cambridge, MA: Blackwell, 1996).

10 Bigness is coined in R. Koolhaas and B. Mau, *S, M, L, Xl* (New York: Monacelli, 1995).

11 W. H. Whyte, *City: Rediscovering the Center*, 1st ed. (New York: Doubleday, 1988), 226.

12 A description of the residence of an elderly lady on the Bagijnestraat, just north of the district in "Hoe Arm Den Haag Woont," *De Stedelijke Courant*, December 3, 1908.

13 A cited comment by architect Carel Weeber on the ministry towers in Gerda van Mast Michiel van der Beek, *Van Ambachtelijk Tot Ambtelijk: Het Spuikwartier Door De Eeuwen Heen* ('s-Gravenhage: Staatsuitgeverij, 1978), 76.

14 Maryanne Conheim, "The Shocking State of the Riverfront: Our Most Abused Asset," *Detroit Free Press*, April 13, 1975.

15 First quotes from Staff Reporter, "Ford Motor Plans 'Save Detroit' Project, $400 Million Housing-Hotel-Office Complex," *Wall Street Journal*, November 26, 1971. Second quote from Michael Maidenberg, "Riverfront Project – Now It's Renaissance Center," *Detroit Free Press*, March 23, 1973.

16 Maryanne Conheim, "Riverfront Center to Be Shielded by 25-Foot Wall," *Detroit Free Press*, October 23; June Hicks, "Grim Wall Is a Challenge," *Detroit News*, December 10, 1976; Dave Anderson, "Renaissance Front Walls to Become Exotic Garden," *Detroit Free Press*, November 15, 1976.

17 Quote from Jay Carr, "Rencen, Don't Turn Your Back on Old Detroit," *Detroit News*, March 20, 1977. National commentary include Thomas C. Fox, "Parking Woes Grow Along with Rencen," *Detroit Free Press*, September 25, 1978; Whyte, *City: Rediscovering the Center*.

18 John Portman, interview by Paul Goldberger, 1988, Transcript in Paolo Riani, "John Portman," 1991.

19 Quote from Carr, "Rencen, Don't Turn Your Back on Old Detroit." See also George Bullard, "An a-Maze-Ing Place to Get Lost," *Detroit Free Press*, April 12, 1981.

20 Quote from "View from the Top," *Detroit Free Press*, April 20, 1978.

21 Peter Gavrilovich, "Marketing a Renaissance – Problem: Take 39 Floors X 4 and Fill . . ." *Detroit Free Press*, August 22, 1976; Jeffrey Hadden and Christopher Willcox, "Older Buildings Feel Effect of Tenant Shift to Ren Cen," *Detroit News*, June 22, 1977. Thomas C. Fox, "Need for Parking Gobbling Dozens of City's Buildings," *Detroit Free Press*, January 29, 1978.

22 On the renovations, see Suzanne Stephens, "Project Diary – Som's Radical Renovation in Detroit, the G.M. Renaissance Center, Raises Hopes for John Portman's Famous Icon of the 1970s," *Architectural Record* 194, no. 2 (2006).

23 Robert M. Fogelson, *Downtown: Its Rise and Fall, 1880–1950* (New Haven: Yale University Press, 2001).

24 Therefore, many urban core policies seek to banish these shutters.

25 E.g. R. M. Hurd, *Principles of Land Values* (New York: The Record and Guide, 1903); Ernest Watson Burgess, Roderick Duncan McKenzie, and Louis Wirth, *The City* (Chicago, IL: University of Chicago Press, 1925); Homer Hoyt, *One Hundred Years of Land Values in Chicago* (Chicago, IL: University of Chicago Press, 1933). For an overview of retail theory, see also Conrad Kickert, "Retail," in *A Research Agenda for New Urbanism*, ed. Talen (Cheltenham: Edward Elgar, 2019).

26 This process is described in far more quantitative detail for Detroit, Birmingham, and The Hague in Conrad Kickert et al., "Spatial Dynamics of Long-Term Urban Retail Decline in Three Transatlantic Cities," *Cities* 107 (2020). Vancouver was left out of this study as its number of retailers increased due to downtown growth.

27 Fringe belts have been discovered in many cities by urban morphologists to decline in economic and morphological activity. JWR Whitehand, "Urban Fringe Belts: Development of an Idea," *Planning perspectives* 3, no. 1 (1988); M. P. Conzen, "How Cities Internalize Their Former Urban Fringers: A Cross-Cultural Comparison," *Urban Morphology* 13, no. 1 (2009).

28 For more on this process, see Chapter 2 and Kickert, "Dream City: Creation, Destruction, and Reinvention in Downtown Detroit."

29 This measurement is of street segments in or adjacent to renewal areas, comparing their average interactivity change during a renewal era (scored fully interactive as 2, semi-interactive as 1, and inactive as 0) to the overall interactivity change of the entire urban core by deduction. Street segments with no interactivity or business frontage left either in 2018 or after their immediate urban renewal were not included in the calculation for mathematical reasons. For more detail, see Kickert, "Active Centers – Interactive Edges."

30 Jane Jacobs, *The Death and Life of Great American Cities* (New York: Random House, 1961).

31 We have calculated a Gini coefficient for street segments as follows:

$$\text{Gini Coefficient}\left(\text{interactivity}\right) = 1 - \frac{2}{n-1}\left(n - \frac{\sum_{i=1}^{n} iy_i}{\sum_{i=1}^{n} y_i}\right)$$

where n is the number of values in the interactivity dataset, i is the bucket of interactivity and y is the interactivity value. This coefficient increased 9% in The Hague, yet 152% in Detroit.

32 New Economics Foundation, *Clone Town Britain: The Loss of Local Identity on the Nation's High Streets* (London: New Economics Foundation, 2004); New Economics Foundation, *Clone Town Britain, the Survey Results on the Bland State of the Nation* (London: New Economics Foundation, 2005).

33 Jacobs, *The Death and Life of Great American Cities*, 251.

34 The Simpson Index is calculated as follows:

$$\text{Diversity} = \frac{\sum_{i=1}^{R} n_i\left(n_i - 1\right)}{N\left(N-1\right)}$$

Where n_i is the number of frontages of type i and N is the total number of frontages in the sample, with R number of types. In Detroit and The Hague recognizes 27 types of land uses, which include four types of retail (run, fun, destination and bar/restaurant) were recognized between 1911 and 2011. The Simpson Index was calculated for a 50 meter radius around each frontage. For more detail, see Kickert, "Active Centers – Interactive Edges."

35 In: Jacobs, *The Death and Life of Great American Cities*, 259.

36 This pattern is similar for accelerated decline of business frontage. See Kickert, "Active Centers – Interactive Edges," 425–32.

37 The definition of 'chance a frontage becomes vacant' is defined as the percentage of active frontages in interval *t-1* that fell vacant in interval *t*. This chance is compared between frontages less than 20 meters from an already vacant frontage and more than 20 meters (66 feet) away. This distance is chosen as it includes buildings across the average street width:

$$\left(\frac{\text{number of newly vacant frontages in interval } t \text{ within } 20m \text{ of } >1 \text{ vacant frontages in interval } t-1}{\text{number of active frontages in interval } t-1 \text{ within } 20m \text{ of } >1 \text{ vacant frontages in interval } t-1} \right)$$

$$\frac{\text{number of newly vacant frontages in interval } t \text{ within } 20m \text{ of } 0 \text{ vacant frontages in interval } t-1}{\text{number of active frontages in interval } t-1 \text{ within } 20m \text{ of } 0 \text{ vacant frontages in interval } t-1} \Big) -1$$

38 The increased chance a building is demolished without replacement within 20 meters of an existing vacant or parking lot is 163.3%. This follows a similar mathematic to the previous calculation.

39 This study was conducted in Birmingham, Detroit, and The Hague, as Vancouver saw significant business growth. Two journal papers have statistically investigated the effects of agglomeration (the number of nearby businesses) on business closure: Conrad Kickert and Rainer vom Hofe, "Critical Mass Matters: The Long-Term Benefits of Retail Agglomeration for Establishment Survival in Downtown Detroit and the Hague," *Urban Studies* 55, no. 5 (2017); Kickert et al., "Spatial Dynamics of Long-Term Urban Retail Decline in Three Transatlantic Cities." Each has taken a slightly different mathematical approach; the 4 to 7% increased closure risk is calculated as follows:

$$Pt(Bx) = (B\_x \text{ (closed)})/(B\_x \text{ (total)})$$

Where $Pt(Bx)$ is the chance a business with characteristics X closes between time interval t and t+1, Bx(closed) is the number of businesses with characteristics X closing between time interval t and t+1, and Bx(total) is the total number of businesses with characteristics X in time interval t. Because the measurement time intervals vary in duration, the chance of business closures is annualized by the formula:

$$P(Bx) = 1 - [\![(1 - Pt(B\_x))]\!]^{\wedge}((1/\Delta t))$$

Where $P(Bx)$ is the annual chance a business with characteristics X closes, and $Pt(Bx)$ is the chance as business with characteristics X closes between time interval t and t+1, and Δt is the time difference in years between time interval t and t+1. The chance of closure is controlled against the average chance of business closure in an interval. This is done as follows:

$$cP(Bx) = (P(B\_x))/(P(B\_all)) - 1$$

Where $cP(Bx)$ is the above/below average annual chance a business with characteristics X closes, $P(Bx)$ is the annual chance a business with characteristics X closes, and $P(Ball)$ is the annual chance any business (i.e. all businesses) closes. Following a panel regression, we find a 4.1% decreased annual chance of a business closing in Detroit per additional business within 50 meters (164 feet), and a 7.0% decreased annual chance of a business closing in The Hague per additional business within 50 meters.

40 On urban attrition see: Jacobs, *The Death and Life of Great American Cities*, 339.

7 COMMERCIAL LIFE
EYE-LEVEL TRANSACTIONS IN THE CITY

Figure 7.0 Commercial life in a Parisian arcade.
Source: Image by Conrad Kickert, 2014.
DOI: 10.4324/9781003041887-7

One of the most visible transformations of the city at eye level has been the decline of storefront commerce, reflecting a shift of consumer transactions to suburbia and cyberspace. We see storefront lights go out at alarming rates, even if we understand that far beyond just 'pure' retailers that sell merchandise, our urban storefronts include food services like bars, restaurants, and coffee shops and personal services like salons and repair shops. Storefront decline is certainly not new: in almost all four cities we just studied, street-level commerce has steadily declined for more than a century, especially beyond their busiest and most central streets. There is a profound sense of loss when storefronts lose their commercial function, and for good reason: shops, bars, restaurants, and services build the kind of mixed-use urbanism that many of us prefer as places to live, work, or at least visit. Storefronts don't just add urban excitement, they are a cornerstone of walkable, sociable, equitable, and innovative cities.[1]

As a result of this key role, most popular, professional, and academic discussions about street-level architecture focus on commercial storefronts. Far beyond architecture and materiality, the decline of street-level commerce is a manifestation of a range of underlying systems that affect the relevance and success of storefronts. Before focusing on the architecture of storefronts, this chapter therefore first presents these systems to better understand how to retain and restore storefront commerce. Over the past century, market conditions, regulatory regimes, and urban spatial structures have all been stacked against the fine-grained street-level commerce we all seek, and current challenges are only mounting. In today's commercial climate, everything has to be just right for a successful commercial storefront, from setting proper expectations to the right location, experience, time, management, policies – and yes, the right design. This chapter describes how choreographing these success factors can help maintain and revitalize existing storefronts and build successful new commercial spaces at street level.

Set the right storefront expectations

First, we need to set our expectations for street-level commerce. Even including food services and personal services (which combined take up more urban storefronts than retailers!), we tend to want too much street-level commercial space. Just look at the average urban plan or design for new or existing districts, and we recognize the public and political pressure for block after block of storefronts. Even if they aren't forced by these policies, developers of new urban projects will gladly comply to build new storefronts at a loss, as they can add upstairs value.[2]

Storefronts are one of the few types of urban development that we seemingly cannot get enough of.

Yet San Francisco urban designer Benjamin Grant explains, "Planners don't create cafes (or restaurants or grocery stores) and for the most part, neither do developers. Entrepreneurs do."[3] We need to understand how entrepreneurs thrive in the fine grained, walkable pattern of shops, bars, restaurants, and services we want, or risk yearning for the reflection of an economic system long gone. Ironically, we seem to long for the fine-grained, fixed, independent storefront (itself but a blip in retail history after market stalls and traveling tradesmen) but resist to understand that the "democratization of luxury" by chains, department stores, and the internet has come at a price to storefronts. Corner store proprietors and their families working around the clock to maintain their shop in light of growing and more efficient competition have become rare species. Nor is the kind of customer that can support their business.[4]

In today's age, there is only so much urban commerce to go around. But how much? Figure 7.1 aims to provide some useful average numbers for cities. Probably the most often-cited statistic is how much retail floor space citizens have at their disposal – a commonly used statistic to demonstrate that America in particular is over-retailed. But instead of relying on national averages, it is far more useful to look at averages of the kind of walkable urban environments we aim for with good street-level architecture – away from the massive superstores and shopping malls that skew results. In walkable cities on either side of the Atlantic, numbers are actually surprisingly consistent. Whether in New York, Amsterdam, or Paris, citizens have about 25 to 35 square feet (2.5 to 3.5 square meters) of commercial space at their disposal (with outliers in more suburbanized cities like Toronto and San Francisco), and there are about 15 to 25 commercial businesses per 1,000 inhabitants (again, with an outlier in Toronto). Remember, these include retailers, but also food services and personal services – any business that activates a storefront. For walkable retail, the *number* of retailers almost matters more than the amount of *space* per capita, as commercial main streets benefit far more from a large number of smaller retailers than the other way around. America's abundant store shelves occupy suburban big box stores rather than urban businesses, which is why the country actually has one of the *lowest* number of retail establishments per capita across the Western world. In planning for retail, think in terms of separate business more than in terms of space.[5]

While commercial establishments per capita are a useful indicator to let us know how many interactive storefronts we can expect, averages can glance over the wide spectrum of locations and types of street-level businesses. A citywide average doesn't tell much about

COMMERCIAL LIFE – EYE-LEVEL TRANSACTIONS IN THE CITY 131

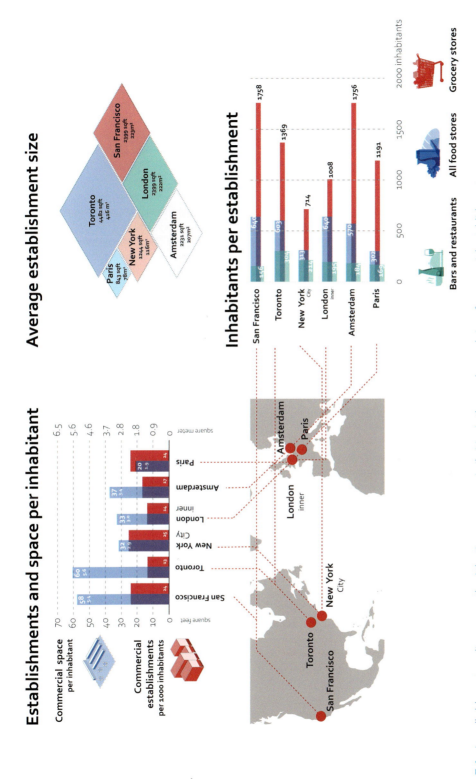

Figure 7.1 In walkable metropolises across the Atlantic, we can see similarities in the number and size of commercial establishments. Source: Diagram by Conrad Kickert, 2021; numbers for 2017–2018, sourced from census records, government and private databases.

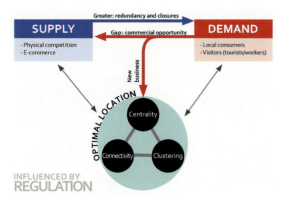

Figure 7.2 For each type of business, commercial success depends on finding a gap between supply and demand, and filling that gap in the right location. Regulation influences all of these factors differently in different markets.
Source: Diagram by Conrad Kickert, 2021.

the success of one specific business in one location, which depends on a complex interaction between supply, demand, space, and regulation (Figure 7.2). For each storefront business, whether existing or new, we need to know their desired location and size; the location and amount of competition; and the location, type, and amount of consumer demand. Successful businesses fill a niche that competitors don't address, and serve the right kind of customers with the right amount of disposable income and willingness to spend. They fill this niche in the right kind of space, permitted by the right regulations. Increasingly advanced models use this logic to calculate the right amount of businesses and space for existing and new storefronts. These models not only know the supply side of locations and competition; they mainly hinge on understanding the demand side through 'psychographic' profiles of a market area, which segments consumer groups along income levels, but also age, education, ethnicity, and other demographic factors. After all, retailers need the right amount of the right kind of consumers: think of boutique cookware stores that rely on a sufficient number of families with a sufficient income level and lifestyle that supports cooking. While knowing when and where to open, close, or refurbish a business remains an intuitive 'art,' these models and profiles now define much of the 'science' of these decisions.[6] They are mainly used by consultants and larger retailers, but also by governments: in many European countries, supply and demand calculations are a planning permission requirement for new commercial developments, especially above a certain size.[7] Unfortunately, access to these advanced models often remains out of reach to smaller and independent businesses.

Different types of street-level commerce have vastly different needs for clientele to survive and thrive. A corner grocer may get by on a few hundred (local) customers, but a comparison store that sells high-end shoes will need thousands if not hundreds of thousands of well-heeled customers. Similarly, our corner pub may function as a neighborhood meeting place; a Michelin-star restaurant needs to draw a national if not international audience. Figure 7.1 compares how many citizens it takes for three types of businesses that satisfy our hunger for local urbanity and nourishment: any food store (including for example ethnic and boutique stores), a full grocery store, and a food service provider like a bar, restaurant, coffee shop, or lunchroom. In these broad categories, we see significant similarities: it takes about 200 citizens to support a bar, restaurant, coffee shop, or lunchroom, and about twice to three times that amount to support a food store, and about four to five times to support a full grocery store. However, we also see significant cultural differences: Parisians are notably more enthralled by food, both supporting more stores (also through national subsidies for independent specialty food stores) and more places to eat and drink. Compared to San Franciscans, Torontonians have less of a public dining and drinking culture, which also aligns with their stricter provincial laws on alcohol consumption.[8] These cultural differences make general averages and rules of thumb difficult to use. This becomes more glaringly apparent when we compare more specialized retailers: fashionable Parisians have nearly five times the number of shoe stores per capita than Torontonians.[9]

In conclusion: the more accurate data we have for supply, demand, space, and regulation, and the more advanced the computer model to process this data, the more accurate estimations will be of the right amount of commercial space, the less chance of storefront redundancy, cannibalization, and vacancy.

Choose the right storefront location

Commerce does not simply thrive in any urban location. Storefront businesses need consumers to be able to easily discover and access them. Besides marketing and running a good business, much of this discovery and access depends on the right location for businesses in the city, which hinges on three key factors we also recognized in the previous chapter. Commerce thrives in the right place in the city (Centrality), on the right street (Connectivity), and with the right neighbors (Clustering). These three Cs actually also strongly interrelate.[10]

As we mentioned before, different types of businesses have different needs for their clientele and trade areas; this also strongly affects their locational needs. Let's return to the food store versus the shoe store we discussed in the previous section. Food stores serve the daily to weekly needs of their direct vicinity of a few hundred to a few thousand customers. Similarly, a local pub or barber fit into this category, which thrives on convenience and proximity to customers. This type of business therefore locates itself relatively evenly throughout the city in a fine-grained pattern of solitary stores or small neighborhood business clusters. In larger cities, people can usually walk or bike to them, although the proliferation of larger supermarkets in North America, along with a culture of weekly grocery trips versus Europe's daily errands prompts the need for car parking. The resulting neighborhood business clusters often also contain specialty retailers that serve a specific ethnicity or income bracket – which may function as citywide or even regional destinations. Non-daily needs businesses need to access a larger trade area to stay in business. Think of destination stores like hardware and furniture stores, higher-end or specialty restaurants, but also stores that sell comparison goods like our shoe store. They need to access far more customers, and they can pay higher rents to be in the right place for this access – from key intersections to our urban cores or our most prestigious shopping malls. Retail and restaurant chains are generally able to pay the highest rents for the most central locations, which is why our intersections, urban cores, and malls are so homogeneous with chains.

The higher up the business food chain, the more we need to think of accessibility beyond a local stroll or bike ride. It is no coincidence that the Parisian department stores are located at the confluence of citywide and regional metro lines; nor can we ignore that regional-serving retailers or restaurants in North America need ample parking. As different types of businesses have different needs and abilities to access customers, we see a constellation of different 'tiers' of centers, each with a stratification of businesses along their ability to afford centrality. Specifically, we see a fine-grained pattern of many smaller daily needs centers in our cities, with fewer larger non-daily centers, all the way to national-serving downtowns and malls where we can compare the greatest range of goods. This phenomenon was first modeled almost a century ago by German economist Walter Christaller and remains at the heart of many public and private strategies and regulations for commerce today (Figure 7.3).[11] In urban settings, tiers of centers and businesses may blend together – think of the neighborhood business street with some nationally renowned specialty stores. Nevertheless, it remains wise to understand what kind of hinterland your existing or new storefront is serving, which strongly influences its rent level, its likely tenant, and its location needs. The more central and accessible your storefront is, the higher its rent is likely to be, which may render it too expensive for local-serving or independent businesses. In return, don't expect a high-end shoe store to thrive in a solitary urban location, either. As mentioned, solitary corner storefronts rarely do well, unless it is a destination business like a hardware store, or there is a very high number of nearby customers.

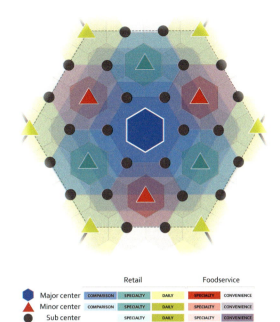

Figure 7.3 Commerce agglomerates into a hierarchy of different centers, which each serve different hinterlands with a different combination of businesses.
Source: Diagram by Conrad Kickert, 2021, based on Christaller, 1933.

Centrality strongly relates to accessibility: being in the right place to be visible and accessible to (potential) customers (Figure 7.4). Business success is more than just about being in a location that is easy to access to consumers. Once they emerge from their bicycle, train, or car, people still need to walk to or past businesses to become customers. This essentially depends on a more detailed definition of the right location: the type of space that attracts pedestrian 'footfall'. All businesses benefit from more people passing by their storefront, but especially businesses that depend on serendipitous purchases are keen to lure them in – especially those non-daily fashion stores or gift shops. Economists have related the amount of footfall to business success for well over a century, which has fueled an industry of pedestrian data counters like Experian and Locatus in Europe, using new technologies like GPS, Bluetooth, and WiFi to study pedestrian behavior.[12]

While counting pedestrian passersby is certainly is a good predictor for retail success, counts cannot predict future pedestrian (consumer) flows when new streets or buildings open. Devised over the past decades, several modeling techniques can increasingly accurately predict pedestrian behavior. Each of these models have their own assumptions and methods, and hence strengths and weaknesses. Early models of pedestrian behavior as a linked series of decisions have evolved into complex computer-powered 'agent-based' models.[13]

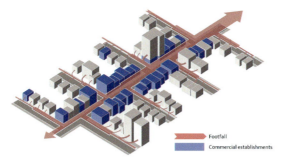

Figure 7.4 Urban commerce thrives on footfall, generated by the thousands of trips between our cities' front doors. Well-connected streets absorb many of our trips, which makes them suitable for business.
Source: Diagram by Conrad Kickert, 2021.

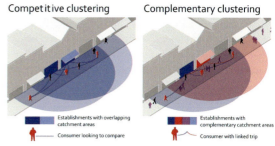

Figure 7.5 Clustering is fueled by competition (left), but also allows complementary businesses to attract more combined customers seeking compatible items or services (right).
Source: Diagram by Conrad Kickert, 2021.

Another approach models pedestrian behavior from the perspective of the 'social logic' or 'space syntax' of the urban configuration of streets and public spaces. Space Syntax research argues that well-connected and well-integrated streets attract pedestrian activity and hence retail activity.[14] In North America, urban researcher Andres Sevtsuk models the 'betweenness' of streets from consumers to destinations, finding that stores are often located en route in his modeled mobility patterns.[15] Of course, beyond the location of the street, the quality of the street itself also strongly affects the success of businesses that line it, as proven by various studies throughout Europe.[16] In practice, the footfall of a street strongly reflects in commercial rent levels, known as A, B, or C streets, with the latter fetching far lower rents, as they attract fewer pedestrians. As we will have seen in the past chapter, the most peripheral streets are at the highest risk of losing their critical mass of retailers.

Perhaps more than anything else, the right neighbors matter to street-level businesses. Clustering is incredibly important to the survival of individual establishments, especially if they sell more specialized items or services that people tend to compare before they buy. A critical mass of surrounding compatible businesses matter at for commercial success at several levels and for several reasons. First, bigger clusters, especially with complementary businesses, simply have a bigger draw to consumers. After Christaller recognized agglomerations, subsequent economists ascribed a gravitational pull to larger centers, as customers love to compare and obtain multiple items and services in one trip.[17] Furthermore, retailers love to locate close to competitors to maximize their catchment area overlap and take business, conveniently minimizing consumers' risk not to find what they need.[18] Beyond competition, retailers also like to benefit from the overflow sales of complementary neighbors, such as the baker that locates next to a butcher, or the popcorn stand next to the cinema. They want to become part of our linked purchase trip, which actually makes up the majority of our shopping trips through cities (Figure 7.5).[19] Business complementarity builds the success of our markets and food halls, but also our entertainment districts. Key commercial and noncommercial destinations such as department stores and supermarkets, but also public buildings such as libraries or city offices can draw bigger crowds and subsequently generate significant commercial spill-over sales. Together with source points like transit stations and parking facilities, these are considered anchors to a successful commercial area. Mall operators actually subsidize these anchors to attract customers to smaller businesses that pay most of the mall rent. Knowing and fine tuning the 'affinities' between anchors and other businesses increases the amount of money spent per commercial trip, but centralized mall ownership makes this a far easier task than herding dozens or hundreds of independent urban retail landlords. More about this later.[20]

At street level, clusters also matter physiologically, visually, and psychologically. First, commercial clusters tend to restrict to a walkable size of about a quarter mile (or 500 meters), as customers do not want to walk further from other means of transportation, especially carrying merchandise.[21] Of course, clusters can blend together, especially in urban cores extending into longer commercial ribbons. Second, the case study cities have demonstrated what happens when gaps appear in formerly continuous business streets: they experience accelerated decline, as consumers may think the business cluster has ended and turn around, and they may feel an area is on the decline in general. Our case studies also demonstrated that clustering has been the single most powerful predictor of business survival of all of the three C locational factors, especially for pure retailers.[22]

It is therefore imperative to make sure that business remains clustered. When planning new storefronts (only if there is need for them, as mentioned in the previous section), they should be located close if not adjacent to existing storefront businesses. Almost any business benefits from clustering – even local-serving businesses

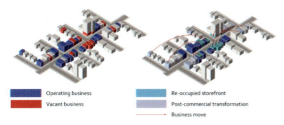

Figure 7.6 When commercial vacancies mount, commercial re-concentration can ensure the symbiosis of a more compact business cluster.
Source: Diagram by Conrad Kickert, 2021.

like grocers can spin off sales to nearby specialty stores. After calculating the number and type of businesses and sales space needed, the resulting amount should be clustered according to the proposed tier of cluster and the type of business (e.g., a small convenience cluster or a larger comparison shopping cluster). Balancing the right amount of space and establishments for the right tenants is very important: if clusters are planned too small, the success rate of businesses will suffer due to a lack of agglomeration and spillover between businesses; if clusters are planned too large, businesses may scatter and harm their own viability.

When vacant storefronts appear along existing business streets, they should be filled as soon as possible, or when gaps are too big, businesses should consider reconsolidating into a smaller yet contiguous cluster. Reconsolidating raises significant legal and financial difficulties, which usually requires government intervention to overcome. Yet this is easier said than done. Over the past few years, many European municipalities have tightened the boundaries of their legally defined and protected retail cores to re-concentrate remaining businesses within, and open storefronts to post-commercial transformations beyond (Figure 7.6). This land use re-designation may take years to prompt an actual commercial shift, but it can set the wheels in motion for more assertive reconsolidation strategies. For example, German, French, Spanish, and Dutch cities are experimenting with 're-parceling' retail business and building owners, by assembling and then strategically redistributing retail zoning rights – essentially, redistributing the building values that rise or fall with a commercial designation.[23] European and North American cities and regions have also actively acquired vacant retail properties to recirculate them into retail or repurpose them for other street-level uses – more about this later.[24]

Mix the right storefront business

While we have discussed *how many* street-level storefront businesses can thrive in a place and *where* they can thrive, location and space are only part of the picture for the future of our storefronts. We need to look ahead to understand *what kind* of businesses are likely to thrive in the nearby future, and why. The street-level commercial landscape is changing more rapidly than ever before, with the rise of e-commerce and the experience economy providing us with an array of challenges and opportunities. This section describes what kind of tenants we should expect over the next decade – about as far as we can reasonably look ahead.

While they tend to take up less than half of the storefronts in our cities,[25] much of the current discourse on street-level commerce focuses on the rapid transformation of the 'pure' retail industry, comprising stores that sell merchandise to consumers. They take up the brunt of street-level commercial decline, and their decline is only accelerating.[26] Yet instead of a 'retail apocalypse', we should see ourselves in the midst of a retail revolution, not unlike past revolutions like permanent stores, fixed pricing, and self-service.[27] E-commerce is the biggest presumed structural threat to physical retail, yet its impacts vary widely across different retail categories. Especially physical sales of durable, non-daily purchases that are easy to ship and useful to compare before buying, like office supplies, consumer electronics, home and leisure goods, and fashion, have suffered from the rise of e-commerce. In these categories, physical (chain) stores offer few service and ambiance advantages.[28] The urban effects of the loss of durable retailers highly vary by country, as American cities have moved these to suburban malls decades ago, yet European urban centers should brace for impact.[29] E-commerce mostly impacts middle-class stores, prompting a 'bifurcation' of physical retail toward low-end and high-end stores. Again, the European High Street with its chain stores is notably vulnerable here.[30]

Most of our consumer spending goes to our basic daily needs: groceries. Grocery delivery is seen as the next frontier for e-commerce: it is notoriously difficult to profitably pick and ship groceries due to their odd sizes and thin margins, and consumers remain hesitant to buy fresh items before seeing them in person. Yet, the incredible size of this market has prompted larger corporations to make big leaps in order-picking and last-mile delivery technology. The COVID-19 pandemic only accelerated their push. Expect aggressive investments by larger retailers to overtake smaller urban grocers and specialty food stores that cannot pay the high cost of online fulfillment infrastructure.[31] The fine-grained landscape of walkable grocery stores may be under threat. However, ubiquitous online grocery delivery may also combat inequalities in food access, which helps livability in low-income food deserts.[32] Furthermore, a countermovement has emerged to online and chain dominance in food access, focusing on sustainable, local, and healthy foods, fueling the rise of vibrant and often innovative urban food markets and hybrid online-physical formats – at least to those who can afford it.[33] Grocery e-commerce may still leave room for fine-grained convenience retail, which can in turn expect to see the rise of automation – for those retailers that can afford to keep up.

Physical and e-commerce is not necessarily adversarial, nor binary. Online-first and traditional retailers both understand the value of physical stores, which can offer consumers instant gratification, better service, physical interaction with merchandise, and social interaction with others. Successful retailers now blend the best of online and physical retail 'channels' in multichannel or omnichannel strategies. Physical retailers open online storefronts, using their shops as showrooms and collection points, and virtual retailers open physical storefronts to let consumers interact with their merchandise, staff, and brand.[34] Besides convenience, physical retail benefits are hence mainly experiential. Saturated with all the goods they need, a growing cohort of middle-class consumers now looks for novelty, authenticity, and differentiation in the "experience economy".[35] Experiential retail makes the shopping environment as important as the product or service for sale, transforming stores from places to make a sale to places to show yourselves to passersby and interact with products. This changes the role of storefronts from places of transaction to what retail expert Heather Arnold calls "three-dimensional advertisements", places to connect consumers to merchandise and brands.[36]

Especially urban storefronts with a sense of place have an experiential edge, as retailers seek to connect their brand or offerings to this experiential value. In the attention economy of screens and swipes,[37] the immersive experience of a remarkable urban storefront counts – especially in destinations that attract well-heeled customers. The average experiential store can be smaller, as retailers have to keep fewer items on their shelves, instead focusing on maximizing their (window) displays. Even suburban big-box retailers are now willing to shrink their massive floorplates to come closer to middle-class urban audiences (Figure 7.7). Whatever doesn't fit in the store can be ordered from the store for home delivery; vice versa, physical stores serve as online order pick-up points.

While this omnichannel, experiential future may sound like the saving grace of our urban storefronts, its blessings are mixed. Like with grocery deliveries, the expensive infrastructure to make omnichannel retail work hurts the chances of smaller and independent retailers to keep up. Big boxes entering urban markets will inevitably siphon off sales from dozens of independent competitors. Furthermore, many retail startups may forgo physical stores altogether and just sell their goods online.[38] This is a shame, as research consistently shows that independent businesses often activate and enliven sidewalks more than chains through their intimate knowledge of and interest in passersby. Furthermore, they contribute more of their sales back into the local economy, and in turn provide more inclusive entrepreneurial opportunities.[39] Cities and national governments have devised a range of policies to protect independent commerce, from San Francisco's outright ban on chains with more than ten outlets in defined areas to more widespread curbs on the size of commercial spaces, making them less attractive to space-hungry chains. Thus far, these regulations have mixed results as chains find loopholes and independent retailers are not necessarily more affordable or useful to local residents, especially those with lower disposable incomes. Instead, vibrant and accessible commercial clusters rely on a balance of chains and independent businesses.[40]

Beyond changing the retail landscape, the experience economy has fueled the meteoric rise of food service establishments like restaurants, bars, coffee shops, and lunchrooms in urban storefronts, especially those with a strong experiential value. For example, the number

Figure 7.7a–b (a) Online-first glasses retailer Warby Parker has opened physical stores in young professional destinations throughout the United States, including this store in Cincinnati's Over-the-Rhine neighborhood. **(b)** Big box warehouses shrink their formats to cater to urban dwellers, such as this Target store in Cincinnati's Clifton Heights neighborhood, below two floors of offices. *Source: Both images by Conrad Kickert, 2020.*

of specialty coffee shops in America has increased by double digits almost each year since the 1990s, and other countries are not far behind. Craft breweries are seeing similar growth rates.[41] After decades of growth, food services now occupy between a quarter to a third of our urban storefronts, and despite economic and health disruptions we can expect this number to only rise further. Often catering to younger, upscale urbanites, our corner grocer may well have turned into the next coffee house or microbrewer on the block. Food and beverage establishments are more than just spaces to consume, they often form neighborhood 'third places' that facilitate meaningful social and business encounters, serving as cornerstones in the creative economy.[42] These establishments can also become focal points for 'foodie culture', drawing visitors and residents to urban districts.[43]

As Europe and North America's appetite has moved from kitchens to restaurants over the past decades, the experiential shops-to-hops transition can bring new public life to streets and storefronts, but also raise the pressure to convert sidewalk space for outdoor drinking and dining – more about this at the end of this chapter. Furthermore, the rise of eating and drinking establishments may clash with nearby residents' need for quiet, which poses a permitting challenge for cities and a design opportunity for architects. Last but not least, gentrification by upscale coffee houses, bars, and microbreweries pose an even more complex dilemma, which can only be resolved in close collaboration with the community.[44]

Bars, restaurants and personal services can pick up some of the loss of pure retail use of storefronts. America can be seen as leading in this movement, as retail has left many urban storefronts decades ago and most revitalization strategies have since focused on food services and entertainment uses.[45] Even in Chicago, one of America's remaining viable retail cores, there are nearly twice as many food and beverage establishments as retail shops. Downtown Detroit's revival hinged on bars and restaurants, not on retail stores. Similarly, American urban neighborhoods are seeing a continued transformation from retail to food and beverage offerings.[46] For example, the revitalization of Cincinnati's Over-the-Rhine neighborhood hinged on its hip bars and restaurants, followed by compatible retailers that mostly serve experiential merchandise such as locally produced items and curated fashion. While the redevelopment process has attracted criticism over gentrification, Over-the-Rhine has become a regional leisure and experiential retail destination, which has propelled Cincinnati's most coveted dwellings upstairs – although residents are not universally happy with the neighborhood's nighttime focus (Figure 7.8).[47]

Like any experiential business that effectively thrives on discretionary spending, bars and restaurants are not immune to economic, social, and hygienic turmoil. Then again, concepts like food trucks and food hall stalls that we now hold for granted actually popularized during the 2008 recession. We can expect new concepts to emerge in future recessions – albeit with unknown consequences for permanent storefronts with higher fixed costs.[48] Food and beverage establishments are also certainly not immune to e-commerce disruption, with meal kits and delivery services eager to get their piece of the market.[49] Economic and e-commerce disruptions present mixed trends for personal services like banks, hair salons, and dry cleaners, which can take up more than a quarter of urban storefronts combined. Some of these businesses remain stable in recessions and the growth of e-commerce, as they supply us with physical necessities such as haircuts. Some even thrive in otherwise unstable times, like repair shops. Some see a structural decline, such as banks (due to ongoing virtualization of banking) and drycleaners (due to changing fashion trends). In general, this makes the fate of personal services harder to generalize. Market analysts like IBISWorld, CBRE, and Colliers present outlooks per business type.[50]

In conclusion, street-level commercial trends strongly depend on the type of business. Especially 'pure' retail stores see different trajectories. Stores that sell durable merchandise such as fashion, electronics, or household goods are losing their role as places we *need* to go for purchases, so they should become places we *want* to go for interaction – either with staff, products, and brands, but also with each other. This transition may impact European urban cores (and to a lesser extent, Canadian downtowns) more than American downtowns, as they still contain a significant amount of durable merchandise retailers. Furthermore, this experiential transition will be unequal. We can expect high-value, high-experience larger retail clusters like larger historic urban cores to thrive (albeit

Figure 7.8 Many of the revitalized storefronts in Over-the-Rhine in Cincinnati now host food and drink establishments, leading to a renewed public life, but also spurring gentrification and noise concerns for nearby residents.
Source: Image by Conrad Kickert, 2020.

with fewer retailers) as regional fun-shopping, food service, and cultural destinations. Neighborhood clusters for daily needs like groceries are now seeing the kind of e-commerce disruption that downtowns saw decades ago, but they serve an ongoing physical role in the walkable city. But especially the clusters in between – too big to just serve as local convenience centers, too small or indistinct to serve as regional destinations – will struggle to retain their relevance.[51] Similarly, retail clusters that serve lower-income markets may need public support to remain viable, or risk virtualization or closure.

Manage street-level commerce the right way

Now that we know how much street-level commerce we need, where this retail should be located, and what type of retailers are likely to thrive, how do we build and maintain a vibrant commercial street? After all, we cannot rely on single businesses, developers, or designers to create a mutually supportive ecosystem of storefronts. A successful commercial storefront cluster hinges on a mixture of acquisition, collaboration, promotion, and maintenance – tasks that require an overarching management structure. To optimize the functioning of the 'hardware' of our storefronts and the 'software' of their commercial tenants, we need coordinating 'orgware'.[52] This can take various shapes, depending on the level of control and the tasks of managing organization.

The most powerful way to manage a full cluster of urban storefronts is to simply own it. As mentioned before, mall owners benefit from being able to acquire the right business mix to maximize the destination value of their holdings and optimize spillover sales. Larger owners see the bigger picture: storefronts are a value-adding portion of their overall holdings; even when they make a loss they add value to other storefronts and upstairs spaces. However, consolidated ownership is rare for urban commercial settings, where storefronts are usually owned by a variety of different people with an even bigger variety of viewpoints and engagement. The exceptions show a significant benefit to storefront vitality. In Cincinnati's Over-the-Rhine, a single nonprofit organization owns, fills, and manages dozens of commercial spaces within the district, allowing it to pursue a more holistic mixture of compatible and attractive businesses. As demonstrated in Chapter 2, Dan Gilbert's holdings in downtown Detroit follow a similar model, where he can absorb losses from certain street-level anchor businesses to ensure a greater overall attraction to his clientele (which also live and work upstairs, often for Gilbert himself). In Toronto, a single development company has purchased and repurposed a historic distillery into a mixture of retail, leisure, dwellings, and workplaces. To target a creative class clientele, this Distillery District has attracted only independent retailers

and art galleries and studios (with subsidized rents), food and beverage establishments, and theaters. Through careful central management, the district offers its visitors a 'three-hour experience' of entertainment and discovery, including through frequent events, while bolstering the value of upper-floor condominiums and offices.[53]

Large owners can be single investors like Gilbert in Detroit, private entities like the distillery district's owner, or nonprofit institutions like Over-the-Rhine's developer and social housing corporations that own large swaths of Dutch storefronts.[54] Large owners with a social mission can inspire creative solutions for struggling commercial districts. When the Dutch neighborhood of Klarendal in Arnhem struggled with crime, drug trade, and prostitution, a partnership between residents, the city, and the neighborhood's housing corporation that owned most of its central storefronts yielded a fashion district run and occupied by recent graduates from a local arts university. Vacant storefronts were renovated and rented to a new generation of fashion designers, who were often able to live upstairs. This big push was followed by new anchor destinations like a fashion hotel, art gallery and workspace, and a street redesign. While neighborhood residents have been apprehensive of gentrification, the area now counts dozens of fashion stores and has become an award-winning national destination (Figure 7.9).[55] Nonprofits and governments can emulate consolidated ownership by land-banking vacant storefronts. In many American legacy cities, community development corporations (CDCs) have bought up clusters of empty storefronts, allowing them to reshape commercial clusters. In Europe, for example the London borough of Hackney has bought up vacant storefronts along its commercial corridors to help curate the right mix of new business tenants.[56] Of course, we can also see the downsides of consolidated ownership, as putting too many properties in the hands of a single owner increases risk of homogenization and larger impact of an owner failure.

Most commonly in cities, we see partnerships between multiple owners, governments, and dedicated managers to rebuild commercial districts. With the right approach, these partnerships can still manage acquisition, promotion, and maintenance of districts even without owning any building, simply by convincing owners and businesses that the sum of a successful commercial street is greater than its parts. The late Nel de Jager almost single-handedly introduced commercial street management in the Netherlands in the 1980s, when she propelled the city's Haarlemmerdijk from its urban renewal-induced nadir to one of the city's most vibrant commercial destinations. Initially volunteering to match some municipal building ownership and financial support to a new cohort of storefront businesses, de Jager ultimately invented her own full-time job to convince individual owners to look beyond immediate rental income for the greater good of the street. For decades,

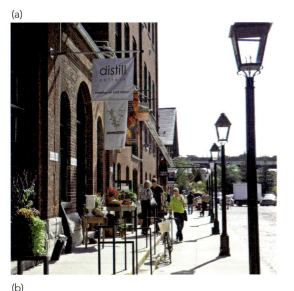

Figure 7.9a–b (a) The power of single ownership: the carefully managed historic character of Toronto's Distillery District boosts its attractiveness to visitors, residents, and workers. Many historic buildings in the former warehouse district have higher windows and fewer doors, leading to innovative solutions to creating eye-level vibrancy. (b) The power of partnerships: the Fashion District in Arnhem transformed a formerly vacant commercial district into a symbiosis between artists and visitors.
Source: Image (a) from Flickr by Payton Chung, CC-BY-2.0. Image (b) by author, 2020.

owners followed her successful vision of the street as a common "organism that grows over time" reflecting the "DNA of the neighborhood".[57] De Jager's hard work to "grease the wheels" of a commercial street has evolved into organizations that manage, promote, and beautify commercial streets. Most notably, Business Improvement Districts (BIDs) have become a staple in Canada and the United States, and they increasingly influence European commercial streets. BIDs are a step up from store owners' associations, as they are generally funded by all building owners within a defined area to prevent 'freeloading'. They also increasingly take on more tasks than beautification and promotion. While they rarely own properties outright, more than three-quarters of American BIDs do market storefronts to the right tenant mix on behalf of owners, and more than half directly engage in recruiting tenants. Yet without ownership, their toolkit for the right tenant mix remains limited.[58] BID success is not universal, and these organizations have been critiqued for prioritizing the needs of building owners (which tend to fund BIDs) over retail tenants, especially those who are smaller and less able to pay rising rents.[59]

BIDs and other management organizations are helpful in promoting districts through events and branding. As we have seen in our four case study cities, branding can be a powerful tool to bring in a larger and more targeted audience, such as the ethnic branding in Vancouver, Birmingham, and The Hague's Chinatowns and Detroit's Greektown, but also branding the aforementioned Fashion District in Arnhem. While branding can be a powerful tool to bring visitors, regeneration, and reinvestment, rebranding may risk simulation and inauthenticity.[60] The combination of economic development, design, organization, and branding mentioned in this section are the four pillars behind the Main Street approach of the American National Trust for Historic Preservation, which is used in hundreds of smaller and larger commercial centers across the country.[61] In Europe, management models vary widely between countries, usually dependent on how much local and central governments are involved in boosting commercial streets.

Choose the right time frame

As we have seen in our case study cities, storefront tenants change over a lot faster than the buildings they occupy. In a rapidly changing urban economy, business models need to adapt or perish, and turnover is simply part of the business life cycle. For example, about a third of American restaurants fail within the first year.[62] On the other hand, we welcome hundreds of thousands of new street-level commercial businesses a year, adding new blood and excitement to our urban commercial streets. Successful sidewalks should welcome newcomers, which is more than just about providing the right storefront design. Startup storefront success hinges on three C's: *curation* ensures that the right new businesses are attracted to the right market; *coaching* maximizes their chance of success; and *connections* to accessible, low-risk storefronts and financing minimizes newcomers' barrier to entry.

A new generation of organizations focuses on these three C's to find and support startup businesses to become part of our eye-level commercial experience. In the Netherlands, the Streetwise Foundation is funded by participating municipalities to connect moving and startup retailers with building owners and investors, acting as a curator and coach for successful business ideas. Streetwise's high success rate resonates with storefront owners and lenders, connecting hundreds of their 'graduates' to the right space and financing.[63] Understanding the value of startup retailers to enliven a new urban neighborhood in Gothenburg, Sweden, the developer actively sought out and coached new businesses.[64] Often, organizations have a wider social purpose such as promoting ethnic or minority business startups. For example, Buffalo nonprofit WEDI runs the West Side Bazaar to support new immigrant stores and restaurants in one of the city's most ethnically diverse neighborhoods with affordable space and an incubator kitchen, where members can prepare foods in a commercially compliant kitchen. Several of these businesses have since expanded into full-sized storefronts.[65] Similarly, Cincinnati's MORTAR is a training and resource center for starting and running African American businesses, including retail.[66] With foundation support, nearby nonprofit Findlay Market supports an incubator kitchen, and has launched "Findlay Launch" in two nearby storefronts it owns, focusing on startups that want to enter a full-time business. In one restaurant and one retail space, Launch curates applicants and requires them to have prior experience, draft a business plan, provide financials, and maintain regular opening hours – steps to ensure success.[67]

Startup businesses usually do not have the financing to afford a full-sized retail space on the best corner of town. Like other independent businesses, they tend to find space along more peripheral streets and in smaller spaces that fit their budget. Larger storefronts can be divided into smaller spaces that are affordable to startups, or several businesses can become co-tenants in one space. In the food service industry, food trucks have lowered the barrier to business entry (Figure 7.10). Affordable rents are not the panacea to startup commercial success, as they tend to make up less than a quarter of business costs. They should be considered in conjunction with curation and coaching. Furthermore, startups can benefit from short-term 'pop-up' spaces to test their markets and business models. Traditionally associated with a high 'churn' rate that predates commercial decline, pop-ups have grown more popular with retailers, consumers, and even storefront owners in recent years. They can reduce risk for (startup) businesses when sales don't pan out as planned; they raise the visibility of otherwise vacant spaces for their owners looking to land a permanent tenant; and their constantly changing tenants satisfy increasing passerby cravings for new experiences – if well executed.[68]

Britain has risen as a global leader in pop-up spaces due to a stringent law borne out of the 2008 recession that forces vacant storefront owners to pay full property taxes after a three-month grace period. This has fueled a 'meanwhile' industry of organizations that offer to take vacant spaces off landlords' hands, in turn renting them to short-term tenants. For example, London-based Meanwhile Space uses this model to provide short-term spaces for entrepreneurship, community building, and local access to opportunity, especially focusing on disadvantaged neighborhoods and new businesses. They can often lease out spaces at half the price of commercial rents, and at lower-risk, shorter lease periods.[69] The organization actively trains and coaches the businesses they support, which range from retailers to designers, makers, artists, community groups, and workspaces. After initial government backing, Meanwhile Space is now mostly supported by (unsubsidized) rental income from tenants (Figure 7.11).[70] Coopolis in Berlin similarly curates, coaches, and connects landlords of vacant small

Figure 7.11 In collaboration with the British government, Meanwhile Space repurposed a vacant Stoke-on-Trent storefront for art pop-ups, social enterprises, and meeting space. Throughout the United Kingdom, Meanwhile Space rents out storefronts for uses beyond retail, focusing on social impact above rental income.
Source: Image annotated by Conrad Kickert, courtesy of Meanwhile Space from Open Doors Pilot Programme Report, published by the Ministry of Ministry of Housing, Communities & Local Government.

Figure 7.10 Food trucks serving the lunch crowd in downtown Minneapolis.
Source: Image courtesy of Minneapolis Public Works, CC-BY-2.0.

storefronts in the up-and-coming Neukölln district with startups, also keeping rents affordable by asking tenants to renovate the spaces themselves. Aiming to increase the district's social capital, Coopolis targets more than retailers, hosting creative tenants like makerspaces, youth and music clubs, galleries, and cafes. They also increasingly focus on longer-term leases to protect tenants from Neukölln's rapid gentrification.[71]

Despite the combination of curation, coaching, and connections, significant failure rates should be expected from short-term and startup tenants. This is simply part of starting a new business, and planners and designers should anticipate rapid turnover.[72] The tentative nature of short-term leases can also obscure thinking of long-term business viability, which is why for example Streetwise prefers tougher curation and more intense coaching of new businesses into permanent storefronts. Fitting out a vacant space for a new retail business, especially bars and restaurants, costs tens of thousands, which can only be recouped over a longer time frame.[73] Furthermore, pop-up spaces can prevent the realization for owners that a permanent commercial tenant is simply no longer viable, obstructing a meaningful transition to the kind of post-commercial uses we will discuss in the next chapter.[74] Nevertheless, in a shrinking renters market, the average retail lease period is drastically shortening and percentage leases are becoming more common, which increasingly blends pop-up, startup, and permanent retail features. We can expect our urban commercial streets to change faster than ever as a result.[75]

Design the right commercial space and the right frontage

To maximize the chances of successful commercial spaces, architects need to balance the right layout, size, and designs for street-level commerce. As mentioned, commerce thrives in well-connected, well-accessible locations. If possible, new storefronts should hook into existing pedestrian flows by locating within direct eyesight and access of existing commercial clusters, unobstructed by gaps and barriers like parking lots and noncommercial frontages, but also blank walls on the side of corner stores. In other words, the commercial street wall should be continuous. Following pedestrian flows, commercial storefronts should ideally be strung between access points and destinations (Figure 7.12). Depending on the cultural context, access points include car parking lots and garages and public transit stations. On the other end of the pedestrian flows, traditional anchor destinations such as department stores have made way for a larger variety of destinations like libraries, museums and theaters (for nighttime commerce), key public spaces such as parks and riverfronts, but also food halls. Larger new developments can build in these anchors, as shopping malls have done for decades.[76] In new non-retail districts, commerce should locate in the most visible and central spots, usually at the corners of blocks where they can be seen from multiple streets.

When we want to create the right tenant mix, we also need the right mix of commercial unit sizes, as different tenants have different space needs. Figure 7.13 demonstrates the widely differing need for space for startup and independent businesses, food service providers, chain stores (including so-called Mid-Size Units of larger chains), and anchor spaces. All of these business

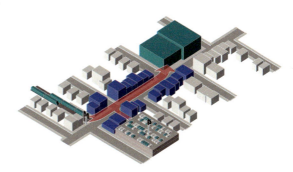

Figure 7.12 Commerce thrives on footfall generated from pedestrian flows between source points and destinations.
Source: Diagram by Conrad Kickert, 2021.

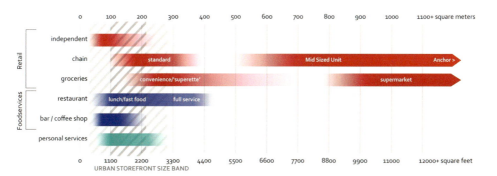

Figure 7.13 Size bands for key street-level commercial types.
Source: Diagram by Conrad Kickert, 2021.

types have a role along vibrant commercial sidewalks, as they mutually draw and reinforce more visitors and sales. Existing, repurposed, and new storefronts should therefore include a gamut of sizes, from micro-units (including kiosks and food trucks) that welcome startups and independents,[77] average-sized units for independent stores and chains, 'mid-sized units' that can accommodate chain flagship stores, to larger units for, for example, grocery stores and other anchors. If the last century of retail change is any indication, retail size requirements will only go up – especially as stores increasingly function as omnichannel fulfillment centers. Restaurant size requirements strongly vary on the way in which they serve customers. A walk-up coffee counter may need no seating, but a sit-down restaurant requires between 10 and 20 square feet (0.9 to 1.8 square meters) per patron. Bars may not need much space for servers and storage, but a restaurant should account for more than a third of its space for back-of-house operations like a kitchen, storage, and offices. If several adjacent commercial spaces are repurposed or built at once, they should be designed flexibly to accommodate tenants of different sizes. If a city or developer wants to prevent the intrusion of chains, store sizes should remain under 1,500 to 2,200 square feet (140 to 200 square meters); to prevent big-box stores like supermarkets and discount warehouses, sizes should remain below 15,000 square feet (1400 to 1500 square meters) – a common size cap in European regulations and one advocated in America (Figure 7.13).[78]

Despite their wide variety in sizes, storefronts should be between 20 and 25 feet wide (6 to 8 meters) in general, and certainly no more than 30 to 45 feet (10 to 15 meters) wide. This allows pedestrians a new storefront experience roughly every four to ten seconds on average. Obstructing this rhythm with much wider storefronts or noncommercial gaps will diminish the sensory stimulation for shopping passersby, prompting many to turn around. The depth of commercial spaces then defines the size and layout of retail spaces. Traditionally, commercial tenants have looked for narrower, deeper spaces to maximize their space in narrow plots. Most traditional retail spaces tend to be about 45 to 75 feet (about 15 to 25 meters) deep, with a depth up to four times the width of a storefront, leading to typical spaces between 1,000 and 2,000 square feet (about 90 to 180 square meters).[79] But commerce can take place in much smaller and shallower spaces as well, as long as there are enough passersby: think of newspaper stands less than a meter or three feet deep, food or drink counters (also known as transactional facades) fronting spaces only a few meters or feet deep, or micro-units that house independent businesses.[80]

We increasingly see shallower, wider commercial spaces in new developments – ideal for bars and restaurants where patrons can enjoy more sunlight, and ideal for activating more frontage along the street per establishment. Shallower commercial units can also serve

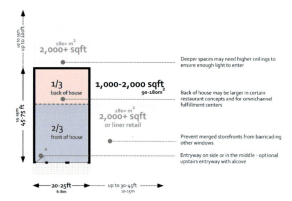

Figure 7.14 The dimensions of a typical urban retail unit.
Source: Diagram by Conrad Kickert, 2021.

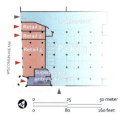 

Figure 7.15 Local design guidelines ensured that a large supermarket in Washington, D.C., was raised above liner retail units to maintain storefront continuity along a main retail street. The supermarket can be entered through a corner staircase and rear parking.
Source: Floor plan by Conrad Kickert, image annotated on original by Eric Fisher via Flickr, CC-BY-2.0.

as 'liners' for otherwise inactive uses behind them like parking or larger stores; more about this later. Figure 7.14 displays the floorplan diagram for a typical urban retail unit.

Older retail spaces tend to be smaller, as the average size of commercial units has risen dramatically over the past century. As we have seen, modern, especially chain retailers tend to require more space: around 2,600 square feet (around 250 square meters) on average in Europe and even more in the United States. If needed, smaller spaces can be expanded toward the back. Alternatively, two or more adjacent spaces can be merged into one larger space, but merged unit entrances will likely be closed and tenants should not be allowed to barricade entire merged storefronts with shelving and stickering. Even larger uses like supermarkets and other anchors can be accommodated through a regular-width entrance, either behind adjacent shallow 'liner' units, or up or down a floor from regular-sized units. Liner retailers can enliven the street and often benefit from their larger neighbor (Figure 7.15). Especially supermarkets can be tricky urbanites, as they thrive in larger floorplates, and prioritize shelf space over window interaction. Smaller 'superette' formulas work in many

European and Canadian cities; larger supermarkets can place an interactive café in the front of their space. These interventions allow cities to maintain around ten commercial units and entrances per 300 feet (roughly 100 meters) of block length – a common mandate in zoning codes and design guidelines.[81] Larger units may need emergency exits and loading zones; these should not be placed in the active frontage area. To allow light to enter deep retail floorplates and to leave room for HVAC and lighting technology, new street-level commercial space should be around 12 to 15 feet (4 to 5 meters) tall; double-height retail spaces with mezzanines can extend even higher.[82]

As the interface of commercial units and the street, the design of storefronts themselves should balance communication and coherence. Centuries of storefront design evolution has resulted in a highly similar set of architectural elements and proportions that maximize passerby interaction. Successful storefronts are *the materialization* of Gehl's touted three-mile-per-hour architecture, designed to inform, excite and seduce passersby.[83] They distinguish themselves from upper floors through different materials, proportions, and a horizontal band that may include space for awnings, a cornice, fascia or frieze, and advertising. Yet most of the storefront communication takes place at the eye level 'attention zone' that roughly spans between two to seven feet (60 to 210 centimeters) above the ground (as we typically look slightly downward). The retail adagio that 'eye level is buy level' counts for storefronts as much as store shelves: the attention zone should have a high level of transparency (usually half to three-quarters of a façade) and attention to detail to convert passersby to patrons. Passerby seduction happens in two ways: by storefronts directly showing the items, services, and experiences on offer inside, and by communicating the business brand identity. Global brands increasingly assume passerby associate a mere logo with the offerings inside and sticker off their entire storefront, numbing the sidewalk experience. Instead, successful storefronts balance branding and transparency by allowing passersby to look at least three to four feet (about a meter) inside, unobstructed by reflective glass or too many stickers and posted advertisements – which effectively act as blank walls.[84] The gaze of passersby can be captured and framed through exciting window displays, also known as visual merchandising – an art as much as a science, perfected over the last century by designers from Victor Gruen and Norman Bel Geddes to Salvador Dali. Display competitions can raise the bar for merchants to create exciting displays. In bars and restaurants, patrons themselves (and their food and drink) are the visual merchandise, as smart entrepreneurs fill their tables from the frontage inward to show off patrons having a good time (Figure 7.16).[85]

Vertical elements like columns and posts besides and within storefronts help to distinguish individual businesses and articulate the storefront itself. As we scan

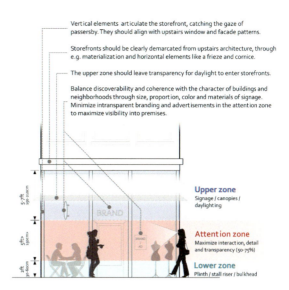

Figure 7.16 Storefront design diagram.
Source: Diagram by Conrad Kickert, 2021.

our surroundings mostly horizontally, vertical storefront elements help to stop and catch our gaze. Indentations and niches can extend the size of storefronts and allow for more display space at different angles, leading pedestrians into a recessed entrance (which may also access upstairs units). Historic facades often contain these vertical elements and articulations; their preservation can accentuate the unique character of a storefront – an important asset in today's experience economy. Transparent shutters can still allow passersby to see storefront contents after business hours, which in fact helps to prevent vandalism and feelings of unsafety. Signage in and above storefronts should balance communicating brand identity with matching the character of a commercial cluster, and respecting the pedestrian scale. Signs should not insult passersby with huge lettering aimed at drivers, but they also should not bombard them with information they cannot digest in a few seconds. Cities (and at times, larger property owners) tend to have detailed storefront design and signage guidelines in place for size, color, character, lighting, and accessibility. Furthermore, many cities have façade improvement grants or loans that can entice building or business owners to align their storefronts with the design tricks mentioned here, as well as the character of an area codified into local guidelines. Façade improvement programs are proven to increase business, improve the impression and character of an area, and improve community pride (Figure 7.17).[86] Like the architecture of its host building, storefront design is susceptible to stylistic evolution, which has impacted the design of ornamentation, materialization, and even the layout of the façade over the past century. Load-bearing elements should be uncoupled from storefronts to enable designs

Figure 7.17a–e Storefronts in the OMA-designed Rijnstraat 8 building in The Hague (a) suffer from a lack of distinction with upper floors, a flat façade without many vertical elements and articulation, and a low ceiling height. You'd barely know stores are there! This is night and day compared to a well-articulated storefront mere blocks away (b). Large storefronts are frequently occupied by chain tenants which tend to sticker off windows with logos and advertisements, prioritizing brand recognition and internal shelf space over passerby excitement. At a supermarket in The Hague, parked bicycles and trolleys finish the job (c). Façade improvements can project trust, progress, and drastically improve business, like in Detroit (d and e).

Source: Image (a) by author, 2020. Image (b) by author, 2012. Image (c) by author, 2014. Image (d) by author, 2012. Image (e) by Matteo Marrocco, 2021.

COMMERCIAL LIFE – EYE-LEVEL TRANSACTIONS IN THE CITY   145

Figure 7.18a–c Frontage zones can be used to communicate and introduce merchandise, from billboards in Birmingham (a), books in Paris (b), to an entire sidewalk plant sales stand in Buffalo (c). *Source:* Image (a) by Conrad Kickert, 2017. Image (b) by Conrad Kickert, 2012. Image (c) by Conrad Kickert, 2021.

Figure 7.19 Frontage zones can also spill out patrons from eating and drinking establishments, from small two-person bistro tables on a narrow two-foot sidewalk in The Hague (a) to a wider six-foot seating area (b) and an entire leisure square nearby (c). The COVID-19 pandemic reminds us of the relevance of outdoor drinking and dining for the social and economic life of cities.
Source: Images (a) and (b) by Conrad Kickert 2014; image (c) by Ben Bender via Wikimedia Commons, cc-by-sa-3.0 2021.

to adapt to change, while design review and preservation should ensure spatial and temporal coherence.[87]

Successful street-level commerce hinges on high quality public space that provides room, comfort, and excitement to pedestrians. In our four case study cities and their peers across the Western Hemisphere, investments in high-quality sidewalks, squares, and pedestrianized streets have resulted in significant street-level commercial growth. Besides their environmental, social, and health value, the economic value of well-designed public spaces has been proven time and again, and street-level businesses now routinely fund streetscape improvements through BIDs.[88] In street design, the interface between public space and storefronts is frequently referred to as the frontage zone, which extends into the street and into the commercial space itself. This zone is the place where commerce blends with the street in the form of advertisements and merchandise displays (Figure 7.18), but also of outdoor drinking and dining patios (Figure 7.19). In this zone, passersby can gather an

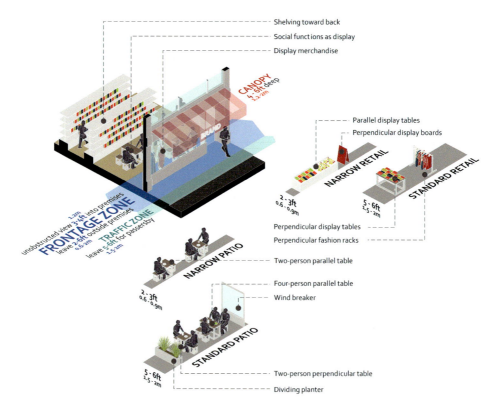

Figure 7.20 Defining, designing, inhabiting, and enforcing the frontage zone.
Source: Diagram by Conrad Kickert, 2021.

impression of the services, merchandise, and experience on offer inside commercial spaces.

As the width of sidewalks is constrained in most dense cities, this zone should leave a five- to six-foot right of way to allow people to pass, especially with wheelchairs and baby carriages. It is amazing to see how much can be achieved within the space left for frontage zones. Even with less than three feet (90 centimeters) available, sales racks and displays can lure passersby into stores or accommodate direct outdoor transactions. Simple plantings in the frontage zone can increase sales in stores by improving their image. Averaging around only 100 square feet (less than 10 square meters), Parisian patios famously add sights, sounds, and tastes to streets and boulevards, inspiring global aspirational peers. Above-ground-floor patios, umbrellas, and awnings can shelter passersby from the weather, as well as further define storefronts, although over-application can spur darkness and monotony. Alternatively, storefronts can be recessed to create arcades that shelter passersby from the weather and create a more enclosed shopping environment. Horizontally, windbreakers similarly protect patios, and American regulations often mandate barriers around patios where alcohol is served. These horizontal definitions can even merge with awnings into virtually enclosed verandas, complete with heating and ventilation systems. Increasingly, cities also support the conversion of parking spaces into 'parklet' patios. When space allows, for example along wider boulevards, fully pedestrianized streets and larger public spaces, larger patios, and outdoor sales areas can truly blur the division between public space and private enterprise. While extending commerce into the street can improve business success and generate tax revenue, cities need to balance public and private interests to safeguard universal access to public spaces. This balance needs to be enforced frequently to prevent 'café creep': the tendency of businesses to encroach lucrative patios further into public space. Clear design guidelines for frontage zone elements can ensure visual coherence between elements themselves, their host building, and the overall character of an area (Figure 7.20).[89]

New commercial spaces need to carefully balance flexibility to house a variety of storefront tenants, with the need to project a certain esthetic to a target audience. After decades of relatively innocuous façade design that maximized tenants' ability to define their storefronts, postmodern retail designers began to reclaim façade design as a stylistic frame, like the 'visceral reality' of the late Jon Jerde's highly stylized malls to the current trend of shipping container stores and food trucks. Especially the latter can be excellent tools to (temporarily) enliven gaps in retail areas. However, architectural style should not overwhelm storefront communication, and an overdesigned shell may struggle to keep up with the

Figure 7.21 As the world's first pop-up mall, BoxPark in Shoreditch creates a new wall of shipping container stores in front of an otherwise blank viaduct.
Source: Image by Fred Romero via Wikimedia Commons, CC-BY-2.0.

faster pace of tenant rebranding, refits, and reshuffles.[90] Regardless of style, commercial space and storefront design should allow different tenants to thrive in different-sized units, while maintaining a rhythm of new storefront experiences for passersby, ensuring that tenants fully communicate with the street through transparent storefronts and lively frontage zones (Figure 7.21). Yet we also need to face the inevitable truth that with a shrinking pool of storefront businesses, the future of our city at eye level is increasingly post-transactional. The next chapter will demonstrate why this is not as bad for our cities as we might think.

Notes

1. For a wider assessment of the value of urban retail, see Conrad Kickert, "Introduction: The Urban Retail Predicament," in *Streetlife: The Future of Urban Retail*, eds. Conrad Kickert and Emily Talen (Toronto: University of Toronto Press, 2023); Andres Sevtsuk, *Street Commerce: Creating Vibrant Urban Sidewalks* (Philadelphia, PA: University of Pennsylvania Press, 2020).
2. Street-level commerce is increasingly seen as an amenity for upstairs development. See e.g. Patrick Sisson, "In the Apartment Amenity Arms Race, Service and Technology Win Out," *Curbed*, March 26, 2019; Bendix Anderson, "Do First Floor Retail Spaces Pencil out for Multifamily Developers?" *National Real Estate Investor*, March 15, 2016.
3. Benjamin Grant, "Designing at Ground Level," *The Urbanist*, no. 534 (2014).
4. Quote from Ann Satterthwaite, *Going Shopping: Consumer Choices and Community Consequences* (New Haven: Yale University Press, 2001). On the history of American retailing, see e.g. R. W. Longstreth, *City Center to Regional Mall: Architecture, the Automobile, and Retailing in Los Angeles, 1920–1950* (Cambridge, MA: MIT Press, 1997); Richard W. Longstreth, *The Drive-in, the Supermarket, and the Transformation of Commercial Space in Los Angeles, 1914–1941* (Cambridge, MA: MIT Press, 2000); R. W. Longstreth, *The American Department Store Transformed, 1920–1960* (New Haven, CT: Yale University Press, 2010); Vicki Howard, *From Main Street to Mall: The Rise and Fall of the American Department Store* (Philadelphia, PA: University of Pennsylvania Press, 2015). For Europe, see e.g. R. Miellet and M. Voorn, *Winkelen in Weelde: Warenhuizen in West-Europa 1860–2000* (Zutphen: Walburg Pers, 2001); Peter Coleman, *Shopping Environments: Evolution, Planning and Design* (Amsterdam, Boston and London: Architectural Press, 2006). Retail transformation has followed a series of 'revolutions' over the past century, including fixed pricing and self-service: Dorothy Davis, *A History of Shopping* (Toronto: University of Toronto Press, 1966). On models of organizational change in retail, see Stephen Brown, "Institutional Change in Retailing: A Review and Synthesis," *European Journal of Marketing* 21, no. 6 (1987); Ellen McArthur, Scott Weaven, and Rajiv Dant, "The Evolution of Retailing: A Meta Review of the Literature," *Journal of Macromarketing* 36, no. 3 (2016).
5. C. Kickert and E. Talen, *Streetlife – The Future of Urban Retail* (Toronto: University of Toronto Press, 2023).
6. William Applebaum, "Methods for Determining Store Trade Areas, Market Penetration, and Potential Sales," *Journal of Marketing Research* 3, no. 2 (1966); Mark Birkin, Graham Clarke, and Martin P. Clarke, *Retail Geography and Intelligent Network Planning* (Hoboken, NJ: John Wiley & Sons, 2002); Tony Hernández and David Bennison, "The Art and Science of Retail Location Decisions," *International Journal of Retail & Distribution Management* 28, no. 8 (2000); Patrick M. Dunne, Robert F. Lusch, and James R. Carver, *Retailing* (Boston, MA: Cengage Learning, 2013); David L. Huff, "A Probabilistic Analysis of Shopping Center Trade Areas," *Land economics* 39, no. 1 (1963). See also Conrad Kickert, "Retail," in *A Research Agenda for New Urbanism*, ed. Emily Talen (Cheltenham: Edward Elgar Publishing, 2019).
7. Calculation models are often gravity based, and are based on a mixture of business data to model the supply side, and consumer profiles (psychodemographics) to model the demand side: "Retail."; D. Evers, D. Kooijman, and E. Van der Krabben, *Planning Van Winkellocaties En Winkelgebieden in Nederland* (The Hague: Sdu, 2011); Hernández and Bennison, "The Art and Science of Retail Location Decisions."
8. The reason these categories are so broadly defined is that food consumption, both from stores and foodservice providers, varies significantly between countries. For example coffee shops, often desired

in Anglo-Saxon contexts, are actually far scarcer in Paris or Amsterdam: from about one shop per 2,000 people in dense American and British contexts, to only one per 4,000 people in Amsterdam (excluding cannabis-selling 'coffeeshops') and only one shop per 8,000 in Paris – appropriately named "Salon de Thé."

9 There is one shoe store per 2,181 Parisians versus one shoe store per 10,193 Torontonians in 2018. Please note that these examples are skewed as these large cities welcome thousands of annual tourists, not to mention millions of daily commuters – not to mention the strong influence of regional and national differences in regulation. Clifford M. Guy, "Controlling New Retail Spaces: The Impress of Planning Policies in Western Europe," *Urban Studies* 35, no. 5–6 (1998); Jesse W. J. Weltevreden, "Substitution or Complementarity? How the Internet Changes City Centre Shopping," *Journal of Retailing and Consumer Services* 14, no. 3 (2007); Ken Jones and Tony Hernandez, "Dynamics of the Canadian Retail Environment," in *Canadian Cities in Transition*, eds. Trudi E. Bunting and Pierre Filion (Oxford: Oxford University Press, 2000); D. Evers et al., *Winkelen in Megaland*, ed. Rijksplanbureau (Rotterdam: NAi Uitgevers, 2005).

10 Scientifically, the locational decision-making process and the subsequent success of retailers are known as emergent phenomena: the coinciding and interaction between retail businesses and external forces. Sevtsuk, *Street Commerce: Creating Vibrant Urban Sidewalks*; Jane Jacobs, *The Death and Life of Great American Cities* (New York: Random House, 1961); Hillier and J. Hanson, *The Social Logic of Space* (Cambridge [Cambridgeshire] and New York: Cambridge University Press, 1984).

11 Christaller's original theory focused on urban and rural economies in general: W. Christaller, *Die Zentralen Orte in Suddeutschland. Translated by Carlisle W. Baskin, 1966, as Central Places in Southern Germany* (Englewood Cliffs, NJ: Prentice Hall, 1933). This work was expanded and developed by A. Lösch, *The Economics of Location* (New Haven: Yale University Press, 1940). Criticisms include whether consumers rationally choose nearest locations, travel patterns, differences in branding, and the role of center attributes beyond retail offerings, like experiential value: I. D. H. Shepherd and C. J. Thomas, "Urban Consumer Behaviour," in *Retail Geography*, ed. John A. Dawson (London: Halstead Press, 1980); D. Kooijman, "Het Recreatieve Einde Van Christaller," *Rooilijn* 3 (2000); Sevtsuk, *Street Commerce: Creating Vibrant Urban Sidewalks*, 71. Central Place Theory was validated in the mid-20th century for American urban retail centers: B. J. L. Berry and W. L. Garrison, "The Functional Bases of the Central Place Hierarchy," *Economic Geography*

34 (1958); "Recent Developments of Central Place Theory," *Papers in Regional Science* 4, no. 1 (1958). The continued use may be due to a cycle of adoption of Central Place Theory, which in turn validates it further. Similarly, the stratification of businesses according to their need and ability to pay for centrality that we saw in the previous chapter has been theorized into economic "bid-rent" models. For a further review, see Stephen Brown, "Retail Location Theory: Evolution and Evaluation," *International Review of Retail, Distribution and Consumer Research* 3, no. 2 (1993).

12 Reinhard Baumeister, *Stadt-Erweiterungen in Technischer, Baupolizeilicher Und Wirthschaftlicher Beziehung* (Ernst & Korn, 1876); R. M. Hurd, *Principles of Land Values* (New York: The Record and Guide, 1903); Carlo Ratti and Matthew Claudel, *The City of Tomorrow: Sensors, Networks, Hackers, and the Future of Urban Life* (New Haven: Yale University Press, 2016); S. C. Van der Spek et al., "Sensing Human Activity: Gps Tracking," *Sensors* 9, no. 4 (2009). Footfall measurements remain popular with retailers, as they correlate with potential sales: S. J. Thornton, R. P. Bradshaw, and M. J. McCullagh, "Pedestrian Flows and Retail Turnover," *British Food Journal* 93, no. 9 (1991); E. J. Bolt, *Winkelvoorzieningen Op Waarde Geschat* (Merkelbeek: Bakker, 2003).

13 A. Borgers and H. Timmermans, "A Model of Pedestrian Route Choice and Demand for Retail Facilities Within Inner-City Shopping Areas," *Geographical Analysis* 18, no. 2 (1986); Michael Batty, "Agent-Based Pedestrian Modeling," *Environment and Planning B: Planning and Design* 28, no. 3 (2001); Michael Batty, *The New Science of Cities* (Cambridge, MA: MIT Press, 2013).

14 See a.o. Hillier and A. Leaman, "The Man-Environment Paradigm and Its Paradoxes," *Architectural Design* 78, no. 8 (1973); Hillier and Hanson, *The Social Logic of Space*; Hillier, *Space Is the Machine: A Configurational Theory of Architecture* (Cambridge and New York: Cambridge University Press, 1996). For research that has corroborated the link between various Space Syntax measures, pedestrian activity and retail, see e.g. A. Van Nes, *Road Building and Urban Change: The Effect of Ring Roads on the Dispersal of Shop and Retail in Western European Towns and Cities* (Agricultural University of Norway, Department of Land Use and Landscape Planning, 2002); Alan Penn and Alasdair Turner, "Space Syntax Based Agent Simulation," in *Pedestrian and Evacuation Dynamics*, eds. Michael Schreckenberg and Som Deo Sharma (Berlin: Springer-Verlag, 2002); Sophia Psarra, Conrad Kickert, and Amanda Pluviano, "Paradigm Lost: Industrial and Post-Industrial Detroit – an Analysis

of the Street Network and Its Social and Economic Dimensions from 1796 to the Present," *Urban Design International* 18, no. 4 (2013). Criticisms and branches from Space Syntax focus on its lack of land use focus, which the movement presumes is derived from the street configuration: Carlo Ratti, "Space Syntax: Some Inconsistencies," *Environment and Planning B: Planning and Design* 31, no. 4 (2004); Bill Hillier and Alan Penn, "Rejoinder to Carlo Ratti," ibid.; Lars Marcus et al., "Location-Based Density and Differentiation – Adding Attraction Variables to Space Syntax," in *24th Isuf International Conference. Book of Papers* (Valencia: Editorial Universitat Politècnica de València, 2018). A response has been Place Syntax: Alexander Ståhle, Lars Marcus, and Anders Karlström, "Place Syntax: Geographic Accessibility with Axial Lines in Gis" (paper presented at the fifth international space syntax symposium, 2005).

15 Andres Sevtsuk, "Location and Agglomeration: The Distribution of Retail and Food Businesses in Dense Urban Environments," *Journal of Planning Education and Research* 34, no. 4 (2014); Andres Sevtsuk, *Street Commerce – Creating Vibrant Urban Sidewalks* (Philadelphia: University of Pennsylvania Press, 2020).

16 E.g. J. Gehl, *Life Between Buildings: Using Public Space* (New York: Van Nostrand Reinhold, 1987); J. Gehl, *Cities for People* (Washington, DC: Island Press, 2010); Matthew Carmona et al., "The Value of Urban Design" (A Research Project Commissioned by CABE and DETR to Examine the Value Added by Good Urban Design, 2001).

17 This approach to modeling the value of retail clustering in a tiered system of centers has allowed for more empirical corroboration: Brown, "Retail Location Theory: Evolution and Evaluation."

18 This was seen as a socially detrimental effect, as it places vendors further away from customers. Hurd, *Principles of Land Values*; H. Hotelling, "Stability in Competition," *The economic journal* 39, no. 153 (1929).

19 One survey in Uppsala, Sweden demonstrated between 32% and 73% of shopping trips were multipurpose: Susan Hanson, "Spatial Diversification and Multipurpose Travel: Implications for Choice Theory," *Geographical Analysis* 12, no. 3 (1980).

20 R. L. Nelson, *The Selection of Retail Locations* (New York: FW Dodge Corporation, 1958); Conrad Kickert and Rainer vom Hofe, "Critical Mass Matters: The Long-Term Benefits of Retail Agglomeration for Establishment Survival in Downtown Detroit and the Hague," *Urban Studies* 55, no. 5 (2017); W. Alonso, "A Theory of the Urban Land Market," *Papers in Regional Science* 6, no. 1 (1960); M. Anikeeff, "Shopping Center Tenant Selection and Mix: A Review," *Research Issues in Real Estate* 3 (1996); Sevtsuk, *Street Commerce: Creating Vibrant Urban Sidewalks*, 79–83. In mall planning jargon, spillovers are defined by "affinity groups" of retailers that have a complementary offer. Anchors pay 10% or less of non-anchor spaces: James D. Vernor et al., *Shopping Center Appraisal and Analysis* (Chicago, IL: Appraisal Institute, 2009); Urban Land Institute – Research Division. and International Council of Shopping Centers, *Dollars & Cents of Shopping Centers / the Score 2008* (Washington, DC: Urban Land Institute, 2008). For a contemporary overview of clustering between urban retailers, see Sevtsuk, *Street Commerce: Creating Vibrant Urban Sidewalks*, 91. Table 6.

21 This is why the average shopping mall has this as its longest length between anchors: Victor Gruen and Larry Smith, *Shopping Towns USA; the Planning of Shopping Centers*, Progressive Architecture Library (New York,: Reinhold Pub. Corp., 1960).

22 See also Conrad Kickert et al., "Spatial Dynamics of Long-Term Urban Retail Decline in Three Transatlantic Cities," *Cities* 107 (2020).

23 After an independent valuation of current values of all retail buildings in a re-parceled district, building owners will be guaranteed their current share of value in the newly re-concentrated district. Re-parcelation is a highly complex process, which as of writing has prevented its widespread adoption by cities and into national legislation. Barbara Heebels and Suzanne van Dusseldorp, *Experiment Aangename Aanloopstraten – Eindrapportage* (The Hague: Platform31, 2016), 61; E. W. T. M. Heurkens, *Private Sector-Led Urban Development Projects – Management, Partnership & Effects in the Netherlands and the UK* (Delft: TU Delft, 2012), 396–97; Peter Nieland, "Retail Issues and Shop Re-Parcelling," in *The City at Eye Level*, eds. Meredith Glaser, et al. (Delft: Eburon, 2012). Interview with Joost Nicasie, July 2, 2020. Researcher Andres Sevtsuk proposes redistributing property rights through co-ops, but acknowledges this model has not been tried before: Sevtsuk, *Street Commerce: Creating Vibrant Urban Sidewalks*, 100–1. Downzoning in the United Kingdom is mostly decentralized, fitting the current political climate of localization. Most recently, Town Centre Investment Zones have been proposed as public-private partnerships to redistribute retail into smaller areas. Communities and Local Government Ministry of Housing, *National Planning Policy Framework* (London: Her Majesty's Stationary Office, 2019); H. M. Treasury, *Budget 2014* (London: Her Majesty's Stationary Office, 2014); *Budget 2013* (London: Her Majesty's Stationary Office, 2013); L. Peace, "High Street Armageddon – Are Town Centre Investment Zones the Answer?" *Planning in London*

177 (2021). The Dutch government has initiated a national Retail Agenda with local and regional "retail deals" to reduce or halt the growth of floor space allocations, initiatives to explore other uses of storefronts in peripheral retail areas and streets, and other innovation and capacity building projects. The Retail Agenda started in 2016, and has been renewed in 2018. Ministerie van Economische Zaken en Klimaat, *Retailagenda 2018–2020 – Vervolgaanpak in Vijf Thema's* (The Hague: Sdu, 2018). See also Hanneke van Rooijen et al., *De Nieuwe Binnenstad* (Den Haag: Platform31, 2018).

24 American city land banks have held retail for decades: Julie A. Tappendorf and Brent O. Denzin, "Turning Vacant Properties into Community Assets through Land Banking," *Urb. Law.* 43 (2010). For the Netherlands, see Arjen Raatgever, *Winkelgebied Van De Toekomst* (The Hague: Platform31, 2014).

25 For the United States, see Conrad Kickert, "What's in Store: Prospects and Challenges for American Street-Level Commerce," *Journal of Urban Design* 26, no. 2 (2021). For Europe, see Experian or Locatus data.

26 Establishment closure estimates vary between market analysts UBS, CoreSight and eMarketer, but all agree on significantly accelerated decline. Suzanne Kapner and Sarah Nassauer, "Coronavirus Finishes the Retail Reckoning That Amazon Started," *The Wall Street Journal*, May 14, 2020.

27 Sabrina Helm, Soo Hyun Kim, and Silvia Van Riper, "Navigating the 'Retail Apocalypse': A Framework of Consumer Evaluations of the New Retail Landscape," *Journal of Retailing and Consumer Services* 54 (2020).

28 Koen Pauwels and Scott A. Neslin, "Building with Bricks and Mortar: The Revenue Impact of Opening Physical Stores in a Multichannel Environment," *Journal of Retailing* 91, no. 2 (2015); Scott A. Neslin et al., "Challenges and Opportunities in Multichannel Customer Management," *Journal of Service Research* 9, no. 2 (2006).

29 On American shopping malls, see e.g. Ellen Dunham-Jones and June Williamson, *Retrofitting Suburbia: Urban Design Solutions for Redesigning Suburbs* (Hoboken, NJ: Wiley Publishing, 2008). On the British High Street, see e.g. Mary Portas, *The Portas Review: An Independent Review into the Future of Our High Streets* (Department for Business, Innovation and Skills, 2011); Matthew Carmona, "London's Local High Streets: The Problems, Potential and Complexities of Mixed Street Corridors," *Progress in Planning* 100 (2015).

30 Kasey Lobaugh et al., "The Great Retail Bifurcation – Why the Retail "Apocalypse" Is Really a Renaissance," in *Deloitte Insights* (New York: Company Report, 2018).

31 Market shares of online groceries varies between countries, with the United States trailing European markets, especially the United Kingdom. Nielsen, *What's in-Store for Online Grocery Shopping – Omnichannel Strategies to Reach Crossover Shoppers* (New York: Nielsen, 2017); Nielsen and Food Marketing Institute, *The Digitally Engaged Food Shopper* (Arlington, VA: Nielsen and Food Marketing Institute, 2018); Russell Redman, "Meal Kit Players Adapt to Changing Market," *Supermarket News*, November 30, 2018.

32 For example, a federal pilot program in the United States offers grocery delivery to low-income families: United States Food and Nutrition Service, "USDA Launches Snap Online Purchasing Pilot," *News Release*, April 18, 2019.

33 Cushman & Wakefield, *The Global Food & Beverage Market* (London: Cushman & Wakefield, 2017). The number of American farmers markets have grown over 2,500% between 1970 and 2019: USDA, *National Farmers Market Directory* (Washington, DC: USDA, 2019).

34 Consumers want to search, decide and buy their merchandise through various channels: the presence of a physical store significantly boosts sales for online-first companies, and vice versa. Peter C. Verhoef, Pallassana K. Kannan, and J. Jeffrey Inman, "From Multi-Channel Retailing to Omni-Channel Retailing: Introduction to the Special Issue on Multi-Channel Retailing," *Journal of retailing* 91, no. 2 (2015); Pauwels and Neslin, "Building with Bricks and Mortar"; CACI, *The Halo Effect – Online Sales More Than Within a Store's Catchment* (London: CACI, 2020). China is a global leader in omnichannel retail, bypassing legacy physical store ecosystems: Michael Cheng, "Ecommerce in China – the Future Is Already Here," in *Total Retail 2017* (Hong Kong: PWC, 2017); Sara Belghiti et al., "The Phygital Shopping Experience: An Attempt at Conceptualization and Empirical Investigation" (Paper presented at the Academy of Marketing Science World Marketing Congress, 2017).

35 B. Joseph Pine and James H. Gilmore, *The Experience Economy* (Boston: Harvard Business School Press, 1999); Robert V. Kozinets, "Brands in Space: New Inking About Experiential Retail," in *Brick & Mortar Shopping in the 21st Century*, ed. Tina Lowrey (New York: Psychology Press, 2007).

36 Andrew Lipsman et al., *The Future of Retail 2019* (New York: eMarketer, 2018); Robin Lewis and Michael Dart, *The New Rules of Retail: Competing in the World's Toughest Marketplace* (New York: St. Martin's Press, 2014).

37 T. H. Davenport and J. C. Beck, *The Attention Economy: Understanding the New Currency of Business* (Cambridge, MA: Harvard Business School Press, 2001).

38 Craig M. Parker and Tanya Castleman, "Small Firm E-Business Adoption: A Critical Analysis of Theory," *Journal of Enterprise Information Management* 22, no. 1/2 (2009); Nancy M. Levenburg, Vipin Gupta, and Simha R. Magal, "The Uptake of Electronic Commerce in the Retail Industry: Enhancing Our Understanding," *Journal of Global Business and Technology* 7, no. 1 (2011). Large online marketplaces like Amazon, Etsy and eBay see themselves as the small retail storefronts of the future – a contentious proposition: Shan Wang et al., "A Literature Review of Electronic Marketplace Research: Themes, Theories and an Integrative Framework," *Information Systems Frontiers* 10, no. 5 (2008); Jeffrey P. Bezos, 2017. However, small businesses keep an edge of unique products, localization, service, ambiance and often convenience over their chain rivals – advantages that overlap with the benefits of physical storefronts in general. Corporations are hot on their tail with technology that allows for personalized customer interaction, seen as "the future of retail": Kickert, "What's in Store: Prospects and Challenges for American Street-Level Commerce."

39 Sevtsuk, *Street Commerce: Creating Vibrant Urban Sidewalks*; Civic Economics, *Economic Impact Analysis: A Case Study – Local Merchants Vs. Chain Retailers* (Chicago, IL and Austin, TX: Liveable City AIBA, 2002); Vikas Mehta and Jennifer K. Bosson, "Third Places and the Social Life of Streets," *Environment and Behavior* 42, no. 6 (2010); LOCO BC, *The Economic Impact of Local Businesses* (Vancouver, BC: LOCO BC, 2019); Vikas Mehta, "Small Businesses and the Vitality of Main Street," *Journal of Architectural and Planning Research* 28 (2011). Small businesses continue to thrive in ethnic communities. See e.g. Suzanne M. Hall, "Super-Diverse Street: A 'Trans-Ethnography' Across Migrant Localities," *Ethnic and racial studies* 38, no. 1 (2015).

40 For San Francisco's protection of independent business, see City of San Francisco, "Formula Retail Uses," in *303.1* (San Francisco: American Legal Publishing Corporation, 2014). On the effects of anti-chain regulation, see e.g. Raffaella Sadun, "Does Planning Regulation Protect Independent Retailers?" *Review of Economics and Statistics* 97, no. 5 (2015); Colin Horgan, "Retail Revolution: Should Cities Ban Chain Stores?" *The Guardian*, April 20, 2017. On American independent business and space affordability, see Olivia LaVecchia and Stacy Mitchell, *Affordable Space – How Rising Commercial Rents Are Threatening Independent Businesses, and What Cities Are Doing About It* (Minneapolis, Portland and Washington: Institute for Local Self-Reliance, 2016). For a European review of commercial regulation, including anti-chain regulation, see Guy, "Controlling New Retail Spaces: The Impress of Planning Policies in Western Europe"; Pedro Guimarães, "Revisiting Retail Planning Policies in Countries of Restraint of Western Europe," *International Journal of Urban Sciences* 20, no. 3 (2016). Anti-chain regulation has a fruitless history in the United States: Satterthwaite, *Going Shopping: Consumer Choices and Community Consequences.*

41 Statistics and definitions on specialty coffee shops slightly vary between numbers by Specialty Coffee Association of America, the US Census, and Allegra private reports. Current coffee shop growth has decreased, as the market reaches saturation. On craft breweries, see Brewers Association, "National Beer Sales & Production Data."

42 Ray Oldenburg, *The Great Good Place: Cafes, Coffee Shops, Bookstores, Bars, Hair Salons, and Other Hangouts at the Heart of a Community* (Philadelphia, PA: Da Capo Press, 1999); Daniel Aaron Silver and Terry Nichols Clark, *Scenescapes: How Qualities of Place Shape Social Life* (Chicago: University of Chicago Press, 2016); R. L. Florida, *The Rise of the Creative Class: And How It's Transforming Work, Leisure, Community and Everyday Life* (New York: Basic Civitas Books, 2002).

43 Priscilla Boniface, *Tasting Tourism: Travelling for Food and Drink* (New York; London: Routledge, 2017).

44 Edward L. Glaeser, Hyunjin Kim, and Michael Luca, "Nowcasting Gentrification: Using Yelp Data to Quantify Neighborhood Change" (Paper presented at the AEA Papers and Proceedings, 2018); Samuel Walker and Chloe Fox Miller, "Have Craft Breweries Followed or Led Gentrification in Portland, Oregon? An Investigation of Retail and Neighbourhood Change," *Geografiska Annaler: Series B, Human Geography* 101, no. 2 (2019). For a broader perspective on the relation between retail, food and beverage, consumerism and gentrification, see: Sharon Zukin, "Consuming Authenticity – from Outposts of Difference to Means of Exclusion," *Cultural Studies* 22, no. 5 (2008); Sharon Zukin, Philip Kasinitz, and Xiangming Chen, *Global Cities, Local Streets: Everyday Diversity from New York to Shanghai* (New York and London: Routledge, 2016).

45 John Hannigan, *Fantasy City: Pleasure and Profit in the Postmodern Metropolis* (London: Routledge, 2010).

46 Food and beverage establishments are classified as "eating and drinking" establishments in Chicago. Department of Planning & Development, *Citywide Retail Market Analysis* (Chicago, IL: City of Chicago, 2013).

47 Personal interviews with Kathleen Norris in 2019 and 2020; see also www.urbanfastforward.com and

www.3cdc.org. For European policies on welcoming foodservices, see e.g. Portas, *The Portas Review: An Independent Review into the Future of Our High Streets*; Cathy Hughes and Cath Jackson, "Death of the High Street: Identification, Prevention, Reinvention," *Regional Studies, Regional Science 2*, no. 1 (2015); David Evers et al., *De Veerkrachtige Binnenstad* (Den Haag: PBL, 2015).

48 Clare Cho and Jessica Todd, "Food Away from Home During the Great Recession," in *America's Eating Habits: Food Away from Home*, eds. Michelle J. Saksena, Abigail M. Okrent, and Karen S. Hamrick (Washington, DC: United States Department of Agriculture, 2018). Food halls have grown particularly fast in North America: Garrick H. Brown, *Food Halls of North America* (New York: Cushman & Wakefield, 2019).

49 Andrew M. Charles, *Delivery: Dining in Is the New Dining Out* (New York: Cowen Inc., 2018).

50 For deeper insight for the United States, see Kickert, "What's in Store: Prospects and Challenges for American Street-Level Commerce." For broader industry prospects, consult market analysis such as IBISWorld.

51 We already see smaller British and French towns disproportionately suffering from durable goods retail decline: Matthieu Delage et al., "Retail Decline in France's Small and Medium-Sized Cities over Four Decades. Evidences from a Multi-Level Analysis," *Cities* 104 (2020). Hughes and Jackson, "Death of the High Street: Identification, Prevention, Reinvention."

52 For more on this triad in urban environments, see a.o. Im Sik Cho, Chye-Kiang Heng, and Zdravko Trivic, *Re-Framing Urban Space: Urban Design for Emerging Hybrid and High-Density Conditions* (New York: Routledge, 2015); Meredith Glaser et al., *The City at Eye Level: Lessons for Street Plinths* (Delft: Eburon Uitgeverij BV, 2012).

53 Willie Macrae, "The Distillery District Toronto," in *The City at Eye Level: Lessons for Street Plinths*, eds. Hans Karssenberg, Jeroen Laven, Meredith Glaser, Matthijs van 't Hoff (Delft: Eburon, 2012).

54 See also the entrepreneur who transformed the Meent in Rotterdam: Robin von Weiler, "Meent Rotterdam," in *The City at Eye Level: lessons for street plinths*, eds. Hans Karssenberg, Jeroen Laven, Meredith Glaser, Matthijs van 't Hoff (Delft: Eburon, 2012).

55 Berry Kessels. "Klarendal Arnhem," in *The City at Eye Level: lessons for street plinths The City at Eye Level: lessons for street plinths*, eds. Hans Karssenberg, Jeroen Laven, Meredith Glaser, Matthijs van 't Hoff (Delft: Eburon, 2012), correspondence with Berry Kessels July 2020. Dany Jacobs, Ewan Lentjes, and Esther Ruiten, "Fashion District Arnhem:

Creative Entrepreneurs Upgrading a Deprived Neighbourhood," in *Creative Districts Around the World: Celebrating the 500th Anniversary of Bairro Alto* (Breda: NHTV, 2014).

56 Regeneration Team, *High Streets & Town Centres – Adaptive Strategies* (London: Great London Authority, 2019).

57 The Haarlemmerdijk won a 2014 award for the Netherlands' best shopping street. Nel de Jager. "The comeback of an urban shopping street," in: *The City at Eye Level: Lessons for Street Plinths*, eds. Hans Karssenberg, Jeroen Laven, Meredith Glaser, Matthijs van 't Hoff (Delft, Eburon, 2012). Floor Millikowski, "Nel De Jager (1953–18 September 2019)," *De Groene Amsterdammer*, October 2, 2019.

58 Urban scholar Andres Sevtsuk recommends setting up a coop model, a similar model to the aforementioned reparcelling: Sevtsuk, *Street Commerce: Creating Vibrant Urban Sidewalks*, 98–103.

59 Lorlene Hoyt and Devika Gopal-Agge, "The Business Improvement District Model: A Balanced Review of Contemporary Debates," *Geography Compass* 1, no. 4 (2007); Kevin Ward, "Business Improvement Districts: Policy Origins, Mobile Policies and Urban Liveability," ibid., no. 3; Abraham Unger, *Business Improvement Districts in the United States: Private Government and Public Consequences* (London: Palgrave Macmillan, 2016); Sevtsuk, *Street Commerce: Creating Vibrant Urban Sidewalks*, 96–98.

60 See also Hannigan, *Fantasy City: Pleasure and Profit in the Postmodern Metropolis*.

61 For more information, see www.mainstreet.org.

62 HG Parsa et al., "Why Restaurants Fail," *Cornell Hotel and Restaurant Administration Quarterly* 46, no. 3 (2005).

63 Streetwise has a 90% success rate of graduates after two years of tenancy; the organization also coaches and brokers space for existing businesses. More information on Heebels and Dusseldorp, "Experiment Aangename Aanloopstraten – Eindrapportage," 50–51. www.stichtingstreetwise. nl; interview and date from Leonie Kuepers, November 16 and 18, 2020.

64 David Sim, *Soft City: Building Density for Everyday Life* (Island Press, 2019). See also the developer's website www.nextstep.se.

65 See Erkin Özay, "Rust Belt Cosmopolitanism: Resettlement Urbanism in Buffalo," in *Buffalo at the Crossroads*, ed. Peter H. Christensen (Ithaca, NY: Cornell University Press, 2020). And www. westsidebazaar.com.

66 More information on www.wearemortar.com.

67 Almost all of the businesses supported by Findlay Kitchen and Findlay Launch are women, minority, and/or immigrant owned. Launch is the next

step toward a full-time business, and includes a business training curriculum. Information from conversation with Findlay Market CEO Joe Hansbauer, March 2021. More information on www.findlaylaunch.org and www.findlaykitchen.org.

68 Keiko Morris, "Retailers Looking to Test Run Stores See Opportunity in Short-Term Leases," *The Wall Street Journal*, September 1, 2018.

69 CREW Regeneration Wales, "Meanwhile Use in Wales: Summary and Guidance," (Cardiff: CREW Regeneration Wales, 2015); Nicolas Bosetti and Tom Colthorpe, *Meanwhile, in London: Making Use of London's Empty Spaces* (London: Centre for London, 2018).

70 City at Eye Level meanwhile space chapter, Meanwhile Space, *Meanwhile Space – Creating Better Places to Live and Work* (London: Meanwhile Space, 2018); Garyfalia Palaiologou, *Meanwhile Space: Ten Years in Practice* (London: Meanwhile Space, 2019). The Meanwhile Foundation has expanded this approach to community groups in other cities in the United Kingdom.

71 CEL Coopolis chapter, correspondence with Stephanie Raab, 2019.

72 For Dutch experiences with pop-up retail failures, see Nikki Sterkenburg, "Pop-Upstores Laten Zien Hoe De Winkelstraat Voorgoed Verandert," *Vrij Nederland*, April 3, 2020.

73 Interview with Leonie Kuepers, November 16, 2020. British pop-up retail space provider Sook aims to lower the cost of short-term retail occupancy by providing display shelving and interactive screens to advertise brands and merchandise. Spaces can be rented even by the hour. www.sook.space.

74 Pop-up spaces and existing storefronts are useful amenities after emergencies, and to activate new districts. For example, war-torn Rotterdam had several temporary shopping walks during the 1940s. Astrid Aarsen, *60 Jaar Lijnbaan* (Rotterdam: Architectuurzaken, 2013). Following the destruction of a 2011 earthquake, Christchurch built a shipping container shopping mall that remained open until 2018: Liz McDonald, "Christchurch Container Mall Tenants Scatter as Six-Year-Old 'Temporary' Community Ends," *The Press*, January 31, 2018.

75 On retail lease lengths, see e.g. Esther Fung, "Retail Rent Breaks May Last," *The Wall Street Journal*, June 16, 2021; Nicole LaRusso, Michael Slattery, and Hironori Imaizumi, "Manhattan Retail, Q1, 2021," in *CBRE Marketview* (New York: CBRE Company Report, 2021).

76 For more explanation on the internal makeup of pedestrian flows, see Sevtsuk, *Street Commerce: Creating Vibrant Urban Sidewalks*. For an historical reference on anchors, see Gruen and Smith, *Shopping Towns USA; the Planning of Shopping Centers*.

77 Smaller units help spur retail start-ups: Impresa Inc. Preservation Green Lab, Basemap, Gehl Studio, State of Place, *Older, Smaller, Better – Measuring How the Character of Buildings and Blocks Influences Urban Vitality* (Chicago: National Trust for Historic Preservation, 2014).

78 All noted sizes are Gross Floor Area, with a quarter to a third taken out for back-of-house spaces such as storage and kitchens. On common space requirements, see e.g. Coleman, *Shopping Environments: Evolution, Planning and Design*; Bill Beckeman, *How Much Space You Should Lease for Your Retail Business* (Burlington, MA: Linear Retail, 2012). Locatus data (The Netherlands). In The Netherlands, chain stores seek a minimum size of about 2600 square feet (250 square meters): Evers, Kooijman, and Van der Krabben, *Planning Van Winkellocaties En Winkelgebieden in Nederland*.

79 Coleman, *Shopping Environments: Evolution, Planning and Design*, 293–95; Fiona Cousins et al., *Laying the Groundwork – Design Guidelines for Retail and Other Ground-Floor Uses in Mixed-Use Affordable Housing Developments* (New York: Design Trust for Public Space – New York City Department of Housing Preservation & Development, 2015).

80 For examples, see Sim, *Soft City: Building Density for Everyday Life*.

81 For a comprehensive overview of frontage width, entrance and storefront design guidelines in the United States, see New York City Department of City Planning, *Active Design – Shaping the Sidewalk Experience: Tools and Resources* (New York: New York City Department of City Planning, 2013). In Europe, frontage dimensions tend to be part of overall design and character guidelines drawn by municipalities and regions. Liner retail can also line other non-active functions in the city. Historically, large church buildings had lining retailers, and today, liner retail can wrap around parking and institutional buildings: Sim, *Soft City: Building Density for Everyday Life*.

82 Coleman, *Shopping Environments: Evolution, Planning and Design*, 296–97. Zoning can incentivize or even mandate a minimum floor height in specified districts: Grant, "Designing at Ground Level."

83 The term three-mile-per-hour architecture is coined in J. Gehl, "Close Encounters with Buildings," *Urban Design International* 11 (2006).

84 Vancouver encourages visibility into premises in various urban design guidelines, e.g. in its HA-1A Design Policies amended in 2018. In some guideline documents, it sets a minimum visibility into premises, e.g. one foot. San Francisco has set a "visibility zone" at about four foot (1.2 meters) high, mandating 75% of a frontage allows people to see four feet in: San Francisco Planning, *Standards for Storefront Transparency* (San Francisco, CA: San Francisco Planning, 2013).

85 On window display and visual merchandising history and theory, see Tony Morgan, *Visual Merchandising Third Edition: Windows and in-Store Displays for Retail* (London: Laurence King Publishing, 2016); Paco Underhill, *Why We Buy: The Science of Shopping*, Updated and rev. ed. (New York: Simon & Schuster, 2009); Leonard S. Marcus, *The American Store Window* (New York: Whitney Library of Design, 1978); Dion Kooijman, *Machine En Theater: Ontwerpconcepten Van Winkelgebouwen* (Rotterdam: Uitgeverij 010, 1999); Claus Ebster, *Store Design and Visual Merchandising: Creating Store Space That Encourages Buying* (New York: Business Expert Press, 2011). Indentations and niches gained popularity in modernist storefront architecture: M. Jeffrey Hardwick, *Mall Maker: Victor Gruen, Architect of an American Dream* (Philadelphia: University of Pennsylvania Press, 2004); J. G. Wattjes, *Constructie En Architectuur Van Winkelpuien* (Amsterdam: Kosmos, 1926). In recent years, high-rent stores occupied by chains have flattened facades, replaced entrances with air curtains, and removed entrances to upstairs units (whose rent did not compensate for the lost space of ground-floor stairways). However, articulation and upstairs entrances are making a comeback as downtown living and historic preservation becomes attractive to residents and regulators alike.

86 For British design and signage guidelines, see e.g. Jan Kattein et al., *Design Spd 8: Shop Front Guidance* (London: London Borough of Merton, 2016). In the United States, storefront design guidelines tend to be written for historic districts, which can mandate design standards, e.g. Landmarks Preservation Commission, *Guidelines for Storefront Design in Historic Districts* (New York: City of New York, 2019). The Dutch railway architect has a retail design guide for all stations: Bureau Spoorbouwmeester, "Handboek Retail En Services," in *Visie Op Informatie* (Utrecht: Bureau Spoorbouwmeester, 2016). Façade improvement support has been surveyed as the most effective Main Street program in 40 American cities (as recommended by the National Trust for Historic Preservation): Kent A. Robertson, "The Main Street Approach to Downtown Development: An Examination of the Four-Point Program," *Journal of Architectural and Planning Research* 21 (2004).

87 See e.g. Gabrielle M. Esperdy, *Modernizing Main Street Architecture and Consumer Culture in the New Deal* (Chicago: University of Chicago Press, 2008); Richard Mattson, "Store Front Remodeling on Main Street," *Journal of Cultural Geography* 3, no. 2 (1983); J. J. Jehee, *Winkelpuien in Nederland: Ontwikkeling En Architectuur* (Zwolle: WBooks, 2015).

88 See e.g. Carmona et al., "The Value of Urban Design"; Helen Elizabeth Woolley, *The Value of Public Space: How High Quality Parks and Public Spaces Create Economic, Social and Environmental Value* (London: Commission for Architecture and the Built Environment, 2004); Matthew Carmona, "Place Value: Place Quality and Its Impact on Health, Social, Economic and Environmental Outcomes," *Journal of Urban Design* 24, no. 1 (2019). On the mixed success of pedestrianization, see Kelly Gregg, *Pedestrianized Streets – from Shopping to Public Space* (Dissertation, Toronto: University of Toronto, 2019). On business-funded streetscape improvements, see Ward, "Business Improvement Districts: Policy Origins, Mobile Policies and Urban Liveability." For general reading on public space, see Gehl, *Life Between Buildings: Using Public Space*; *Cities for People*; W. H. Whyte, *City: Rediscovering the Center*, 1st ed. (New York: Doubleday, 1988).

89 The maximum width of a frontage zone tends to be defined by the minimum width it leaves on sidewalks, e.g. 1.5m in Paris, 15–2m in San Francisco, and 2.5m in New York. Frontage zones are part of American Complete Streets guidelines, see National Association of City Transportation Officials, *Urban Street Design Guide* (New York: Island Press, 2013). For American patio layout guidelines, see e.g. Department of Consumer Affairs, *Sidewalk Café Design and Regulations Guide* (New York: New York City, 2013); Department of Planning and Development Review, *Sidewalk Café Design Guidelines* (Richmond, VA: City of Richmond, 2012). For European guidelines, see e.g. Mairie de Paris, *Reglement – Terrasses Et Étalages* (Paris: Mairie de Paris, 2020). On awnings, see e.g. Robert J. Gibbs, *Principles of Urban Retail Planning and Development* (Hoboken, NJ: John Wiley & Sons, 2012), 117–18. On café creep, see Jerold S. Kayden, "Zoning Incentives to Create Public Spaces – Lessons from New York City," in *The Humane Metropolis – People and Nature in the 21st-Century City*, ed. Rutherford H. Platt (Amherst and Boston: University of Massachusetts Press, 2006).

90 Jerde Partnership International and Jon A. Jerde, *The Jerde Partnership International: Visceral Reality* (Milano: L'Arca, 1998). University of Edinburgh professor of contemporary visual cultures Richard Williams derides shipping container stores as "hipster modernity", calling them "not even particularly cheap. (. . .) To use them for architecture is rarely the convenience their proponents make it out to be. So let's call it what it is: a matter of aesthetics." Richard J. Williams, "The Sinister Brutality of Shipping Container Architecture," *The New York Times*, August 14, 2019.

8 LIFE BEYOND TRANSACTIONS
NEW DESTINATIONS IN THE CITY

Figure 8.0 An artist studio in a former Berlin storefront connects production to exposure.

DOI: 10.4324/9781003041887-8

A vibrant city at eye level does not only comprise storefronts. In fact, the past chapters have demonstrated that the role of storefronts continues to dwindle in street-level architecture, as retail decline is accelerating, and bars and restaurants can only partially offset this loss. Whether we like it or not, the hegemony of transactional frontages is coming to an end. As British architect MacCormac already lamented decades ago, the transactions that underlie our urban economy are simply shifting out of sight, from storefronts to headquarters, warehouses, and now cyberspace.[1] We need to come to terms that our street-level architecture should, can, and already does serve many more key roles for the city and its citizens than just facilitating consumption. Successful ground floors can accommodate creativity, learning, production, socialization, and communication – all without a cash register in sight. Understanding the post-transactional life of frontages is not just key to maintaining and restoring the relevance of our current struggling commercial cores but to building economically and socially resilient future buildings and cities.

The next two chapters explore the many different roles that street-level architecture can fulfill besides selling items, experiences, and services. This chapter explores the ways in which ground floors find urban relevance as spaces of socialization, creativity, production, and culture, while the next chapter focuses on ground floors as living spaces. Both chapters will demonstrate that planning, developing, and designing frontages for life beyond commercial transactions is certainly not less worth pursuing. In fact, introducing new ground-floor uses to our most accessible streets and frontages makes our cities and their buildings more resilient, creative, and exciting. Each post-transactional street-level function has its own ability to interact with public space, its own financial bandwidth to occupy street-level spaces, and its own layout requirements and challenges. With the right function, the right tenant, the right design and layout, and the right enforcement, our street-level architecture can continue to excite, invite, and inspire passersby and the city in general. But the success of post-transactional frontages requires a shift in what we expect from our buildings at street level.

First step: acceptance
Second step: balance.

This paradigm shift is easier said than done. Perhaps the biggest hurdle to acknowledging the post-transactional value of frontages is the common consensus on storefronts as the holy grail of street-level frontages. As design guidelines, planning mandates, and development ambitions continue to push for more storefront units in an already oversaturated market, dozens of existing storefront businesses are shutting down every day. We seem to be so stuck in our belief that street-level commerce is the only way to enliven and give purpose to sidewalks that we cannot even see the value of post-transactional futures for our growing stock of vacant storefronts – let alone for new ground floors.

We have hardly passed through the stages of grievance when we are confronted with vacant storefronts. Squarely in the denial stage, vacant storefronts are too often seen as a temporary sign of failure rather than a permanent reflection of our economic evolution. The pain is real: vacant storefronts hurt the livability of neighborhoods and the image of streets. They held amenities and still hold memories. Vacant storefronts in central and often historical locations can symbolize the entire city and region. And as we discussed in the previous chapter, vacant storefronts significantly hurt nearby businesses as they erode continuous business clusters and their footfall. But the panacea is too often a mirage, as we continue to plan, develop, and design to magically fill up storefronts with a shrinking pool of potential commercial tenants. We are struggling to accept the inevitable and think of new uses for vacant storefronts that don't involve consumption, which is often the only way to bring life back to our most central spaces.

Part of this acceptance struggle is political, as governments are still searching for support and tools to reimagine what storefronts could be. Hard-hit by e-commerce and the COVID-19 pandemic, the United Kingdom has been leading the philosophical and practical quest for post-transactional storefront futures. Even British retail experts now understand that their venerable High Streets should retain their relevance as "an activity-based community gathering place" that is "clearly . . . about much more than retail".[2] In London, retailers and food services already make up less than a fifth of its commercial corridor tenants, prompting economist Mariana Mazzucato to reflect on the "public value" of these High Streets as social and economic ecosystems in a government report, openly asking: "Who are the streets for?"[3] British policy incentives offer some early, if crude answers. Storefront conversions to dwellings and offices no longer require planning permission, which has led to mixed early results.[4] A national Future High Streets Fund includes support to transitioning retail properties to post-commercial uses, even allowing local governments to plan, purchase, and repurpose storefronts by themselves.[5] The Irish government similarly subsidizes residential conversions of storefronts.[6] Similarly, Dutch regional and national governments are beginning to understand the merits of post-commercial planning and development incentives.[7] Across the board, government policies to reimagine storefronts for post-transactional futures are in early stages and face little enthusiasm among developers and the general public. In North America, post-transactional horizons for storefronts have yet to be widened by leaders and administrators.

The lack of political and regulatory momentum to repurpose vacant storefronts is also fueled by financial difficulties. Most post-transactional uses for storefronts will not be able to afford the same rents that departing retailers paid, and it is difficult to convince building owners and governments to take the haircut. Owners have vacant storefront spaces in their books – or worse, in the books of their lenders – at inflated property values, calculated from equally inflated assumptions of retail rental incomes that may never materialize again. Lower post-retail rents may prompt an expensive devaluation of the building, while maintaining the vacant status quo won't prompt angry phone calls from lenders or accountants, and lost rental income due to vacancy is often tax deductible. Instead of promoting vacancy, fiscal policy could prod owners to shift their views on vacant storefronts. Fiscal penalties have been proven to prod building owners to think about commercial and post-commercial solutions. Local governments can often be hesitant to levy fines to support conversions away from retail use, and they too may count on a fictional retail occupant for their tax revenues. Solutions may come from higher up the institutional ladder, as we have seen with the British national tax penalty on vacancy in the last chapter.[8] Fiscal policies and more aggressive interventions to prompt transformations of vacant storefronts should carefully deflate what could be a commercial property bubble.[9] They should also be careful not to take storefront transformation too far, as high housing and office pressures are beginning to force even viable retailers out of their spaces without protection, eroding otherwise continuous retail clusters.[10]

Most of all, our storefront transformation struggles are philosophical. Right in our faces, vacant storefronts force us to rethink the role of our most visible and central public and private spaces. What do we want from our urban cores, their sidewalks, and their storefronts, if we cannot spend money in them? And if not for storefronts, what should the ground floors of our new buildings hold to make them interact with the city?

In our process of grievance, we are still in the early stages of answering these questions. While the experience economy and e-commerce has already reframed our urban cores and their ground floors from places we *have* to go to places we *want* to go in the experiential revolution, we need to think beyond consumption to bolster of our most accessible spaces, even beyond downtown.[11] This chapter aims to offer alternatives to transactional storefronts by showing the potential of ground floors as social infrastructure, places for creation, culture, growth, and gathering – all while exciting and inviting passersby. Each of these alternatives are post-transactional, and are currently seen as less interactive than storefront businesses. However, the right tenants, the right strategies, and the right design can ensure that they support public life, each in their own way and often even more than transactional spaces.

Storefronts as social infrastructure

At the interface between our buildings and the city, ground floors are among the most logical places for social encounters. The previous chapter framed social interaction in the context of consumption, as pubs, bars, restaurants, lunchrooms, and coffee houses serve as neighborhood "third places" – those areas beyond the home and the workplace that allow us to meet friends and encounter strangers.[12] But to socialize, we do not always have to spend money. For example, public surveys indicate that downtown Vancouver's pedestrians visit to spend time with friends and family up to nearly twice as much as to shop.[13] Even without the need for consumption, our urban ground floors are cornerstones of the city's "social infrastructure": offering spaces that shape how we interact with friends and strangers, negotiate similarities and differences, and build trust.[14] In many ways, our ground floors can and do serve as interior public spaces.

The most well-known indoor public space is surely the public library. While libraries have traditionally been housed in dedicated buildings, they are increasingly coming into ground floors of existing buildings, including storefronts. Several trends make libraries increasingly interesting uses for ground-floor spaces. Libraries have expanded from places to simply borrow books to places for knowledge exchange, learning, personal growth, and innovation, which reposition them as the "living room of the city".[15] Libraries now facilitate co-work, homework, job access, skills and entrepreneurship training, after-school programs, local health and civic programs, and even innovation through makerspaces. Libraries are among the few indoor places where one can work, read, and learn in a safe, quiet – and, most importantly, a free environment for people of all ages and backgrounds.[16] While their need for physical book circulation has decreased, most libraries tend to take up more than a single storefront space, as they now host so many new functions. Nevertheless, small, flexible libraries can transform over the course of the day to serve different audiences, like freelancers, children, and the elderly.[17] From a temporary library running on a few thousand donated books and local design and development activists in Boston to more permanent libraries in smaller cities and towns, libraries can thrive in storefront spaces. However, full-service libraries tend to need more space than a typical urban storefront can offer. Larger retail buildings can be repurposed as libraries, and new library spaces can serve as the ground floor of new construction. In general, libraries can connect through the street by placing their most public meeting functions in the front, such as shared work tables and even in-house coffee shops. Shelving and lecture spaces can be located further back (Figure 8.1).[18]

Libraries often serve as neighborhood community centers, but these centers can also stand on their own in frontages. Increasingly moving away from dedicated

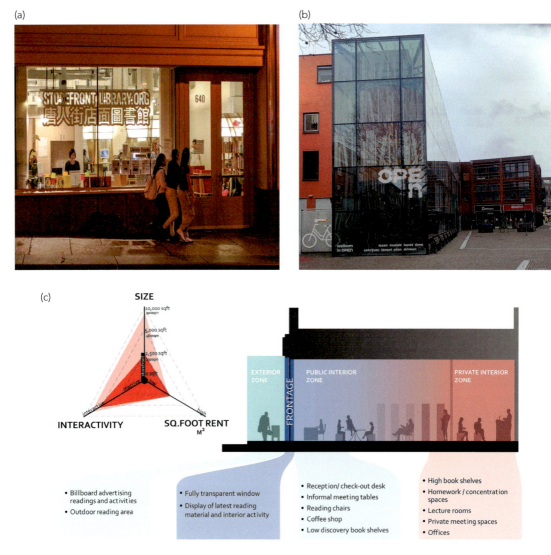

Figure 8.1a–c (a) Boston's Chinatown Library was started to prove the merit of a library space in an underserved neighborhood. Started with a donation of only a few thousand books and $30,000 in a 3,000-square-foot (270 square meter) space, the Chinatown library's interior was designed by university students and operated three months from a donated storefront.) **(b)** A former supermarket and office building in Delft, Netherlands, was repurposed as a more than 50,000-square-foot (5,500 square meter) library, arts, music, and community center, wrapped by a glass atrium that invites passersby and several liner storefronts. **(c)** With the right design and layout, libraries can interact with public space, although they are not able to afford expensive space.[19]
Source: (a) Image by Trevor Patt via Flickr, CC BY-NC-SA 2.0. (b) Image by Conrad Kickert, 2020. (c) Diagram by Conrad Kickert, 2021.

buildings into ground floors of new construction or former storefronts, community centers at eye level can better serve as the social and cultural heart of neighborhoods. In North America, community organizations are finding their way into former commercial storefronts to reach their target audiences. Youth and writing centers offer safety, relaxation, and educational opportunities to improve the lives of struggling inner-city teenagers. In Europe, community centers are similarly opening up to the sidewalk. For example, The Hague is increasingly relocating community centers into storefronts out of fiscal prudence, partnering with existing schools, cultural institutions, sports clubs, and health care organizations. In either case, ground-floor community centers can activate frontages and demonstrate community investment and cohesion.[20]

Similarly, places of worship are becoming sidewalk staples as mosques, temples, and churches increasingly occupy former storefronts. While struggling with stigma and often haphazard design, storefront places of worship can interact and add life to sidewalks if well designed with transparent front meeting rooms.[21] Community centers can temporarily occupy storefront spaces as well. Funded by foundations, developers, and governments, CultureHouse in Boston has set up several "indoor pop-ups" in vacant storefronts to invite passersby to play, work, meet others, or "just . . . hang out". Their "non-transactional" spaces "where someone can simply exist without spending money", target people of all ages and walks of life with a homely design, frequent events, seats and tables, play spaces, reading material, and free hot drinks.[22] In the United Kingdom, a joint venture between governments and the Meanwhile Foundation yielded an open call for community organizations to locate in pop-up storefront spaces we discussed in the previous chapter.[23] New construction can greatly benefit from community spaces at street level, both adding value to upstairs dwellings and workspaces and anchoring a building in the neighborhood. It may take enforcement to keep ground-floor community space open to non-residents and workers of new buildings. Community space can be mandated within new development, or developers can be required to contribute to a community center fund.[24] When designing for community centers, it is key to maintain a close-grained relationship to the sidewalk by placing the most public functions like meeting and leisure spaces in the front of the space, keeping spaces for concentration like offices and homework cubicles in the rear. Some community centers have even opened retail areas in the front, selling items that relate to and financially support the activities in the back (Figure 8.2).[25]

Storefronts for health, wellness, and care

Increasingly, our urban ground floors help us live healthier lives by accommodating health and wellness centers, as well as small medical and dental tenants. For better or worse, our spending on health and wellness has increased steadily over the past decades. For example, the global health club industry revenue has risen by almost 50% over the past decade, prompting a growth of health and fitness clubs (including yoga studios) in cities across the Atlantic by around 25%. While online competitors are lurking, especially after the COVID-19 pandemic, fitness and yoga culture's inherent social characteristics continue to call for physical spaces. In contemporary Western culture, fitness is a lifestyle statement like any other, and fitness and yoga studios have increasingly opened up to the sidewalk to see and be seen. Furthermore, fitness and yoga studios can support a wealth of health-focused commercial neighbors as well, making them attractive tenants for commercial streets that have vacancies. However, many fitness and yoga studios take up more space than the average urban storefront space.[26] As described in the previous chapter, personal service providers like nail and hair salons are also becoming more prominent in storefronts, as their offerings are not easily replicated online. They often straddle the line between retail and wellness (Figure 8.3).

Ground floors also increasingly house health care providers such as doctors and dentists, allowing them to locate closer to patients. In the more commercial American health care market, many singular general practitioners and dentists have evolved into chains that advertise their services to passersby through inviting storefronts and lobbies, looking to attract walk-in patients. The number of American outpatient health care centers has grown by more than half over the past decade alone.[28] Even in the European state-led health care model, doctors, dentists, and physical therapists are co-locating into modernized buildings to save on overhead such as a shared receptionist and an in-house apothecary. These practices increasingly find their way into the urban ground floor, taking up between 2,500 and 4,000 square feet (about 240 to 370 square meters) for most modern buildings – more space than a typical urban storefront could accommodate, but easy to fit within new construction. Increasingly, health care centers are joined with welfare functions and municipal functions to create 'one-stop-shops' for clients as well.[29] Costs to retrofit spaces for medical uses can run very high, making already-cramped and potentially leased storefront conversions less appealing than new construction for medical and dental users.[30] From a street-level architecture perspective, medical and dental spaces need to balance frontage interactivity with the privacy and focus needs of patients and providers, for example by moving more public functions such as reception and an apothecary to the front of the unit, leaving the back for consultations and waiting rooms (Figure 8.4).

Growth and learning

The ground floors of our cities are also spaces where we can grow and learn at all ages. Increasingly, educational and childcare facilities connect to public space in former storefronts and new street-level spaces. From childcare facilities to university classrooms, growth, and learning are becoming more visible in our cities at eye level. For example, daycare facilities have become a common sight in ground-floor spaces, reflecting and bolstering the family-friendly nature of cities. At street level, it is easy to drop off and pick up your child without the need for stairs and elevators, and frontages can provide exciting intergenerational connections between young children and passersby. The daycare industry is highly regulated between countries to protect the well-being of children, which strongly affects the spatial layout and standards for daycares. In general, regulations mandate 25 to 35 square feet (roughly 2,5 to 3,5 square meters) of space per child, which allows around 25 to 40 children (or about two separate groups) into the average storefront space and more in dedicated newly built spaces. As daycare efficiency

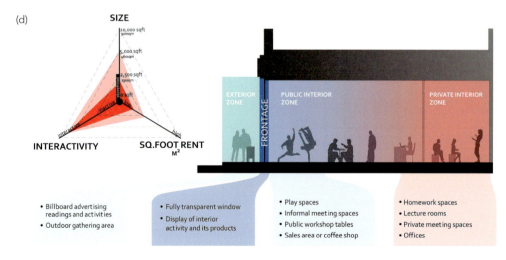

Figure 8.2a–d A community center or 'neighborhood laboratory' occupies a former corner storefront in The Hague and accommodates a neighborhood newspaper, meeting spaces at a nominal fee and events (a). Churches can open up to the city, like in The Hague's Attention Center, a church-led meeting space in a storefront, welcoming people of all walks of life (b). The CultureHouse Kendall Street space, opened between 2019 and 2020 in Boston, was deliberately designed as welcoming, yet intimate to draw in passersby (c). Community centers should place their most public functions in front of the building to welcome passersby (d).

Source: Image (a) by Conrad Kickert, 2021. Image (b) by Conrad Kickert, 2021. Image (c) courtesy of CultureHouse. Diagram (d) by Conrad Kickert, 2021.

Figure 8.3a–c (a) Fitness is a social activity that can be visible from the sidewalk, like this studio in Manhattan. (b) An Amsterdam boxing gym opens up to the sidewalk for ventilation and views of the action. (c) With interactive design, wellness spaces like fitness and yoga studios can connect well with the sidewalk, and operators can often afford premium spaces.
Source: Image (a) courtesy Billie Grace Ward via Flickr, public domain. Image (b) by Conrad Kickert, 2021. Diagram (c) by Conrad Kickert, 2021.[27]

increases with scale, daycares tend to need more space than a single storefront, and regulations on ventilation and daylight can make narrow, deep retail spaces difficult to convert to daycares. Daycares also greatly benefit from outdoor play space, which may limit their ability to locate in densely built up commercial corridors.[31]

Looking to connect with urban environments, universities are also increasingly locating micro-campus locations in urban ground floors. Urban locations makes universities more visible and may tie in with urban engagement missions. Chapter 6 already described a new street-level university retrofitted in a former office building in The Hague, which was a deliberate effort by a nearby university to connect its public administration students with the Dutch government capital at eye level. The new space contains an open meeting space and workspaces at the ground floor, with classrooms and lecture halls that require more concentration on higher floors. Similarly, American universities are bringing classroom and meeting spaces into urban environments. One of these spaces focuses on arts education; we will discuss this in an upcoming section. When designing either childcare or education spaces, public functions such as play rooms and meeting spaces should be located in the front, and the privacy of children and students should be carefully balanced with the need to engage with the sidewalk (Figure 8.5).

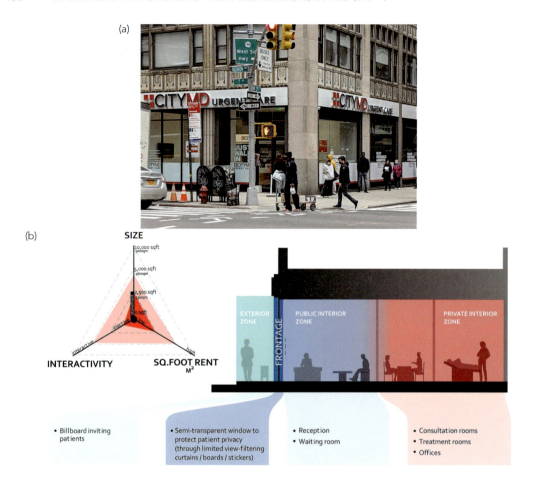

Figure 8.4a–b A CityMD urgent care facility in New York City balances a transparent corner storefront with privacy for waiting patients (a). Medical and dental spaces need to be carefully designed to welcome passersby, yet protect the privacy of patients (b).
Source: Image (a) 2020 by Jim Naureckas via Flickr, CC-BY-2.0. Diagram (b) by Conrad Kickert, 2021.

Ideation and collaboration

Besides socialization, learning, and growth, our urban ground floors are also excellent spaces for creating and collaborating on new ideas. Especially the rapid transformation of the nature of offices due to changing corporate culture, real estate evolution, and the COVID-19 pandemic open up possibilities to reinvigorate workspaces on urban ground floors. Far from the office desks and cubicles of yesteryear, our workplace can now unfold on a coffee shop table or chair, a co-working 'hot' desk, or a micro-office. If planned and designed correctly, workplaces can enter the city at eye level, facilitating interaction and collaboration and "make the economy visible" to passersby and potential collaborators – a term coined by the Project for Public Spaces.[32] Workplaces can become interactive street-level tenants, if we understand that productivity hinges on more than just focus, which tends to shun contact with outsiders. Research has proven that workplace productivity actually mostly hinges on collaboration, socialization, and learning – social processes facilitated by workspaces connected to the city at eye level. These processes are especially crucial for offices in the innovation and creative sector, and for smaller startup businesses.[33] When Jane Jacobs famously wrote "new ideas need old buildings", she meant that new ideas needed the urban interconnection and affordability that street-level spaces can bring.[34] Connecting the workplace to the city at eye level depends on finding the right tenant understanding of the value of public space, occupying the right space with the right design and the right frontage.

To see how extraverted and urban our workplace has become, we only need to visit our local coffee shop. Evolving from spaces to enjoy coffee and a conversation, coffee shops have become de facto workspaces for a growing generation of freelancers.[35] While not all coffee shops are happy with their new professional tenants, the coffee shop environment helps many freelancers (and for that matter, road warrior employees) be more productive and creative for a variety of reasons, including ambient noise levels, watching others work, and of course plenty of available sugar and caffeine.[36] Beyond

Figure 8.5a–c The transparent street-level frontage of an Amsterdam daycare shows off the creative work of its children to passersby and proud parents (a). Leiden University has constructed a campus in The Hague's government district, entered through a transparent and welcoming street-level frontage with workplaces and meeting places (b). Childcare spaces can become interactive neighborhood hubs, although the privacy and focus of children needs to be protected. Educational spaces for older children and adults act similarly to workspaces: place reception and meeting areas in the front (c).
Source: Images and diagram by Conrad Kickert, 2021.

facilitating individual work, coffee shops enable planned and serendipitous interactions as "third places", which have been proven to improve innovation and creativity. In fact, a new generation of innovation districts hinges on street-level coffee shops to facilitate their production of new ideas and products. Increasingly, tech companies and campuses are getting rid of private canteens to nudge their employees to meet each other in public street-level spaces like coffee shops and lunchrooms. Eindhoven's innovation park has concentrated its dining facilities in a central strip to generate "managed serendipity" between tech workers; Twitter now occupies the upper floors of a former San Francisco department store on top of a street-level market hall, similar to Google in New York.[37]

A big step up from the informal coffee shop table, co-working or flexible workspaces offer subscription-based desks, meeting spaces, and private offices. Co-working spaces combine the benefits of flexible work arrangements and chance encounters in coffee shops with the greater stability and ability to focus on a desk. Since their inception in the tech world in the mid-2000s, co-working spaces have seen double-digital annual growth across the Atlantic, benefiting from the labor-market shifts during the 2008 Great Recession and increasing corporate interest in flexible spaces. In the United States, almost a third of new office leases were signed for flexible co-working spaces in 2019, and growth is even higher in Europe. Originally population in the creative and tech economy of big cities, co-working spaces are finding their way into more sectors and smaller cities as well, and the COVID-19 pandemic has prompted more companies to diversify their workplace portfolio to embrace co-working spaces.[38] Co-working operators have professionalized from grass-roots communities of like-minded tech workers to subsidiaries of the world's largest office space owners, although successful spaces continue to focus on like-minded communities such as artists, coders, musicians, or women. Importantly for cities, co-working spaces especially locate and thrive in dense, walkable, transit-oriented environments with ample surrounding amenities.[39] Sustainable co-working spaces rely on economies of scale – especially in terms of membership numbers. This explains why three quarters of co-working spaces exceed the size of a storefront.[40] Co-working spaces often occupy several floors of larger buildings, but they often build an interactive street-level presence by placing meeting spaces and a coffee shop in the front. Like retail, co-working spaces are also becoming a coveted street-level amenity for new development, adding value to upstairs dwellings or offices.[41]

Beyond accommodating informal coffee shop workplaces or co-working spaces, ground floors can also house more conventional dedicated offices at various sizes. Even a storefront can comfortably fit up to around ten employees – making up the vast majority of businesses, especially in the creative sector.[42] Keeping a fine-grained cadence of seven to ten entrances per 300 feet (or 100 meters) of frontage in mind, street-level workplaces can easily grow over 5,000 square feet (500 square meters) with deeper units, although daylighting can become problematic. Street-level clusters of small businesses can serve as incubators, benefiting from knowledge spillovers and shared facilities. Many smaller companies may value their visibility from the street as they look for accessibility and exposure as part of a walk-in trade business model. Coined by Dutch zoning standards as having a "counter function", offices that rely on walk-in trade include real estate agencies, banks, and travel agents, but it is easy to recognize other offices that accept walk-in clients such as designers, accountants, lawyers, and the aforementioned doctors and dentists.[43] The transparency of office frontages that embrace walk-in trade reflects the "transactional value" that we have discussed in this book's introduction, which relates the amount of transactions between buildings and public space to the interactivity of its interface.[44] Offices that welcome visitors at least somewhat frequently will make sure their frontage feels welcoming, and even offices that do not rely on walk-in trade can open themselves up to the street, especially if they seek collaboration and visibility. Furthermore, office tenants can always be reminded of their civic duty to maintain openness to the sidewalk with design guidelines. In Amsterdam, office tenants moving into vacant storefronts were hand-curated by a neighborhood-wide coordinator, and lease agreements ensured that they could not draw their blinds to the sidewalk, which inherently attracted open-minded

tenants to move in. New street-level workspaces include a rentable storefront space for meetings, co-working and eating, and socially engaged film production company Visual Gain.[45] Learning from its retail brokerage experience, Cincinnati consultancy Urban Fast Forward set up their offices in a vacant storefront, maximizing their transparency to invite clients and advertise available spaces in front of a welcoming reception area. As founder Kathleen Norris commented: "We're about connectivity and the energy of the street. Plus, we wanted passing traffic to be able to see us and our listings."[46] Like many of the other spaces we discuss in this chapter, the key to ensuring workspaces interact with the sidewalk is to place more public uses toward the frontage, from entire (coffee) shops and reception areas to dedicated meeting rooms, displays of office work and simply viewing working desks. Smart placement of displays can also balance privacy and interaction (Figure 8.6). Street-level workspaces can also be part of new live-work units that interact with the street. More about this in the following chapter.

Production

Besides producing new ideas and innovations, the city can produce more tangible items at eye level as well, as ground-floor spaces can house a wide range of manufacturers and artisans. Instead of the typical smokestacks, docks, and warehouses we associate with manufacturing, production is (re-)entering urban environments with exciting hybrids between production, collaboration, and consumption. Especially a new wave of small manufacturers and artisans that grew from the 2008 recession, known as the Maker Movement, has a strong potential to enliven urban storefronts. Coalescing into vibrant maker districts from Barcelona (Poblenou) to Brooklyn (Navy Yard) and Abu Dhabi (Makers District), makers' focus on mixing production and consumption and the movement's relatively light manufacturing methods – often through advanced machinery – make them better neighbors and sidewalk activators than their industrial predecessors.[47] Makers adapt the centuries-old mixture of production, repair, and consumption we have seen in our case study cities – surviving as shoe repair shops, bakers, and framers – to the experience economy by focusing on artisanal production. Production often happens within the same storefront that goods are sold, as in the case of micro-breweries, coffee roasters, bicycle and leather goods manufacturers. Watching the production process proves to be a fascinating sight for passersby, helping them understand and appreciate local production processes.[48] Furthermore, makers can also promote a resilient and diverse urban economy, innovation, sustainable production, and inclusive economic opportunities with better jobs than in the retail industry.[49] Like with storefront desktop workspaces, the key to ensuring interactive maker frontages is finding the right street-level storefront maker tenant, providing them with

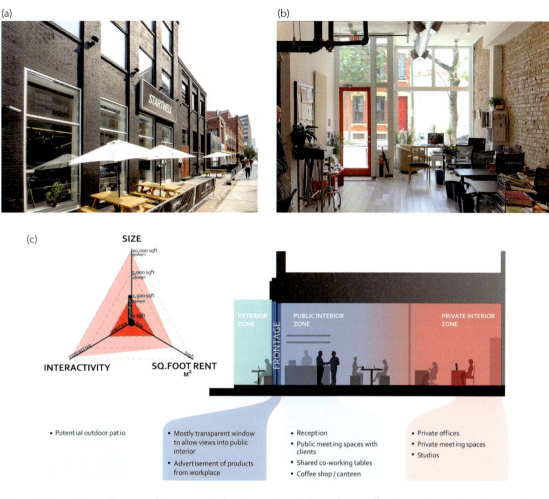

Figure 8.6a–c Startwell's co-working space in downtown Toronto has a front coffeeshop with a patio where members and visitors can meet, collaborate, and relax (a). Cincinnati's Urban Fast Forward has placed its reception and meeting area in an open-format storefront office (b). Workspaces can interact with public space through careful placement of more public functions such as meeting spaces, receptions, and coffee shops (c).
Source: Image (a) courtesy of StartWell Toronto, see www.startwell.co. Image (b) courtesy of John Yung at Urban Fast Forward. Diagram (c) by Conrad Kickert, 2021.

the right space, and managing a mutually beneficial relationship between their activities and the sidewalk.

In other words, we need to ensure makers can be of interest to the sidewalk, and the sidewalk can be interesting to makers. Especially small startup makers and those focusing on arts and artisanal production stand out as good candidates for this symbiosis. Similar to the co-working space, small manufacturing ideas can take root and grow at makerspaces, collaborative spaces that allow for sharing of amenities, tools, and expensive machinery. Makerspaces can also include incubator kitchens that welcome new producers to the food industry. Makerspaces form the social infrastructure of the maker community but they can rarely get by from membership and auxiliary fees. Furthermore, the cost of equipping a makerspace can be very high. Therefore, they often operate as part of libraries, schools, community centers, or other public and nonprofit entities. Self-sufficient makerspaces that support their own investment and staff are usually larger than a typical storefront, and they will struggle to afford retail rents. They can instead occupy larger ground-floor spaces built to suit their needs. Like with co-working spaces, we increasingly see makerspaces as a (subsidized) street-level amenity for new residential developments.[50] Makerspaces can interface with the city by directly revealing the maker process through transparent windows, but often spaces are fronted by a small sales area that displays goods made in the space, and supplies for makers.

One step up from the makerspace are storefront micro-units of 400 to 1,000 square feet (35 to 90 square meters) that allow a single maker to produce items and sell them in the same space. Similar to makerspaces, these artisan units often cannot support full retail rents: storefront conversions may need supporting funding, or units can be purpose-built on the ground floor of less central buildings.[51] Appreciating the value that small makers have for economic growth, innovation, and urban vitality, various cities have a strategy to support makers with affordable spaces and technical assistance. For example, Amsterdam has partnered with nonprofit agencies and brokers to support more than 60 incubators employing and inspiring thousands of artists, designers, makers, and other creatives.[52] Makers can also help activate new buildings and put a neighborhood on the map. When the street-level frontage of the new Westerdok development in Amsterdam struggled to attract commercial tenants before many residents had moved in, the developer leased 15 street-level retail spaces at below-market rates for ten years to artists and makers, who in turn promised to interact with the sidewalk and the neighborhood as a whole.[53] Below the famous Promenade Plantée on top of a disused railway, the Paris economic development agency SEMAEST curated artists and makers to occupy more than 50 roughly 1,000-square-foot arches at affordable rates. After a slow start, a new wave of makers and artists has turned the almost mile-long corridor into a showcase of French arts and crafts.[54] Besides directly selling their own products, storefront manufacturers and artisans can increase their revenue by programming classes and events, or by selling compatible merchandise, further blurring the boundaries between production, collaboration, and consumption, and finding another way to interact with the city.

Successful street-level production hinges on zoning, regulation, and stimulation as much as on careful design. Zoning often needs to be updated to accommodate the Maker Movement, as most regulations still see manufacturing as an irritant, incompatible with nearby residents and workers, and a threat to frontage transparency and retail continuity. An increasing number of North American and European cities are creating new 'artisan zones' to enable makers to locate in storefronts and small-scaled buildings. In fact, cities understand the value of street-level production to reinvigorate existing commercial districts, branding areas as maker districts.[55] Often, rezoning comes with reevaluating environmental regulations, adopting nuisance agreements, smart design, construction, and scheduling to avoid conflicts and encourage higher-density environments that incorporate making without denying that manufacturing needs space and tolerance to thrive.[56] Often, cities need to go even further to protect existing makers and bring new ones in, as small manufacturing is one of the first uses to get priced out of a gentrifying neighborhood. We have seen how Birmingham has tried to protect small manufacturing in its southern urban core. Similarly, San Francisco has adopted a 'Production, Distribution and Repair' zoning and incentive strategy to maintain space for these businesses in various mixed zones. Other public stimulus tools include direct grants or loans, promotion of temporary small manufacturing in storefronts, and logistics support. Increasingly, developers come to understand that like street-level retail and co-working

spaces, urban manufacturing can raise the value of nearby homes and offices, and they may integrate production into larger developments as a loss leader.[57] In terms of design, interactive maker frontages can vary from a window display or sales room of manufactured products (especially if makers are wary of intellectual property theft) to a full view into the manufacturing process. It's what fits best with the values of the makers themselves, and interactivity can be cast into zoning overlays as well as (affordable) rental agreements. Furthermore, cities should understand that manufacturing frontages will not always be transparent or neatly manicured, but can still add to sidewalk life and excitement (Figure 8.7).[58]

Art and culture

As we have seen from the introduction onward, frontages are excellent communication devices. From storefront branding to displays of trust in residential front stoops, street-level architecture always carries a message. These messages can be personal and social, but frontages are also excellent places to communicate cultural values, including through art and creative expression. Art is an excellent way to occupy vacant storefronts, either temporarily or permanently, and it can invigorate creative life into new developments as well. Instead of plywood or brown paper on vacant storefront windows, artworks can stimulate the senses of passersby sufficiently to maintain a sense of continuity in retail streets that are struggling with vacancy. Beyond being a good neighbor, vacant storefront owners can also gather visibility for their properties by opening up to artists. As the creative director of a New York organization that places pop-up art exhibits in vacant storefronts explains, "We've found the currency building owners care about most is cash, but not far behind that is [good] publicity."[59] Furthermore, arts can keep a vacant storefront occupied and taken care of, which reduces its risk of vandalism and squatting.[60] Storefront art exhibits can be as simple as convincing storefront owners to display artworks in front their otherwise vacant and still-closed windows. While potential tenants can still see the commercial unit behind, store window art can create significant buzz from passersby as well as the selection process, which tends to be highly competitive as artists crave the kind of exposure that well-located store windows can provide them. Funded by the National Endowment for the Arts, the City of San Francisco ran the Art in Storefronts program for several years. Hundreds of artists vied for around two dozen store window spots, many of which became social media hits. Store window art exhibits like Art on the Ave in New York allow artists to sell their displayed artworks with significant success. Some storefront owners may be worried about insuring potentially expensive artworks, which other cities resolved by displaying print reproductions of artworks. In various permutations, store window art has now been a success in a range of American and European cities.[61] Furthermore, mural

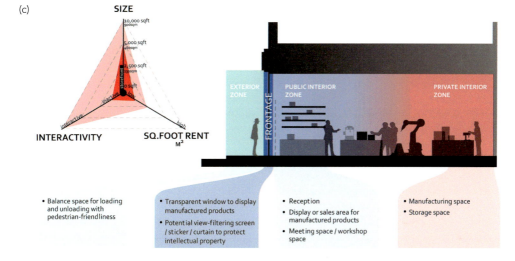

Figure 8.7a–c The Amsterdam Westerdok street-level artisan spaces include social manufacturing and prototyping workshop CRE-8, which allows passersby to see the making process as well as a display of finished products (a). And sometimes, a small manufacturer simply wants to show off their process to the city, opening up their workshop for light, air, and views (b). Urban makerspaces can interact with public space by displaying the making process, by inviting passersby to join this process in workshops, and by selling the made products. Careful visual filtering can protect intellectual property (c).
Source: All images by Conrad Kickert, 2021.

programs can give otherwise blank walls new meaning and relevance in cities, supporting creative expression while building destinations and bolstering safety and building community pride.[62]

One step beyond store window art displays and murals, street-level spaces can fully open up to display, experience, and potentially sell artworks on a pop-up basis. Owners will need to open up their spaces for artists, their installations, and their patrons, but in return they gather even more visibility and publicity for otherwise vacant spaces. This win-win model has been quite successful in the United States, where an increasing number of foundations, nonprofits, and governments understand the mutual benefits of pop-up art spaces for artists and building owners. New York's Chashama has negotiated vacant storefront leases to artists since 1995, allowing artists to fully occupy these spaces for temporary exhibits and installations for free or a nominal fee. Other organizations in New York and other cities have picked up the idea and Chashama has expanded to other American cities as well.[63] Following the United Kingdom's strict taxation of vacancy, temporary storefront uses have included arts projects for years, supported by tax breaks. For artists, these pop-up spaces have "become the only way to do a project relatively cheaply in much of London", which of course also demonstrates the problematic position of arts spaces in high-rent markets.[64]

Moving from a temporary to a permanent street-level use is more challenging for arts projects, as they tend to rely on variable grant and public funding. Furthermore, art spaces in storefronts need significant rent concessions from owners, which they are unlikely to extend indefinitely. Policy, partnerships, and long-term funding can help to make arts a permanent fixture at eye level. Permanent arts organizations can make the leap into storefront or other street-level spaces, opening as nonprofit art galleries that welcome artists to display and create their work on a rotating basis without the need for constant transactions. Art spaces can also broaden their scope to creative education and meeting spaces to connect with more people. Started from Montreal in partnership with a local university, Art Hives have been constructed as 'community art studios' across the globe to welcome visitors of all ages and backgrounds to make, display, and grow with art.[65] A fixture in New York City, the freely accessible Storefront for Art and Architecture hosts regularly rotating exhibits in a 100-foot (30 meter) dynamic façade designed in 1993 by artist Vito Acconci and architect Steven Holl. The storefront invites and challenges passersby on often critical topics through exhibits and frequent events.[66] Public policy can help solidify the arts at eye level as well. To protect the role of arts and culture even in new development, the new Hafencity district in Hamburg supports street-level spaces for cultural use through development policy, including the construction of various exhibition and performance spaces. Together with local organizations, the district now permanently supports making, exhibiting, performing and selling art.[67] Like with many of the other uses we have seen in this chapter, singular new developments may also significantly benefit from the cultural capital of a street-level arts space for upscale dwellings, and more affordable artist loft developments similarly benefit from the practical value of exhibition space.[68] Either way, the sidewalk benefits (Figure 8.8).

Conclusion

Each in their own way, the street-level uses in this chapter add to the social, cultural, and economic life of cities, while interacting with passersby with communicative, social, and sometimes even transactional frontages. Like stores, bars, and restaurants, many of these post-transactional functions can thrive in clusters – think of the benefits of clustered incubator spaces, offices, and makerspaces. These functions can bring more relevance and public life to central streets and public spaces, giving people more reasons to visit them. As such, they can enliven commercial areas, like a library or a community center that draws in a steady flow of patrons, or storefront art spaces that generate buzz and footfall in otherwise struggling retail areas.

The post-transactional city at eye level comes with new dynamics and challenges. Financially, it is inevitable that many of these post-transactional functions cannot afford the same rents or purchase prices as retailers or restaurant owners. Increasingly, the street level is turning from a primary business case that generates its own profits, to a secondary business case that adds value to upstairs developments, neighborhoods, and entire cities. The private and public sectors will need to acknowledge this shift and ensure. Furthermore, most post-transactional uses do not naturally interact with the sidewalk as much as transactional storefronts would. It takes the right tenant who understands the value of public space, the right designs and layouts to allow these tenants to interact with public space, and the right enforcement of these designs and layouts to ensure their interaction will last. The blinds will go down before you know it, breaking the critical mass of street-level interaction between buildings and public space and potentially starting a downward spiral of introversion. Even then, these post-transactional uses need to be carefully blended with transactional storefronts to avoid disrupting storefront continuity. Last but not least, many of these new uses may be too large for existing storefront spaces. Post-transactional futures may require consolidating vacant storefronts, or extending to upper floors. The design of new street-level spaces needs to remain flexible, not only to maximize the ability to host the functions in this chapter, but to allow urban tenants we do not yet even know about to introduce themselves to the future city. Design spaces with flexible sizes and ample opportunity to engage with the sidewalk to give the floor to this new generation.

Notes

1 R. MacCormac, "Urban Reform: Maccormac's Manifesto," *Architects Journal* 15 (1983).

2 First quote from retail veteran Bill Grimsey in Communities and Local Government Committee Housing, *High Streets and Town Centres in 2030* (London: House of Commons, 2019). Second quote from Regeneration Team, *High Streets & Town Centres – Adaptive Strategies* (London: Great London Authority, 2019), 19–21.

3 These numbers are from the Office for National Statistics. Mariana Mazzucato, "Public Value and the High Street," in *High Streets & Town Centres – Adaptive Strategies*, ed. Regeneration Team (London: Great London Authority, 2019). See also Mary Portas, *The Portas Review: An Independent Review into the Future of Our High Streets* (London: Department for Business, Innovation and Skills, 2011); Bill Grimsey, *The Grimsey Review – an Alternative Future for the High Street* (Corham: Company Report, 2013); Bill Grimsey et al., *The Grimsey Review 2 – It's Time to Reshape Our Town Centres* (Corham: Company Report, 2018); Andrew Stone, "Can Resi and Mixed-Use Breathe New Life into Ailing High Streets," *PropertyWeek*, July 18, 2019.

4 India Block, "Law Allowing Conversion of Shops to Homes Without Planning Permission 'Truly Disgraceful' Says Riba," *Dezeen*, July 21, 2020; Building Beautiful Commission Building Better,

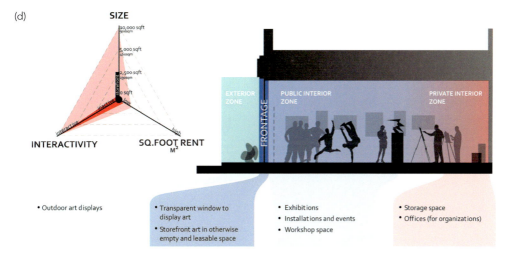

Figure 8.8a–d San Francisco's storefront art exhibits became social media successes, like Hui-Ying Tsai's "Eulogy on My Humble Abode" in 2010 (a). One of the newly constructed street-level art spaces in HafenCity is designxport, an exhibition, event, and meeting venue for Hamburg's design profession, supported by the city (b). The Storefront for Art and Architecture's hybrid façade opens and engages with Manhattan passersby (c). While unable to pay significantly for street-level spaces, art at eye level can invigorate sidewalks like no other, from displaying art to inviting passersby to engage in interactive installations or workshops (d).
Source: Image (a) by San Francisco Arts Commission, City of San Francisco. Image (b) courtesy of Laura Müller. Image (c) by Artandarch via Wikimedia Commons, cc-by-2.0. Diagram (d) by Conrad Kickert, 2021.

Living with Beauty (London: Communities and Local Government Ministry of Housing, 2020).

5 Communities and Local Government Ministry of Housing, *Future High Streets Fund – Call for Proposals* (London: Communities and Local Government Ministry of Housing, 2018); Housing, *High Streets and Town Centres in 2030*, 24–25; ibid. Every year, hundreds of retail storefronts are transformed into homes: Simon Williams, "Retail to Residential Conversions Set to Rise," *Boodle Hatfield*, www.boodlehatfield.com/the-firm/articles/retail-to-residential-conversions-set-to-rise/.

6 This subsidy is part of a larger initiative to increase the number of residents in Ireland's largest urban cores. Irish Tax and Customs, "Living City Initiative," in *10–31–01* (Dublin: Irish Tax and Customs, 2020).

7 Dutch policies remain ad hoc and national legislation and funding lag behind the United Kingdom: Barbara Heebels and Suzanne van Dusseldorp, *Experiment Aangename Aanloopstraten – Eindrapportage* (The Hague: Platform31, 2016).

8 A Dutch vacancy ordinance is relatively weak due to its discretionary nature, the amount of work to administer fines, and the relatively low cost of fines: Sandra Suijkerbuijk and Johan Groot Nibbelink, *Aanpak Leegstand in Zuid-Hollandse Winkelstraten* (The Hague: Provincie Zuid-Holland, 2019). American cities like San Francisco, Washington D.C., and New York are now experimenting with registries and penalties for vacant storefronts, with varying levels of success: Larisa Ortiz Associates, *Storefront Vacancies Best Practices* (Cambridge, MA: Community Development Department, 2018).

9 Jennifer Shea, "The Commercial Real-Estate Market's Impending Crash," *JSTOR Daily*, May 27, 2020; John M. Griffin and Alex Priest, "Is Covid Revealing a Cmbs Virus?" *SSRN* (2020): 115; Cezary Podkul, "Commercial Properties' Ability to Repay Mortgages Was Overstated, Study Finds," *The Wall Street Journal*, August 11, 2020; Joe Rennison, "Destruction of Value in Us Real Estate Revealed," *Financial Times*, September 27, 2020; Katy O'Donnell, "The Next Economic Crisis: Empty Retail Space," *Politico*, 2020. For Europe, see Green Street, *Fundamentals in Flux – Pan-European Commercial Property Price Index* (London: Green STreet, 2020). On Manhattan, see Derek Thompson, "How Manhattan Became a Rich Ghost Town," *The Atlantic*, October 15, 2018.

10 Stone, "Can Resi and Mixed-Use Breathe New Life into Ailing High Streets"; Housing, *High Streets and Town Centres in 2030*; Rebecca McDonald, "Converting Shops into Houses Is Not the Panacea for Struggling High Streets," *Centre for Cities*, www.centreforcities.org/blog/converting-shops-into-houses-is-not-the-panacea-for-struggling-high-streets/. The replacement of peripheral retailers by housing reminds us of the bid-rent curve, which is far steeper for retailers than for dwellings. As the curve sharpens for retailers due to re-concentration, dwellings can now outbid peripheral storefronts – even when they present locally desirable amenities.

11 Dutch retail consultant Joost Nicasie questions the "goals to visit" urban cores along two axes: needs versus wants, and material/commercial versus immaterial/noncommercial: Joost Nicasie to LinkedIn Pulse, June 23, 2020.

12 Ray Oldenburg, *The Great Good Place: Cafes, Coffee Shops, Bookstores, Bars, Hair Salons, and Other Hangouts at the Heart of a Community* (Philadelphia, PA: Da Capo Press, 1999).

13 This is the result of a 2017–2018 survey of downtown pedestrians. Socializing with friends and family was cited as the main reason to visit downtown, yet half also responded they interacted with someone they never met before. J. Gehl, *Downtown Vancouver Public Space & Public Life* (Vancouver: City of Vancouver, 2020), 50, 60.

14 Eric Klinenberg, *Palaces for the People: How Social Infrastructure Can Help Fight Inequality, Polarization, and the Decline of Civic Life* (New York: Broadway Books, 2018).

15 Ken Worpole, *Contemporary Library Architecture: A Planning and Design Guide* (New York; London: Routledge, 2013), 80.

16 James Fallows and Deborah Fallows, *Our Towns: A 100,000-Mile Journey into the Heart of America* (Vintage, 2018). and the Urban Libraries Council via www.urbanlibraries.org. For the United Kingdom, see Libraries Taskforce, *Libraries Deliver: Ambition for Public Libraries in England 2016–2021* (London: Cultura Department for Digital, Media & Sport, 2016).

17 David Giles, Jeanette Estima, and Noelle Francois, *Re-Envisioning New York's Branch Libraries* (New York: Center for an Urban Future, 2014), 54; Worpole, *Contemporary Library Architecture: A Planning and Design Guide*.

18 Fred Schlipf and John A. Moorman, *The Practical Handbook of Library Architecture: Creating Building Spaces That Work* (Chicago: ALA Editions, 2018); Worpole, *Contemporary Library Architecture: A Planning and Design Guide*.

19 Image (a) by Trevor Patt via Flickr, CC BY-NC-SA 2.0. Image (b) by author, 2020. For more on the Chinatown Library, see www.storefrontlibrary.org and Meghan E. Irons, "For Chinatown, a New Chapter," *Boston Herald*, September 21, 2009. Image (c) by author, 2020. On the Delft library, see www.archdaily.com/266672/mediatheek-delft-dok-architecten and https://dokarchitecten.nl/en/project/media-library-delft. In America, suburban big-box stores are ideal for library transformations due to their floorplate size. Some multilevel (urban) department stores are more difficult to reuse due to the large weight of book shelves. Image (c) by author. Diagram by author.

20 Gemeente Den Haag, *Buurthuis Van De Toekomst: Het Fundament* (The Hague: Municipality of The Hague, 2014).

21 On storefront churches, see Ira E. Harrison, "The Storefront Church as a Revitalization Movement," *Review of Religious Research* 7, no. 3 (1966); Asha

22 CultureHouse, *Culturehouse Kendall – Impact Report* (Boston: CultureHouse, 2020), 4. ohn Surico, "From Dead Store to Pop-up 'Social Infrastructure'," *Bloomberg CityLab*, September 10, 2019; CultureHouse, *Culturehouse Kendall – Impact Report*; CultureHouse, *Culturehouse Manual* (Boston: CultureHouse, 2018).

21 Kutty, "Sanctuaries Along Streets: Security, Social Intimacy and Identity in the Space of the Storefront Church," *Journal of Interior Design* 45, no. 1 (2020).

23 The pilot project ran between spring 2019 and spring 2020 in five storefronts: Communities and Local Government Ministry of Housing and Rt. Hon. Jake Berry MP, "High Streets Open Doors to Community Projects," *News Release*, 2019.

24 See Larry Beasley and Frances Bula, *Vancouverism* (Vancouver: On Point Press, 2019); A. Lehnerer, *Grand Urban Rules* (Rotterdam: 010 Publishers, 2009).

25 This is common for American writing centers that teach writing skills. See e.g. the 826 writing centers in several American cities and DISCO in Birmingham, Alabama.

26 In 2019, revenue was estimated at $96.7 billion: Racquet & Sportsclub Association International Health, *2018 Ihrsa Global Report* (Boston, MA: IHRSA, 2018), 32; *2020 Ihrsa Global Report* (Boston, MA: IHRSA, 2020). On the spatiality of fitness, see Roberta Sassatelli, "Fitness Culture," In *The Blackwell Encyclopedia of Sociology* (Malden, MA: Blackwell, 2007); Jennifer Smith Maguire, *Fit for Consumption: Sociology and the Business of Fitness* (London: Routledge, 2007); Katherine Rosman, "The Boutique Fitness Boom," *The New York Times*, June 17, 2019.

27 Image (a) courtesy Billie Grace Ward via Flickr, public domain. Image (b) by Conrad Kicket, 2021. Diagram by Conrad Kickert, 2021.

28 Caroline Lewis, "The Dentist's Office Gets the Urgent-Care Treatment," *Crain's New York Business*, December 11, 2017; CBRE Research, *2018 U.S. Medical Office Buildings* (Los Angeles, CA: CBRE, 2018). The US urgent care industry has grown annually by over 6% between 2014 and 2019, although this growth is expected to slow: Anna Miller, *Urgent Care Centers – Report Od5458* (New York: IBISWorld Inc., 2019).

29 This average size is calculated from submissions to the 2016 building award for the Dutch Association of General Practitioners. See also Lex van Waarden and Judith van Empel, *Handboek Bouw Gezondheidscentra* (Utrecht: Landelijke Huisartsen Vereniging, 2015).

30 Coy Davidson, "Leasing Retail Space for Medical Use," *Colliers International*, www.coydavidson. com/healthcare-real-estate/leasing-retail-space-medical-use/.

31 Space requirements include secondary spaces like hallways, storage for children's belongings, sanitary and administrative rooms. Maximum group sizes and design standards strongly vary between ages, countries and states. For example, for the United States, see Linda Cain Ruth, *Design Standards for Children's Environments* (New York: McGraw-Hill, 2000); Public Buildings Service – Office of Child Care, *Child Care Center Design Guide* (Washington, DC: U.S. General Services Administration, 2003). For The Netherlands, see e.g. Ministerie van Binnenlandse Zaken en Koninkrijksrelaties, *Bouwbesluit 2012 – Kinderopvang* (The Hague: Ministerie van Binnenlandse Zaken en Koninkrijksrelaties, 2012); Ine van Liempd and Ed Hoekstra, *Ruimten Maken Voor Nul Tot Vier Jaar* (Amsterdam: Uitgeverij SWP, 2011).

32 Nate Storring, "Placemaking and the Evolution of Innovation Districts," Project for Public Spaces; Nate Storring and Meg Walker, "8 Placemaking Principles for Innovation Districts," Project for Public Spaces.

33 Ben Waber, Jennifer Magnolfi, and Greg Lindsay, "Workspaces That Move People," *Harvard Business Review*, 2014; Christine Congdon, Donna Flynn, and Melanie Redman, "Balancing We and Me," *Harvard Business Review* 92, no. 10 (2014); Judith H. Heerwagen et al., "Collaborative Knowledge Work Environments," *Building Research & Information* 32, no. 6 (2004); Andreas Andreou et al., *2008 Workplace Survey – United States* (Washington, DC: Gensler, 2009).

34 Jane Jacobs, *The Death and Life of Great American Cities* (New York: Random House, 1961).

35 On the changing nature of freelance working: Patricia Leighton and Duncan Brown, *Future Working: The Rise of Europe's Independent Professionals* (London: United Kingdom, 2013). The gig economy employs significant numbers of desk workers: Elka Torpey and Andrew Hogan, *Working in a Gig Economy* (Washington, DC: United States Bureau of Labor Statistics, 2016).

36 David Burkus, "Why You Can Focus in a Coffee Shop but Not in Your Open Office," *Harvard Business Review*, 2017; Emma Felton, *Filtered: Coffee, the Café and the 21st-Century City* (London: Routledge, 2018); Ravi Mehta, Rui Zhu, and Amar Cheema, "Is Noise Always Bad? Exploring the Effects of Ambient Noise on Creative Cognition," *Journal of Consumer Research* 39, no. 4 (2012).

37 On Eindhoven's business park, see Jacques van Dinteren and Paul Jansen, "Considerations for Science Parks to Remain Competitive," (36th IASP World Conference, Nantes, France, 2019); Bert-Jan Woertman, "Brain Belts: The Many Innovation Centers That Will Take on Silicon

Valley," *VentureBeat*, October 16, 2016. On Twitter in San Francisco, see David Sim, *Soft City: Building Density for Everyday Life* (Washington, DC: Island Press, 2019). On innovation and urban connections, see Bruce Katz and Julie Wagner, "The Rise of Innovation Districts: A New Geography of Innovation in America," in *Metropolitan Policy Program* (Washington, DC: Brookings Institution, 2014); T. A. Hutton, "The New Economy of the Inner City," *Cities* 21, no. 2 (2004); Julie Wagner, Bruce Katz, and Thomas Osha, *The Evolution of Innovation Districts* (Washington, DC and Lugano: Global Institute on Innovation Districts, 2019). See also Daniel Aaron Silver and Terry Nichols Clark, *Scenescapes: How Qualities of Place Shape Social Life* (Chicago: University of Chicago Press, 2016).

38 Andrew Nelson and Ron Zappile, "U.S. Flexible Workspace and Coworking: Established, Expanding and Evolving," in *Research Report* (San Francisco, CA: Colliers International, 2019); Tom Sleigh, Damian Harrington, and Andrew Hallisey, "The Flexible Workspace Outlook Report 2019," in *Colliers Insight* (London: Colliers International, 2019); Waber, Magnolfi, and Lindsay, "Workspaces That Move People." In smaller cities, profitability remains lower than larger cities: Casten Foertsch, *2019 Profitability of Coworking Spaces* (Berlin: Deskmag, 2019). For The Netherlands, see Yanti Rabelink, "De Win-Win Van Flexwerken in Retailcentra En Hotels," *Stadszaken*, May 22, 2019. On the COVID effects on co-working, see OfficeRnD and LiquidSpace, *2020 State of the Flexible Workspace Industry Report* (Atlanta, GA: OfficeRnD and LiquidSpace, 2020).

39 Gretchen Spreitzer, Peter Bacevice, and Lyndon Garrett, "Why People Thrive in Coworking Spaces," *Harvard Business Review* 93, no. 7 (2015); Minou Weijs-Perrée et al., "Analysing User Preferences for Co-Working Space Characteristics," *Building Research & Information* 47, no. 5 (2019); Steve King, "Coworking Is Not About Workspace – It's About Feeling Less Lonely," *Harvard Business Review* 16 (2017).

40 Many smaller co-working spaces are run as a nonprofit or as auxiliary income to another business such as the office of a lead tenant or a retailer. Alessandro Gandini, "The Rise of Coworking Spaces: A Literature Review," *Ephemera* 15, no. 1 (2015). On sizes of coworking spaces, see the 2018 Global Coworking Survey by DeskMag, one of the largest co-working organizations and journals in the field. In 2018, 28% of co-working spaces was smaller than 2,500 square feet (roughly 250 square meters; the typical size of a large storefront), and the historical trend is downward: DeskMag, *Ultimate Coworking Space Data Report* (Berlin, Germany: DeskMag, 2018). On profitability, see Foertsch, *2019 Profitability of Coworking Spaces*.

41 Kaarin Vembar, "Take Care: How an Indie Store Is Merging Coworking and Retail," *RetailDive*, 2019; James D. Cook, Scott Homa, and Keisha McDonnough Virtue, "Can Coworking Work at the Mall?" in *Retail Research Point of View* (Chicago, IL: Jones Lang LaSalle, 2018).

42 Companies with fewer than ten employees make up more than three-quarters of American firms, and nearly 85% of firms that operate mostly at desks. In the creative sectors, the percentage of businesses below ten employees is even higher. Desk businesses in the United States are counted as NAICS 51 (Information), 52 (Finance and Insurance), 53 (Real Estate and Rental and Leasing), 54 (Professional, Scientific and Technical Services), 55 (Management of Companies and Enterprises). The definition of creative sectors varies between organizations within the United States. See Christine Harris, Margaret Collins, and Dennis Cheek, *America's Creative Economy* (Oklahoma City, OK: National Creativity Network Creative Alliance Milwaukee, 2013). Furthermore, these numbers are comparable in Canada and Europe, per Eurostat and Statistics Canada.

43 Dutch regulators argue that a strong 'baliefunctie' essentially turns office tenants into commercial service providers, which brings them in line with retailers in terms of parking requirements and attracting traffic: Municipality of Amsterdam, "Bestemmingsplan Water," in *NL.IMRO.0363. A1103BPSTD-VG01* (Amsterdam, Netherlands: Municipality of Amsterdam, 2020).

44 MacCormac, "Urban Reform: Maccormac's Manifesto." Offices with walk-in trade and a counter function often need to adhere to stricter zoning and building regulations, including barrier-free access, bathroom facilities and parking requirements: Thomas Dolan, *Live-Work Planning and Design: Zero-Commute Housing* (Hoboken, NJ: John Wiley & Sons, 2012), 137.

45 Between 2010 and 2013, storefront vacancy decreased from twelve to three. The frontage approach has won two awards for its transformative and communicative capacities. Joost Nicasie, *Winkelvastgoed Als Instrument – Het Effect Van Vastgoedcoordinatie in De Amsterdamse Transvaalbuurt* (Doorn: Areaal Advies, 2014).

46 Interview with Kathleen Norris and John Yung, July 20, 2020; www.urbanfastforward.com.

47 Laura Wolf-Powers et al., "The Maker Movement and Urban Economic Development," *Journal of the American Planning Association* 83, no. 4 (2017); Dale Dougherty, "The Maker Movement," *Innovations: Technology, Governance, Globalization* 7, no. 3

(2012); Chris Anderson, *Makers: The New Industrial Revolution* (New York: Crown Business, 2012).

48 Manufacturing visibility is a key learning point for building a circular economy and for showing diverse job and entrepreneurial opportunities. Barbara Heebels and Janneke ten Kate, *Aan De Slag Met De Nieuwe Maakindustrie* (The Hague: Platform31, 2019); Ben Croxford et al., *Foundries of the Future: A Guide for 21st Century Cities of Making* (Delft: TU Delft Open, 2020).

49 *Foundries of the Future: A Guide for 21st Century Cities of Making*; Alex Hutchinson et al., *Made in Place – Small-Scale Manufacturing and Neighborhood Revitalization* (Washington, DC: Smart Growth America, 2017). In the United States, the Urban Manufacturing Alliance promotes urban manufacturers with many of these arguments: www.urbanmfg.org. Urban manufacturing presents entrepreneurial and employment opportunities to minorities and immigrants, paying more than retail wages: Doug Saunders, *Arrival City: How the Largest Migration in History Is Reshaping Our World* (New York, NY: Vintage, 2011); Croxford et al., *Foundries of the Future: A Guide for 21st Century Cities of Making*; Mark Muro et al., *America's Advanced Industries: What They Are, Where They Are, and Why They Matter* (Brookings, 2015).

50 Howard Davis, *Working Cities: Architecture, Place, and Production* (London: Routledge, 2020); Jenifer Buckley, H. Christopher Peterson, and R. James Bingen, "The Starting Block: A Case Study of an Incubator Kitchen," *International Food and Agribusiness Management Review* 17, no. 1030–2016–82972 (2014); Morgan M. Hynes and Wendy J. Hynes, "If You Build It, Will They Come? Student Preferences for Makerspace Environments in Higher Education," *International Journal of Technology and Design Education* 28, no. 3 (2018).

51 Urban manufacturing expert Ilana Preuss calls these small-scaled artisanal spaces "micro-retail", and regards them as urban assets worth subsidizing by developers and cities to bolster the urban economy and project bottom line: Ilana Preuss, "Artisan Businesses and Equitable Neighborhood Development: An Important Formula," in *How to Do Creative Placemaking*, eds. Jason Schupbach and Don Ball (Washington, DC: National Endowment for the Arts, 2016).

52 Bureau Broedplaatsen, *Revised Studio and Creative Incubator Policy for Amsterdam 2015–2018* (Amsterdam: City of Amsterdam, 2016).

53 The "breeding place" Westerdok was brokered by Urban Resort, a nonprofit artist space developer and manager with ties to the creative and squatter scene in Amsterdam: Urban Resort, *Geschiedenis Van Urban Resort* (Amsterdam: Urban Resort, 2017).

More information on the Westerdok in Jeroen Laven et al., *The City at Eye Level in the Netherlands* (Wageningen: Blauwdruk, 2017).

54 Jeffrey T. Iverson, "Parisian Walkways: The Rebirth of the Le Viaduc Des Arts in the 12th Arrondissement," *France Today*, October 24, 2017; Alexandra Michot, "Il Faut Sauver Le Viaduc Des Arts," *Le Figaro*, October 22, 2012. See also www.leviaducdesarts.com.

55 At the time of writing, North American cities include Ottawa, Canada's zoning for light industrial in specific commercial corridors; Cincinnati's "Urban Mix" zone; "Artisan zones" (often tailored to specific industries such as food and beverage production) in Indianapolis, IN, Nashville, TN, Bozeman, MT, San Diego, CA, Kansas City, MO; form-based codes in Peoria, IL, Overland Park, KS, Beaufort, NC, Somerville, MA and Fort Worth, TX; and the mentioned PDR zones in San Francisco. European examples include "co-location zones" in London and "zones for economy mixed use" in Brussels: Croxford et al., *Foundries of the Future: A Guide for 21st Century Cities of Making*, 132–33; Johnny Magdaleno and Lee Wellington, *An Urban Revival: How Land Use Tools and Real Estate Strategies Are Fueling the Resurgence of Light Manufacturing in Greater Boston* (New York: Urban Manufacturing Alliance, 2018).

56 Croxford et al., *Foundries of the Future: A Guide for 21st Century Cities of Making*, 132–35; Heebels and Kate, "Aan De Slag Met De Nieuwe Maakindustrie." The Dutch Board of Government Advisors suggests a triad between "calm, noise and bustle" to mix living, working, and manufacturing: Marco Broekman et al., *Guiding Principles Metro Mix* (The Hague: College van Rijksadviseurs, 2019).

57 Croxford et al., *Foundries of the Future: A Guide for 21st Century Cities of Making*, 170–71; Preuss, "Artisan Businesses and Equitable Neighborhood Development: An Important Formula"; Peter Hirshberg, Dale Dougherty, and Marcia Kadanoff, *Maker City: A Practical Guide for Reinventing American Cities* (Berkeley: Maker Media, Inc., 2016), Chapter 7; The City and County of San Francisco, "Pdr Districts," in *Sec. 210.3* (San Francisco: American Legal Publishing Corporation, 2020).

58 Croxford et al., *Foundries of the Future: A Guide for 21st Century Cities of Making*, 170–71; 78–79; Robert N. Lane and Nina Rappaport, eds., *The Design of Urban Manufacturing* (New York: Routledge, 2020).

59 Quote from Smart Space's Creative Director Ellen Scott: Jacob E. Osterhout, "New 'Borderland' Art Exhibit Finds Home on Broome Street, Focuses on Cable-Access Tv Show Concept," *Daily News*, March 22, 2011.

60 CREW Regeneration Wales, *Meanwhile Use in Wales: Summary and Guidance* (Cardiff: CREW

Regeneration Wales, 2015); Nicolas Bosetti and Tom Colthorpe, *Meanwhile, in London: Making Use of London's Empty Spaces* (London: Centre for London, 2018).

61 San Francisco Arts Commission, *Art in Storefronts Toolkit* (San Francisco: San Francisco Arts Commission, 2013); Colleen Powers, "Storefront Art Programs Reflect Cities' Changes & Challenges," *Creative Exchange*, February 8, 2017. The first competition was held in Cambridge 2019; it ran again in 2020: Cambridge Community Development Department, "Vacant Storefront Creative Design Contest," www.cambridgema. gov/CDD/econdev/vacantstorefrontresources/ vacantstorefrontcreativedesigncontest; Amelia F. Roth-Dishy, "The Art of Vacant Storefronts," *The Harvard Crimson*, April 20, 2019. For Art on the Ave, see www.artontheavenyc.com.

62 Maura E. Greaney, "The Power of the Urban Canvas: Paint, Politics, and Mural Art Policy," *New England Journal of Public Policy* 18, no. 1 (2002); Eynat Mendelson-Shwartz and Nir Mualam, "Taming Murals in the City: A Foray into Mural Policies, Practices, and Regulation," *International Journal of Cultural Policy* 27, no. 1 (2021).

63 For more information, see www.chashama.org. See also Jotham Sederstrom, "Anita's Way: Douglas Durst's Eldest Daughter Merges Art with Real Estate," *Commercial Observer*, June 19, 2012. For example in Boston, SpaceUs, started by two MIT graduates rents vacant storefronts for a mixture of workspaces, exhibition spaces and sales areas: www. spacesus.co, Lilly Smith, "Want to Get Rid of Vacant Storefronts? Let Artists Take Over," *FastCompany*, January 7, 2020.

64 Bosetti and Colthorpe, "Meanwhile, in London: Making Use of London's Empty Spaces," 8, 9.

65 The original Art Hive in Montreal is co-sponsored by Concordia University and a range of government and philanthropic funders. Students earn credits as instructors. Janis Timm-Bottos and Rosemary C Reilly, "Learning in Third Spaces: Community Art Studio as Storefront University Classroom," *American Journal of Community Psychology* 55, no. 1–2 (2015).

66 Quote from www.storefrontnews.org/general-info/ about-storefront. See also https://architizer.com/ projects/storefront-for-art-and-architecture/.

67 Marichela Sepe, "Urban History and Cultural Resources in Urban Regeneration: A Case of Creative Waterfront Renewal," *Planning Perspectives* 28, no. 4 (2013); HafenCity GmbH, "Vorhang Auf: Die Hafencity Als Bühne Für Kultur," www. hafencity.com/de/leben/vorhang-auf-die-hafencity-als-buehne-fuer-kultur.html.

68 Ground-floor galleries as part of affordable artist housing: Maria Rosario Jackson and Florence Kabwasa-Green, "Artist Space Development: Making the Case," in *Leveraging Investments in Creativity* (Washington, DC: Urban Institute, 2008).

9 LIVING AT EYE LEVEL
PROSPECT AND REFUGE

Figure 9.0 Residents enjoying the street in the Netherlands in 2012.
DOI: 10.4324/9781003041887-9

We have seen how the city at eye level can host transactions, socialization, innovation, production, and culture – but mostly, our frontages actually host us as dwellers. Especially beyond our main streets, a lot of the everyday sidewalk life in our cities actually takes place in front of homes. But some homes interact with the sidewalk a lot better than others, which strongly depends on the design of the public-private interface. This chapter first describes the ways in which dwellings and their residents interact with the city on the ground floor, before offering design suggestions to maintain and improve this interaction at various levels, densities, and project types.

The life of dwelling at eye level

Living at eye level can benefit the vibrancy of cities in a variety of ways, as residential frontages can fulfill a range of useful roles. At the most basic level, the street-level frontage allows residents to enter their homes. They serve as a place of *transition* from public space like sidewalks and streets to the private realm of their home. This happens not just through placing doors, but in transition zones in front of (and behind) doors that act as a physical and psychological filter between homes and the city. In front of the home, we can see 'hybrid zones' like stoops, porches, and yards. Behind the front door, home layouts can place more public functions like cooking and dining in front (Figure 9.1). Over the past century, the physical way in which we access our homes in cities has changed considerably, as the type and density of urban dwellings has radically shifted. The single-family home, whether free-standing or connected to others in rows, directly connected to the street with its own front door and transition zone has increasingly made way for denser multifamily buildings in the heart of our cities. Especially from the mid-20th century onward, modernist designers removed direct dwelling entrances from the street, which they considered obsolete, usually only leaving storage, parking or outright blank walls at eye level. A lack of trust in public life only exacerbates this introversion, and higher densities make connecting individual dwellings and the street increasingly difficult. Team X and Structuralist architects began to reappreciate the interaction between dwellings and the city for social life and control, resulting in experiments to bring back street-level entrances to at least lower-floor units. As we have seen in our case study cities, direct street-level residential entrances have indeed risen again over the past decades, often prompted by designers and urban policy. Nevertheless, as Dutch architecture scholar Birgit Jürgenhake calls it, the personal "face" of individual urban dwellings has increasingly become hidden behind an anonymous "mask" of larger multi-unit buildings, as our urban densities have increased. Furthermore, the loss of individual dwelling entrances and transition zones like yards, stoops, and porches directly in front has resulted in a loss of ability for residents to connect with the city (Figure 9.2).[1]

The inability of residents to interact with the city right in front of their dwellings is especially a social loss.

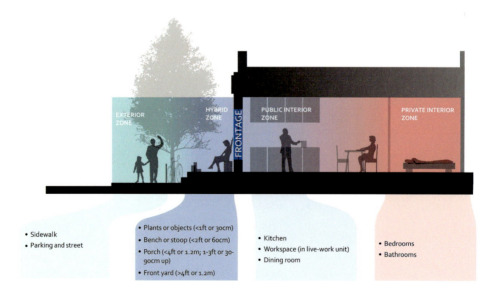

Figure 9.1 The residential public-private transition starts in the hybrid or transition zone in front of the home, continuing in the frontage and the interior, where more public uses can be placed toward the front of the house. When this natural transition cannot take place, residents will ensure privacy and territory through more stringent measures such as fences, black-out curtains, or even walls.
Source: Diagram by Conrad Kickert, inspired by Eric van Ulden and Sander van der Ham, "De Stoep in Vogelvlucht," in De Stoep, eds. Eric van Ulden, Daniel Heussen, and Sander van der Ham (Rotterdam: NAi010, 2015).

Entrances, but especially the transition zones in front of them, are a hub for neighborhood social life. Research has proven that 80% of our neighborhood informal contacts start right in our front yards, porches, and stoops.[2] Indeed, streets with transition zones have significantly more social life than those without them. In fact, many residents tend to prefer front yards to back yards, as they offer opportunities to socialize with neighbors.[3] In North America, porches are an essential part of the social life of neighborhoods, allowing residents to enjoy themselves and engage with passersby, roles that only intensified during the COVID-19 pandemic.[4] Social contacts in front of homes tend to be more informal and less committed than in the home itself, but are an important part of the social glue of neighborhoods. These contacts build what sociologists call public familiarity: knowing the faces and being able to guess the lifestyles and viewpoints of neighbors, which adds to feelings of

(a)

(b)

(c)

(d)

Figure 9.2a–d Dwellings and the street through time: among the first hybrid spaces for expression, transition, and storage were created in front of Dutch medieval homes, soon coined stoops (a); single-family dwellings in Buffalo with a porch in front indicate and reinforce strong social ties (b); multifamily dwellings on top of parking in Detroit signal distrust and disconnection (c); street-level dwelling entrances and hybrid zones are reintroduced in high-density Vancouver projects through urban design guideline mandates (d).
Source: Image (a) by Conrad Kickert, 2021. Image (b) by Conrad Kickert, 2020. Image (c) by Conrad Kickert, 2014. Image (d) by Conrad Kickert, 2017.

neighborhood rootedness and safety. Furthermore, the more social connection, the more responsibility residents feel for the sidewalk.[5] Of course, socialization in front of the house should happen on terms that residents are comfortable with, which differs from one person to the next. Essentially, the zone in front of their homes offers a prospect to the street and neighbors, backed by the refuge of one's home – an evolutionarily preferred human condition.[6] Beyond building adults' connections, transition zones are important in the socialization of children, as they make their first social steps from the home to the city.[7]

Front doors and transition zones are also excellent spaces for personal expression, allowing residents to communicate their esthetic, personal, and even political viewpoints to the city. As residents customize their environment, they also exert control over the urban environment to fit their needs.[8] Expressions almost always take up space outside the home in the transition zone, and can range from a simple flower pot in front of a home, to placing furniture (which of course also helps socialization) and even entire front yard displays of political beliefs. Expressions are certainly not always allowed by law, as they may coopt public space and altering building facades. Austrian artist-architect Hundertwasser proposed a "Fensterrecht" (Window Law) to allow renters to change their façade as far as their arms could reach out their windows.[9] Even without these laws in place, most residents still go to amazing lengths to make the vicinity of their homes their own. A recent study of more than 6,000 streets in Rotterdam, the Netherlands demonstrates that residents frequently coopt sidewalks in front of their homes with more than just bicycles and trash bins, enlivening sidewalks with personal expressions, planting, and furniture. These expressions generate significantly more social life and improve residents' satisfaction with their living environment.[10] Rotterdam aligns with international studies that demonstrate the correlation between personal expressions on and in front of homes and positive evaluations of neighborhoods, as they give "environmental messages" of care, homeliness and safety. Expressions can help passersby understand the lifestyles and identities of dwellers (Figure 9.3).[11]

Of course, residents do not only customize their dwellings to express themselves and welcome visitors, but also to signal their territory and protect their privacy. The street-level dwelling hence constantly negotiates between engaging and retreating from others.[12] Dutch environmental psychologist Machiel van Dorst describes how street-level dwellings relate to the street with different "privacy zones", which operate at various scales between the home and the city. The layering and shaping of these zones balance territoriality with the desire to socialize with neighbors and passersby.[13] The need for privacy highly varies between people, cultures, and locations. People can be introverted or extraverted, cultures can have specific gender and family roles, as well as value modesty over expression, and busy or dangerous locations can encourage barricading.[14] Territory and privacy can be regulated in the frontage itself by opening or closing windows and doors, but is easier to demonstrate and regulate in the transition zone through cues like personalization, fencing, and signage. If dwelling frontages or transition zones do not allow residents to control their own privacy (e.g., by using windows that are too large, or locating right next to a busy street), residents experience stress and tend to withdraw inside their house or erect barriers to protect their privacy, effectively ending the ability to interact with neighbors and the city.[15] Territoriality also improves the safety of homes and streets beyond just 'eyes on the street'. Danish architect David Sim explains "while windows are eyes on the street, I would add that doors means 'arms and legs on the street. . .' sending a stronger signal of security, warning would-be perpetrators and assuring potential victims, not only that you will be seen, but that you can be reached as well."[16] As early as the 1970s, researchers discovered that neighborhoods with a clear sense of territory, personalization, and ownership of their publicly accessible spaces experienced less crime. Since then, these elements commonly found in street-level dwellings and well-used transition zones have consistently been proven to protect homes from vandalism and burglary, and public spaces from perceived and real crime.[17] Of course, territorializing spaces in front of the home can also raise questions of equity, as transition zones and personal expressions can increase spatial segregation and can signify social privilege and status.[18]

New life at eye level

Now that we know the myriad ways that street-level dwellings can add to the social life, expressivity, and sense of rootedness and safety of residents, neighbors, and passersby, how do we make sure that new street-level architecture reaches this potential? Successful eye-level dwelling hinges on a few key elements, as noted next:

- **Direct access to public space.** While higher urban density calls for stacked dwellings accessed through internal horizontal and vertical systems, there is no reason that new buildings should be devoid of street-level dwellings with direct doors to the street. What the Dutch call 'ground-bound housing', a house with a direct connection to public space, is paramount to the liveliness of residential streets, and can easily be integrated at the foot of larger buildings. Vancouver's design guidelines for new downtown development demonstrates that even in taller buildings, a podium of rowhouses with a dense pattern of street-level doors and transition zones is possible. As mentioned in our Vancouver chapter, the city mandates rowhousing with

Figure 9.3a–c Residents shape their dwellings and the spaces in front of them to express themselves (a), socialize (b), and to set territory and privacy boundaries (c).
Source: All images in Buffalo, NY, by Conrad Kickert, 2021.

entrances roughly 25 to 30 feet (6 to 10 meters) apart in most new dense developments, enlivening the sidewalk at the foot of otherwise high-rise blocks. While developers were initially wary of building so close to the city's busy public spaces, the homes have proven a huge success. While only contributing to 2% of new housing stock, these rowhouses have an outsized benefit to the social life of streets.[19] The transition zones in front of individual home entrances are far more personalized than for shared entrances, which reflects their greater sense of personal ownership. In return, as David Sim rightfully states, "immediate access to the street is what makes city life so attractive", especially for families with children and disabled dwellers, who can benefit from (nearly) level access to public space. Dwellings should anticipate lining the street in their street-level floor plans, placing more public functions like kitchens, living rooms, (and as discussed soon, home offices) in front. Furthermore, they should comprise multiple levels, to keep more private spaces like bedrooms and bathrooms sufficiently removed from public space.[20]

- **Street-level façades that balance welcoming, individuality, access, and privacy.** At the threshold of the home and the city, the building façade has both a communicative role, a technical role, and a filtering role. Facades should communicate personal beliefs (as mentioned in for example Hundertwasser's Fensterrecht) but also more formal design choices that delineate homes from one another through horizontal and vertical articulation that breaks up larger volumes. Attractive street-level facades communicate trust in public space through transparency and personalization, offer a sufficient level of complexity in their façade expression to visually excite passersby, and a sufficient level of care and upkeep.[21] As mentioned, street-level facades also (usually) fulfill the technical role of entryways. As buildings have become denser and technology has evolved, the pressure has increased on the street-level frontage to accommodate the entry and exit of people, but also vehicles, garbage, and packages. The entry of people should be prioritized by consolidating vehicular and service entrances, and preferably placing them in lesser-used parts of the frontage. More about this later in this chapter. Doors should have minimal thresholds to public space, but placing floors slightly above street level increases the level of privacy. Vancouver has overcome this paradox between universal access and privacy by raising street-level dwellings, but also giving them secondary, barrier-free access to parking.[22] The right amount of transparency in a residential frontage varies strongly between cultures, people, location, and even the time of day, but in general, frontages that are too transparent are simply barricaded by residents with curtains, privacy stickers, or worse. After all, residents have a right and a desire for street-level privacy. On the other hand, residents crave light and air to enter their dwellings, and they can be as interested in seeing passersby as the other way around.[23] Inside otherwise large windows, louvers, shutters, blinds, and curtains can maximize residents' leeway to open or close windows according to their needs, giving them control of their exposure to the street.[24] A significant determinant of their ultimate decision depends on what happens right outside these windows in the transition zone.

- **The right transition zone between homes and the city.** As we have seen in the first part of this chapter, a key element of sociable, communicative, and sheltered homes at eye level is the zone in which the private home transitions into the public spaces of the city. While we have seen that the public-private transition even starts inside by placing more guest-friendly kitchens and living rooms in the front of the home, the zone especially impacts the city outside the front

door. Like many other elements of successful street-level dwellings, designing the right transition zone depends on culture, location, climate, and the needs of individual residents. The beloved American porch, which can be up to 15–20 feet (4 to 6 meters) deep with a front lawn, may not fit into narrow European streets. Vice versa, American domestic culture may be less amenable than Dutch extraversion to placing the home almost directly up to sidewalks. The transition zone can allow space for personal expression even in the tiniest spaces, lifting a small sidewalk tile for vertical greening or potted plants. In general, transition zones begin to be able to fulfill a social role when furniture can be placed, like a bench or a little chair at about two feet (less than a meter) wide. From there onward, more space means more room for socializing with more people, and transition zones begin to blossom socially between three to six feet (one to two meters) wide – the typical width of Vancouver's mandated transition zones and Rotterdam's most successful transition zones.

Transition zones can house for chairs, tables, play space for children, and unobtrusive bicycle or bin storage, and it should include permeable garden space as well. In Rotterdam, transition zones wider than six feet (or two meters) became increasingly coopted by residents as their own private space, barricading them with fences and hedges, resulting in a similar introversion to homes placed too close to the sidewalk. Of course, in many American cities, the transition zone can be wider without this barricading tendency, as its neighborhoods have a culture of keeping front yards more open. As mentioned, transition zones can benefit from being raised slightly to further demarcate private space, and to filter views into homes. Vancouver's zones are raised between two to three feet (about 0.5 to 1 meter) from the street. However, raising the transition zone also raises issues of universal access and segregation between private and public space. Do not mistake hybrid zones with ambiguous zones: transition zones should connect directly with the main street-level entryway of homes, as this is where residents enter and exit every day. Last but not least, zones should have the right solar orientation and be sheltered from wind, providing residents sufficient comfort to interact with the street.[25]

Existing streets may not have sufficient space for transition zones. However, existing streets can accommodate personalization and socialization with a redesign that reallocates space for cars toward wider sidewalks and transition zones. The Dutch 'woonerf' comes to mind, a concept from the 1970s that reimagined streets as curb-free shared spaces for people of all ages and abilities to not just move through, but inhabit. Cities across the world are adopting shared

Figure 9.4a–d Even at a foot wide, transition zones can already express identity through planting. This also helps green the city, and city programs in Belgium and the Netherlands provide free planting and advice (a). Another foot also allows for a seat or a bench (b). Three or more feet, a meter, and we have space for tables and more chairs for socialization, like in Amsterdam's specifically designed transition zones in front of new homes. These can also be recessed into arcades in higher density projects (c). And at six or more feet, two meters wide – and a few steps up – porches can function as outdoor social rooms (d). Front yards allow even more space for expression, although design guidelines and enforcement should prevent barricading larger spaces and placing obtrusive bins, bicycles, or cars.
Source: Image (a) CC-BY-2.0 via Wikimedia by Opuntia, 2007. Images (b) and (c), Buffalo, NY by Conrad Kickert, 2021. Image (d) Amsterdam, by Conrad Kickert, 2021.

space residential streets to encourage safety and socialization.[26] Started in Ghent, Belgium, Living Streets are temporary street closures that allow residents to reimagine their street spaces for socialization, personalization, and greening. This process has inspired similar projects elsewhere, admittedly prompting questions of permanence and gentrification.[27] Successful street-level dwelling encompasses all scales, from maintaining public-private transitions within the dwelling floor plan to balanced façades, sociable, personalizable, and privacy-aware transition zones and streets (Figure 9.4).

Street-level dwellings at higher densities

When urban densities go up, many of the axioms of successful street-level dwelling become more difficult to accomplish. With the wrong design, higher population densities jeopardize social bonds at street level as unfamiliar passersby, whether motorized or not, begin to crowd out known neighbors.[28] Taller residential buildings may also deteriorate the comfort of public spaces by causing wind tunnels or obstructing sunlight. Architecturally, tall residential buildings force more residents to share the same amount of street-level frontage for entry doors, but also for parking garages, places to deposit trash, access utilities, emergency exits, and increasingly, package deliveries. This high-rise pressure risks transforming the street-level façade from a place of social interaction and personal expression to an anonymous transition zone for people, vehicles, and goods. This creates what Australian urbanists Kim Dovey and Felicity Symons call "density without intensity".[29] The same deterioration of social life occurs internally in high-rise residential buildings, as corridors and lobbies may be shared by too many people to build fine-grained networks of recognition and interaction. Paradoxically, high-rise living hence places more people closer together, yet actually decreases socialization between themselves and with the city.[30]

Above a certain density, maintaining interactive street-level architecture, especially residential architecture, therefore needs proper design guidelines.[31] These guidelines ensure that high-density architecture has the right function at eye level, at the right scale, and with the right transition zone. In many cases, the loss of street-level and internal social life due to high-density housing can be offset by commercial and other amenity spaces at street level, as described in the previous chapters. Developers understand the value of street-enlivening functions like retailers, but also co-working spaces, makerspaces, and other urban amenities at the base of their buildings, which add to the attractiveness of upstairs dwellings even if these amenities run at a loss. Furthermore, many cities negotiate with developers to include otherwise loss-making street-level "planning gain" amenities like schools and community centers in high-density developments – although developers should be prevented from making them only available to their tenants.[32] High-rise residential frontages should define the street, and hence not be set back too much, which would disrupt an otherwise continuous street wall. On the other hand, the form of buildings should ensure proper wind and sunlight conditions. Utilities like parking, package deliveries, and trash collection should be minimized behind as few doors as possible, ideally placed along side or back streets. Cities like Seattle, San Francisco, and Rotterdam have active policies in place to ensure that high-rise buildings have continuous and humanly scaled 'podiums' of only a few stories tall, which contain interactive uses and minimize disruptions by car parking, blank walls, trash collection, and emergency exits.[33] Ottawa, Canada, rightfully makes a distinction between the 'expression' that high-rise buildings seek in the skyline, versus the 'experience' they shape at eye level.[34] Vancouver's design policy understands that not all frontages can hold commerce or public amenities. Instead, their high-rise policy "domesticates the high-density streetscape" by encouraging densely built up rowhouses with individual entrances and well-designed transition spaces at the basis of mid-rise or high-rise residential developments. As we discussed in this chapter and in Chapter 5, these guidelines have been quite successful in Vancouver, although their replication in other cities has more mixed results. Furthermore, incentivized residential frontages along busy Vancouver traffic arterials have barricaded their front yards and facades. Ultimately, residential frontages only thrive in the right location, for the right people, and in the right culture (Figure 9.5).[35]

(a)

(b)

(c)

Figure 9.5a–c Dwellings in our busiest public spaces are best situated atop public amenities. A residential tower on top of a six-story mixed retail and residential podium marks a key intersection in The Hague (a). High-rise dwellings are recessed from a defined retail and amenity plinth in downtown Detroit (b). There are limits to urban living at eye level: town house residents at the foot of a Vancouver high-rise along a busy arterial have all drawn their blinds and do not use their hybrid zones (c).
Source: Image (a) by Conrad Kickert, 2012. Image (b) by Conrad Kickert, 2014. Image (c) by Conrad Kickert, 2017.

Mixing living and working

Increasingly, urban dwellings are mixed with street-level workspaces. This combination has taken on renewed relevance with the rise of freelance workers and the distribution of office space after the Great Recession and the COVID-19 pandemic. A variety of live-work configurations exist, mostly defined by the amount of separation between the two functions. Most relevant for street-level architecture is what architect Thomas Dolan calls the "live-near proximity type", where a house sits on top of a separately accessible street-level workplace. These street-level spaces should be designed flexibly to accommodate office use or retail use with sufficient consumer support – a question of a flexible architecture as well as flexible zoning.[36] Live-work units that are not separated are less flexible, as they require tenants to occupy both spaces simultaneously. This arrangement has become more popular with the rise of freelance work and working from home, leading to the rise of integrated live-work homes in the United Kingdom, Germany, and the Netherlands – often in conjunction with progressive self-build development models. Special care should be taken that street-level work spaces don't turn into living spaces, or worse, storage. Also, as mentioned in the previous chapter, design guidelines and their enforcement should ensure that live-work office frontages continue to interact with the sidewalk (Figure 9.6).[37] Live-work combinations can also be excellent solutions for transforming former storefronts into dwellings, as we will see at the end of the next section.

Residential transformations

As the demand for workplaces and retail changes in cities, an increasing number of offices, factories, and stores are transformed into dwellings. This presents mixed opportunities for enlivening the city at eye level. Transforming large and often introverted office buildings into dwellings can yield a remarkable street-level reinvigoration with the right design, but in a roundabout way. Taller office buildings can often accommodate hundreds of upstairs dwelling units, which in turn allow street-level spaces to hold more storefronts, but also non-retail amenities such as daycares, gyms, and co-working spaces. Provided that these amenities are also accessible to passersby, they can bring new life to formerly vacant facades.[38]

We have previously discussed the ample supply of vacant storefronts, which is only likely to grow. In the Netherlands, real estate lenders and consultants estimate that up to 10,000 long-term vacant retail stores can be transformed into much-needed homes.[39] Storefronts are located in walkable, central locations, and they are accessible to people of all ages and abilities. However, converting vacant storefronts into dwellings presents a different set of challenges. In the United Kingdom, the national government has permitted storefront (and office) conversions into dwellings by right, prompting a wave of conversions throughout the country. Many of these conversions have unfortunately disrupted the continuity of retail corridors for small dwellings with relatively little daylight or garden access. Despite their oft-disappointing outcomes, converting underutilized retail spaces to alleviate increasing housing pressures continues to entice policy makers in Britain, and are inspiring peers abroad.[40] Successful storefront-to-dwelling conversions require careful design.

Besides their difficult ground-floor layouts that often lack front and rear yard space, storefront conversions into dwellings present a typological mismatch at the frontage level. Converting a transparent, extraverted retail frontage that seeks to grab the attention of passersby into a frontage that seeks to balance this welcoming with individuality, access, and privacy is easier said than done. The large plate glass expanses of a storefront directly abutting the sidewalk may let in sunlight, but also unwelcome peeks into the private residential domain. As a result, storefront residents usually resort to a variety of filtering techniques, which can quickly escalate into projecting a sense of distrust toward the sidewalk (Figure 9.7). Successful storefront dwelling designs need to allow people to define their own level of comfort with the sidewalk by still enabling them to project their identity to the sidewalk and socialize, while ensuring their privacy. Beyond the above resident alterations, this balance can be designed in various manners. Most redesigns require retrofitting the storefront window, which may raise issues of cost, preservation, and reversibility. Some urban store windows and retail spaces have actually been retrofitted into or added onto existing residential buildings, which can simply be converted back.[41] Storefront additions can be removed to recreate the original hybrid zone between dwellings and the street. Where the existing building is built up to the sidewalk, front windows can be reduced in

Figure 9.6 A vacant storefront by Paul Pettigrew Architect and ZED Architects in Chicago has been recessed to feature a live-work space that contains both a (smaller) retail store and a dwelling unit behind an inviting front porch. Image courtesy of ZED Architects.

Figure 9.7a–d The typological mismatch of storefront dwellings prompts residents to block views into their homes, while still expressing themselves to the sidewalk. The outcome can vary from a careful filtering with objects, screens, and sheer curtains (a) and constructing internal walls for a front storage area (b) to constructing a fence in front of the storefront (c), or even bricking in a store window – an ultimate sign of distrust (d).
Source: Images (a) and (b) in The Hague by Conrad Kickert, 2021. Image (c) in Toronto by Conrad Kickert, 2019. Image (d) in Cincinnati by Conrad Kickert, 2018.

size to filter views, and the storefront can be moved back to create a patio nook that allows for socialization and privacy. If store windows have to be preserved in their full size, front spaces can be used to exhibit art by residents, or be turned into live-work units (Figure 9.8).

Conclusion

With the right design, ground-floor dwellings can signify and imbue trust and sociability to the sidewalk. As they make up the majority of our frontages, good design makes a big difference in our urban eye-level experience and the social life of streets. The key to designing the right residential frontages lies in balancing residents' needs to socialize and express themselves, but also set boundaries of privacy and territory – an evolutionary balance between prospect and refuge. There is no one-size-fits-all solution, as this balance varies strongly by culture, by neighborhood, and even by the type of street that dwellings line. However, successful living at street level has a

LIVING AT EYE LEVEL – PROSPECT AND REFUGE   185

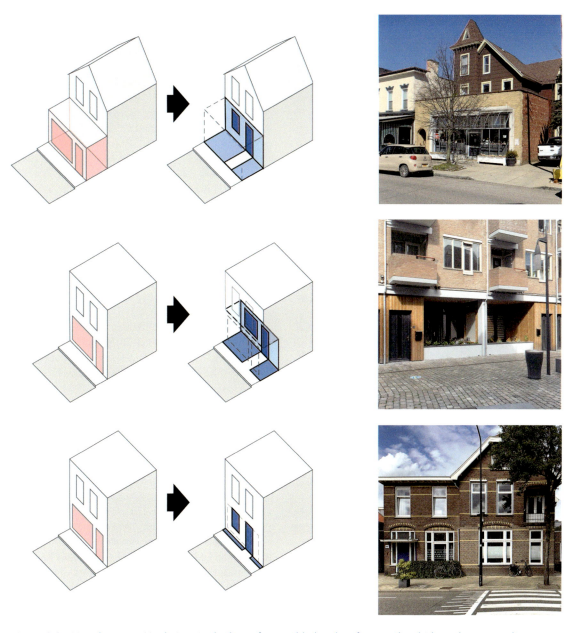

Figure 9.8 Many homes in North America had storefronts added to their front yards, which can be removed to reintroduce a street-level residential façade and hybrid zone (top). When there is no front yard, former retail facades can be recessed to introduce an arcaded hybrid zone, like in the Dutch city of Goes (middle). Many larger store windows were retrofitted into residential buildings. These can be returned to their original, smaller windows, like in the Dutch city of Zeist. Note the lighter brick was a former bicycle store (bottom).
Source: Diagram and images (a) and (b) by Conrad Kickert, 2021. Image (c) courtesy of Joost Nicasie, 2020.

few common denominators. The balance between private and public life should permeate the entire design of the street-level dwelling, from the interior layout behind the front door, the façade itself, to the 'hybrid zone' in front of the dwelling and the design of the street. Only homes with a successful public-private continuum will accept the sidewalk as a space to socialize and express themselves, prompting interactive frontages and a sense of responsibility for the sidewalk. Otherwise, curtains are drawn and fences are built before we know it. At higher densities and at larger building scales, the intricate morphological and social 'neighborliness' between dwellings, residents, and the street may suffer from too much traffic and too many strangers. High-density block layouts and street designs can make an express effort to create more 'domestic' streets and public spaces such as mews or courtyards that enable street-level living. However, along our busiest streets, residential frontages should therefore give way to more public and commercial street-level amenities. Designers should hence understand and reflect the hierarchy of streets and public spaces in our city with a compatible hierarchy of public and private street-level uses.

Notes

1 Etymologically, the English-American term 'stoop' is derived from the Dutch term 'stoep', which has traditionally served as a transition zone between homes and public space. For a history of the relationship between dwellings and the city, see Wijnand Galema, "Overgang Tussen Huis En Straat – De Stoep in Historisch Perspectief," ibid.; Birgit Jürgenhake, "De Gevel – Een Intermediair Element Tussen Buiten En Binnen: Over Het Tonen En Vertonen Van Het Twintigste-Eeuwse Woongebouw in Nederland," *A+ BE – Architecture and the Built Environment*, no. 16 (2016); Amos Rapoport, *House Form and Culture* (Englewood Cliffs, NJ: Prentice-Hall, 1966); N. J. Habraken and Jonathan Teicher, *The Structure of the Ordinary: Form and Control in the Built Environment* (Cambridge, MA: MIT Press, 1998); M. Bobić, *Between the Edges: Street-Building Transition as Urbanity Interface* (Bussum: Thoth Publishers, 2004); K. Scheerlinck, "Depth Configurations. Proximity, Permeability and Territorial Boundaries in Urban Projects" (PhD Dissertation, URL Barcelona, 2012).

2 Oddvar Skjaeveland and Tommy Garling, "Effects of Interactional Space on Neighbouring," *Journal of Environmental Psychology* 17, no. 3 (1997).

3 The link between social life and frontage zones is the outcome of several studies in Scandinavia, Canada, and Australia: J. Gehl, "Soft Edges in Residential Streets," *Housing, Theory and Society* 3, no. 2 (1986); J. Gehl, F. Brack, and S. Thornton, "The Interface Between Public and Private Territories in Residential Areas," In *Department of Architecture and Building* (Melbourne: University of Melbourne, 1977); Elizabeth Macdonald, "Street-Facing Dwelling Units and Livability: The Impacts of Emerging Building Types in Vancouver's New High-Density Residential Neighbourhoods," *Journal of Urban Design* 10, no. 1 (2005). For front versus back yards, see Ralph B. Taylor and Roger R. Stough, "Territorial Cognition: Assessing Altman's Typology," *Journal of Personality and Social Psychology* 36, no. 4 (1978).

4 Vikas Mehta, "The New Proxemics: Covid-19, Social Distancing, and Sociable Space," *Journal of Urban Design* 25, no. 6 (2020); Tina Govan to Social Life Project, July 7, 2020, www.sociallifeproject.org/porch-life-building-social-neighborhoods/.

5 Ulden and Ham, "De Stoep in Vogelvlucht," 18–37; Thaddeus Müller, "The Empire of Scrounge Meets the Warm City: Danger, Civility, Cooperation and Community Among Strangers in the Urban Public World," *Critical Criminology* 20, no. 4 (2012); Claude S Fischer, "The Public and Private Worlds of City Life," *American Sociological Review* (1981): 306–16; Susan D. Greenbaum and Paul E. Greenbaum, "The Ecology of Social Networks in Four Urban Neighborhoods," *Social networks* 7, no. 1 (1985); Gwen van Eijk, "Contact En Herkenning – De Stoep in Stadssociologisch Perspectief," in *De Stoep*, eds. Eric van Ulden, Daniel Heussen, and Sander van der Ham (Rotterdam: NAi010, 2015), 125–30.

6 Paul Keedwell, *Headspace: The Psychology of City Living* (London: Aurum Press, 2017), 37; Ulden and Ham, "De Stoep in Vogelvlucht"; Jay Appleton, *The Experience of Landscape* (London: J. Wiley & Sons, 1975).

7 Machiel van Dorst, *Een Duurzaam Leefbare Woonomgeving* (Delft: Eburon Uitgeverij BV, 2005); Barbara B. Brown, John R. Burton, and Anne L. Sweaney, "Neighbors, Households, and Front Porches: New Urbanist Community Tool or Mere Nostalgia?" *Environment and Behavior* 30, no. 5 (1998).

8 Customization of residential environments hence aligns with Kevin Lynch's concept of good city form, which requires fit and control by residents: K. Lynch, *Good City Form* (Cambridge, MA: The MIT Press, 1984).

9 The Fensterrecht was part of a manifesto: Friedensreich Hundertwasser, *Verschimmelungsmanifest Gegen Den Rationalismus in Der Architektur* (Wiesbaden: Galerie Renate Boukes, 1958). See also van Dorst, *Een Duurzaam Leefbare Woonomgeving*, 298.

10 Eric van Ulden and Daniel Heussen, "6231 Straten – Een Ruimtelijke Analyse," in *De Stoep*, eds. Eric van Ulden, Daniel Heussen, and Sander van der Ham (Rotterdam: NAi010, 2015).

11 Term from F. D. Becker and C. Coniglio, "Environmental Messages. Personalization and Territory," *Humanitas* 11 (1975). See also Charles J. Holahan, "Environmental Change in a Psychiatric Setting: A Social Systems Analysis," *Human Relations* 29, no. 2 (1976); E Sadalla, W. J. Burroughs, and M. Quaid, *House Form and Social Identity*, eds. R. E. Stough and A. Wasserman, Optimizing Environments (Washington, DC: Environmental Design Research Association, 1980); Daniel D Arreola, "Fences as Landscape Taste: Tucson's Barrios," *Journal of Cultural Geography* 2, no. 1 (1981). For a wider discussion on expression and meaning, see semiotics studies such as Amos Rapoport, *The Meaning of the Built Environment: A Nonverbal Communication Approach* (Tucson, AZ: University of Arizona Press, 1990); Umberto Eco,

"Function and Sign: The Semiotics of Architecture," in *The City and the Sign*, eds. M. Gottdiener and A. P. Lagopoulos (New York: Columbia University Press, 1986); Jürgenhake, "De Gevel – Een Intermediair Element Tussen Buiten En Binnen: Over Het Tonen En Vertonen Van Het Twintigste-Eeuwse Woongebouw in Nederland."

12 This relates to the philosophical theories of Georg Simmel about urban engagement with strangers: Georg Simmel, "The Stranger," in *The Sociology of Georg Simmel*, ed. Kurt H. Wolff (New York: Free Press, 1950). See also Lyn H. Lofland, *A World of Strangers – Order and Action in Urban Public Space* (Prospect Heights, IL: Waveland Press, 1985); Kim Dovey and Stephen Wood, "Public/Private Urban Interfaces: Type, Adaptation, Assemblage," *Journal of Urbanism: International Research on Placemaking and Urban Sustainability* 8, no. 1 (2015).

13 van Dorst, *Een Duurzaam Leefbare Woonomgeving*.

14 On personal roles, see Carl Matthews et al., "Personal Bias: The Influence of Personality Profile on Residential Design Decisions," *Housing and Society* 37, no. 1 (2010). On culture, see Rapoport, *House Form and Culture*, 70–72, 80, 132–33; van Dorst, *Een Duurzaam Leefbare Woonomgeving*.

15 *Een Duurzaam Leefbare Woonomgeving*; Ulden and Ham, "De Stoep in Vogelvlucht"; Clare Cooper Marcus, *House as a Mirror of Self: Exploring the Deeper Meaning of Home* (Berkeley, CA: Conari Press, 1995).

16 David Sim, *Soft City: Building Density for Everyday Life* (Washington, DC: Island Press, 2019), 102.

17 Oscar Newman, *Defensible Space; Crime Prevention through Urban Design* (New York: Macmillan, 1972); Barbara B. Brown and Irwin Altman, "Territoriality, Defensible Space and Residential Burglary: An Environmental Analysis," *Journal of Environmental Psychology* 3, no. 3 (1983); Gehl, "Soft Edges in Residential Streets"; Sander van der Ham, "Van Wie Is De Stoep? De Stoep in Stadspsychologisch Perspectief," in *De Stoep*, eds. Eric van Ulden, Daniel Heussen, and Sander van der Ham (Rotterdam: NAi010, 2015). Note that ownership in this paragraph is not used as a legal term, but a psychological one, depicting (signaled) responsibility over a space. See also Timothy Crowe and Lawrence J. Fennelly, *Crime Prevention Through Environmental Design*, 3rd ed. (Amsterdam: Elsevier, 2013).

18 Richard Sennett, *The Uses of Disorder: Personal Identity & City Life* (New York: Norton, 1970). See also Ulden et al., *De Stoep*, 54–55, 136–37, 87.

19 Macdonald, "Street-Facing Dwelling Units and Livability."

20 Sim, *Soft City*, 124; Ulden et al., *De Stoep*, 25, 190–93; Macdonald, "Street-Facing Dwelling Units and Livability," 36.

21 Psychological research has linked these communicative properties to passersby preference for facades: Arthur E. Stamps III, "Physical Determinants of Preferences for Residential Facades," *Environment and Behavior* 31, no. 6 (1999); Aysu Akalin et al., "Architecture and Engineering Students' Evaluations of House Façades: Preference, Complexity and Impressiveness," *Journal of Environmental Psychology* 29, no. 1 (2009); Hieronymus C. Borst et al., "Relationships Between Street Characteristics and Perceived Attractiveness for Walking Reported by Elderly People," *Journal of Environmental Psychology* 28, no. 4 (2008). On façade communication, see also Jürgenhake, "De Gevel – Een Intermediair Element Tussen Buiten En Binnen"; Rapoport, *The Meaning of the Built Environment*.

22 Macdonald, "Street-Facing Dwelling Units and Livability"; Larry Beasley and Frances Bula, *Vancouverism* (Vancouver: On Point Press, 2019). Like many other countries, Dutch building code mandates level residential access with hardly any threshold: Ulden and Ham, "De Stoep in Vogelvlucht," 39.

23 Ham, "Van Wie Is De Stoep? De Stoep in Stadspsychologisch Perspectief," 190. A study of a preferred window-to-wall ratio in homes in Mu'tah University in Jordan resulted in a moderate ratio of 40 to 50%, but results did not differentiate the street level, and they will likely vary elsewhere: Majdi M. Alkhresheh, "Preference for Void-to-Solid Ratio in Residential Facades," *Journal of Environmental Psychology* 32, no. 3 (2012).

24 See for example the Barcelona Window: Sim, *Soft City*, 160.

25 On the various activities that can take place in different widths of transition zones, see ibid. On Vancouver's transition zone dimensions, see Planning Department, *Downtown South Guidelines (Excluding Granville Street)* (Vancouver: Planning Department, 1991); Macdonald, "Street-Facing Dwelling Units and Livability." On Rotterdam's study of transition spaces, see Ulden et al., *De Stoep*, 19–34, 90–97. The transition zone is also called a 'hybrid zone': van Dorst, *Een Duurzaam Leefbare Woonomgeving*. On American front yards and culture (focusing mostly on suburban areas), see Cynthia L. Girling and Kenneth I. Helphand, *Yard, Street, Park: The Design of Suburban Open Space* (New York: J. Wiley, 1994).

26 The Dutch woonerf was inspired by British traffic theory in the 1960s, and has made an impact on street design across the world: Eran Ben-Joseph, "Changing the Residential Street Scene: Adapting the Shared Street (Woonerf) Concept to the Suburban Environment," *Journal of the American Planning Association* 61, no. 4 (1995).

27 Dries Gysels, "The Ghent Living Streets: Experiencing a Sustainable and Social Future," in *Handbook of Sustainable Transport* (Cheltenham: Edward Elgar Publishing, 2020); Cedric Goossens, Stijn Oosterlynck, and Lieve Bradt, "Livable Streets? Green Gentrification and the Displacement of Longtime Residents in Ghent, Belgium," *Urban Geography* 41, no. 4 (2020). The Rotterdam study of transition zones found that streets that were either too narrow (less than 12m) or too wide (more than 20m) saw fewer personalization in front of homes and resident satisfaction. This may be partly explained by the likelihood of more traffic along wider streets, which inhibits social life: Ulden et al., *De Stoep*, 26–30, 194; D. Appleyard, M. S. Gerson, and M. Lintell, *Livable Streets* (Berkeley: University of California Press, 1982).

28 van Dorst, *Een Duurzaam Leefbare Woonomgeving*, 316.

29 Kim Dovey and Felicity Symons, "Density without Intensity and What to Do About It: Reassembling Public/Private Interfaces in Melbourne's Southbank Hinterland," *Australian Planner* 51, no. 1 (2014).

30 Robert Gifford, "The Consequences of Living in High-Rise Buildings," *Architectural Science Review* 50, no. 1 (2007); Nancy M Wells and Annie Moch, "Housing and Mental Health: A Review of the Evidence and a Methodological and Conceptual Critique," *Journal of Social Issues* 59, no. 3 (2003).

31 A fact readily acknowledged by Vancouver planner Larry Beasley: Beasley and Bula, *Vancouverism*.

32 James T. White and Bilge Serin, *High-Rise Residential Development – an International Evidence Review* (Glasgow: UK Collaborative Centre for Housing Evidence, 2021).

33 For Seattle, see City Planning and Development, "23.49 Downtown Zoning," in *Land Use Code* (Seattle: City of Seattle, 2021). For San Francisco, see San Francisco Planning Department, "Urban Design Element," in *San Francisco General Plan* (San Francisco: City of San Francisco, 1972). The City of Rotterdam also mandates that residents have to pass through a semi-public 'meeting square' from parking to dwellings to prevent anonymity: Gemeente Rotterdam, *Hoogbouwvisie 2019* (Rotterdam: City of Rotterdam, 2019).

34 Development and Construction Department of Planning, *Urban Design Guidelines for High-Rise Buildings* (Ottawa, Canada: City of Ottawa, 2018).

35 Quote from Beasley and Bula, *Vancouverism*, 257; Macdonald, "Street-Facing Dwelling Units and Livability"; John Punter, *The Vancouver Achievement – Urban Planning and Design* (Vancouver: UBC Press, 2003); Robert M. Walsh, "The Origins of Vancouverism: A Historical Inquiry into the Architecture and Urban Form of Vancouver, British Columbia" (PhD Thesis, University of Michigan, 2013); James T. White and John Punter, "Toronto's Vancouverism: Developer Adaptation, Planning Responses, and the Challenge of Design Quality," *Town Planning Review* 88, no. 2 (2017).

36 Thomas Dolan, *Live-Work Planning and Design: Zero-Commute Housing* (Hoboken, NJ: John Wiley & Sons, 2012).

37 Jonathan Tarbatt, "Live-Work: Understanding the Typology," *Urban Design*, no. 136 (2015). For mixing housing with small-scaled manufacturing, see Ben Croxford et al., *Foundries of the Future: A Guide for 21st Century Cities of Making* (Delft: TU Delft Open, 2020), 200–1.

38 Derek Gilley et al., *Design Parameters for Urban Office to Residential Conversion* (Washington, DC: Gensler Research Institute, 2018). One extreme example is the conversion of Lower Manhattan's office buildings into hotels and dwellings after September 11, 2001. Office closures unexpectedly enlivened public life as building conversions more than doubled the number of residents, hotel rooms, and tourist visits: Konrad Putzier, "Out of the Ashes, a New Downtown New York," *The Wall Street Journal*, September 10, 2021.

39 Chris Lanting, Vincent Ollefers, and Martijn Pustjens, *Transformatie Van Winkels Naar Woningen* (Amsterdam: Colliers International, 2020); Christian Lennartz, Sandra Koenraadt, and Arjen Ouwehand, "Transformatieatlas Retail," in *Economisch Onderzoek*, ed. RaboResearch (Utrecht: Rabobank, 2018).

40 B. Clifford et al., "Research into the Quality Standard of Homes Delivered Through Change of Use Permitted Development Rights," Ministry of Housing, Communities & Local Government: London, UK, 2020. In California, State Assembly Bill No. 68 allows by-right conversions of multifamily building storefronts into dwelling units. The policy was enacted in 2020; other bills are currently under debate for other retail type conversions.

41 J. J. Jehee, *Winkelpuien in Nederland: Ontwikkeling En Architectuur* (Zwolle: WBooks, 2015); R. W. Longstreth, *The Buildings of Main Street: A Guide to American Commercial Architecture* (Washington, DC: Preservation Press, 1987).

References

Akalin, Aysu, Kemal Yildirim, Christopher Wilson, and Onder Kilicoglu. "Architecture and Engineering Students' Evaluations of House Façades: Preference, Complexity and Impressiveness." *Journal of Environmental Psychology* 29, no. 1 (2009): 124–32.

Alkhresheh, Majdi M. "Preference for Void-to-Solid Ratio in Residential Facades." *Journal of Environmental Psychology* 32, no. 3 (2012/09/01/ 2012): 234–45.

Appleton, Jay. *The Experience of Landscape*. [in English] London: J. Wiley & Sons, 1975.

Appleyard, D., M. S. Gerson, and M. Lintell. *Livable Streets*. Berkeley: University of California Press, 1982.

Arreola, Daniel D. "Fences as Landscape Taste: Tucson's Barrios." *Journal of Cultural Geography* 2, no. 1 (1981): 96–105.

Beasley, Larry, and Frances Bula. *Vancouverism*. Vancouver: On Point Press, 2019.

Becker, F. D., and C. Coniglio. "Environmental Messages. Personalization and Territory." *Humanitas* 11 (1975): 55–74.

Ben-Joseph, Eran. "Changing the Residential Street Scene: Adapting the Shared Street (Woonerf) Concept to the Suburban Environment." *Journal of the American Planning Association* 61, no. 4 (1995): 504–15.

Bobić, M. *Between the Edges: Street-Building Transition as Urbanity Interface*. Bussum: Thoth Publishers, 2004.

Borst, Hieronymus C., Henk M. E. Miedema, Sanne I. de Vries, Jamie M. A. Graham, and Jef E. F. van Dongen. "Relationships Between Street Characteristics and Perceived Attractiveness for Walking Reported by Elderly People." *Journal of Environmental Psychology* 28, no. 4 (2008): 353–61.

Brown, Barbara B., and Irwin Altman. "Territoriality, Defensible Space and Residential Burglary: An Environmental Analysis." *Journal of Environmental Psychology* 3, no. 3 (1983): 203–20.

Brown, Barbara B., John R. Burton, and Anne L. Sweaney. "Neighbors, Households, and Front Porches: New Urbanist Community Tool or Mere Nostalgia?" *Environment and Behavior* 30, no. 5 (1998/09/01 1998): 579–600.

Clifford, B., P. Canales, J. Ferm, N. Livingstone, A. Lord, and R. Dunning. "Research into the Quality Standard of Homes Delivered through Change of Use Permitted Development Rights." Ministry of Housing, Communities & Local Government: London, UK, 2020.

Crowe, Timothy, and Lawrence J. Fennelly. *Crime Prevention Through Environmental Design*. Amsterdam: Elsevier, 2013.

Croxford, Ben, Teresa Domenech, B. Hausleitner, Adrian Vickery Hill, Han Meyer, Alexandre Orban, V. Muñoz Sanz, Fabio Vanin, and Josie Warden. *Foundries of the Future: A Guide for 21st Century Cities of Making*. Delft: TU Delft Open, 2020.

Department of Planning. *Downtown South Guidelines (Excluding Granville Street)*. Vancouver: Department of Planning, 1991.

Department of Planning, Development and Construction. *Urban Design Guidelines for High-Rise Buildings*, 15. Ottawa, Canada: City of Ottawa, 2018.

Department, San Francisco Planning. "Urban Design Element." In *San Francisco General Plan*. San Francisco: City of San Francisco, 1972.

Development, City Planning. "23.49 Downtown Zoning." In *Land Use Code*. Seattle: City of Seattle, 2021.

Dolan, Thomas. *Live-Work Planning and Design: Zero-Commute Housing*. Hoboken, NJ: John Wiley & Sons, 2012.

Dovey, Kim, and Felicity Symons. "Density without Intensity and What to Do About It: Reassembling Public/Private Interfaces in Melbourne's Southbank Hinterland." *Australian Planner* 51, no. 1 (2014): 34–46.

Dovey, Kim, and Stephen Wood. "Public/Private Urban Interfaces: Type, Adaptation, Assemblage." *Journal of Urbanism: International Research on Placemaking and Urban Sustainability* 8, no. 1 (2015): 1–16.

Eco, Umberto. "Function and Sign: The Semiotics of Architecture." In *The City and the Sign*, edited by M. Gottdiener and A. P. Lagopoulos. New York: Columbia University Press, 1986.

Eijk, Gwen van. "Contact En Herkenning – De Stoep in Stadssociologisch Perspectief." In *De Stoep*, edited by Eric van Ulden, Daniel Heussen, and Sander van der Ham. Rotterdam: nai010, 2015.

Fischer, Claude S. "The Public and Private Worlds of City Life." *American Sociological Review* (1981): 306–16.

Galema, Wijnand. "Overgang Tussen Huis En Straat – De Stoep in Historisch Perspectief." In *De Stoep*, edited by Eric van Ulden, Daniel Heussen, and Sander van der Ham. Rotterdam: nai010, 2015.

Gehl, J. "Soft Edges in Residential Streets." *Housing, Theory and Society* 3, no. 2 (1986): 89–102.

Gehl, J., F. Brack, and S. Thornton. "The Interface Between Public and Private Territories in Residential Areas." In *Department of Architecture and Building*. Melbourne: University of Melbourne, 1977.

Gifford, Robert. "The Consequences of Living in High-Rise Buildings." *Architectural Science Review* 50, no. 1 (2007/03/01 2007): 2–17.

Gilley, Derek, Greg Zielinski, Sarah Palmer, Duncan Lyons, Jeff Barber, and Bill Talley. *Design Parameters for Urban Office to Residential Conversion*. Washington, DC: Gensler Research Institute, 2018.

Girling, Cynthia L., and Kenneth I. Helphand. *Yard, Street, Park: The Design of Suburban Open Space*. New York: J. Wiley, 1994.

Goossens, Cedric, Stijn Oosterlynck, and Lieve Bradt. "Livable Streets? Green Gentrification and the Displacement of Longtime Residents in Ghent, Belgium." *Urban Geography* 41, no. 4 (2020): 550–72.

Govan, Tina. "Porch Life: Building Social Neighborhoods." In *Social Life Project*, edited by Fred Kent and Kathy Madden. New York, 2020. Online article.

Greenbaum, Susan D., and Paul E. Greenbaum. "The Ecology of Social Networks in Four Urban Neighborhoods." *Social networks* 7, no. 1 (1985): 47–76.

Gysels, Dries. "The Ghent Living Streets: Experiencing a Sustainable and Social Future." In *Handbook of Sustainable Transport*. Cheltenham: Edward Elgar Publishing, 2020.

Habraken, N. J., and J. Teicher. *The Structure of the Ordinary: Form and Control in the Built Environment*. [in English] Cambridge, MA: MIT Press, 1998.

Ham, Sander van der. "Van Wie Is De Stoep? De Stoep in Stadspsychologisch Perspectief." In *De Stoep*, edited by Eric van Ulden, Daniel Heussen, and Sander van der Ham. Rotterdam: nai010, 2015.

Holahan, Charles J. "Environmental Change in a Psychiatric Setting: A Social Systems Analysis." *Human Relations* 29, no. 2 (1976): 153–66.

Hundertwasser, Friedensreich. *Verschimmelungsmanifest Gegen Den Rationalismus in Der Architektur*. Wiesbaden: Galerie Renate Boukes, 1958.

Jehee, J. J. *Winkelpuien in Nederland: Ontwikkeling En Architectuur*. [in Dutch] Zwolle: WBooks, 2015.

Jürgenhake, Birgit. "De Gevel – Een Intermediair Element Tussen Buiten En Binnen: Over Het Tonen En Vertonen Van Het Twintigste-Eeuwse Woongebouw in Nederland." *A+ BE – Architecture and the Built Environment*, no. 16 (2016): 1–596.

Keedwell, Paul. *Headspace: The Psychology of City Living*. London: Aurum Press, 2017.

Lanting, Chris, Vincent Ollefers, and Martijn Pustjens. *Transformatie Van Winkels Naar Woningen*. Amsterdam: Colliers International, 2020.

Lennartz, Christian, Sandra Koenraadt, and Arjen Ouwehand. "Transformatieatlas Retail." In *Economisch Onderzoek*, edited by RaboResearch. Utrecht: Rabobank, 2018.

Lofland, Lyn H. *A World of Strangers – Order and Action in Urban Public Space*. [in English] Prospect Heights, IL: Waveland Press, 1985.

Longstreth, R. W. *The Buildings of Main Street: A Guide to American Commercial Architecture*. Washington, DC: Preservation Press, 1987.

Lynch, K. *Good City Form*. Cambridge, MA: The MIT Press, 1984.

Macdonald, Elizabeth. "Street-Facing Dwelling Units and Livability: The Impacts of Emerging Building Types in Vancouver's New High-Density Residential Neighbourhoods." *Journal of Urban Design* 10, no. 1 (2005): 13–38.

Marcus, Clare Cooper. *House as a Mirror of Self: Exploring the Deeper Meaning of Home*. Berkeley, CA: Conari Press, 1995.

Matthews, Carl, Caroline Hill, F. Duncan Case, and Tom Allisma. "Personal Bias: The Influence of Personality Profile on Residential Design Decisions." *Housing and Society* 37, no. 1 (2010): 1–24.

Mehta, Vikas. "The New Proxemics: Covid-19, Social Distancing, and Sociable Space." *Journal of Urban Design* 25, no. 6 (2020): 669–74.

Müller, Thaddeus. "The Empire of Scrounge Meets the Warm City: Danger, Civility, Cooperation and Community among Strangers in the Urban Public World." *Critical Criminology* 20, no. 4 (2012/11/01 2012): 447–61.

Newman, Oscar. *Defensible Space; Crime Prevention Through Urban Design*. New York: Macmillan, 1972.

Punter, John. *The Vancouver Achievement – Urban Planning and Design*. [in English] Vancouver: UBC Press, 2003.

Putzier, Konrad. "Out of the Ashes, a New Downtown New York." *The Wall Street Journal*, September 10, 2021.

Rapoport, Amos. *House Form and Culture*. Englewood Cliffs, NJ: Prentice-Hall, 1966.

———. *The Meaning of the Built Environment: A Nonverbal Communication Approach*. Tucson, AZ: University of Arizona Press, 1990.

Rotterdam, Gemeente. *Hoogbouwvisie 2019*. Rotterdam: City of Rotterdam, 2019.

Sadalla, E., W. J. Burroughs, and M. Quaid. *House Form and Social Identity. Optimizing Environments*, edited by R. E. Stough and A. Wasserman. Washington, DC: Environmental Design Research Association, 1980.

Scheerlinck, K. "Depth Configurations. Proximity, Permeability and Territorial Boundaries in Urban Projects." PhD Thesis, URL Barcelona, 2012.

Sennett, Richard. *The Uses of Disorder: Personal Identity & City Life*. [in English] New York: Norton, 1970.

Sim, David. *Soft City: Building Density for Everyday Life*. Washington, DC: Island Press, 2019.

Simmel, Georg. "The Stranger." In *The Sociology of Georg Simmel*, edited by Kurt H. Wolff. New York: Free Press, 1950.

Skjaeveland, Oddvar, and Tommy Garling. "Effects of Interactional Space on Neighbouring." *Journal of Environmental Psychology* 17, no. 3 (1997): 181–98.

Stamps III, Arthur E. "Physical Determinants of Preferences for Residential Facades." *Environment and Behavior* 31, no. 6 (1999): 723–51.

Tarbatt, Jonathan. "Live-Work: Understanding the Typology." *Urban Design*, no. 136 (2015): 32–35.

Taylor, Ralph B., and Roger R. Stough. "Territorial Cognition: Assessing Altman's Typology." *Journal of Personality and Social Psychology* 36, no. 4 (1978): 418.

Ulden, Eric van, and Sander van der Ham. "De Stoep in Vogelvlucht." In *De Stoep*, edited by Eric van Ulden, Daniel Heussen, and Sander van der Ham. Rotterdam: nai010, 2015.

Ulden, Eric van, and Daniel Heussen. "6231 Straten – Een Ruimtelijke Analyse." In *De Stoep*, edited by Eric van Ulden, Daniel Heussen, and Sander van der Ham. Rotterdam: nai010, 2015.

Ulden, Eric van, Daniel Heussen, and Sander van der Ham. *De Stoep: Ontmoetingen Tussen Huis En Straat.* [in Dutch] Rotterdam: 010 Publishers, 2015.

van Dorst, Machiel. *Een Duurzaam Leefbare Woonomgeving.* Delft: Eburon Uitgeverij BV, 2005.

Walsh, Robert M. "The Origins of Vancouverism: A Historical Inquiry into the Architecture and Urban Form of Vancouver, British Columbia." PhD Thesis, University of Michigan, 2013.

Wells, Nancy M., and Annie Moch. "Housing and Mental Health: A Review of the Evidence and a Methodological and Conceptual Critique." *Journal of Social Issues* 59, no. 3 (2003): 475–500.

White, James T., and John Punter. "Toronto's Vancouverism: Developer Adaptation, Planning Responses, and the Challenge of Design Quality." *Town Planning Review* 88, no. 2 (2017): 173–200.

White, James T., and Bilge Serin. *High-Rise Residential Development – an International Evidence Review.* Glasgow: UK Collaborative Centre for Housing Evidence, 2021.

10 CONCLUSION
LIVING IT UP

Figure 10.0 The Plaats in The Hague – a gathering place.
DOI: 10.4324/9781003041887-10

Even though street-level architecture makes up a fraction of our urban floor space, it shapes the vast majority of our urban experience. Traversing the city, we see, hear, smell, and feel our buildings mostly at eye level. We should design the way we experience the city, focusing far more on what is right in front of us. By improving the interface between architecture and the city, we can lay another cornerstone to the walkable, lively, sustainable, and inclusive city. Interactive street-level frontages improve our cities not just esthetically, but also by feeding economic, social, and cultural life. Some frontages are the destinations where we meet others, share ideas, grow, and live; others make our walk on the way more exciting. Interactive frontages give us a sense of purpose and safety, they allow us to express ourselves, and they allow us to socialize. Our street-level architecture is both the barometer of the life of a city and the key to this life.

It is worth summarizing the lessons on street-level architecture we have covered in this book, which help us understand, plan, program, design, and manage more exciting, interactive, and inclusive frontages. Of course, the quantitative and formalistic canon of frontages remains useful. But the true lessons of interactive frontages go beyond the formalism of glass and doorways. Interaction between buildings and public space is enabled by form, but interaction is activated by inhabitants who communicate and trust the city in their everyday lives. Interaction hence hinges far more on what happens in front or behind a frontage than what a frontage itself looks like (see also Figure 1.2). As sociologist Richard Sennett rightfully observes, plate glass may allow you to see inside a building, but it does not necessarily allow you to interact with one. We should aim for true porous architecture, enabling buildings and their inhabitants to express themselves, communicate, socialize, and transact beyond merely offering tantalizing views. As Sennett states, "Making buildings more porous will be one of the great challenges of 21st century architecture; porosity could make buildings more truly urban."[1]

Creating this porosity takes far more than just design – it takes curation, programming, and management to create the preconditions for interaction and trust between the city and its buildings, but more importantly, between the city and its inhabitants. It takes understanding what currently obstructs porosity and how we can overcome these obstructions. It takes a thorough understanding of the dynamics that shape street-level spaces, but also the dynamics that influence their inhabitation and their embrace of the city. As the precondition for street-level life and trust, good design can start and reinforce a positive momentum of trust between buildings and public space. But only by understanding frontages as a complex interplay among space, inhabitation, and connotation, we can pull the right levers toward more porous and interactive street-level architecture. This interplay can be summarized into the following nine key themes.

The cards are stacked against interactive street-level architecture

As we have seen in four cities on both ends of the Atlantic, the interaction between buildings and public space has drastically deteriorated over the past century. Despite significant cultural, geographic, and regulatory differences, surprisingly similar forces have deactivated frontages. Interconnected, systematic, and often self-reinforcing, these forces have chipped away at the form, function, and connotation of our cities at eye level. They have reduced the amount of interactive street-level frontages and entrances, and increased the number of blank walls, vacancy, and street-level distrust. Understanding these systems is crucial to building counter-systems to improve street-level architecture. The following key forces are working against the interactive city at eye level:

- *The changing street-level economy.* The most significant driver behind the loss of interactive frontages is the century-long decline of small-scaled retailers along our city streets, first in lieu of larger urban department and chain stores, then in lieu of suburban competition (especially in North America), and now in lieu of e-commerce. Similarly, the loss of small manufacturing in cities has reshuffled the economies of urban neighborhoods. Beyond directly leaving vacant frontages, these economic shifts often prompted large-scale urban renewal projects that reinforced street-level deactivation. Future strategies should acknowledge that the decline of small-scaled retail will continue, instead anticipating a new street-level economy and relevance, based on a mixture of (creative) production, living, socialization, and care. Plans and designs should allow buildings to remain flexible to future economic shifts as well, as the only constant at eye level is rapid change.

- *Changing technology.* While the invention of rail and streetcar technology was a powerful centralizer that bolstered the commercial vibrancy of urban cores, their automobile successor accomplished the opposite. Unlocking near-unlimited swaths of land for suburbanization, the car first challenged the hegemony of urban dwellings, retailers, and offices. In many countries, a subsequent wave of urban revenge followed, when planners, architects, and engineers forced automobiles into cities and their cores. Architecture soon followed the viaducts and parking lots. The cities that were able to counter this auto-centric spiral by investing in human-scaled infrastructure and development emerge as street-level winners, from a social, economic, and esthetic perspective. But cars were not the only technology that impacted cities. Refrigerators killed the corner store from the 1930s onward; air curtain technology negated the need for store windows and doors from the 1940s onward; the internet has vacated our retail streets while packing our residential porches and lobbies. Rather than be blinded by new technology, we should design around the evolutionary constant of human perception and interaction with the built environment. Do not let new technology disrupt, let alone define urban form if this erodes the human experience. Today, do not allow parked or moving cars to get between us and our buildings. Tomorrow, remain critical of the experiential impact of new technology, from autonomous vehicles to drone deliveries.

- *Consolidation and coarsening*. As urban land pressure and value grows, street-level interaction rarely benefits, as denser architecture tends to fuel coarser urbanism. Taller and larger buildings require the land that dozens if not hundreds of smaller predecessors took up; capital accumulation and public powers pave the way for the required land consolidation. As former fine-grained urbanism makes way for singular visions, commercial vibrancy – no matter how ragged – is often internalized, leaving too many streets for service access and parking. Frontages become wider and less interactive; entrances become rare; access becomes controlled. Higher density hence rarely fuels higher street-level intensity, as Australian urbanist Kim Dovey has demonstrated.[2] Urban policies and new neighborhood designs should aim to prevent large, consolidated development parcels if possible. But in many cases, denser, larger-scale development is here to stay. Plans and designs should leverage the benefits of large-scale visions, such as the ability to curate, distribute, manage, and cross-subsidize street-level commerce and amenities, the ability to create spatial and architectural cohesion, and the ability for higher urban density. At the same time, plans and designs should combat the negative side-effects of larger, denser developments, mandating articulated and well-designed frontages and hybrid zones, a minimum number of entrances (typically around three to four per 100 feet (30 meters) of street wall), a minimization of street-level parking and service uses, and frontage uses calibrated to a hierarchy of publicly accessible spaces. If maintaining historic fine-grained urban fabric is paramount, preservation regulations can help.

- *Distrust and introversion*. As street-level retail dwindles, people drive rather than walk, and buildings become bigger, the fine-grained relationship between buildings and streets easily unravels. Ever-larger developments can internalize the lucrative upsides of urbanity such as commerce, productivity, and human interaction, while externalizing downsides such as poverty, traffic, and pollution. Add the increasingly social, racial, and ethnic division of recent decades, and a spiral of distrust between architecture and the city is easily entered – yet surprisingly difficult to revert. Transparency and entrance mandates are a good start to revert this cycle, but as we will discuss later in this conclusion, true trust and extraversion require a combination of accessibility, transparency, inhabitation, and communication. It also requires reckoning with larger socioeconomic divides that feed distrust.

- *Changing architectural and urban planning paradigms*. While design and planning professionals tend to be the usual suspects for the decreasing relationship between buildings and public space, their influence is surprisingly beholden to the forces mentioned earlier. Architects didn't close urban stores; fleeing customers and retailers did. Planners didn't automobilize the city; manufacturers, marketers, lobbyists, and engineers did.[3] Few designers or planners were responsible for the capital and power accumulation that enabled the redevelopment of entire blocks and districts; politicians, financial markets, and developers were. Similarly, very few architects deliberately design introverted buildings; their clients, their budgets, or their technological constraints asked them to. Nevertheless, designers and planners often reinforced rather than mitigated these forces, especially around the mid-20th century. They pioneered introverted suburban malls and aloof office lobbies; they salivated over deleterious urban freeways; they loved the opportunity to raze and redesign entire urban districts into an acontextual mirage of perfection and control. Instead of gazing at blueprints or skylines, a new generation of designers and planners should stay focused on refining the city at eye level, focusing on bolstering fine-grained interactions among buildings, inhabitants, and the street (Figure 10.1).

The deteriorating relationship between buildings and public space is self-reinforcing

The relationship between buildings and the street is not just defined at the doorstep. Instead, street-level architecture is influenced by a building's location in an urban ecosystem, which quickly disintegrates into a spiral of introversion and vacancy if disrupted due to the forces mentioned in the previous section. Several of the mechanisms of decline are self-reinforcing, influenced by both the exponential deterioration of activity and the contagion of inactivity. Understanding these spirals and acting upon them at the right time is paramount to maintaining and (re)building interactive frontages. These spirals are as follows:

- *Contagious inactivity*. Once inactive elements like parking lots, garages, major infrastructure, or blank walls enter a street, they disrupt the much-needed continuity and hence the functioning of interactive frontages like storefronts and homes. Footfall decreases, retail failures go up, home values go down,

(a)

(b)

Figure 10.1a–b A century of economic change, consolidation, introversion, and stylistic evolution yielded the Main Place Mall in Buffalo, New York. The now closed mall replaced two blocks with hundreds of business and residents (a) with one introverted superblock at the base of an office tower (b).
Source: Image (a) 1911 by W.H. Brandel, courtesy of Library of Congress Prints and Photographs Division, id ds05281. Image (b) by Conrad Kickert, 2021.

and a downward spiral is easily set in motion. Detroit's scattering of parking lots from the 1910s had amalgamated into a veritable ring by the 1930s, but so did Birmingham's rash of blank walls by the 1960s, and The Hague's storefront vacancies may soon follow. Zoning, design guidelines, and ultimately designs should minimize the street-level presence of inactivity at the level of the building, the block, and the district. Deactivation beyond design, such as vacancies

or barricading, should be halted as soon as possible through programming and management.

- *Fragile activity.* Part of the self-accelerating decline of interactive frontages is fueled by the fragile ecosystems of footfall, interaction, transaction, and trust that support frontage interactivity in the first place. Retail success depends on a critical mass of nearby storefronts. If the continuity of retail streets is disrupted by an inactive element, failure rates skyrocket as the symbiosis between compatible retailers is lost and customers turn around. Dwellings and other fine-grained uses that interact with the street similarly require continuity to connect with neighbors and build trust. Plans and designs should build and maintain this critical mass – we will discuss the strategies for this soon.
- *Stratification.* Frontage decline is not equally distributed. Especially retail and other commercial frontages decline faster along more peripheral and poorly connected streets. A natural gradation from buzzing commercial cores to quieter, but still interactive residential streets has made way for a confined retail core surrounded by a ring of service frontages, parking, and infrastructure. In economic terms, the bid-rent curve has become steeper. At the finer grain, certain streets and even building frontages gain or maintain interactivity at the expense of others, pushing loading docks, parking, and blank walls into side streets. Add contagious inactivity, and a dichotomy between 'winner and loser' streets soon appears. Plans and designs should not deny the economic and technological reasons behind the stratification of interactivity, but carefully plan for which streets need to be protected from decline, and which streets can devolve into service and parking corridors. If possible, design new city blocks at a sufficient size to internalize services into alleyways or consolidated entrances, so no public street is forced to take up these deleterious frontage uses.
- *Homogenization.* The same economic processes that stratify interactivity also homogenize the frontage uses along a street. A city's most central streets often become the sole territory of national chain retailers that can afford top rents, feeding a global similarity.[4] Around the corner is the 9 to 5 monoculture of high-rent office lobbies. Only a block or two away, the pressure to service these high-rent uses fuels a similar inactive and low-rent monoculture of concrete and tarmac docks, lots, garages, flyovers, and vacancy. Further afield, the residential city begins. The sweet spot between success and failure that creates the mixture between consumption, production, socialization, and dwelling has become more elusive. And with homogenization comes increased risk of failure, as certain monocultural uses suddenly lose their relevance. Designs and policies should aim for mixed use in all senses of the word, allowing a mixture of tenants at all rent levels, all functions, and all sizes. These

(a)  (b)

Figure 10.2a–b One by one, commercial buildings at the fringe of downtown Buffalo, New York, were felled for the parking demands of the central business district, ultimately consolidated into a parking garage. Self-reinforcing decline amplified by urban renewal powers marked the end of this former commercial hub.
Source: Image (a) 1935, Collection of the Buffalo History Museum, General Photograph Collection. Image (b) by Conrad Kickert, 2021.

are the areas that make the city unique, resilient, and inclusive.
- *Heavy-handed renewal.* Not long after the edges of urban cores began to fray, large-scale renewal plans began to emerge in the mid-20th century. All four of our cities saw urban freeways, district-wide removal of historic buildings for modern campuses and parking, and privatized megastructures gobbling up urban vibrancy. Whether they were publicly or privately driven, whether modern or postmodern, these urban renewal plans further deteriorated the interaction between buildings and public space – often significantly so, both within and beyond their perimeters. American urbanist Jane Jacobs was right: large-scale renewal plans were simply incapable of replicating the fine-grained diversity of street-level activity they replaced.[5] Instead, they created vacuums of vibrancy that reverberated blocks away. Future renewal plans should aim for a fine grain of buildings and frontages, embedded into a connective and permeable urban tissue that connects rather than rejects the city (Figure 10.2).

Street-level commerce only thrives in the right ecosystem

Designers, planners, developers, and citizens love street-level storefronts. For good reason, as retailers, bars, and restaurants add neighborhood amenities and walkable destinations, support social life and entrepreneurship, and often support social equity. As a result, street-level commercial space is often oversupplied in strategic visions, designs, and new developments. Similarly, we expect too much from our existing storefronts: we tend to resist the inevitable declining demand for physical retail establishments. The outcome is clear in both cases: vacant storefronts, old and new. For a storefront to be filled with a commercial tenant, a lot of things need to come together, before we even get to design them:

- *Street-level commerce is about more than retail.* When we think of storefronts, we tend to think they are occupied by retailers selling merchandise. As merchandise sales are shifting online, physical stores are changing rapidly into service, branding, and fulfillment centers, and their century-long dwindle has only accelerated. Instead, most street-level commerce now offers experiences rather than physical products. Bars, restaurants, coffee shops, and personal services like hair salons and repair shops already make up the majority of our urban commercial streets, and their dominance will only solidify with the loss of 'pure' merchandise retailers. The shift from merchandise to experiences will affect the design of storefronts and streets, especially toward wider, shallower floor plates, more open facades, and more outdoor bar and restaurant patios. This shift may also require rethinking zoning and mitigating hindrance regulations.
- *New and existing commerce should meet clear customer demand.* This demand may be less than most might imagine. Even in our most walkable and fine-grained cities, a typical bar or restaurant needs hundreds of people to stay in business; a grocery store needs hundreds if not thousands more. Demand strongly fluctuates between cultures and between commercial

business types. Furthermore, businesses tend to have quite specific target audience needs. As much as we'd want that bar or grocery on our key square or corner, the choice is ultimate made by models that estimate demand with the demographics of an area, its connectivity, and physical and virtual competition.

- *Commerce only thrives in locations that are accessible and well-connected to their specific clientele.* Businesses need customers to be able to reach them easily, or to see them on their way to somewhere else. They should hence be well located within the urban street network, and between source points and destinations. Different types of businesses have different hinterlands, hence different demands for accessibility and connectivity, and different abilities to pay for their location. Our most central urban locations are the territory of businesses that serve thousands of customers, whereas specialty or local businesses can be located in less central locations. Very few customer-serving businesses can survive in very inaccessible or invisible locations. Connectivity and accessibility strongly rely on national and regional infrastructure policies, which can bolster urban retail by promoting centralizing (transit) systems, bikeability and walkability, or harm urban retail by promoting decentralizing (road) systems and drivability.
- *Stores need the right amount and the right kind of neighbors to thrive.* Clustering is one of the key drivers of commercial success, especially for retailers. Complementary retailers benefit from spillover sales and cumulative attractiveness to comparing consumers. Retail stores can hook into the pedestrian flows generated by other stores, continuing an upward cycle. Besides peer businesses, larger anchors can attract more people to an area. These do not have to be just retailers but also, for example, railway stations, libraries, museums, historical monuments, and parks.
- *Commercial areas need the right developer and manager.* Single development and ownership of an entire area allows an organization to fine-tune the right mix of businesses and the right design. Usually, urban areas usually have a variety of owners, which require careful coordination to mix, maintain, and market an area.
- *Street design matters.* People-oriented public space hugely matters to commercial success. As retail architect Victor Gruen once remarked, "Cars don't buy anything."[6] Car traffic should be mitigated to allow more space for strolling and sojourning, which (among many other social benefits), helps consumption. Full pedestrianization, especially in North America, should be approached with care.[7]
- *Bring fresh blood into commercial districts.* Storefront tenants change over at a rapid pace, and attracting the right new tenant is crucial for the life of a commercial street. Furthermore, commercial streets can offer excellent entrepreneurial opportunities to disadvantaged groups. Attracting newcomers is about more than just offering low rents, as new commercial businesses should be carefully curated, coached, and connected to storefronts. Commercial businesses can start in pop-up spaces, but they should be able to mature in more permanent spaces, at the right price (Figure 10.3).

Critical mass matters

Architecture rarely interacts and never trusts the sidewalk in a vacuum. Buildings need to be part of a sufficient cluster of other buildings that exude trust and interaction to start and maintain an upward spiral. Building tenants look to their neighbors to see whether a sidewalk is worth engaging with. Only together they can create a critical mass of interaction, trust, and subsequent foot traffic to make this engagement worth it. This is valid for all interactive frontage uses, but none more so than for street-level commerce. Storefronts need to be surrounded by compatible peers and competitors to offer passersby a larger selection of items, maximizing overflow sales while reducing consumers' risk of not finding what they need. When business clusters are broken up, the chance of further business closure increases rapidly. Furthermore, significant gaps between street-level businesses can give shoppers or patrons the sense a district has ended and make them turn around. Maintaining a critical mass can be ensured as follows:

- *Don't start too big.* Start a new commercial district with a critical mass of stores. This often means starting small and growing from there, instead of oversupplying the amount of street-level retail. This only scatters stores and deprives them of the benefit of clustering. Retail clusters have a natural size limit of about 500 meters or a quarter mile, as this is the furthest most customers are willing to walk. Larger clusters can amalgamate from sub-clusters, often aimed at different audiences.
- *Don't plan too small.* Instead of spreading out individual commercial establishments to minimize walking distances, combine establishments in clusters to match market demand and the type of retail (e.g., smaller convenience or larger comparison clusters).
- *Prevent gaps* in existing commercial clusters by restricting parking, blank walls, major infrastructure, and other less-interactive uses along an otherwise continuous retail wall through design guidelines and zoning. Many of these uses are an essential part of commercial districts, but they can be placed behind more interactive frontages or, in the worst case, moved to peripheral streets. Gaps of vacant storefronts should be addressed as soon as possible by replacing (temporary) retailers. When vacancy gaps are too big, consider reconsolidating retailers into a smaller,

Figure 10.3a–c Street-level commerce thrives in the right location, with the right neighbors, the right street design, and the right management. This lively street corner in Birmingham has a national railway hub a block away (in the background), traffic-calmed streets, an active management organization, and a cluster of bars and restaurants. Nary a shop in sight, by the way (a). Retail is becoming less about hosting transactions, more about experiences and brand advertisement. Even after closing at night, this online-first pet company advertises its products and its brand in Miami (b). Pop-up storefronts can bring exposure to new ideas. For example, Pop-Up Britain showcased the products of ten online startups per week in a central London storefront (c).
Source: Image (a) by Conrad Kickert, 2018. Image (b) by Conrad Kickert, 2020. Image (c) by Wilhelm Lappe. 2013, via Flickr, CC-BY-2.0.

continuous cluster. This is a highly complex process in areas with scattered ownership.
- *Corners matter.* Many urban corner buildings have a clear distinction between an active front and an inactive side. Make sure stores, bars, and restaurants turn corners with a contiguous transparent frontage, instead of closing a side wall that disrupts frontage continuity and chokes side streets.
- *Critical mass matters for more than just retailers.* Critical mass is crucial to enable successful street-level living and working. Social bonds created in hybrid zones and interactive residential facades are only viable if

Figure 10.4 The loss of critical mass is killing for frontages, especially if they contain retail. Wedged between shuttered storefronts along an almost fully vacant Buffalo commercial block, this solitary store defiantly confirms its existence.
Source: Image (a) by Conrad Kickert in Buffalo, 2021. This store is at the base of figure 10.1's mall.

there are enough neighbors to socialize with. Interactive residential developments should therefore also be planned in sufficient clusters. The same goes for street-level workspaces and studios, which benefit from cross-pollination with neighbors (Figure 10.4).

Commercial unit and facade design benefits businesses, neighbors, and the city

Once a commercial unit is located in the right place to thrive, it should be designed to maximize its chance of commercial success and the success of its environment. Commercial units should be designed at the right size and the right layout for a tenant. Similarly, commercial windows should interact and communicate with the sidewalk in the right way, which benefits the commercial cluster as a whole. The right storefront excites, invites, informs, interacts, and blends the sidewalk with the store. This follows a set of design axioms that are quite similar across cultures, as they relate to basic human perception, behavior, and evaluation. These axioms are as follows:

- *Size*. Commercial spaces should be designed at the right size to accommodate a specific type of businesses, both in terms of the merchandise or services they sell and whether they are independent or part of a chain. Units can range from a simple sales window of less than 100 square feet (9 square meters), to a full unit of less than 500 square feet (45 square meters) for an independent business, to tens of thousands of square feet for a major supermarket. Furthermore, the right size is highly dependent on the cultural, regulatory and market context of a space. As the nature of retail is ever-changing, spaces should be designed flexibly to adapt to new size and layout demands. A healthy commercial street should have a variety of sizes holding a variety of compatible businesses.
- *Rhythm*. No matter the size of the commercial unit, their width should be limited to between 20 and 30 feet (6 and 10 meters) to allow passersby a new experience every few seconds at walking pace. Generally, aim for about ten units per 300 feet of block length. Adding more space per unit can hence only come from adding depth, up to four times the width. This also allows 'back-of-house' space for storage and kitchens. However, bar and restaurant spaces are becoming shallower and wider to allow light and air to patrons. Units should never be wider than 45 feet (15 meters) without significant other engagement with the sidewalk, for example, through patios, secondary entrances, and walk-up windows. Older commercial spaces tend to be smaller. When (often chain) businesses want to merge these smaller spaces to make a larger unit, understand that this decreases the amount of street-level entrances, and mitigate the barricading of merged units with shelving and stickering.
- *Liner commercial units*. Many commercial districts will have larger or wider stores, as well as inactive parking and service uses. Line these with commercial units that perpetuate the 20- to 30-foot rhythm. As liner stores tend to be shallow, they are often smaller, and hence great opportunities for independent businesses. They can often complement the use behind them.
- *Façade design*. The design for commercial facades should balance communication and coherence. In the eye-level 'attention' zone between two and seven feet (0.5 to 2.1 meters) tall, commercial windows should be as interactive and transparent as possible – at least 50 to 75%. This zone should allow passersby to see into the space at least three feet in, preventing shelving and stickering from obstructing views and ensuring that commercial windows communicate their actual contents beyond just their brand. Visual merchandising and display competitions can be very useful to draw in the gaze of passersby. Above this 'attention zone', signage and canopies can be more prevalent.
- *Signage*. Storefront advertisements should similarly balance communication and coherence. Signage scale should be aimed at passersby instead of drivers; signs should dose their message instead of bombard passersby with information; and store windows should communicate the contents of a store beyond just the brand. Signs should be coherent within a retail cluster. Signage guidelines, preferably connecting with broader design guidelines for an entire district, can help achieve this.
- *Frontage zone*. Commercial units can extend their draw into the street by using the area in front of the unit for advertisement, merchandise, and patio seating.

A frontage zone of just two to three feet (less than a meter) wide already allows businesses to blend indoor and outdoor space; more space can allow for more generous patio seating and sales racks. The frontage zone should leave a five- to six-foot (about two meters) unobstructed passage for people of all ages and abilities. Furthermore, the dimensions of frontage zones, especially patios, should be carefully enforced to prevent encroachment and obstruction.
- *Shutters.* After business hours, transparent shutters should allow passersby to still see into commercial units. Transparent shutter materials like polycarbonate can prevent break-ins, and still exude more trust and safety than traditional steel shutters.
- *Funding.* Street-level commerce is increasingly cross-subsidized by developers, as the right retail presence adds value to upstairs and nearby uses. This subsidization allows commercial space to become more accessible to new and independent businesses. Façade improvement grants can help fund store window design improvements, which have been proven to increase business, improve the impression of an area, and bolster community pride. Finally, business improvement districts can help fund district-wide management and certain street improvements (Figure 10.5).

There is life beyond street-level commerce

Interactive frontages are often conflated with storefronts. Indeed, street-level commerce tends to interact with the sidewalk the most, as business owners seek to lure in customers and patrons. But we are not all shopping, dining, or drinking all the time. As sales go from bricks to clicks, we need to think of street-level public amenities and destinations that go beyond transactions. A variety of street-level uses ensures that an area becomes or remains attractive to a greater variety of visitors. As the most accessible spaces in a city, frontages allow us so much more than just to spend money; they allow us to socialize, to grow, to heal, to learn, to be productive, and to express ourselves. There are ample people and organizations waiting to connect with the city without immediately looking to make a sale. They require various space sizes, accessibility, and layouts, but the connection with the city through frontage transparency and permeability should be non-negotiable. The key lessons to building and retrofitting non-transactional spaces that interact with the city are as follows:

- *First and foremost: acceptance.* Financial and political resistance to non-transactional uses at street level is significant, especially if they are retrofitted into commercial spaces. Most non-transactional street-level uses are not able to pay typical retail rents. Retrofitting non-transactional

Figure 10.5a–b The right storefront fits the needs of its tenants, invites passersby, and blends interior and exterior space. This bookseller in Valencia, Spain, allows passersby to start their exploration outside by rummaging through books, but invites them in through window displays and a view deep into the store itself (a). Patios help extend commercial life onto the sidewalks, allowing patrons to enjoy outdoor space and talk with passersby – as long as they maintain a five- to six-foot (1.5 to 2 meter) sidewalk clearance. In Park City, Utah, patios even span two floors (b).
Source: Image (a) by Pim van den Berg, 2019. Image (b) in Park City, Utah by Terry Ott via Flickr, CC-BY-2.0.

uses into storefronts hence lowers their book value, however fictional and unsustainable they may be in a post-retail landscape. Public incentives may be required to spur change, both in the form of penalizing vacancy and incentivizing transformation. This takes public and political acceptance of non-transactional uses as urban assets rather than disruptions or stopgap measures to stem oft-inevitable retail decline. Public leaders often need to alter zoning to allow post-transactional uses in former retail districts, and they need to approve the carrots and sticks to instigate change.

- *The post-transactional trifecta.* Find the right *use* that needs the city and vice versa, provide the right *design* for this use to thrive and connect with the city, and if needed, *enforce* that users indeed continue to interact with the city at a critical mass. If one of these three are missing, the blinds are likely to be drawn on non-transactional street-level uses, negating most value for the city. There are ample non-transactional uses that embrace the city, from libraries to co-working spaces, health spaces, small manufacturers, art spaces, and daycares. Each needs to be carefully laid out to maximize their trust and connection with the city.
- *Balance interaction with privacy and focus.* Facades should allow passersby to understand what happens inside spaces, while ensuring privacy and preventing interruptions. This requires careful thought on the filtering techniques behind, in, and in front of the façade. Lay out the most public functions at the front of non-transactional spaces, like communications, front desks, reception areas, event spaces, and meeting rooms. Filter windows through advertisements or semi-transparent curtains and blinds, and, if appropriate, build outdoor transition zones.
- *Cross-subsidize.* Just like commercial units, street-level uses like co-working, daycare, and art spaces are valuable urban amenities that can command premiums on upper floor offices or apartments. Developers increasingly understand and support them as loss leaders; make sure these amenities are also accessible to passersby.
- *Locate non-transactional uses correctly.* Ensure that non-transactional street-level uses amplify rather than disrupt commercial storefront continuity. Uses like workspaces relate to the street differently and often attract a different audience than shoppers or diners; place these at the periphery of (right-sized) retail districts to prevent disrupting continuous commercial clusters. Each use will have its own ideal location, both for its own functioning and its benefits to the city. Some uses like libraries and art spaces actually function as destinations in themselves; these can bolster the heart of retail districts. Some non-transactional uses internally benefit from clustering, like co-working and manufacturing spaces (Figure 10.6).

Living at eye level enriches the life of cities and citizens

The vast majority of our street-level architecture doesn't hold commerce or public amenities, but actually contain homes, either solely at ground level or connecting to upper floors. Street-level living is a cornerstone of urban life, if residents can interact with the street properly. The most fruitful interactions between dwellings and the sidewalk

(a)

(b)

Figure 10.6a–b A photo studio office next to a yoga studio – both uses interact and transact with the street in their own way, but both remain transparent and welcoming (a). Storefront spaces can even communicate political messages, like a social democratic party office window in The Hague (b).
Source: Image (a) in Cambridge, MA by Didriks via Flickr, CC-BY-2.0. Image (b) by Conrad Kickert, 2014.

balance prospect and refuge: the need for residents to socialize, customize, and express themselves to their environment, balanced with their need for privacy and territoriality. If this balance is not struck by designers, residents will do so on their own by barricading their frontage with curtains, fences, or worse. A balanced street-level dwelling can be designed, planned, and developed as follows:

- *Design a public-private continuum.* For trust to grow, residents need to be able to open up to the city when and how they want to, but withdraw when they need to as well. This requires designing ample space for socialization, expression, demarcation, and withdrawal to accommodate an ebb and flow of urbaneness along a spatial public-private continuum. This continuum begins inside with the placement of more public functions like the kitchen in the front of the house; a direct entryway between the home and public space, and a hybrid zone in front of the home.

- *Design the right hybrid zone.* Hybrid zones should allow residents to customize their environment and socialize with neighbors, while ensuring privacy and territoriality with filtered facades and markers such as short hedges, fences, and steps. Balance a clear division between public and private with the ability of residents to shape this division. Hybrid zones should at least offer room for personalization at about one foot (about 30 centimeters) wide, but preferably room for socialization at three or more feet (a meter) wide. Hybrid zones can be recessed into the façade if there is not enough space on the street for them.
- *Do not mistake hybrid zones for ambiguous zones.* Each hybrid zone should be clearly and directly connected to an individual dwelling entrance. The best hybrid zones also have the right solar orientation to allow residents to enjoy sunlight for most of the day, but especially in afternoons and evenings. Make sure that these hybrid zones are not used for bin, bicycle, or car parking by providing space for these items elsewhere. Hybrid zones are demarcated through visual cues like planting or low fencing. Furthermore, they can be a few steps up from the street to demarcate territory and filter views into the house. This does raise accessibility issues, which can be resolved through a secondary entrance.
- *Design density with intensity.* At higher densities, the fine-grained social bonds of street-connected dwellings become more difficult to maintain, as relatively fewer units can have direct street access, more units share a common entryway and streets may be busier with fewer known neighbors. Furthermore, higher-density living increases pressure at street level for parking, service, and mail access. Avoid 'density without intensity' with careful street-level design. Consolidate inactive service and parking entrances, and, if possible, place them along less busy sides of the building. At the neighborhood scale, design blocks large enough to allow services to take place within the block. Residential podiums with direct street access to lower units can maintain domestic qualities on quieter streets. But as densities and street traffic goes up, dwellings may be best placed on top of public street-level commercial and other public amenities.
- *Design the right storefront dwelling retrofit.* Fitting dwellings into storefronts presents a typological mismatch between an open glass façade originally meant to lure in passersby, and tenants that seek to balance expression and socialization with privacy and territoriality. Storefront dwellings can mitigate this mismatch by either retrofitting windows with (often original) smaller windows, careful filtering while maintaining expression (e.g., through art or objects in the storefront), or introducing a hybrid zone in front of the storefront. The latter can be recessed as patios if streets are too narrow. Storefronts can also house workspaces at the front of a live-work home (Figure 10.7).

(a)

(b)

Figure 10.7a–b Pull out all the stops to make eye-level dwellings interact and trust the street. Hybrid zones should be directly connected to entrances, have the right dimensions, the right context, and the right solar orientation. Two street corners in Vlissingen show how new development with consolidated entrances, few shelters against notorious sea wind, and only morning sun has relatively few signs of residents personalizing and interacting with the street (a). Just around the corner, benches, bicycles, plants, and even toys show a close relationship between homes and the street (b). *Source: Both images by Conrad Kickert, 2020.*

Dead or alive?

Not every frontage in our cities can be interactive. The density, technology, and development dynamics of modern cities place a lot of pressure on its street-level architecture. Beyond leading us to lively storefronts, inviting porches, and vibrant workspaces, frontages also need to provide access to parking spaces, loading docks, access ramps, workshops, and sometimes simply to nothing at all. Not even to mention the frayed edges of cities in flux: the vacant storefront, the construction scaffolding, and the holdover lot. And as we have seen in our four case study cities, the legacy of decades of poor design, planning, and development decisions will linger in our eye-level experience of cities for decades more to come. Despite our best intentions, our cities will always have a significant number of inactive street-level uses and frontages. There are several ways to approach and improve these uses:

- *Accept that some of our street-level architecture will not interact with pedestrian passersby.* Our most vibrant storefronts have to be filled by trucks every once in a while; our thirst for online delivery is fueling a finer-grained logistics chain that requires package and mail sorting and delivery access; our waste needs to be collected somewhere; manufacturing is coming back in our cities; and whether they are autonomous or electric, we still need to park vehicles in the foreseeable future. If their frontages cannot be mitigated, inactive street-level uses should be carefully located in the city, near but sufficiently separated from dwellings and commerce.[8] They should certainly not be allowed to break up a critical mass of more interactive uses. In many cities, essential but inactive uses are located in service alleys behind a more formal block façade. Make sure through zoning and design guidelines that existing streets do not slowly devolve into these alleys, as we have often seen in our case study cities. At the neighborhood design level, design blocks large enough to internalize these uses.
- *Many inactive uses can be hidden behind, above, or below more interactive liner functions.* For example, large retail units, parking garages and lots can be enlivened with fine-grained liner retail units to heal a discontinuous retail cluster. Liner buildings can also contain noncommercial uses, like residential liner buildings wrapped around parking structures, known colloquially as Texas Doughnuts. Liner buildings are shallower than usual to receive sufficient light and air from the front, and they should not make block sizes too large. Large, inactive buildings can also be retrofitted to interact with the city more. For example, large and otherwise hardly active office facades open up to the city through shared workspaces, restaurants, and event spaces. Similarly, parking lots can be lined with active uses (Figure 10.8).

Figure 10.8a–b For years, food carts wrapped around a parking lot disrupting otherwise vibrant downtown Portland, Oregon (a). Das Packhaus in Vienna has transformed half of a long-vacant ten-story office building into a "new work" ecosystem of smaller and larger companies – from a desk chair to an enclosed office. The roughly 7,000 square feet (700 square meters) street level houses co-working, meeting, and common spaces for upstairs tenants to comingle and meet with external clients, but also to enjoy leisure time and organize events such as exhibits, presentations, and screenings (b).
Source: Image (a) 2017, courtesy of Daderot via Wikimedia Common, public domain. Image (b) courtesy of Verein Paradocks, 2016.[9]

- *Inactive frontages can also be celebrated by turning them into canvases for mural art or fertile ground for green walls.* Like the storefront art programs mentioned in Chapter 8, mural programs can become tremendous urban visitor draws, express the values of a city or neighborhood, and launch the careers of new artists. For example, the Wynwood Walls art campus transformed an industrial Miami district into an international art, tourism, living and creative destination. Similarly, green walls can offer a softer, more environmentally conscious alternative to blank walls. Green walls should be carefully situated and require significant maintenance, but they provide numerous environmental and esthetic benefits over blank walls, including reducing pollution, mitigating urban heat island effects and stormwater runoff, and improving acoustics.[10]

Building an architecture of trust

Ultimately, the relationship between our buildings and the street is like any relationship: built on trust. Interactive frontages achieve far more than just hosting transactions. They signal a sense of trust to passersby, neighbors, and the city at large. Frontages act as a barometer to the social and economic health and equality of a city, as the public-private street-level interface both depends and reflects on the public life of the city itself. Interactive street-level architecture is the signifier of the open, equitable, and inclusive city, as well as the precondition for this openness, equity, and inclusiveness. In the words of sociologist Richard Sennett, our frontages should aim to become porous like a border, a place that balances territorial demarcation with enabling interaction between different groups.[11]

This is not possible without trust, which begins as a social and psychological, rather than physical phenomenon. Without safe and sociable streets, dwellings barricade their front yards, their windows, and their front doors. Offices erect safety perimeters. Even the holy grail of frontages, the retail store, will fortify itself. Conversely, open dwellings, open offices, open storefronts signify and amplify trust and safety. With the right societal conditions, the right place, at the right time, and the right participants, the right design will start or reconfirm the right upward spiral between trusting architecture and the open city.

First of all, this requires us to understand the difference between design and inhabitation. Designers and planners don't open shops, entrepreneurs do. We don't liven up porches and office lobbies, residents and companies do. Good design creates the precondition for inhabitation that is open to the city, as Structuralists have argued for decades.[12] This book has provided ample lessons for properly situating and designing street-level spaces for a variety of tenants. Ultimately, our work should align with the trust that these tenants have in the city, and it should reinforce this trust. The right designs will maximize the interaction between street-level inhabitants (from business owners to dwellers, workers, and patrons), the street, and by extension, the city. The spaces that we create should allow inhabitants to express themselves and communicate, but also to control their environment and demarcate their boundaries.[13] Ultimately, it's an inhabitant's choice to use our spatial cues to embrace the city. We should not design either too naively, nor too defensively. Nor should we design too loosely, nor to constrictively. The right design should enable interactive, trusting inhabitation through the following strategies:

- *Read the city and its society*. Architects, planners, and developers should be highly cognizant of the social conditions of the areas they plan to intervene in. This requires understanding the stability and trust between citizens, neighborhood residents, and passersby. This requires active conversations with citizens, but also measuring signals of trust in the street, like personalization and territorial demarcation. New and renovated street-level architecture should be commensurate with existing stability and trust and aim for reasonable improvements. We should not be naïve in our designs, but we should also understand the potential of design in improving social conditions. In low-trust, high-crime areas, tenants will barricade frontages that are designed too openly; in high-trust areas, overly defensive frontages would unnecessarily confine tenants behind overly defensive frontages. Find the sweet spot to reinforce trust between frontages and the city, one that convinces tenants to join an upward cycle.

- *Read the street*. It takes two to build the right relationship between the street and its lining architecture. As a microcosm of the city, the traffic, the social life, and the design of streets are hugely important to the type of tenant that would line this street, how this tenant views the street and vice versa, and hence, how street-level spaces should be designed. Busy streets are best lined with commerce, quieter streets best lined by dwellings – the "movement economy" as British urbanist Bill Hillier calls it.[14] This is not just because of traffic, but also the 'cosmopolitanism' of these streets – the ability of busier streets to welcome and 'bridge' newcomers, versus quieter streets that 'bond' neighbors. Newcomers are welcome customers to retailers, neighbors are welcome to dwellers.[15] As we have seen in previous chapters, street design also strongly affects the type and success of tenants. If this trifecta between street traffic, social dynamics, and design do not align with tenants' desires, barricading and failure soon follow. Dwellings will simply draw their blinds on busy streets with many strangers and narrow sidewalks (see for example Figure 9.5c), and commerce will wither on quiet streets, even if they can greet a neighbor. Design the right spaces for the right street; design the right street for the right spaces.

- *Instigate design for trust*. Often, starting an upward cycle of trust takes more than asking people to open their blinds or take a sticker off their storefront. Too many streets are in a chicken-and-egg rut, in which defensive designs breed distrustful inhabitation and vice versa. Designers often need to take the first step to create the right preconditions for tenants to inhabit and trust the street and the city. The right space is fertile soil for trust to grow, far more easily than trust can sufficiently mend the wrong space to grow more trust.[16] We cannot expect residents to tend a front yard of an introverted apartment building or a business owner to open up the walls at the base of a fortress office complex. However, we can expect them to embrace the city in interactive dwellings and storefronts we design. Design street-level architecture to maximize the chances for inhabitants to trust and embrace the city, but on their own terms. Allow residents to personalize and interact, but also allow them shelter and territoriality. Allow and encourage workers to see the city as a useful extension of their offices and workshops. Provide more street-level spaces in the city to build up social bonds, to learn, to grow, and to heal. Finally, support street-level commerce in its efforts to interact with the city, balancing the need for communication with coherence. When design interventions are too heavy-handed or too expensive, try one of many temporary, tactical strategies to liven and open up the city at eye level. Just make sure that these strategies can lead to permanent change.

- *Trust only works at a critical mass.* Trust is not defined or earned by a single tenant or a single building. Trust depends on an ecosystem of mutual positive understanding between tenants, buildings, and passersby. As part of the trifecta between form, function, and connotation, trust requires a critical mass of urbane tenants and frontages to blossom. A welcoming, embracing porch inspires neighbors to tear down their fences and walls, just as much as an inviting storefront prompts more neighboring retail activity. Therefore, trust is built up and maintained at a larger scale of the street, the block, the neighborhood, and the city.

Figure 10.9a–c Distrust quickly kills the relationship between buildings and the street. Surrounded by heavy traffic, strangers, or (perceived) crime, homes soon barricade themselves against the city with hedges, fences, and foreboding signs (a). But so do retailers, the type of urban use that typically interacts with the city the most (b). Ultimately, the architecture of trust relies on more than space or transactions – it needs and feeds city life itself (c).
Source: Image (a) by Conrad Kickert in Vancouver, 2017. Image (b) by Conrad Kickert in Detroit, 2017. Image (c) by Conrad Kickert in Buffalo, 2021.

Design buildings to become cornerstones or beach-heads of trust, also using urban design guidelines, zoning, and community development to expand this trust into a self-supporting system of a sufficient scale (Figure 10.9).

- *It takes a team.* Just like a critical mass of interactive street-level frontages goes beyond a single building; it also goes beyond just a single designer. It takes a team to ensure that the trifecta of form, function, and connotation work symbiotically: a team ensures that the right architecture supports the right tenant, which has the right attitude of trust toward the street. Besides providing the right street-level space, planners, policy makers, and managers curate the right street-level tenants to inhabit this space, and incentivize (or enforce) that this tenant welcomes the street. These team members also influence the social and economic conditions that enable flourishing frontages to begin with. Of course, the ultimate partner is the tenant itself – our teams simply create the preconditions for tenants to trust the city.
- *Continue to learn.* As we mentioned earlier, the only constant in the city at eye level is change. As our economies continue to turn upside down, our technologies continue to offer new challenges and opportunities to our cities and their streets, our societies evolve or devolve along with their culture of urbanity, our street-level frontages should be ready to host the next tenant, interact with the next passersby, in the next context. Climate change will call for new solutions, cultural change will as well. Remain in constant conversation with the city and its inhabitants to measure trust and find ways to improve it. Frontages should be flexible to changing attitudes, but so should we. Stay hungry, stay tuned.

Notes

1 Richard Sennett, "The Public Realm," in *The Blackwell City Reader*, eds. Gary Bridge and Sophie Watson (London: Wiley, 2010).

2 Kim Dovey and Stephen Wood, "Public/Private Urban Interfaces: Type, Adaptation, Assemblage," *Journal of Urbanism: International Research on Placemaking and Urban Sustainability* 8, no. 1 (2015).

3 Peter D. Norton, *Fighting Traffic: The Dawn of the Motor Age in the American City* (Cambridge, MA: MIT Press, 2008).

4 New Economics Foundation, *Clone Town Britain: The Loss of Local Identity on the Nation's High Streets* (London: New Economics Foundation, 2004).

5 Jane Jacobs, *The Death and Life of Great American Cities* (New York: Random House, 1961).

6 A comment made to business owners fearful of pedestrianizing the Kärntner Straße in Vienna in the 1970s.

7 J. Gehl, *Life Between Buildings: Using Public Space* (New York: Van Nostrand Reinhold, 1987); J. Gehl, *Cities for People* (Washington, DC: Island Press, 2010). On the perils of pedestrianization, see Kelly Gregg, "Conceptualizing the Pedestrian Mall in Post-War North America and Understanding Its Transatlantic Transfer through the Work and Influence of Victor Gruen," *Planning Perspectives* 34, no. 4 (2018): 551–77; Kelly Gregg, *Pedestrianized Streets – from Shopping to Public Space* (University of Toronto, 2019).

8 Dutch planners are distinguishing cities between areas of quiet, areas of vibrancy, and areas of noise (Rust, Reuring and Ruis): Marco Broekman et al., *Guiding Principles Metro Mix* (The Hague: College van Rijksadviseurs, 2019).

9 On Das Packhaus, see Michael Matzenberger, "Das Packhaus: Vom Bundesrechenzentrum Zum Kreativlabor," *Der Standard*, October 19, 2014; Agnes Matoga, "How Media Shape the Perception of Temporary Uses: A Qualitative Media Analysis on Vacancy and Temporary Uses in Vienna," *disP-The Planning Review* 55, no. 1 (2019).

10 Katia Perini and Paolo Rosasco, "Cost – Benefit Analysis for Green Façades and Living Wall Systems," *Building and Environment* 70 (2013).

11 R. Sennett, *The Fall of Public Man* (New York: Knopf, 1977); Richard Sennett, *Building and Dwelling: Ethics for the City* (New York: Farrar, Straus and Giroux, 2018).

12 See e.g. Christopher Alexander, Sara Ishikawa, and Murray Silverstein, *A Pattern Language: Towns, Buildings, Construction* (New York: Oxford University Press, 1977); N. J. Habraken and Jonathan Teicher, *The Structure of the Ordinary: Form and Control in the Built Environment* (Cambridge, MA: MIT Press, 1998); Herman Hertzberger, Laila Ghaït, and Ina Rike, *Lessons for Students in Architecture* (Rotterdam: Uitgeverij 010, 1991).

13 See Richard Sennett's concept of the open city: Sennett, *Building and Dwelling*, as well as the importance of *fit* and *control* in urban design in K. Lynch, *Good City Form* (Cambridge, MA: The MIT Press, 1984).

14 Hillier and J. Hanson, *The Social Logic of Space* (Cambridge [Cambridgeshire] and New York: Cambridge University Press, 1984); Hillier, *Space Is the Machine: A Configurational Theory of Architecture* (Cambridge and New York: Cambridge University Press, 1996).

15 Bridging and bonding are key social functions of urban spaces, building social capital. Bridging reaches out to newcomers and embraces cosmopolitanism, bonding strengthens the ties between people and

groups that know one another: Robert D. Putnam, *Bowling Alone* (New York: Simon & Schuster, 2000).

16   In environmental psychology, space creates affordances for human behavior and evaluation, far more powerfully than the opposite: Roger Garlock Barker, *Ecological Psychology; Concepts and Methods for Studying the Environment of Human Behavior* (Stanford, CA: Stanford University Press, 1968); Hillier and A. Leaman, "The Man-Environment Paradigm and Its Paradoxes," *Architectural Design* 78, no. 8 (1973).

References

Alexander, Christopher, Sara Ishikawa, and Murray Silverstein. *A Pattern Language: Towns, Buildings, Construction.* New York: Oxford University Press, 1977.

Barker, Roger Garlock. *Ecological Psychology; Concepts and Methods for Studying the Environment of Human Behavior.* Stanford, CA: Stanford University Press, 1968.

Broekman, Marco, Floris Alkemade, Berno Strootman, and Daan Zandbelt. *Guiding Principles Metro Mix.* The Hague: College van Rijksadviseurs, 2019.

Dovey, Kim, and Stephen Wood. "Public/Private Urban Interfaces: Type, Adaptation, Assemblage." *Journal of Urbanism: International Research on Placemaking and Urban Sustainability* 8, no. 1 (2015): 1–16.

Foundation, New Economics. *Clone Town Britain: The Loss of Local Identity on the Nation's High Streets.* London: New Economics Foundation, 2004.

Gehl, J. *Cities for People.* Washington, DC: Island Press, 2010.

———. *Life Between Buildings: Using Public Space.* New York: Van Nostrand Reinhold, 1987.

Gregg, Kelly. "Conceptualizing the Pedestrian Mall in Post-War North America and Understanding Its Transatlantic Transfer through the Work and Influence of Victor Gruen." *Planning Perspectives* (2018): 1–27.

———. *Pedestrianized Streets – from Shopping to Public Space.* Toronto: University of Toronto, 2019.

Habraken, N. J., and J. Teicher. *The Structure of the Ordinary: Form and Control in the Built Environment.* [in English] Cambridge, MA: MIT Press, 1998.

Hertzberger, Herman, Laila Ghaït, and Ina Rike. *Lessons for Students in Architecture.* [in English] Rotterdam: Uitgeverij 010, 1991.

Hillier. *Space Is the Machine: A Configurational Theory of Architecture.* Cambridge and New York: Cambridge University Press, 1996.

Hillier, and J. Hanson. *The Social Logic of Space.* Cambridge [Cambridgeshire] and New York: Cambridge University Press, 1984.

Hillier, and A. Leaman. "The Man-Environment Paradigm and Its Paradoxes." *Architectural Design* 78, no. 8 (1973): 507–11.

Jacobs, Jane. *The Death and Life of Great American Cities.* New York: Random House, 1961.

Lynch, K. *Good City Form.* Cambridge, MA: The MIT Press, 1984.

Matoga, Agnes. "How Media Shape the Perception of Temporary Uses: A Qualitative Media Analysis on Vacancy and Temporary Uses in Vienna." *disP-The Planning Review* 55, no. 1 (2019): 85–96.

Matzenberger, Michael. "Das Packhaus: Vom Bundesrechenzentrum Zum Kreativlabor." *Der Standard*, October 19, 2014.

Norton, Peter D. *Fighting Traffic: The Dawn of the Motor Age in the American City.* [in English] Cambridge, MA: MIT Press, 2008.

Perini, Katia, and Paolo Rosasco. "Cost – Benefit Analysis for Green Façades and Living Wall Systems." *Building and Environment* 70 (2013/12/01/ 2013): 110–21.

Putnam, Robert D. *Bowling Alone.* [in English] New York: Simon & Schuster, 2000.

Sennett, Richard. *Building and Dwelling: Ethics for the City.* New York: Farrar, Straus and Giroux, 2018.

———. *The Fall of Public Man.* New York: Knopf, 1977.

———. "The Public Realm." In *The Blackwell City Reader*, edited by Gary Bridge and Sophie Watson. London: Wiley, 2010.

Index

African Americans 15n19, 22, 24, 26–7, 29, 35, 36n5, 38, 121, 140; *see also* inequality

Alexander, Christopher 2, 13, 16, 90, 92, 100, 149, 207–8

apartments *see* dwellings, apartments

Appleyard, Donald 2, 13, 16, 188–9

automobile-oriented design 4, 32, 33, 70, 109

banks 36, 42, 82–3, 137, 150, 164

Birmingham: Bull Ring 43–4, 49–53, 59–62, 111; general 5, 7–8, 26, 41–62, 97–8, 104–15, 121–7, 139, 145, 166, 171, 196, 199; Inner Ring 45–59, 69–71

blank walls 2, 8–9, 12, 27, 32, 35, 62, 87, 89–92, 108, 110–11, 115, 119, 120, 122, 141, 143, 167, 176, 182, 194–8, 204

bottom-up *see* co-creation

clearance *see* demolition

co-creation 1, 33, 90

contagious decline 1, 12, 122–4, 195–6

convention centers 27, 52, 60, 93

crime 2, 8, 22, 29–30, 35, 39, 62, 71, 80–90, 93, 115, 118, 120, 138, 178, 187, 189–90, 205–6; *see also* trust

critical mass 3, 52, 117, 123, 125, 134, 168, 196, 198–207; *see also* retail, proximity benefits

culture 2, 5–6, 8–9, 15, 17, 22, 26, 29–30, 32–3, 36–9, 42, 44, 50, 52, 55, 60–2, 65, 71, 74, 76, 82, 85, 92, 97, 99, 104, 107, 125–6, 132–4, 137–8, 151, 154, 156–9, 162, 166, 168, 171, 174, 176, 180, 182, 184, 186–7, 189–90, 194, 200, 207

deactivation 2, 8, 10, 12, 31, 76, 104, 109, 111, 124–5, 194, 196; *see also* inactivity

demolition 26–8, 30–4, 36, 38–9, 42, 44–5, 47, 49–50, 56–62, 66, 68–71, 73, 75–6, 78, 104, 109, 111, 114, 116–17, 121–2, 124, 127, 201

design guidelines *see* policy, design guidelines

Detroit: Black Bottom 26–9, 38, 121; general viii, 2–3, 8, 14, 18, 21–42, 66, 77, 85, 97, 104–27, 137–9, 144, 148–9, 177, 182, 196, 206; Renaissance Center 29–35, 39, 111, 117–21, 126

distrust *see* trust

downtown *see* urban core

dwellings: apartments 26, 30–1, 33, 50, 52, 60, 68, 70, 73, 82–3, 85, 87, 89, 97, 104, 108, 115, 117, 144, 147, 202, 205; condominiums 92, 100, 138; porches 9, 92, 176–7, 180–3, 186, 189, 195, 204–6; transition zone 176–88, 195, 199, 202–3

e-commerce 104, 107, 124, 135–38, 156–7, 194; *see also* retail

economy: experience economy 33, 107, 135–6, 143, 157, 164; general vi–vii, 2, 8–10, 14–18, 22, 29, 32–9, 42, 45–8, 50, 52, 54, 59, 61–4, 66–71, 76, 87–91, 95–8, 101, 104–8, 111, 114, 117–26, 130, 135–9, 143, 145, 148–51, 154, 156–7, 162–73, 194, 196, 205, 207

entertainment *see* culture; food and beverage; theaters

environmental psychology: general 4, 7, 14–15, 17–19, 134, 150, 174, 176, 186–90, 195, 200, 205–8; sensory stimulus 4–5, 14, 19, 142, 166, 194

expression 5–6, 13, 92, 166–7, 177–82, 186, 202–3

expressways *see* freeways

fear *see* trust

fine-grained *see* granularity

food and beverage 2, 5, 7, 10, 12, 14, 18, 23, 32–3, 52, 65, 71–3, 83, 92, 107, 120–3, 127, 130, 132–3, 136–43, 151–2, 156–7, 168, 170, 197–9, 200, 204; *see also* patios

freeways 7, 26–30, 32–3, 36–8, 42, 47–8, 59, 68, 71, 76, 87–90, 95–9, 108–10, 116, 119–20, 124–5, 195, 197

fringe *see* urban core, periphery

Gehl, Jan 2, 4–5, 13–18, 109, 125, 143, 149, 153–4, 170, 186–9, 207–8

granularity 2–3, 5–6, 22–3, 27, 29, 32–3, 36, 43, 45, 47, 49–50, 65, 68, 71, 73, 82, 87, 89, 92–3, 95, 104, 107, 111, 113–17, 119, 121–2, 124, 130, 133, 135, 164, 182, 195–7, 203–4

hardware and software vi, 13, 138

highways *see* freeways

homes *see* dwellings

homogenization vi, 5, 16–17, 122, 124, 138, 143, 172, 196

hotels 24, 29–33, 40, 47, 52, 58, 73, 82–3, 89, 98, 100, 115, 117, 126, 138, 152, 172, 188

hybrid zone *see* dwellings, transition zone

inactivity 2, 12–13, 23, 27, 31, 35, 50, 53, 66, 84–5, 89, 93, 117, 120–6, 142, 195–6, 199–200, 203–4; *see also* blank walls; deactivation; vacancy

inequality 2, 22, 26, 29, 34–7, 50–1, 93, 95, 122, 170, 178, 180

infrastructure *see* freeways; traffic, engineering

inhabitation vi, 2–8, 10, 12–13, 95, 125, 146, 180, 194–5, 205–7
internet *see* e-commerce; technology
introversion 1–2, 6, 24, 27–35, 47–55, 66, 69–71, 74–6, 87, 89, 107–8, 114–15, 118–20, 124, 126, 143, 168, 176, 178, 183, 195–6, 204–5; *see also* inactivity; real estate

Jacobs, Jane 2, 4, 13, 17, 82, 92, 111, 122–3, 126, 148, 162, 171, 197, 207–8

land value *see* real estate
libraries viii, 5, 15, 18, 22, 29, 50–2, 60, 62, 73, 83, 93, 101, 108, 114, 134, 141, 149, 154, 157–8, 165, 168, 170, 196, 202
logistics 2, 7, 111, 114, 120–1, 135–7, 150–2, 166, 204; *see also* manufacturing

MacCormac, Richard 6, 10, 15–18, 104, 125, 168, 172
management vi, 13, 44, 78, 99, 130, 138–9, 147–51, 172–3, 194, 196, 199–201; *see also* hardware and software; orgware
manufacturing 7, 10, 22–3, 30, 34, 42, 45, 50, 60–1, 64, 76, 83, 96, 108–9, 117, 138–9, 164–7, 173, 188, 202, 204; *see also* logistics
masterplans 26, 30–2, 38, 49, 62; *see also* urban renewal
mixed use 47, 52, 62, 65, 75, 83, 89, 111, 115–17, 122, 130, 173, 196
modernism vi, 15, 18, 26–9, 32, 44–7, 53, 59, 66, 68–73, 76–9, 82, 86–7, 90, 108, 110, 115, 119–21, 142, 154, 159, 176, 197

New Urbanism 2, 125–6, 147, 186, 189

offices: co-working 7, 162–6, 172, 182–3, 202, 204; general vi, 2, 6, 7, 9–11, 15–6, 18, 22–35, 38, 42, 44, 47–52, 58, 60–1, 64–76, 82–100, 104, 108–22, 126, 134–8, 142, 149, 156–72, 179, 183, 188–9, 194–6, 202, 204–6
Oldenburg, Ray 5, 14, 18, 151, 170; *see also* third places
orgware 13, 138

parks *see* public space, parks
parking: garages 7, 15, 18, 28, 33, 38, 66, 72, 109, 114, 120, 197; general 2, 6–9, 12, 15–18, 25–39, 44, 47–50, 66–7, 70–3, 76, 84–5, 87, 89–90, 95, 98, 108–9, 114, 117–27, 133–4, 141–2, 146, 153, 172, 176–7, 180, 182, 188, 194–200, 203–4;; *see also* automobile-oriented design
patios 5, 33, 72, 92, 108, 145–6, 154, 165, 184, 197, 200–3; *see also* food and beverage
pedestrianization 26, 30, 38, 50, 53, 60–1, 70, 74, 90, 99, 116, 145–6, 154, 198, 207–8
perception *see* environmental psychology
periphery 9–10, 19, 25–38, 44–5, 48–9, 52–3, 67–71, 74, 85–90, 95, 110, 115, 119–26, 134, 140, 150, 170, 196–202

plate glass 2, 8, 44, 183, 194; *see also* storefronts
policy: design guidelines 47, 53, 55, 61, 90–3, 95, 100, 109, 142–3, 146, 153–6, 164, 178–82, 196–200, 204, 207; fiscal 26, 31–2, 38–9, 43, 46–7, 54, 140, 146, 157, 167, 170; general vi, vii, 2, 4, 8, 13–18, 24, 35–7, 42, 52, 59, 61, 67, 71–80, 83, 90, 100, 106–11, 115, 125–6, 130, 132–3, 136, 142, 146, 148–9, 151–61, 166, 168, 170–8, 182–3, 188, 195–8, 207; zoning vii, 9, 15, 17, 23–6, 30, 37, 62, 72, 85–7, 90, 92, 97–9, 108–9, 122, 135, 143–6, 153–4, 164, 166, 172–3, 176–8, 180–8, 196–204, 207
politics 8–9, 24–30, 32, 38–9, 42, 44–5, 50, 54–62, 68, 70–1, 74–6, 80, 82, 85–92, 95–9, 104, 130, 149, 156–7, 170, 178, 195, 201–2
porches *see* dwellings, porches
porosity 2, 7, 194, 205; *see also* Sennett, Richard
privacy 5–7, 10, 13, 159–64, 176–84, 202–3
privatization 2, 29, 53, 115, 197
public space: general vi, 2, 4–12, 15, 22, 29, 32, 35–6, 52–4, 64, 71–6, 92–5, 101–11, 114–17, 120, 124–5, 134, 141, 145–6, 154–9, 162–8, 176–80, 182, 185–6, 194–8, 202; parks 4, 14–18, 26–30, 38–9, 50–2, 82–5, 90, 92, 95, 100, 109–10, 113, 141, 154, 163, 171–3, 187, 189, 197–8, 201, 204; plazas 2, 22–5, 28–33, 36, 42, 52–3, 60–1, 66, 71–3, 77, 89–93, 101, 111–19, 125, 130, 142, 145–6, 153, 158–9, 164–6, 172, 188, 198, 200, 204; sidewalks 2, 5, 10, 22, 24, 30–3, 50, 92–3, 104, 125, 136–9, 142–69, 176–80, 183–5, 198–205

real estate vii, 2–4, 6–8, 12, 24, 32–6, 42, 46–54, 58, 60, 62, 70, 74, 76, 82, 87–95, 98–100, 108–11, 114–15, 119–20, 130, 138, 140, 142, 147, 152, 156, 159, 162–6, 173, 179, 182–3, 188, 191, 195–201, 205
Renaissance Center *see* Detroit, Renaissance Center
residential *see* dwellings
resilience vi, 111, 117, 156, 164, 197
restaurants *see* food and beverage
retail: arcades 6, 14, 17, 24, 27, 42–4, 47, 58, 64, 71, 73, 77, 79, 114, 129, 146, 181, 201; department stores 22–30, 32, 36, 44, 53, 58, 65–8, 70–1, 76, 82–5, 89, 95, 108, 111–14, 130, 133–4, 141, 163, 170; proximity benefits 7, 13, 15, 18, 49, 52, 82, 127, 132–8, 143, 149, 183, 186, 190, 198–204; shopping malls 28, 30, 33, 35, 39, 49, 50–3, 58, 60–2, 70, 89, 98–9, 104, 106–7, 115, 117, 130, 133–5, 138, 141, 146–50, 153–4, 172, 195–6, 200, 207–8; *see also* storefronts

safety vi, 2, 4–8, 24, 29–35, 42, 48, 50, 80, 92, 101, 108, 113–16, 120, 157–8, 167, 171, 178, 181, 194, 201, 205
Scheerlinck, Kris 7, 15, 18, 186, 190
security *see* safety
segregation *see* inequality
Sennett, Richard vi–vii, 7, 15, 18, 187, 190, 194, 205–8
sense of place vi, 8, 136
shops *see* retail

skyscrapers 15, 19, 22–4, 26, 31–3, 35–6, 66, 83, 85, 108, 111, 114, 125; *see also* dwellings, apartments; offices

slums 24, 27, 42, 44, 47, 57, 62, 66–70, 77–8, 85, 95, 121

socialization 2, 5, 6–7, 13, 16, 72, 76, 92, 130, 141, 156, 157, 162, 170, 176–90, 194, 197, 200–7

standardization *see* homogenization

storefronts 2, 5–6, 9–10, 13, 22–7, 30–5, 47, 59, 64–75, 82–3, 87, 90–5, 105–12, 120–5, 130–74, 183–8, 195–206

street management *see* management

streets *see* public space

structuralism 7, 15, 176

suburbanization 13, 16–18, 22–38, 42–50, 56, 59, 68, 70, 78, 82–7, 95–8, 106–7, 117, 123, 130, 135–6, 150, 170, 187, 189, 194–5

sustainability 4–5, 95, 125, 135, 164, 187–90, 194, 207–8

technology 1, 6, 9–10, 35–6, 76, 104–11, 115, 122–4, 135, 143, 147, 151, 172–3, 180, 194–6, 204; *see also* automobile-oriented design; e-commerce

territory 7, 15, 18, 92, 111, 122, 176–9, 184–90, 196, 198, 203–6; *see also* dwellings, transition zones

theaters 22, 24, 26, 29–32, 36, 39, 44–5, 48, 50, 52, 56, 59–60, 71, 99, 107, 115, 117, 134, 137–41, 154; *see also* culture

The Hague: general 6–8, 11, 14, 18, 37, 42, 47, 55, 63–80, 103–27, 139, 144–50, 155, 158, 160–3, 170–3, 182, 184, 193, 196, 202, 207–8; Spuikwartier 80, 115–17, 125

third places 92, 137, 157, 163; *see also* Oldenburg, Ray

traffic: engineering 4 26, 27, 33, 38, 45, 49, 50, 52, 58, 66–71, 93–6, 101, 104, 107–10, 120, 122, 135–6, 157, 165, 170–1, 194–8; general 4, 24, 26, 30–9, 44–8, 52, 54, 59, 61, 64, 66–79, 84, 90, 95, 111–18, 164, 172, 182, 187–8, 195, 198–9, 203–8;; *see also* automobile-oriented design; freeways; parking

transit *see* public transportation

transition zone *see* dwellings, transition zone

transparency 2, 8, 66, 89, 104, 117, 125, 143, 147, 153, 159, 162–6, 180, 183, 195, 199–202

trust vi, 2–8, 30, 35–9, 55–60, 76, 83, 110, 115, 120, 124–5, 139, 144, 153–4, 157, 166, 176–80, 183–4, 194–8, 201–7

urban renewal 26–9, 34–9, 45–50, 53–60, 62, 64, 68–71, 74–9, 87, 95, 98, 104, 107, 110, 114–17, 120–6, 138, 174, 194, 197; *see also* masterplans; modernism

vacancy 2–3, 7–10, 13, 22, 25–35, 39, 49–52, 66–74, 82, 93, 104, 107–15, 119–27, 132, 135, 138–41, 150, 156–9, 164–74, 183, 194–201, 204, 207–8

Vancouver: False Creek 82–5, 90–101; general 8, 26, 55, 81–115, 125–7, 139, 151, 153, 157, 170–1, 177–82, 186–91, 206; West End 82–92, 96–100, 108

visual merchandizing *see* storefronts

walkability 2–7, 13–18, 26, 30, 33, 50, 92, 120, 123, 125, 130–1, 134–8, 153, 159–60, 164, 183, 194, 197–8

zoning *see* policy, zoning

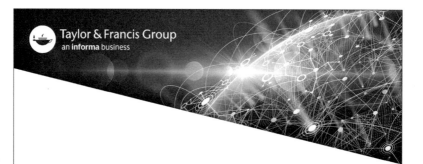